Microsoft® Outlook® 2010

Randy Nordell

Connect
Learn
Succeed™

The McGraw-Hill Companies

Connect
Learn
Succeed™

MICROSOFT® OUTLOOK® 2010
Published by McGraw-Hill, a business unit of The McGraw-Hill Companies, Inc., 1221 Avenue of the Americas, New York, NY, 10020. Copyright © 2012 by The McGraw-Hill Companies, Inc. All rights reserved. No part of this publication may be reproduced or distributed in any form or by any means, or stored in a database or retrieval system, without the prior written consent of The McGraw-Hill Companies, Inc., including, but not limited to, in any network or other electronic storage or transmission, or broadcast for distance learning.

Some ancillaries, including electronic and print components, may not be available to customers outside the United States.

This book is printed on acid-free paper.

1 2 3 4 5 6 7 8 9 0 RJE/RJE 1 0 9 8 7 6 5 4 3 2 1

ISBN 978-0-07-351928-9
MHID 0-07-351928-6

Vice president/Editor in chief: *Elizabeth Haefele*
Vice president/Director of marketing: *John E. Biernat*
Executive sponsoring editor: *Scott Davidson*
Sponsoring editor: *Paul Altier*
Director of development: *Sarah Wood*
Developmental editor: *Alan Palmer*
Freelance developmental editor: *Cindy Nash*
Editorial coordinator: *Allison McCabe*
Marketing manager: *Tiffany Wendt*
Lead digital product manager: *Damian Moshak*
Digital development editor: *Kevin White*
Director, Editing/Design/Production: *Jess Ann Kosic*
Project manager: *Kathryn D. Wright*
Buyer II: *Debra R. Sylvester*
Senior designer: *Srdjan Savanovic*
Media project manager: *Brent dela Cruz*
Cover design: *George Kokkonas*
Typeface: *10.5/13 New Aster*
Compositor: *Laserwords Private Limited*
Printer: *R. R. Donnelley*
Cover credit: © *Lai Leng Yiap, Veer*
Credits: The credits section for this book begins on page 420 and is considered an extension of the copyright page.

Library of Congress Cataloging-in-Publication Data

Nordell, Randy.
  Microsoft Outlook 2010 / Randy Nordell.
    p. cm.
  Includes index.
  ISBN-13: 978-0-07-351928-9 (alk. paper)
  ISBN-10: 0-07-351928-6 (alk. paper)
  1. Microsoft Outlook. 2. Time management—Computer programs. 3. Personal information management—Computer programs. 4. Electronic mail systems—Computer programs. I. Title.
HF5548.4.M5255N67 2012
005.5'7—dc22   2010039980

The Internet addresses listed in the text were accurate at the time of publication. The inclusion of a Web site does not indicate an endorsement by the authors or McGraw-Hill, and McGraw-Hill does not guarantee the accuracy of the information presented at these sites.

www.mhhe.com

Dedication

This book is dedicated to my wife Kelly. Thank you for your support and encouragement during the writing of this book and for the endless hours of proofreading and valuable feedback you provided. This book would not have been possible without you. I'm looking forward to our next 21 years together!

Thank you also to Kelsey and Taylor who keep me young at heart. You two are awesome, and you continually make me proud and grateful to be your dad!

ABOUT THE AUTHOR

Dr. Randy Nordell is a Professor of Business Technology at American River College in Sacramento, California. He has been an educator for over 20 years and has taught at the high school, community college, and university levels. He holds a bachelor's degree in Business Administration from California State University, Stanislaus; a single subject teaching credential from Fresno State University; a master's degree in Education from Fresno Pacific University; and a doctorate in Education from Argosy University. Randy speaks regularly at conferences on the integration of technology into the curriculum. When not teaching, he enjoys spending time with his family, cycling, swimming, skiing, and the California weather and terrain.

BRIEF CONTENTS

CHAPTER 1: OUTLOOK OVERVIEW 2

CHAPTER 2: E-MAIL BASICS 26

CHAPTER 3: E-MAIL SPECIAL FEATURES 58

CHAPTER 4: CONTACTS 86

CHAPTER 5: CALENDAR 118

CHAPTER 6: TASKS AND TO-DO ITEMS 146

CHAPTER 7: FOLDERS, RULES, QUICK STEPS, CATEGORIES, AND FOLLOW UP FLAGS 172

CHAPTER 8: MULTIPLE E-MAIL ACCOUNTS, ADVANCED E-MAIL OPTIONS, AND RSS FEEDS 206

CHAPTER 9: ADVANCED CONTACTS 240

CHAPTER 10: ADVANCED CALENDARS 278

CHAPTER 11: NOTES, JOURNAL, SEARCH FOLDERS, SHORTCUTS, AND ARCHIVING 312

CHAPTER 12: SHARING, SECURITY, SEARCH, AND USER INTERFACE 342

APPENDIX A: SETTING UP OUTLOOK FOR AN ON-SITE OR ONLINE CLASSROOM ENVIRONMENT 379

APPENDIX B: OUTLOOK SHORTCUTS 385

APPENDIX C: OUTLOOK QUICK REFERENCE GUIDE 390

APPENDIX D: EXCHANGE SERVER VERSUS STAND-ALONE USAGE 411

GLOSSARY 417

INDEX 421

CONTENTS

ACKNOWLEDGMENTS xii

OVERVIEW xiii

Chapter 1: Outlook Overview

CHAPTER FLYOVER 2

MAKING OUTLOOK WORK FOR YOU 3

WHAT IS OUTLOOK? 4

WORKING WITH OUTLOOK 4

E-mail 4
Calendar 5
Contacts 5
Tasks 6
Notes 7
Journal 7

NAVIGATING OUTLOOK 7

Outlook Today 8
Outlook Panes 9

Tabs, Ribbons,
and Dialog Boxes 11
Views 12
Folder List 13
Outlook Help 14

WHAT'S NEW IN OUTLOOK 2010 15

OUTLOOK AS A STAND-ALONE PROGRAM 17

OUTLOOK WITH AN EXCHANGE SERVER 18

CHAPTER HIGHLIGHTS 18

WHAT DO YOU KNOW ABOUT OUTLOOK? 20

PUTTING OUTLOOK TO WORK 21

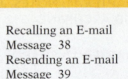

Chapter 2: E-mail Basics

CHAPTER FLYOVER 26

MAKING OUTLOOK WORK FOR YOU 27

TYPES OF E-MAIL ACCOUNTS 28

Microsoft Exchange 28
Post Office Protocol (POP3) 28
Internet Message Access Protocol (IMAP) 28
Hypertext Transfer Protocol (HTTP) 28

SETTING UP AN E-MAIL ACCOUNT 28

CREATING, SENDING, AND RECEIVING E-MAIL 30

Create New E-mail 30
Select Recipients 31
Cc & Bcc 32
Subject Line and Body 33
Formatting Text 33
Sending an E-mail 34
Saving an E-mail Draft 34
Opening E-mail 35
Reply, Reply All, and Forward 35
Saving an E-mail 36
Printing an E-mail 37

Recalling an E-mail
Message 38
Resending an E-mail
Message 39

HANDLING ATTACHMENTS 39

Attaching a File 39
Opening and Saving Attachments 40
Previewing an Attachment 41
Forwarding an E-mail as an
Attachment 42
Attaching Other Outlook Items 43

UNDERSTANDING ARRANGEMENT AND ICONS 44

Arrangement 44
Read/Unread E-mail 45
Mark as Read/Unread 46
Replied to and Forwarded 46
Attachment 46
Flag 46
Importance 46
Reminder 46
Category 47

CLEANING UP YOUR INBOX 47

Deleting E-mail 47
Deleted Items 48
Clean Up and Ignore 48
Empty Deleted Items 48

CHAPTER HIGHLIGHTS 50

WHAT DO YOU KNOW ABOUT OUTLOOK? 51

PUTTING OUTLOOK TO WORK 52

Chapter 3: E-mail Special Features

CHAPTER FLYOVER 58

MAKING OUTLOOK WORK FOR YOU 59

TYPES OF E-MAIL FORMAT 60

Plain Text 60
Outlook Rich Text Format (RTF) 60
Hypertext Markup Language (HTML) 60
Setting Default and Changing Message Format 60

MESSAGE OPTIONS 62

Properties Dialog Box 62
Importance 63
Sensitivity 63
Security 63
Delivery and Read Receipts 64
Delivery Options 66
Follow Up Flag 67
Flag for Recipients 68
Permission 69

VOTING BUTTONS 69

Preset Voting Buttons 69
Customize Voting
Buttons 70
Reply Using Voting Buttons 70
Tracking Voting Responses 71

CUSTOMIZE YOUR E-MAIL 72

Signatures 72
Themes 75
Setting Default Theme and Fonts 75
Desktop Alerts 76
People Pane and Outlook Social Connector 77

CHAPTER HIGHLIGHTS 78

WHAT DO YOU KNOW ABOUT OUTLOOK? 79

PUTTING OUTLOOK TO WORK 80

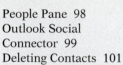

Chapter 4: Contacts

CHAPTER FLYOVER 86

MAKING OUTLOOK WORK FOR YOU 88

WHAT IS A CONTACT? 88

Database Lingo 88
Contacts Versus Global Address List 88

CREATING CONTACTS 89

New Contact 89
New Contact from Same Company 90
From Received E-mail 91
From an Electronic Business Card 92
From Global Address List 93
Duplicates 94

EDITING CONTACT INFO 95

Changing Field Names 95
Address 96
Multiple E-mail Addresses 96
Picture 96
Map 97

People Pane 98
Outlook Social
Connector 99
Deleting Contacts 101

CHANGING VIEWS IN CONTACTS 101

Different Contact Views 101
Modifying Views 102
Sorting Contacts 103

USING CONTACTS 103

Sending E-mail to Contacts 103
Sending a Business Card 104
Creating a Contact Group 105
Using a Contact Group 107
Modifying a Contact Group 107

CHAPTER HIGHLIGHTS 110

WHAT DO YOU KNOW ABOUT OUTLOOK? 111

PUTTING OUTLOOK TO WORK 112

Chapter 5: *Calendar*

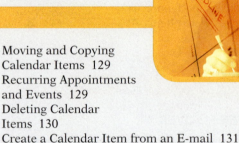

CHAPTER FLYOVER 118

MAKING OUTLOOK WORK FOR YOU 120

BENEFITS OF AN OUTLOOK CALENDAR 120

CALENDAR ITEMS 121

Appointments 121
Events 122
Meeting Requests 122

NAVIGATING THE CALENDAR VIEWS 123

Day View 123
Week View 124
Month View 124
Schedule View 125
Other Views 126

CREATING AND EDITING CALENDAR ITEMS 126

New Appointment 127
New Event 127
Reminders 128

Moving and Copying Calendar Items 129
Recurring Appointments and Events 129
Deleting Calendar Items 130
Create a Calendar Item from an E-mail 131

CREATING AND USING MEETING REQUESTS 131

Creating and Sending a Meeting Request 131
Responding to Meeting Requests 133
Proposing a New Time to a Meeting Request 134
Tracking Meeting Request Respondents 135
Changing and Updating a Meeting Request 137
Deleting a Scheduled Meeting 137

CHAPTER HIGHLIGHTS 138

WHAT DO YOU KNOW ABOUT OUTLOOK? 139

PUTTING OUTLOOK TO WORK 141

Chapter 6: *Tasks and To-Do Items*

CHAPTER FLYOVER 146

MAKING OUTLOOK WORK FOR YOU 147

UNDERSTANDING TASK AND TO-DO ITEMS 148

Tasks 148
Flagged Items 148
Task List 148
To-Do List 149
To-Do Bar 149

CREATING TASKS 149

New Task 149
Edit Task 151
Attach File or Outlook Item 153
Mark a Task as Complete 153
Recurring Task 154
Creating a Task from an E-mail 156
Creating a Task from a Calendar Item 157

VIEWING TASKS AND TO-DO ITEMS 157

Task Views 158
Reading Pane 158
Tasks in Calendar Views 158
Customizing the To-Do Bar 159

MANAGING TASKS 160

Assigning Tasks 160
Accepting Tasks 161
Task Icons 162
Task Status Report 163
Complete Task 164
Task Options 165

CHAPTER HIGHLIGHTS 166

WHAT DO YOU KNOW ABOUT OUTLOOK? 167

PUTTING OUTLOOK TO WORK 168

Chapter 7: *Folders, Rules, Quick Steps, Categories, and Follow Up Flags*

CHAPTER FLYOVER 172

MAKING OUTLOOK WORK FOR YOU 173

USING FOLDERS 174

Creating Folders 174
Moving Folders 175
Deleting Folders 176
Using the Folder List 177

USING RULES AND QUICK STEPS 177

Creating Quick Rules 178
Creating Advanced Rules 179
Modifying Rules 184
Deleting and Turning On/Off Rules 185
Running Rules 185
Ordering Rules 186
Modifying and Using Quick Steps 187

USING CATEGORIES 191

Customizing Categories 191
Assigning Categories 193
Viewing by Categories 194
Setting a Quick Click Category 194

USING FOLLOW UP FLAGS 195

Flagging Items 195
Setting a Quick Click Follow Up Flag 196
View To-Do Items 197

CHAPTER HIGHLIGHTS 198

WHAT DO YOU KNOW ABOUT OUTLOOK? 199

PUTTING OUTLOOK TO WORK 200

Chapter 8: *Multiple E-mail Accounts, Advanced E-mail Options, and RSS Feeds*

CHAPTER FLYOVER 206

MAKING OUTLOOK WORK FOR YOU 207

SETTING UP ADDITIONAL E-MAIL ACCOUNTS 207

Using the Auto Account Setup 207
Troubleshooting E-mail Problems 210
Using Outlook Connector 212

MANAGING MULTIPLE E-MAIL ACCOUNTS 214

Setting the Default Account 214
Sending E-mail Through a Different Account 215
Changing the E-mail Delivery Folder 215
Creating Folders and Using Rules 217
Using Outlook Web Access 217
Texting from Outlook 217

CUSTOMIZING E-MAIL OPTIONS 219

E-mail Options 219
Compose Messages 219
Outlook Panes 221

Message Arrival 221
Conversation
Clean Up 222
Replies and Forwards 222
Save Messages 223
Send Messages 223
MailTips 224
Tracking Options 225
Message Format and Other 225
Out of Office Assistant 225

USING RSS FEEDS 227

Subscribing to an RSS Feed 228
Managing RSS Feeds 230
Sharing an RSS Feed 231
Unsubscribing from an RSS Feed 232

CHAPTER HIGHLIGHTS 233

WHAT DO YOU KNOW ABOUT OUTLOOK? 234

PUTTING OUTLOOK TO WORK 236

Chapter 9: *Advanced Contacts*

CHAPTER FLYOVER 240

MAKING OUTLOOK WORK FOR YOU 241

MANAGING CONTACTS 241

Changing the Default Address Book 242
Using Folders 243
Using Categories 244
Tracking Contact Activities 246
Updating Contacts 247
Customizing Contact Options 247

BUSINESS CARDS 249

Sending Electronic Business Cards 249
Include Your Business Card in Your Signature 251
Customizing Your Business Card 252

IMPORTING AND EXPORTING 255

Importing Contacts 255
Exporting Contacts 260
Exporting and Importing an Outlook Data File 265

USING CONTACTS WITH OTHER OFFICE 2010 PROGRAMS 268

Using Contacts to Create Mailing Labels in Word 268

CHAPTER HIGHLIGHTS 270

WHAT DO YOU KNOW ABOUT OUTLOOK? 271

PUTTING OUTLOOK TO WORK 272

Chapter 10: *Advanced Calendars*

CHAPTER FLYOVER 278

MAKING OUTLOOK WORK FOR YOU 279

USING MULTIPLE CALENDARS 279

Create New Calendar 280
View Multiple Calendars 281

CALENDAR OPTIONS 282

Work Time Options 283
Calendar Options 283
Display Options 284
Time Zones 285
Scheduling Assistant 286
Resource Scheduling 286

PRINTING AND SHARING AN OUTLOOK CALENDAR 287

Print an Outlook Calendar 287
Forwarding an Appointment 288

Share a Calendar 290
Send a Calendar via E-mail 291
Publish a Calendar 293
Viewing Shared Calendars 297

ADVANCED CALENDAR FEATURES 297

Using Categories 297
Attaching Items to a Calendar Item 298
Private Calendar Items 299
Recurring Meetings 300
Using the Scheduling Assistant 301
AutoPick Meeting Times 302

CHAPTER HIGHLIGHTS 303

WHAT DO YOU KNOW ABOUT OUTLOOK? 304

PUTTING OUTLOOK TO WORK 305

Chapter 11: *Notes, Journal, Search Folders, Shortcuts, and Archiving*

CHAPTER FLYOVER 312

MAKING OUTLOOK WORK FOR YOU 314

USING NOTES 314

Creating Notes 314
Editing Notes 315

Categorizing Notes 315
Note Views 316
Forwarding Notes 317
Changing Default Settings on Notes 318

USING THE JOURNAL 319

Manually Record a Journal Entry 320
Automatically Record a Journal Entry 321
Journal Views 322

USING SEARCH FOLDERS 323

Using Existing Search Folders 324
Creating New Search Folders 324
Customizing Search Folders 325
Deleting Search Folders 327

USING SHORTCUTS 328

Creating a New Shortcut 328
Creating a New Group 329
Editing a Shortcut or Group 329

ARCHIVING OUTLOOK FOLDERS 330

AutoArchive Settings 330
Custom AutoArchive Settings 332

CHAPTER HIGHLIGHTS 334

WHAT DO YOU KNOW ABOUT OUTLOOK? 334

PUTTING OUTLOOK TO WORK 336

Chapter 12: *Sharing, Security, Search, and User Interface*

CHAPTER FLYOVER 342

MAKING OUTLOOK WORK FOR YOU 343

SHARING YOUR OUTLOOK WITH OTHERS 344

Understanding Delegates and Permissions 344
Assigning a Delegate 344
Opening Another Outlook User's Folders 346
Creating Outlook Items as a Delegate 347
Removing a Delegate 348

SECURITY 348

Outlook Trust Center 348
Add-Ins 348
Trusted Publishers 349
DEP Setting 349
Privacy Options 350
E-mail Security 350
Attachment Handling 351
Automatic Download 352
Macro Settings 353
Programmatic Access 353
Junk E-mail Options 353
Digital Signatures 356

SEARCHING FOR OUTLOOK ITEMS 358

Instant Search 358
Search Options 359
Advanced Find 360

CUSTOMIZING OUTLOOK TO FIT YOUR NEEDS 361

Outlook Today 361
Navigation Pane Options 362
Favorites Folders 363
Customize Quick Access Toolbar 363
Sorting and Arrangement 364
Add Columns and Field Chooser 365
Show in Groups 367
Customizing Views 368
Creating a Custom View 368

CHAPTER HIGHLIGHTS 370

WHAT DO YOU KNOW ABOUT OUTLOOK? 371

PUTTING OUTLOOK TO WORK 373

APPENDIX A: SETTING UP OUTLOOK FOR AN ON-SITE OR ONLINE CLASSROOM ENVIRONMENT 379

APPENDIX B: OUTLOOK SHORTCUTS 385

APPENDIX C: OUTLOOK QUICK REFERENCE GUIDE 390

APPENDIX D: EXCHANGE SERVER VERSUS STAND-ALONE USAGE 411

GLOSSARY 417

INDEX 421

QUICK TIPS AND TROUBLESHOOTING 430

ACKNOWLEDGMENTS

REVIEWERS

Ken Lavender
East Central Technical College

Karla Brown
Southwestern Illinois College

Debra Giblin
Mitchell Technical Institute

Rhonda Barger
Palomar College

Darrell Abbey
Cascadia Community College

Theresa Savarese
San Diego City College

Richard Smolenski
Westwood College Online

Susan Cully
Long Beach City College

Zoila Rosillo
Long Beach City College

Tod Bruning
Palo Alto College

Melissa Wallace
Lanier Technical College

Judy Settle
Central Georgia Technical College

Peggy Burrus
Red Rocks Community College

Regina Horner
Tennessee Technology Center at Jackson

Carol Ogden
Solano Community College

Mary Jo Slater
College of Beaver County

Janice Rowland
Pellissippi State Technical Community College

Rosalie Westburg
Clover Park Technical College

Karen Everingham
University of Toledo

Margaret Mauldin
Cerro Coso Community College

Neil Gudsen
Washtenaw Community College

Bob Balicki
Cleary University

IdaLynne Gedde
Arapahoe Community College

Tina Dierkes
Southwestern Illinois College

Elaine Mercer
Albany Technical College

Rhoda James
Citrus College

Patricia Partyka
Schoolcraft College

Russell Sabadosa
Manchester Community College

Sue Trakas
University of Cincinnati-Batavia

Theresa Savarese
San Diego City College

Daisy Le
San Diego Mesa College

Crystal Kernodle
North Arkansas College

Darrell Abbey
Cascadia Community College

Tanya Patrick
Clackamas Community College

TECHNICAL EDITORS

Russell Sabadosa
Manchester Community College

Rhoda James
Citrus College

Tina Dierkes
Southwestern Illinois College

Elaine Mercer
Albany Technical College

SUPPLEMENT AUTHORS

Randy Nordell
American River College

Michael-Brian Ogawa
University of Hawaii at Manoa

Linda Mehlinger
Morgan State University

Microsoft® Outlook® 2010 is a textbook born from practical classroom experience and pedagogy. As a computer technology and business professor, I have structured this text in a way to maximize student learning and retention through a systematic introduction of the features of Outlook, detailed visuals, step-by-step directions, and relevant guided and independent practice.

Microsoft Office Outlook 2010 is the industry's leading e-mail and personal information management software, and an increasing number of colleges are offering courses pertaining to this subject matter. Because this textbook is a hybrid between a Microsoft Outlook reference book and an instructor- or self-paced textbook, this text can be used in both the academic setting or in the business environment to train students or employees on the use of Microsoft Outlook.

THE CONTENT
Hybrid Approach

This text is unique in that it is a comprehensive Outlook text and it is a hybrid between a reference book and a step-by-step tutorial textbook, providing instructors and students with the best aspects of these two different types of books. This is a text that can be used for a reference guide without being too wordy, while providing students and instructors with guided reinforcement activities throughout the chapter and independent practice opportunities at the conclusion of each chapter.

Logical Sequence

Students are introduced to Outlook topics in a logical sequence that establishes a strong foundation on the essential aspects of Outlook, and then builds upon these foundational skills as students progress through the text. *Microsoft® Outlook® 2010* provides students with specific instructions and visuals of how to perform specific tasks in Outlook and relevant review exercises to practice the tasks and features taught in each chapter.

Flexible Exercises

Instructors who want the flexibility to be able to teach their course without being required to follow all of the practice exercises commonly found in textbooks of this nature will find this book very user friendly in the classroom environment. This text provides instructors with both guided and independent practice exercises to incorporate and custom tailor to your classroom teaching style. As many colleges are increasing their distance education course offerings, this book could also be used as the text for an online course and can be used in conjunction with ***SimNet***.

THE PEDAGOGY

The instructional features that will be used in each chapter are as follows:

Chapter Flyover. At the beginning of each chapter, the specific topics covered are succinctly listed. This provides both the instructor and students with an overview of chapter learning objectives and serves as a reference guide when using this book.

Making Outlook Work for You. This section provides a brief introduction explaining how and why the topics covered in this chapter are important and relevant to you as an Outlook user.

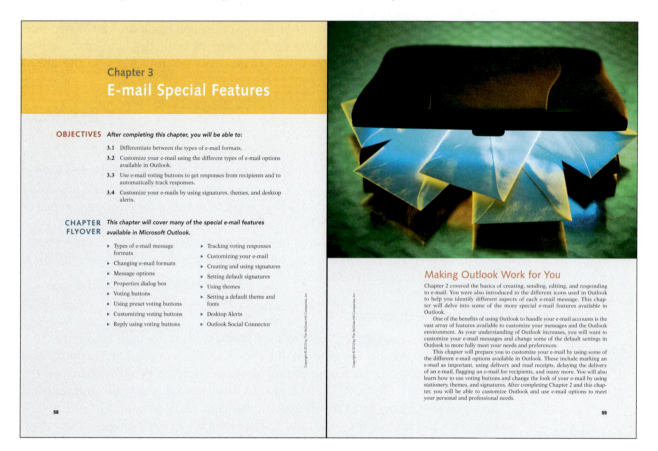

Learning Outlook. This is the main part or body of each chapter and provides both written explanations and visuals of the topics being covered. There is also ancillary marginal information (presented next) included to supplement and reinforce learning objectives.

Chapter Highlights. This serves as a review for the chapter and lists the topics covered and corresponding page numbers.

What Do You Know About Outlook? This section consists of review questions for the chapter and includes a combination of true/false, multiple choice, and short answer questions.

Putting Outlook to Work. This section provides students an opportunity for guided and independent practice. This section is presented in case study format and uses an open-ended approach rather than a step-by-step tutorial.

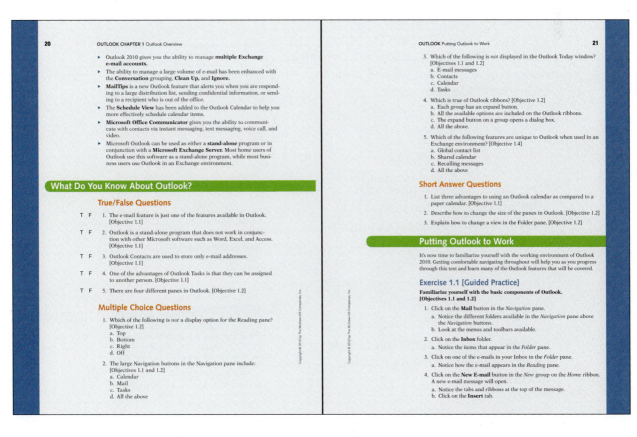

In addition to the preceding chapter information, there is ancillary marginal information throughout each chapter to both reinforce learning and provide additional contextual information. These side notes include:

Step-by-Step. Provides guided steps on how to use the Outlook feature being taught.

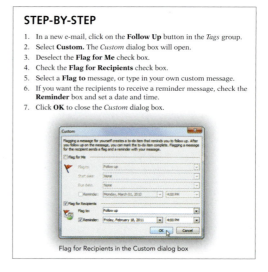

STEP-BY-STEP

1. In a new e-mail, click on the **Follow Up** button in the *Tags* group.
2. Select **Custom.** The *Custom* dialog box will open.
3. Deselect the **Flag for Me** check box.
4. Check the **Flag for Recipients** check box.
5. Select a **Flag to** message, or type in your own custom message.
6. If you want the recipients to receive a reminder message, check the **Reminder** box and set a date and time.
7. Click **OK** to close the *Custom* dialog box.

Flag for Recipients in the Custom dialog box

Netiquette. Provides some e-mail netiquette pertaining to the topic or feature being taught.

NETIQUETTE

The sensitivity marking is only a notification and does not ensure that recipients will treat the information as you have requested.

Shortcut. Provides keyboard and function key shortcuts.

SHORTCUT

Ctrl+Alt+1 will display the calendar in *Day* view.

Another Way. Shows users an alternative method of accomplishing the same task or feature being presented.

ANOTHER WAY

Importance can also be selected from the *Properties* dialog box.

More Info. Presents anecdotal information that references other sections in the book or appendices.

MORE INFO

Don't solely rely on these receipts because read and delivery receipts work only with Microsoft Exchange. This means that you will not receive these notifications from users not using Exchange. Also, just because a recipient opens an e-mail does not necessarily ensure that he or she will read the e-mail.

Changing the default tracking options for receipts will be covered in Chapter 8 on page 225.

Factoid. Provides some interesting information about the topic being discussed.

FACTOID

When you click the small triangle next to a conversation, the message will be expanded to show the related messages in the current folder. When you click on the triangle again, the conversation expands to include related messages in other folders.

THE SUPPLEMENTS

Accompanying this text are relevant supplementary material that will reinforce and enhance your learning of Microsoft Office Outlook 2010. Included with this text is an Online Learning Center, www.mhhe.com/nordell, that contains the following supplementary materials:

- Test bank of questions for each chapter
- Data files for exercises and projects
- Exams and chapter reviews
- Links to current and relevant articles
- Monthly blog article written by the author of the text

The author's blog has an RSS feed available so that both students and professors will be able to subscribe in Outlook to automatically receive any current updates and monthly blog articles.

Microsoft® Outlook® 2010

Chapter 1
Outlook Overview

OBJECTIVES **After completing this chapter, you will be able to:**

1.1 Understand the basic components of Microsoft Office 2010.

1.2 Navigate throughout the Outlook environment and identify the different panes in the Outlook window.

1.3 Identify the changes in Outlook 2010 from previous versions.

1.4 Distinguish between Outlook being used as a stand-alone program and in a Microsoft Exchange environment.

CHAPTER FLYOVER **In this chapter you will learn about:**

► Microsoft Outlook

► E-mail

► Calendar

► Contacts

► Tasks

► Notes

► Journal

► Outlook user interface

► Outlook Today

► Outlook panes: Navigation, Folder, Reading, and People

► Tabs, Ribbons, and Dialog boxes

► Outlook views

► Folder list

► Outlook Help

► What's New in Outlook 2010

► Outlook as a stand-alone program

► Outlook with an Exchange Server

Making Outlook Work for You

Microsoft Outlook (usually referred to as *Outlook*) is the most widely used e-mail and personal management software today. It is used in both the business environment and personal and home environment. Outlook 2010 is part of the Microsoft Office 2010 suite of application software.

This book will cover the different aspects of Outlook and how this software can be used to help manage your electronic communication, schedule your appointments and meetings, organize your personal and business contacts, and arrange your list of to-do items. This chapter provides an overview of the capabilities of Outlook and its working environment.

This first half of this book (Chapters 1–6) introduces you to all the main features of Outlook; the more advanced and special features of Outlook are presented in the second half of the book (Chapters 7–12). After going through the first half of the book, you will be very proficient in using all the main features in Outlook. The remaining chapters will take you more in depth into each of these areas and introduce you to some of the more advanced aspects of Outlook. After going through this book and practicing

> ## ✳ FACTOID
>
> According to the market research firm The Radicati Group, there were an estimated 1.3 billion e-mail users in 2008, and this number is expected to rise to 1.6 billion by 2011.

3

what you are learning, you will become the Outlook expert in your work-place, family, and neighborhood. Hopefully, that's a good thing!

What Is Outlook?

When most people think of or hear about Microsoft Outlook, their first thought is e-mail. One of the main features in Outlook is handling e-mail, but Outlook is so much more! It is personal management software that contains the following features:

- E-mail
- Calendar
- Contacts
- Tasks
- Notes
- Journal

Many users only utilize Outlook to a fraction of its potential. As you work through this chapter, you'll be introduced to the overall capabilities of Outlook.

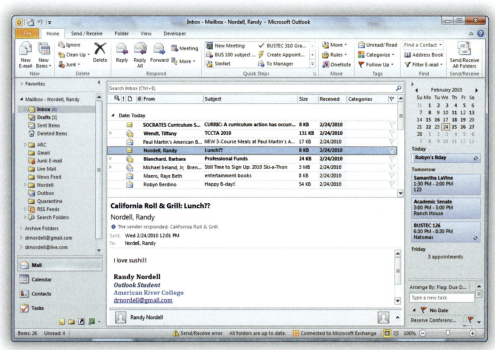

Microsoft Outlook 2010

Working with Outlook

Microsoft Outlook 2010 combines the e-mail, calendar, contacts, tasks, notes, and journal features into one piece of personal management software. Each of these different features in Outlook operates as an independent piece of a personal information management system; yet these different tasks integrate seamlessly together in Outlook. In addition, Outlook can be used in conjunction with Microsoft Word, Excel, Access, and other Microsoft products.

E-mail

E-mail is the commonly used term for **_electronic mail._** Outlook gives users the capability of creating, sending, and receiving e-mail. It can manage a single e-mail account or multiple e-mail accounts. In Outlook, e-mail is activated by clicking on the **Mail** button.

MORE INFO

Chapter 2 will cover the basics of e-mail, while Chapter 3 will go more in depth and cover the special e-mail features available in Outlook. Chapter 7 will discuss the use of rules for handling both incoming and outgoing e-mail, and Chapter 8 will provide the reader with information about setting up the different types of e-mail accounts.

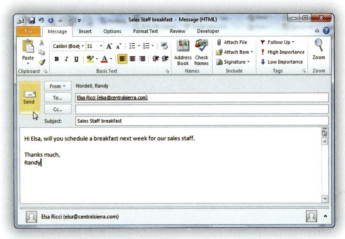

Outlook new e-mail message

Calendar

Most individuals organize their daily, weekly, and monthly schedule with some type of calendar. This might be a daily planner you keep with you or a calendar that hangs on your wall at work or at home. *Outlook Calendar* is an electronic calendar that makes it easy to create appointments or events, edit these items, replicate calendar items, set electronic reminders, create meeting requests, and share calendar items with other Outlook users or other devices. Additional information and details can be stored in a calendar item.

Another advantage of an Outlook calendar is that users can synchronize their work and home calendars. As the popularity of multifunction (smart) cell phones increases, the potential to have your Outlook calendar synchronized between your work, home, and cell phone is not only a reality, but also commonplace for working professionals.

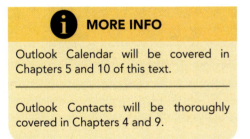

MORE INFO

Outlook Calendar will be covered in Chapters 5 and 10 of this text.

Outlook Contacts will be thoroughly covered in Chapters 4 and 9.

Outlook calendar appointment

Contacts

Outlook also provides an area to keep names, e-mail, phone numbers, and other information about business contacts, coworkers, friends, and family. Similar to the way the Outlook calendar replaces the old paper calendar, *Outlook Contacts* allow users to electronically store personal information. They function as a database, which is a collection of information. One of the many benefits of Outlook contacts is that the user can effectively use them without having any existing knowledge of the organizational structure or database.

Contacts are used to save personal and company information in Outlook and also when populating a recipient list in an e-mail, meeting request, or task request.

Outlook contact record

Tasks

Are you a list person? Do you constantly have a list of things to get done today or this week? Outlook provides a method of keeping track of those things that need to be accomplished with the use of **tasks.** The *tasks* function is very similar to a notepad that you use to write down your to-do items and then cross them off as they are completed. Tasks are included in the Outlook *To-Do List,* which lists both tasks and e-mails that have been flagged for some action.

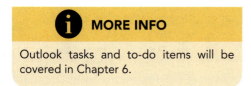

MORE INFO

Outlook tasks and to-do items will be covered in Chapter 6.

Outlook task

Some advantages of using Outlook tasks include:

- Tasks are electronic and can be shared between computers and cell phones.
- Many details, which are not typically written down on a piece of paper, can be added to a task.
- Reminders can be set to alert you to an upcoming due date and time for a task.
- A task can be assigned to another Outlook user.

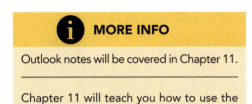

Outlook note

Notes

Outlook Notes are used to keep track of information that does not necessarily or neatly fall into the category of a calendar item, contact, or task. Do you ever end the day with a pocketful of scraps of paper with pieces of information written on them? Do you have sticky notes stuck to your computer monitor or refrigerator? Outlook notes function like electronic sticky notes—actually they look just like them. Notes are an excellent way of storing information such as a username and password to log into a Web site, gift ideas for family and friends, or a list of books you'd like to read.

ⓘ MORE INFO

Outlook notes will be covered in Chapter 11.

Chapter 11 will teach you how to use the Outlook Journal and provide you with ideas of how this feature might be used in the business setting.

Journal

Outlook Journal is a way to keep track of the amount of time spent working on a particular document or project. The journal is primarily used in the business environment and enables you to associate specific Microsoft Office documents to a journal entry.

Outlook journal entry

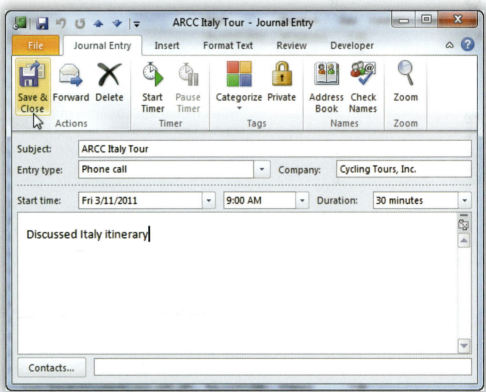

Navigating Outlook

The Outlook working environment has a much different look and feel than that of Microsoft Word, Excel, PowerPoint, and Access. The Outlook user interface is divided into multiple sections, called ***panes.*** As you work through this book and use Outlook, you will become familiar with the Outlook user interface and the different panes available. Outlook has provided much consistency throughout this program to allow you to quickly become comfortable navigating through its working environment.

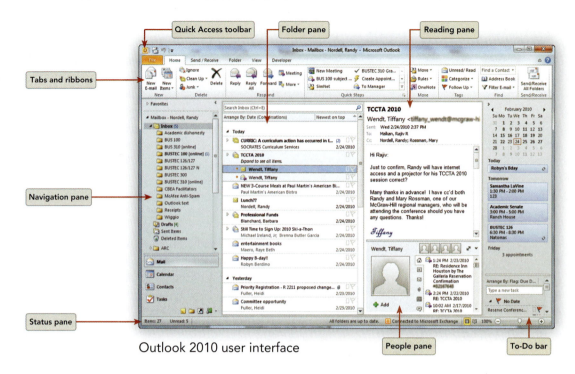

Outlook 2010 user interface

Outlook Today

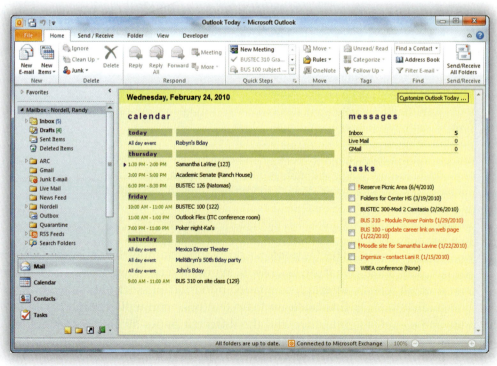

MORE INFO

Chapter 12 will provide more information about customizing **Outlook Today**.

Outlook Today is an introductory screen in Outlook that will provide you with information about your Inbox and other e-mail folders, current calendar items, and upcoming tasks. Outlook Today is displayed in the **Folder pane** and is the default view when you open Outlook each time. Outlook Today can be customized to meet your personal needs.

Outlook Today displayed in the Folder pane

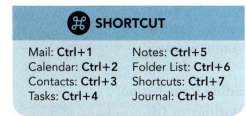

Outlook Panes

The Outlook program window is divided into four main panes: Navigation pane, Folder pane, Reading pane, and the new People pane.

The ***Navigation pane*** is used to help you navigate through the different features available in Outlook. It is located at the left side of the Outlook window, and the buttons at the bottom of the Navigation pane allow you to choose which task you want to work on in Outlook. The main functions in Outlook—***Mail, Calendar, Contacts,*** and ***Tasks***—are represented by large buttons at the bottom of the Navigation pane, while the less commonly used features in Outlook—***Shortcuts, Notes, Folder List,*** and ***Journal***—are represented by smaller icons located below the large buttons.

The look of the Navigation pane changes depending on the feature chosen, but the large and small navigation buttons at the bottom of the Navigation pane remain consistent. The navigation buttons can be customized to better meet your needs, which will be covered in Chapter 12. The width of the Navigation pane can be adjusted using the following steps:

STEP-BY-STEP

1. Click and hold the right border of the *Navigation* pane.
2. Drag the border to the left or right as desired.

The ***Folder pane*** is the main working area in Outlook and displays the contents of the folder selected in the Navigation pane. As a different folder is selected, the contents of the Folder pane change. The following screenshot is an example of the Calendar being selected in the Navigation pane, and the selected calendar is displayed in the Folder pane.

The ***Reading pane*** is an optional pane that is available in most of the different main tasks in Outlook; although it is primarily used with the Mail feature. The Reading pane displays the contents of the item selected in the Folder pane. The Reading pane can be set to appear below or to the right of the Folder pane, or it can be turned **off.** The Reading pane will vary depending on the task (Mail, Calendar, Contacts, etc.) selected in the Navigation pane. Follow these steps to change the location of the Reading pane:

Outlook Navigation pane

Selected Calendar displayed in the Folder pane

that are broken into *groups.* The size of the buttons in each group will vary depending on the size of the open window.

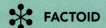 **FACTOID**

Microsoft Outlook 2007 was the only program in the Microsoft Office suite of software that still used pull-down menus and toolbars in its main user interface. Outlook 2010 has now fully integrated tabs and ribbons throughout.

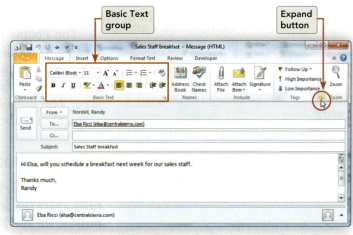

Expand button on the Tags group

Some of the groups on each ribbon have an *expand (or launcher) button* at the bottom right corner of the group. When the expand button is clicked, the *dialog box* for that particular group opens. The opened dialog box contains additional options for the selected group.

 **FACTOID**

The name of the dialog box is not always the same as the name of the group that was expanded. Some dialog boxes contain features that are distributed between a few groups.

Many of the dialog boxes that you will use in Outlook 2010 are the same as or very similar to the dialog boxes used in previous versions of Outlook.

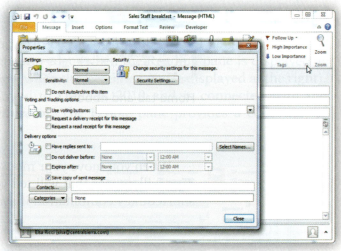

Properties dialog box

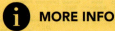 **MORE INFO**

Chapter 12 will cover customizing views, menus, and toolbars.

Views

Each of the different main tasks in Outlook (Mail, Calendar, Contacts, Tasks, Notes, and Journal) has numerous different preset views from which to choose, as well as the option to customize each view or create your own personal view. The selected view will control how the folder selected in the Navigation pane will be displayed in the Folder pane.

Follow these steps to change to a different view in Outlook:

STEP-BY-STEP

1. Click on the **View** tab.
2. Click on the **Change View** button in the *Current View* group.
3. Select the view you want. Notice the different views available; the different views are context sensitive.

E-mail views

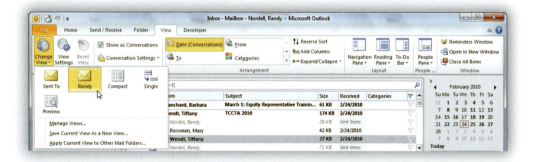

⌘ SHORTCUT

Ctrl+6 will display the Folder list in the *Navigation* pane.

ⓘ MORE INFO

The Folder list will be covered more thoroughly in Chapter 7 when we start using multiple folders for e-mail, contacts, and tasks.

Folder List

The *Folder list* allows you to see all the folders available in Outlook in the Navigation pane. The Folder list button is a small button at the bottom of the pane. When the Folder list button is selected, all the folders for all the items in Outlook appear in the Navigation pane. The benefit of viewing the Folder list is that you can see all folders available in the folder hierarchy in which they reside, rather than viewing just one set of folders at a time. This view can be used to move folders up or down a level or can be used to drag specific items into a folder.

Folder List

Outlook Help

Outlook Help is an online search engine that is available throughout Outlook and will provide you with specific information about topics on which you might have a question or need additional information. The Microsoft Outlook Help button is located in the upper right corner of any open Outlook window.

Microsoft Outlook Help button

When the **Outlook Help** button is clicked, the *Outlook Help* dialog box opens. You will be given the choice of either typing in keywords related to your search or choosing from a list of common Outlook topics.

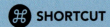 **SHORTCUT**

Pressing the **F1** function key on your computer keyboard will open the *Outlook Help* dialog box.

Microsoft Outlook Help dialog box

MORE INFO

Quick Steps will be covered in Chapter 7.

What's New in Outlook 2010

Outlook 2010 has incorporated some new features and made some improvements in features existing from previous versions of Outlook. The following is a brief list of some of the major additions and improvements made to make Outlook 2010 work more effectively for you.

- **New User Interface:** As mentioned previously, Outlook 2007 was one of the last of the Office applications to use pull-down menus and toolbars in its main user interface. Outlook 2010 fully integrates the *tabs* and *ribbons* interface throughout Outlook. This new user interface makes Outlook more consistent throughout the entire program and more consistent with the other Microsoft Office 2010 applications.

    Outlook 2010 has integrated many global Outlook features that were previously available from the Office button or File menu and consolidated these into the *Office BackStage.* The **File** tab is the tab in the upper left corner of the Outlook window. When the **File** tab is clicked, the *BackStage* window will open. BackStage provides users with many of Outlook's global and special features combined into one window.

Outlook BackStage window

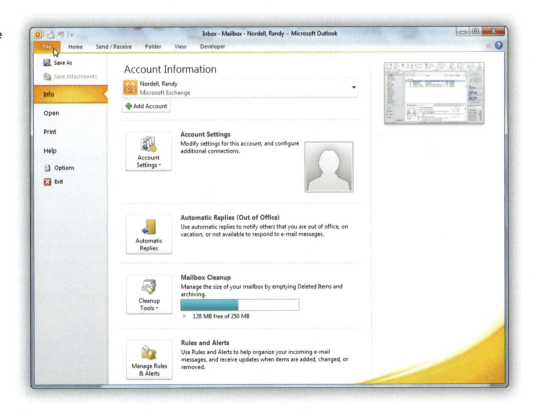

E-mail Quick Steps

- **Quick Steps:** In Outlook 2010, the Quick Steps feature has been added to Outlook Mail. Quick Steps allow you to perform multiple-step actions with a single click. For example, you could create a Quick Step to reply to, categorize, flag, and move an e-mail to a different folder—all in one step. Outlook provides some preset Quick Steps, but you can also create your own or modify existing Quick Steps.

- **People Pane and Outlook Social Connector:** The *People pane* consolidates in one area all Outlook items associated with an individual. These can include e-mails, meetings, contacts, and task requests. In addition the *Outlook Social Connector* (OSC) allows Outlook users to integrate with SharePoint and other social networks, enabling you to manage your professional network within Outlook.

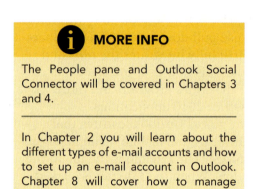

MORE INFO

The People pane and Outlook Social Connector will be covered in Chapters 3 and 4.

In Chapter 2 you will learn about the different types of e-mail accounts and how to set up an e-mail account in Outlook. Chapter 8 will cover how to manage multiple e-mail accounts in Outlook.

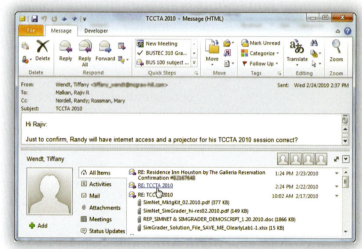

E-mail with People pane displayed

- **Multiple E-mail Accounts:** With each new version of Outlook, the ability to integrate and manage multiple e-mail accounts has improved. In the past, you have been able to manage multiple POP, IMAP, and HTTP accounts, but you were limited to only one Exchange account. A major change in Outlook 2010 is the ability to manage more than one Exchange account.

- **Manage Large Volumes of E-mail:** One of the biggest challenges when using e-mail is to keep up with the ever-increasing number of e-mails received on a daily basis. Outlook 2010 has enhanced some existing features and incorporated new features to help you manage your e-mail. The ability to group e-mail by *Conversation* existed in previous versions of Outlook, but in Outlook 2010 this feature has been greatly enhanced. In addition to better-functioning conversation grouping, Outlook now includes *Clean Up* and *Ignore* features to help you manage your e-mail.

MORE INFO

Conversation, Clean Up, and Ignore features will be covered more thoroughly in Chapter 2.

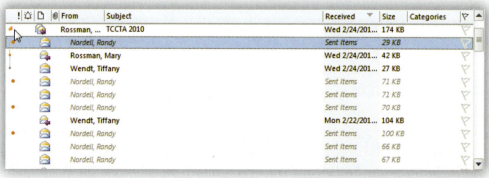

Conversation grouping

- **MailTips:** When responding to an e-mail, have you ever by mistake pressed the Reply All button rather than the Reply button? Outlook 2010 has added *MailTips* to alert you when you are replying to a large number of recipients or distribution list. MailTips will also alert you when you are sending confidential information to someone outside of your company or when you are sending to a recipient who is out of the office.

MORE INFO

MailTips will be covered in Chapters 2 and 8.

- **Scheduling Meetings:** When using Outlook in an Exchange environment, one of the distinct advantages is the ability to share information with others. In Outlook 2010 the ability to view others' calendars to schedule an appointment, event, or meeting has been enhanced with *Schedule View,* which allows you to view shared calendars in a timeline format, which makes scheduling calendar items much easier.

MORE INFO

Using shared calendars to schedule appointments and meetings will be covered in Chapter 10.

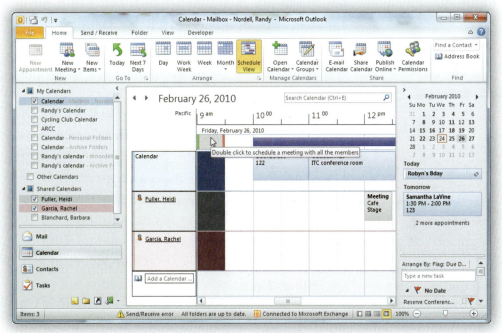

Schedule View

MORE INFO

Microsoft Office Communicator and the enhanced communication capabilities of Outlook 2010 will be covered in Chapter 8.

- **Increased Communication:** Outlook 2010 has expanded its communication capabilities beyond e-mail. It now has the ability to communicate with contacts via instant messaging, text messaging, voice call, or video. These new features of Outlook require the use of *Microsoft Office Communicator.*

Outlook as a Stand-Alone Program

Microsoft Outlook can be used as either a *stand-alone program* or in conjunction with a *Microsoft Exchange Server* (also referred to as an Exchange server or Exchange). Many individuals use Outlook on their home computer, and this is what is meant by stand-alone program. Outlook is still part of the Microsoft Office 2010 suite of software and is still capable of performing all the main functions of this personal management software.

When using Outlook in the home or personal environment, Outlook connects directly with your **Internet Service Provider** (**ISP**) and manages your e-mail through the accounts you set up. Outlook can handle a single e-mail account or multiple e-mail accounts. Some of the more advanced and specialty features in Outlook are only available when Outlook is used in conjunction with Exchange.

Outlook with an Exchange Server

In the business environment, Microsoft Outlook is typically connected to a **Microsoft Exchange Server.** Exchange on a business network handles all the incoming and outgoing mail. Each individual user of Exchange is actually a client of this Exchange network, and the network administrator sets up an account for each individual user. In addition to handling e-mail, Exchange also stores all the data associated with calendars, contacts, tasks, notes, and journals.

Outlook in an Exchange environment has the same user interface as in a stand-alone environment, but Outlook with an Exchange server does allow you more functionality. Some of the enhanced features an Exchange server will enable you to perform include:

FACTOID

Some of the new features in Outlook 2010, such as MailTips and voice mail, require Exchange Server 2010.

MORE INFO

As you progress through this book, you will be informed when Outlook performs functions differently when using Outlook as a stand-alone program or with Exchange. Also, Appendix D provides a summary of Outlook features unique to an Exchange environment.

- Using voting buttons and tracking responses
- Sending meeting requests and tracking responses
- Recalling messages
- Sharing your calendar, contacts, tasks, and e-mail with others
- Using MailTips
- Using a common global contact list

Chapter Highlights

▶ In addition to handling your **e-mail** accounts, Microsoft Outlook 2010 can also be used for the **Calendar, Contacts, Tasks, Notes,** and **Journal** features.

▶ Outlook can be set up to handle multiple e-mail accounts.

▶ The Outlook **Calendar** provides users with some distinct advantages over using a paper calendar. Your Outlook calendar can remind you of appointments, be edited easily, be shared with other Outlook users, and be synchronized with a PDA, cell phone, or other computers.

▶ The **Contacts** feature in Outlook can be used not only to save and store e-mail addresses, but also to store other personal and company information.

- The **Tasks** feature in Outlook allows you to keep a running list of tasks while enabling you to provide additional information about the task, set electronic reminders, and assign a task to another Outlook user.

- Outlook **Notes** are similar to the sticky notes so many of us use regularly. They are used to store information that does not necessarily fall into the category of a calendar item, contact, or task.

- **Outlook Today** is an introductory screen in Outlook that will give you an overview of e-mail, calendar items, and tasks.

- The Microsoft Outlook working environment is set up into sections called **panes.** The four main panes in Outlook are the **Navigation pane, Folder pane, Reading pane,** and **People pane.**

- The **Navigation pane** is on the left edge of the Outlook window and includes buttons to navigate through the different features available in Outlook.

- The **Folder pane** shows the contents of the folder selected in the Navigation pane.

- The **Reading pane** displays the contents of an item selected in the Folder pane. The Reading pane can be displayed at the right or bottom, or it can be turned off.

- The **People pane** is new to Outlook 2010 and displays Outlook items associated with an individual. The People pane is displayed below the Reading pane in the main Outlook interface.

- The size of these panes can be customized by clicking and holding the border of the pane and dragging it to the desired size.

- Outlook uses a combination of **tabs, ribbons,** and **dialog boxes** to provide you with easy access to Outlook features and options.

- Each new item you create (e-mail, calendar, contacts, tasks) will have **tabs** and **ribbons** as the navigational structure to provide you with the different features and actions available.

- Each ribbon is broken into **groups.** Some of the groups have an **expand button,** which can be used to open a **dialog box** that contains more features and options.

- Each of the different main tasks in Outlook has a variety of preset **views** from which to choose. These different views control how the information is displayed in the Folder pane.

- The **Folder list** displays all the folders available in Outlook in the Navigation pane.

- **Outlook Help** is an online search engine that will provide you with help on specific Outlook topics.

- Outlook 2010 has fully integrated the use of tabs and ribbons into its user interface.

- The **BackStage** window will open when the File tab is clicked. Outlook BackStage combines many global and special features into one location.

- **Quick Steps** is a new e-mail feature in Outlook that provides the ability to perform multistep actions with the click of a button.

- The **Outlook Social Connector** and the **People pane** work in conjunction to provide you with consolidated information about your personal and professional contacts.

- Outlook 2010 gives you the ability to manage **multiple Exchange e-mail accounts.**

- The ability to manage a large volume of e-mail has been enhanced with the **Conversation** grouping, **Clean Up,** and **Ignore.**

- **MailTips** is a new Outlook feature that alerts you when you are responding to a large distribution list, sending confidential information, or sending to a recipient who is out of the office.

- The **Schedule View** has been added to the Outlook Calendar to help you more effectively schedule calendar items.

- **Microsoft Office Communicator** gives you the ability to communicate with contacts via instant messaging, text messaging, voice call, and video.

- Microsoft Outlook can be used as either a **stand-alone** program or in conjunction with a **Microsoft Exchange Server.** Most home users of Outlook use this software as a stand-alone program, while most business users use Outlook in an Exchange environment.

What Do You Know About Outlook?

True/False Questions

T F   1. The e-mail feature is just one of the features available in Outlook. [Objective 1.1]

T F   2. Outlook is a stand-alone program that does not work in conjunction with other Microsoft software such as Word, Excel, and Access. [Objective 1.1]

T F   3. Outlook Contacts are used to store only e-mail addresses. [Objective 1.1]

T F   4. One of the advantages of Outlook Tasks is that they can be assigned to another person. [Objective 1.1]

T F   5. There are four different panes in Outlook. [Objective 1.2]

Multiple Choice Questions

1. Which of the following is *not* a display option for the Reading pane? [Objective 1.2]
   a. Top
   b. Bottom
   c. Right
   d. Off

2. The large Navigation buttons in the Navigation pane include: [Objectives 1.1 and 1.2]
   a. Calendar
   b. Mail
   c. Tasks
   d. All the above

3. Which of the following is *not* displayed in the Outlook Today window? [Objectives 1.1 and 1.2]
   a. E-mail messages
   b. Contacts
   c. Calendar
   d. Tasks

4. Which is true of Outlook ribbons? [Objective 1.2]
   a. Each group has an expand button.
   b. All the available options are included on the Outlook ribbons.
   c. The expand button on a group opens a dialog box.
   d. All the above.

5. Which of the following features are unique to Outlook when used in an Exchange environment? [Objective 1.4]
   a. Global contact list
   b. Shared calendar
   c. Recalling messages
   d. All the above

Short Answer Questions

1. List three advantages to using an Outlook calendar as compared to a paper calendar. [Objective 1.1]

2. Describe how to change the size of the panes in Outlook. [Objective 1.2]

3. Explain how to change a view in the Folder pane. [Objective 1.2]

Putting Outlook to Work

It's now time to familiarize yourself with the working environment of Outlook 2010. Getting comfortable navigating throughout will help you as you progress through this text and learn many of the Outlook features that will be covered.

Exercise 1.1 [Guided Practice]

Familiarize yourself with the basic components of Outlook.
[Objectives 1.1 and 1.2]

1. Click on the **Mail** button in the *Navigation* pane.
   a. Notice the different folders available in the *Navigation* pane above the *Navigation* buttons.
   b. Look at the menus and toolbars available.

2. Click on the **Inbox** folder.
   a. Notice the items that appear in the *Folder* pane.

3. Click on one of the e-mails in your Inbox in the *Folder* pane.
   a. Notice how the e-mail appears in the *Reading* pane.

4. Click on the **New E-mail** button in the *New* group on the *Home* ribbon. A new e-mail message will open.
   a. Notice the tabs and ribbons at the top of the message.
   b. Click on the **Insert** tab.

Exercise 1.4 [Guided Practice]

Use the Folder list in the Navigation pane. [Objectives 1.1 and 1.2]

1. Notice the small buttons at the bottom of the Navigation pane below the four main Navigation buttons (Mail, Calendar, Contacts, Tasks).

2. Locate the *Folder List* button. When you put your mouse pointer over a button, a tag will appear with the name of the button.

3. Click on the **Folder List** button.

   a. Notice the list of folders in the *Navigation* pane above the *Navigation* buttons.
   b. Notice that not only are the mail folders available, but also all the folders for Calendar, Contacts, Tasks, Notes, and Journal.
   c. The *Folder List* button appears shaded when it is turned on.

4. Click on the **Calendar** folder in the *Folder* list.

   a. Notice the Calendar appears in the *Folder* pane.
   b. Notice also that the *Folder* list continues to appear in the *Navigation* pane.

5. Click on the **Inbox** folder in the *Navigation* pane. The items in the Inbox appear in the *Folder* pane.

6. Click on the **Mail** button in the *Navigation* pane.

   a. Notice that only the Mail folders now appear in the *Navigation* pane.
   b. To turn off the *Folder list,* another button (e.g., Mail, Calendar, Contacts, Tasks) must be selected.

Exercise 1.5 [Independent Practice]

Modify the Reading pane and view the People pane. [Objective 1.2]

1. Click on the **Mail** button in the *Navigation* pane.

2. Click on the **Inbox** folder in the *Navigation* pane.

3. In the *Folder* pane, click on one of the e-mails in your *Inbox*.

   a. If the *Reading* pane is displayed, notice how the message appears in the *Reading* pane.
   b. Notice the information from the e-mail message that appears in the *Reading* pane.
   c. Notice the buttons on the *Message* ribbon that are available for the message in the *Reading* pane.

4. Change the location of the *Reading* pane so it appears below the *Folder* pane.

   a. Use the *View* ribbon to change the location of the *Reading* pane to appear at the bottom.

5. Turn the *Reading* pane **off.**

6. Turn the *Reading* pane back **on,** and display it at the **bottom.**

7. Adjust the size of the *Reading* page by clicking on and dragging the top edge of the *Reading* pane.

8. Click on the small arrow at the right side of the *People* pane to expand this pane.

   a. The small arrow at the right side of the *People* pane will expand or collapse this pane.

   b. Using the *People Pane* button in the *People Pane* group on the *View* ribbon, the *People* pane can be set to Normal (expanded), Minimized (collapsed), or Off.

9. **Minimize** (collapse) the *People* pane.

Exercise 1.6 [Independent Practice]

Adjust the size of the different panes in the Outlook window.
[Objective 1.2]

1. Click on the **Mail** button in the *Navigation* pane.
2. Increase the width of the *Navigation* pane.
3. Decrease the size of the *Folder* pane.

   a. This will also increase the size of the *Reading* pane.

4. Change the location of the *Reading* pane to appear at the right.
5. Increase the size of the *Folder* pane.
6. Change the location of the *Reading* pane back to the bottom.
7. Adjust the sizes of the *Navigation, Folder,* and *Reading* panes to your preference.

Chapter 2
E-mail Basics

OBJECTIVES   *After completing this chapter, you will be able to:*

2.1   Distinguish between the different types of e-mail accounts.

2.2   Set up an e-mail account in Outlook.

2.3   Use Outlook to create, send, and receive e-mail.

2.4   Understand and incorporate attachments in e-mail.

2.5   Recognize and differentiate e-mail arrangement and icons.

2.6   Understand the importance and process of cleaning up an Inbox.

CHAPTER FLYOVER   *This chapter will introduce you to the basics of e-mail and will cover the following topics:*

- ▶ Types of e-mail accounts
- ▶ Setting up an e-mail account
- ▶ Creating a new e-mail
- ▶ Selecting recipients, Cc, and Bcc
- ▶ Subject line and body of e-mail
- ▶ Formatting text
- ▶ Sending an e-mail
- ▶ Saving an e-mail draft
- ▶ Opening an e-mail
- ▶ Reply, Reply All, and Forward
- ▶ Saving an e-mail
- ▶ Printing an e-mail
- ▶ Recalling an e-mail

- ▶ Resending an e-mail
- ▶ Attaching a file to an e-mail
- ▶ Opening and saving attachments
- ▶ Previewing an attachment
- ▶ Forwarding an e-mail as an attachment
- ▶ Attaching other Outlook items
- ▶ Understanding arrangement and icons
- ▶ Deleting an e-mail
- ▶ Deleted items
- ▶ Clean Up and Ignore
- ▶ Emptying deleted items

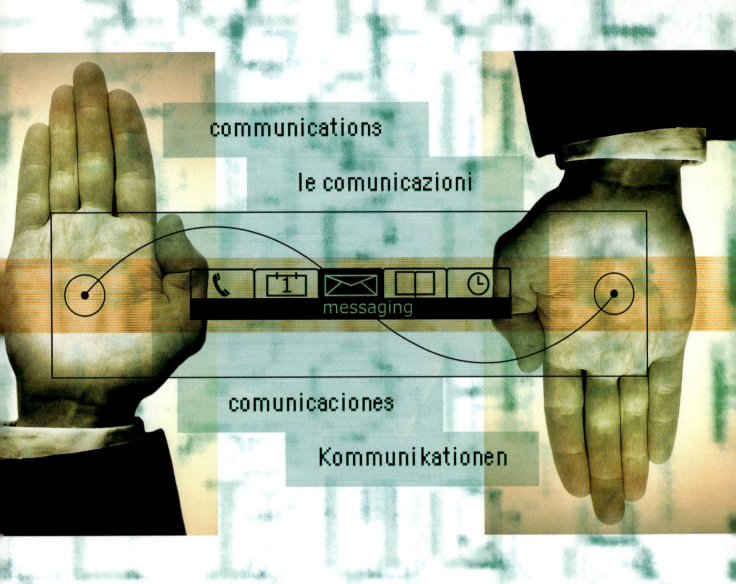

communications

le comunicazioni

messaging

comunicaciones

Kommunikationen

Making Outlook Work for You

Today, most people equate Microsoft Outlook with e-mail, and these two terms have become almost synonymous in their use. E-mail is an integral part of Outlook, but it is much more than just e-mail as you will discover as you continue through this text. Most people use e-mail on a daily basis, and Outlook is widely used in both the business and home environment to manage e-mail accounts.

It is important to remember that Outlook is not e-mail, but rather a computer software program that handles e-mail accounts. Just as your mail carrier is not the mail itself, but rather the person who delivers your mail to your home mailbox, Outlook delivers e-mail received through your existing e-mail account(s). You must have an e-mail account to use Outlook to send and receive e-mail.

Outlook allows you to create and send e-mail, reply to received e-mail, forward e-mail to other recipients, save and manage e-mail, and flag and categorize e-mail. E-mail is also useful as a method of sending pictures and

 **FACTOID**

Average business users of e-mail send/receive 156 e-mails a day (Radicati Group, 2008). E-mail communication is fast and is one of the most common forms of communication in the business environment.

other types of computer files to others. Most individuals cannot imagine their daily work and personal business without the use of e-mail.

Types of E-mail Accounts

There are four different types of e-mail accounts that can be set up in Outlook: *Microsoft Exchange, POP3, IMAP,* and *HTTP.* Multiple e-mail accounts can be set up in Outlook. In previous versions of Outlook, only one Exchange account could be connected, but Outlook 2010 gives you the ability to set up multiple exchange accounts.

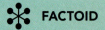 **FACTOID**

Twenty percent of young adults have three or more e-mail accounts (Pew Internet Project, 2008).

Microsoft Exchange

Microsoft Exchange accounts are used primarily in medium- to large-business settings. These e-mail accounts are set up through the company network or e-mail administrator. An Exchange account has an individual mailbox assigned to each user and resides on an Exchange file server. Outlook connects to the Exchange server to retrieve your e-mail. Exchange accounts use Messaging Application Programming Interface (MAPI) and provide enhanced functionality when used with Outlook. Recalling messages, tracking voting responses, and sharing Outlook with others on your Exchange system are features that are associated with Exchange accounts and Outlook.

Post Office Protocol (POP3)

POP3 accounts are Internet e-mail accounts that are associated with your Internet service provider (ISP). If you have an ISP such as Comcast or AT&T, you will have an e-mail account (or multiple e-mail accounts) through your provider. This POP3 account can be set up in Outlook to send and receive e-mail. When using Outlook with this type of account, your e-mail messages are downloaded to Outlook.

Internet Message Access Protocol (IMAP)

IMAP accounts are also Internet accounts but are not always associated with an ISP. IMAP accounts create folders on a server to store and organize messages for retrieval by other computers and give you the option to read message headers only and select which messages to download. These types of accounts are becoming increasingly popular as personal e-mail accounts. Gmail is an example of an IMAP e-mail account.

Hypertext Transfer Protocol (HTTP)

HTTP accounts use the hypertext transfer protocol used on the Web to create, view, send, and receive messages. This type of account is not automatically supported by Outlook but can be configured by installing an add-in. Windows Live Mail is an HTTP account that can be configured to work with Outlook by using the MSN Connector for Outlook.

Setting up an E-mail Account

To create, send, and receive e-mail, Outlook must be set up to recognize your e-mail account. In the past it has been a challenge to get all the specific information needed to set up an e-mail account, but beginning with Outlook

2007 an *Auto Account Setup* feature was added to automatically detect the incoming and outgoing server.

To set up your account, you will need to supply your **e-mail address** and **password** to access the account. This will give Outlook the location of your Exchange or Internet mailbox, and your password provides access to the account. An account only needs to be set up once, and it will be stored in Outlook for future use.

BackStage window used to add e-mail account

Step-by-Step

1. Click on the **File** tab. The *BackStage* window will open.
2. Click on the **Add Account** button. The *Add New Account* dialog box will open.
3. Enter account settings: **Your Name** (as you want it to appear in e-mail), **E-mail address, Password, Retype Password.**
4. Click **Next.**

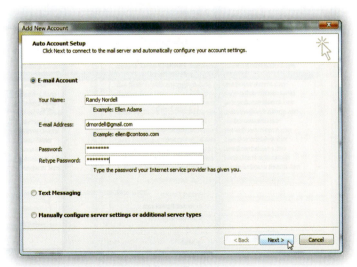

Add New Account dialog box

Cc & Bcc

There are two other options that are available when selecting recipients for your e-mail message: *Copy* (Cc) and **Blind copy** (Bcc). Cc is used when someone is not the main recipient of the message, but they need to be kept informed of the contents of the message or ongoing e-mail discussion.

FACTOID

Cc used to refer to carbon copy. Back in the day of typewriters, the only way to make a copy was to use carbon paper between two sheets of paper in the typewriter.

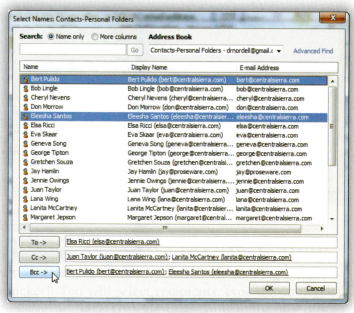

Cc and Bcc fields in the Select Names dialog box

Bcc is used when you do not want those receiving the e-mail message to see other recipients' e-mail address or names. When a recipient receives an e-mail, he or she will be able to see other recipients' names/e-mail addresses in both the To and Cc fields, but the Bcc field is hidden.

NETIQUETTE

Be careful about sharing e-mail addresses with those outside of your organization. Bcc is a great feature to provide confidentiality in e-mail by hiding others' e-mail addresses. To send an e-mail, there must be at least one recipient in one of the recipient fields.

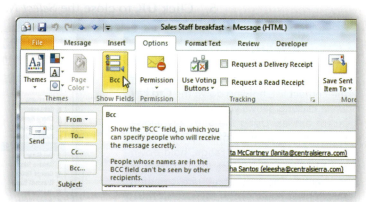

Show Bcc button

The Cc button appears on a new message and can be used like the To button to select recipients. By default, the Bcc button or field is not available when you open a new e-mail message. You can click on either the **To** or **Cc** button to open the *Select Names* dialog box. Once this dialog box is open, the *Bcc* field is available.

ANOTHER WAY

In a new e-mail message, click on the **Options** tab and then click on the **Bcc** button in the *Show Fields* group. Bcc recipients can now be selected by clicking on the **Bcc** button.

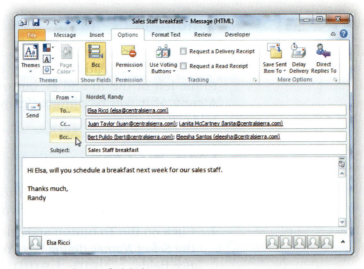

E-mail with Bcc field shown

NETIQUETTE

Use a subject line on every e-mail, and keep it short and descriptive. Your subject line might determine whether or not your message gets read.

Be careful to not overdo it with text formatting in the body of an e-mail message. Depending on the type of e-mail account the recipient has, some of the text formatting might not be visible to the recipient.

Subject Line and Body

The **Subject** line alerts recipients to the subject of the e-mail, and the **Body** contains the contents of the e-mail. When a new e-mail message is created, the e-mail is untitled (top center), but once a subject is typed in, it becomes the message title.

Formatting Text

Outlook provides users many of the same formatting features that are available in Microsoft Word. These text formatting features can be used in the body of the e-mail message. Many of the commonly used formatting features are available on the *Message* ribbon in the *Basic Text* group. This *Basic Text* group can be expanded (by clicking the small box in the bottom right corner of the group) to open the *Font* dialog box.

Formatting options on the Message ribbon

More formatting options are available by clicking on the *Format Text* tab, which opens this ribbon for additional formatting features.

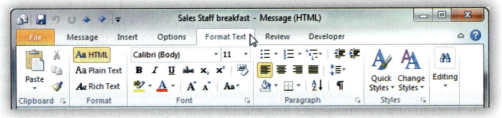

Format Text ribbon

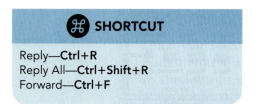

SHORTCUT

Reply—**Ctrl+R**
Reply All—**Ctrl+Shift+R**
Forward—**Ctrl+F**

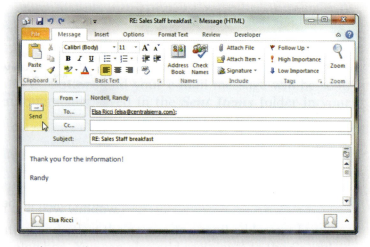

Reply e-mail

To use any of the response options, open the e-mail and choose either Reply, Reply All, or Forward.

Saving an E-mail

When an e-mail message is sent, the original message remains in your Inbox and a copy of the response is automatically saved in the Sent Items folder. There might be times when you want to save an important or sensitive e-mail message outside of Outlook. You can save e-mail messages to a different folder on your computer.

 ## ANOTHER WAY

When viewing a message in the *Folder* or *Reading* pane, the *Reply, Reply All,* and *Forward* buttons are located in the *Respond* group on the *Home* ribbon. Clicking on any of these buttons will open the message.

NETIQUETTE

Use Reply All sparingly and only when it is absolutely necessary that all original recipients receive your response to the original message. Don't unnecessarily clutter up others' e-mail Inboxes.

Saving an e-mail message outside of Outlook using Save As

Step-by-Step

1. Either click on the message to be saved in the *Folder* pane, or open the message into a new window.

2. Click on the **File** tab. The *BackStage* window will open.

3. Click on the **Save As** button. The *Save As* dialog box will open.

4. Browse to the desired location to save the file.

5. By default the *File name* will be the subject line of the e-mail. You can change this if you desire.

6. Click on the **Save** button.

MORE INFO

MailTips, a new feature in Outlook 2010, will alert you if you are replying to a large distribution list. MailTips will be covered in Chapter 8.

Folders can be created in Outlook to store and organize e-mail messages. Creating and using folders will be covered in Chapter 7.

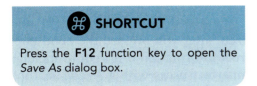

SHORTCUT

Press the **F12** function key to open the *Save As* dialog box.

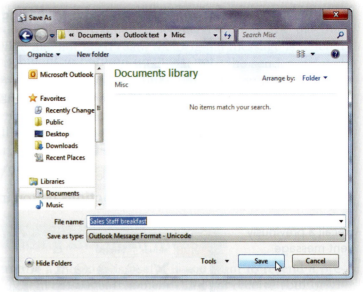

Save As dialog box

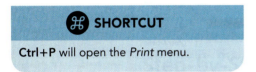

SHORTCUT

Ctrl+P will open the *Print* menu.

Printing an E-mail

If you are on your way to a meeting and need some information from an e-mail in your Inbox, you might want to print the e-mail to take with you. Also, you might want to print the contents of one of your Inbox folders. The Print option in Outlook allows you to print either an individual e-mail in ***Memo Style*** or the contents of a folder in ***Table Style.***

Step-by-Step

1. Select the e-mail or folder to be printed.
2. Click on the **File** tab. The *BackStage* window will open.
3. Click on the **Print** button.
4. Select the type of printout you would like in the *Print What* area.
5. Click on the **Print** button.

Printing options in Outlook

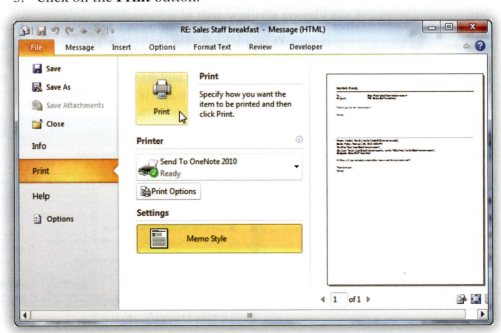

Step-by Step

1. When creating, replying to, or forwarding an e-mail, click on the **Attach File** button in the *Include* group on the *Message* ribbon.
2. Browse through the files on your computer.
3. Select the files (remember the Ctrl and Shift keys can be used to select multiple files).
4. Click **Insert.**

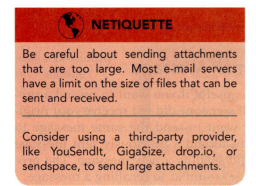

NETIQUETTE

Be careful about sending attachments that are too large. Most e-mail servers have a limit on the size of files that can be sent and received.

Consider using a third-party provider, like YouSendIt, GigaSize, drop.io, or sendspace, to send large attachments.

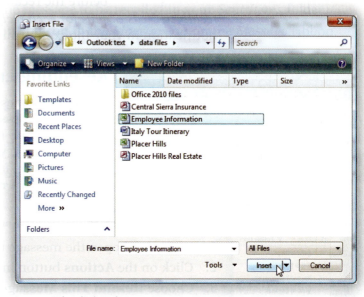

Insert File dialog box

5. The attached files will appear below the subject line.

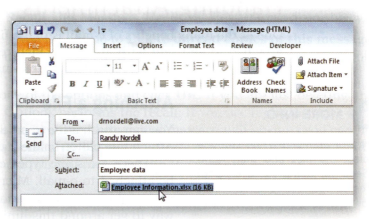

File attached to e-mail

FACTOID

Attachments are usually associated with specific software. For example, if you receive a compressed Access database, you will need to have Access on your computer to be able to open the file.

Opening and Saving Attachments

Usually when an attachment is received via e-mail, you will want to open and/or save the attachment. It will be located below the subject line in the e-mail.

Outlook 2010 has made attachment handling much easier with the new ***Attachments*** ribbon. This ribbon is automatically displayed when the attachment is selected in an e-mail message. Using the Attachments ribbon, you can open, save, print, copy, or remove the attachment.

Step-by-Step

1. With an e-mail message open or in the *Reading* pane, click on the **attachment.** The *Attachments* ribbon is displayed.
2. Click on the **Open** button in the *Actions* group to open the attachment. It will open in a new window.

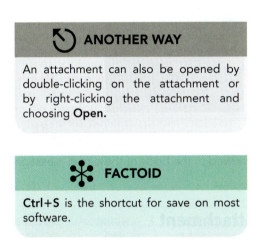

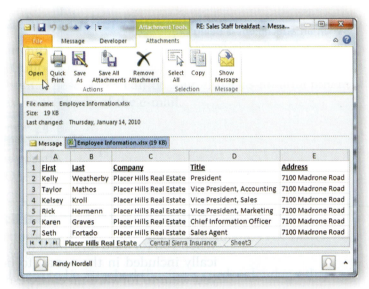

E-mail with attachment. Attachments ribbon displayed and attachment being previewed in body of message.

If an attachment is opened, it can be saved the same way you save any other open document. Typically, you can save an open document by pressing **Ctrl+S** or clicking on the **Save** icon located on the ribbon or *Quick Access* toolbar. Be sure to specify the location where you want the document saved.

An attachment can also be saved without opening it from the e-mail.

Step-by-Step

1. Click on the attachment to be saved. The *Attachments* ribbon will open.
2. Click on the **Save As** button in the *Actions* group. The *Save As* dialog box will open.
3. Choose the desired location to save the file, and specify a file name.
4. Click **Save.**

Previewing an Attachment

Outlook allows you to preview most types of attachments without opening them. When you click on the attachment, the attachment will be displayed in the body of the message. You can return to the e-mail message

ANOTHER WAY

An attachment can also be opened by double-clicking on the attachment or by right-clicking the attachment and choosing **Open.**

FACTOID

Ctrl+S is the shortcut for save on most software.

MORE INFO

Message options will be covered in Chapter 3, which will describe how to use the different features associated with some of the Inbox icons. Chapter 12 will cover how to customize the user interface.

Understanding Arrangement and Icons

As mentioned in Chapter 1, the working environment in Outlook is broken into panes. There are typically four panes open in Outlook: *Navigation, Folder, Reading,* and *People.* There is also the *To-Do bar* that can be open or collapsed.

In the Folder pane, you can arrange e-mails in numerous different ways to meet your needs and preferences. Outlook also provides users with many *icons* to help easily and quickly identify different aspects of an e-mail displayed in the Folder pane. The icons on each e-mail in the Folder pane can tell you if a message has been read, if it has been replied to or forwarded, if there is an attachment, if it is marked *important,* if it is *flagged* for action, or if it is assigned to a *category.*

Arrangement

Arrangement controls the order in which e-mail messages are displayed in the Folder pane. Typically e-mail messages are arranged or sorted with the most recently received e-mail at the top of the list (i.e., arranged by date and time in descending order). The *View* ribbon provides you with different View and Arrangement options. Outlook 2010 has upgraded the arrangement options to make it easier to quickly change the arrangement of e-mails.

View ribbon

Also, Outlook 2010 has greatly enhanced the **Conversation** arrangement. This new default arrangement groups all e-mails related to a particular e-mail conversation (by subject), which is intended to greatly reduce the number of redundant e-mails displayed in the folder list. The Conversation arrangement groups these e-mails together to take up less space in your list of e-mails and gives you the ability to expand the conversation and see all related messages, including those in the Sent Items folder.

MORE INFO

Customizing Folder pane views will be covered in Chapter 12.

Conversation arrangement expanded

When there are multiple e-mails within a conversation, clicking on the small triangle to the left of an e-mail will expand the conversation. The conversation can be collapsed by clicking on the small triangle to the left of the conversation subject in the Folder pane.

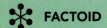 **FACTOID**

When you click the small triangle next to a conversation, the message will be expanded to show the related messages in the current folder. When you click on the triangle again, the conversation expands to include related messages in other folders.

Conversation Thread

Conversation arrangement expanded to include Sent Items

There are many other preset arrangement options available in Outlook. These can be selected from the *Arrangement* group on the View ribbon.

Read/Unread E-mail

When the Inbox (or any other folder) is selected in your Navigation pane, the contents of that folder are displayed in the Folder pane. The icon to the left of the e-mail shows whether or not the e-mail has been read. When an e-mail

Inbox contents displayed in the Folder pane.

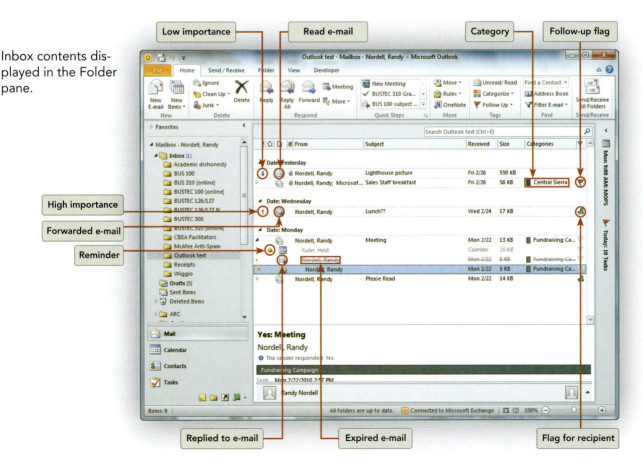

has not been read, the e-mail is bold and has a ***closed envelope*** icon. Once the e-mail has been opened and read, the e-mail will no longer be bold and the icon will be an ***open envelope.***

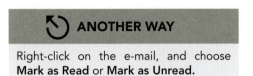

ANOTHER WAY

Right-click on the e-mail, and choose **Mark as Read** or **Mark as Unread.**

Mark as Read/Unread

When an e-mail is opened, Outlook marks it as read. There are times when you might want to mark a message as unread to draw attention to it in the folder or Folder pane. Outlook gives you the option of marking an e-mail as ***Read*** or ***Unread.***

Mark as Unread/ Read button

Step-by-Step

1. Select the e-mail in the *Folder* pane to be marked as **Read** or **Unread.**
2. In the *Tags* group on the *Home* ribbon, click on the **Unread/Read** button.

Replied to and Forwarded

By scanning your e-mail in the Folder pane, you can easily see the response action previously taken on each e-mail. Messages that have been replied to have a ***purple arrow*** on the e-mail icon pointing to the left, and those that have been forwarded have a ***blue arrow*** pointing to the right. See the Inbox contents screen at the bottom of page 45.

MORE INFO

The entire contents of a folder can be marked as Read by either right-clicking on the folder and choosing **Mark All as Read,** or by clicking on the **Mark All as Read** button in the *Clean Up* group on the *Folder* ribbon.

Using follow-up flags and flags for recipients will be covered in Chapter 3 on page 67.

Marking an item for importance will be covered in Chapter 3 on page 63.

Attachment

Outlook uses a ***paper clip*** icon to indicate that an e-mail has an attachment. See the Inbox contents screen at the bottom of page 45.

Flag

When a message is flagged for follow-up or has a flag for recipients, the ***flag*** icon is used. This flag will appear in different shades of red depending on the action of the flag. See the Inbox contents screen at the bottom of page 45.

Importance

There are three levels of importance that can be set for each e-mail: ***High, Low,*** and ***Normal.*** High Importance is indicated by a red exclamation point, Low Importance uses a blue arrow pointed down, and Normal Importance uses no special icon. (Normal Importance is the default on all new e-mail messages.) See the Inbox contents screen at the bottom of page 45.

Reminder

When an e-mail is received that includes a reminder, it is marked with a ***small bell*** icon. An electronic reminder will open on your computer on the reminder day and time. You have the options of **opening** the e-mail, **dismissing** the reminder, or **snoozing** the reminder.

 **MORE INFO**

Categories will be covered in depth in Chapter 7 on page 191.

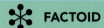 **FACTOID**

A friend recently confessed to having over 18,000 e-mails in his inbox. Yikes! Moral of the story—delete e-mail!

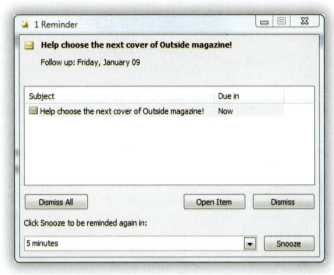

Reminder window

Category

Categories are used to group Inbox items. Colors are used to distinguish categories, and the category names can be customized to meet your individual needs. Categories are not limited to e-mail messages; they can also be advantageous for grouping contacts, tasks, and calendar items. See the Inbox contents screen at the bottom of page 45.

Cleaning Up Your Inbox

It is important to manage your Inbox effectively. When you receive mail (postal mail) at home or work, you read it and then determine what action needs to be taken. Bills need to be paid, some information needs to be filed and saved, junk mail is discarded, and other mail is thrown away when it has been responded to. Your e-mail Inbox is very similar. Throughout this text, you will learn about many different tools to help you effectively manage your Inbox. For now, it is important to learn how to delete an e-mail you no longer need.

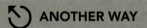 **ANOTHER WAY**

Outlook items can also be deleted by right-clicking on the item and choosing **Delete.**

Deleting E-mail

Select the e-mails to be deleted, and then either click on the **Delete** button in the *Delete* group on the *Home* ribbon or press the **Delete** key (not **Backspace**) on your computer keyboard. When an e-mail is deleted, it is not gone forever. It has been moved from your *Inbox* (or the folder it is in) to your *Deleted Items* folder.

 **SHORTCUT**

Use **Ctrl+D** to delete a selected Outlook item.

Delete button

Deleted Items folder
in the Navigation
pane

Deleted Items

Deleted Items is a folder in your list of *Mail* folders. Deleted e-mail, contacts, tasks, calendar items, and other Outlook items are stored in this folder when they are deleted from another location. By default Outlook does not delete the items in the Deleted Items folder. But, this is not a good location to store items you might need.

Clean Up and Ignore

By default Outlook now arranges e-mails displayed in the Folder pane by conversation. This helps to both group related items together and reduce the clutter and redundant e-mails in your Inbox. Two new features added to further manage conversations in Outlook are ***Clean Up*** and ***Ignore.*** Clean Up will remove redundant messages in an e-mail conversation. Clean Up can also be used on an entire folder and subfolders. Ignore will delete all e-mails related to a specific conversation and delete any new received e-mail that is related to that conversation.

Clean Up menu

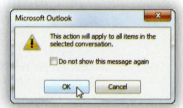

Ignore dialog box

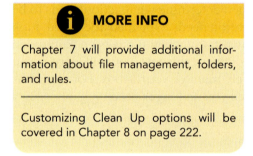

MORE INFO

Chapter 7 will provide additional information about file management, folders, and rules.

Customizing Clean Up options will be covered in Chapter 8 on page 222.

Both Clean Up and Ignore are handy features to help manage the volume of e-mails you receive. By default when you Clean Up or Ignore a conversation, the deleted e-mails are moved to the Deleted Items folder.

Empty Deleted Items

It is a good idea to regularly empty your Deleted Items folder. The items in this folder can be manually deleted.

Step-by-Step

1. Click on the **Deleted Items** folder in the *Navigation* pane.
2. Click on the **Folder** tab.
3. Click on the **Empty Folder** button in the *Clean Up* group. A dialog box will open confirming that you want to empty the Deleted Items folder.

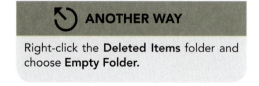

ANOTHER WAY

Right-click the **Deleted Items** folder and choose **Empty Folder.**

Empty "Deleted Items" Folder button

4. Choose **Yes** to delete items in the *Deleted Items* folder.

It is a good idea to have Outlook automatically empty the Deleted Items folder each time you exit Outlook. The default settings in Outlook can easily be changed to do this.

Step-by-Step

1. Click on the **File** tab to open the *BackStage*.
2. Click on the **Options** button at the left. The *Outlook Options* dialog box will open.
3. Click on the **Advanced** button at the left.
4. Check **Empty Deleted Items folder when exiting Outlook.**
5. Click **OK** to close the *Outlook Options* dialog box.

 **MORE INFO**

The Outlook Options dialog box will be used throughout this text. This area will allow you to customize the settings in Outlook. Outlook Options and other Outlook features are located on the *BackStage,* which is accessed by clicking on the **File** tab. Outlook Options will be covered in Chapter 8 on page 219.

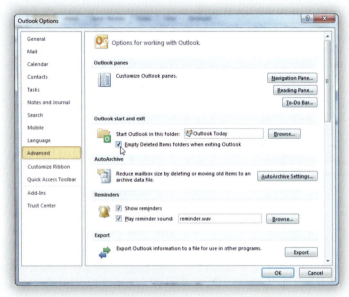

Outlook Options dialog box

Even when Outlook items have been deleted, and the Deleted Items folder has been emptied, Outlook still provides you with the ability to recover deleted items. The ***Recover Deleted Items*** button in the *Clean Up* group on the *Folder* ribbon will allow you to select previously deleted items to recover. These recovered items will be placed in your Deleted items folder.

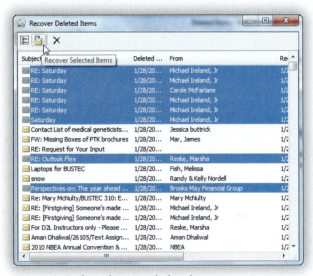

Recover Deleted Items dialog box

Chapter Highlights

▶ There are four different types of e-mail accounts that can be set up in Outlook: **Microsoft Exchange, Post Office Protocol** (POP3), **Internet Message Access Protocol** (IMAP), and **Hypertext Transfer Protocol** (HTTP).

▶ For Outlook to handle your e-mail, it must be set up to recognize your e-mail account. You only need to set up an account once in Outlook, and then you will have full access to that e-mail account.

▶ To set up an e-mail account, you need to go to the **Account Settings menu** and choose **New.** You will provide your e-mail address and password to authenticate your account.

▶ To create a new e-mail message, click on the **New** button on the ribbon (or Ctrl+N) when in the Mail feature of Outlook.

▶ To send an e-mail you must have at least one recipient. You can send to multiple recipients, and you can either type the e-mail addresses in the **To** field or click on the **To** button and choose recipients from your **Contacts.**

▶ The **Cc** (copy) and **Bcc** (blind copy) fields can be used for recipients who are not the main recipients of your e-mail, but would benefit from receiving a copy of the e-mail.

▶ The **Subject Line** of an e-mail contains the main subject of the e-mail, and the **Body** contains the contents of the e-mail.

▶ The text in the body of an e-mail can be formatted with different fonts, sizes, styles, and colors. These formatting options are available on the **Message** and **Format Text** tabs of a new e-mail message.

▶ An e-mail message can be **saved** before sending. Saved e-mail messages are stored in the **Drafts** folder. E-mail messages can also be saved outside of Outlook using **Save As.**

▶ When responding to an e-mail, you have three options: **Reply, Reply All,** and **Forward.**

▶ When using Outlook in an Exchange environment, a sent message can be **recalled.** When a message is recalled, you have the options of recalling the message or recalling and replacing it with a new message.

▶ An Outlook user can also **resend** a message previously sent.

▶ Many different types of files can be sent as an **attachment** to an e-mail message.

▶ When you receive an e-mail with an attachment, you can open or save the attachment. An e-mail received with an attachment can also be forwarded as an e-mail to others.

▶ Outlook also allows you to attach other Outlook items to an e-mail. For example, you can attach contact records to an e-mail and send them to recipients.

▶ The **Conversation** arrangement has been enhanced in Outlook 2010 and is the default grouping in the Folder pane. When e-mail items are arranged by conversation, they are grouped together based on the **subject line.**

- ▶ The conversation can be expanded to view the items in the conversation by clicking on the small triangle to the left of the conversation.

- ▶ Outlook uses **icons** to visually help you identify many different aspects of an e-mail message in the Folder pane. These icons include **Read/Unread e-mail, Replied To** and **Forwarded e-mail, Attachment, Flags, Importance, Reminder,** and **Categories.**

- ▶ A deleted e-mail is moved to the **Deleted Items** folder. Deleted items are stored in this folder until they are permanently deleted. Outlook can be set up to delete items in the Deleted Items folder each time you exit Outlook.

- ▶ **Clean Up** will move redundant e-mail messages in a conversation to the Deleted Items folder. **Ignore** will move an entire conversation to the Deleted Items folder.

What Do You Know About Outlook?

True/False Questions

T F 1. If you have a personal e-mail account, it is most likely an Exchange account. [Objective 2.1]

T F 2. Multiple Exchange accounts can be set up in Outlook. [Objectives 2.1, 2.2]

T F 3. To send an e-mail message, you must have at least one e-mail recipient. [Objective 2.3]

T F 4. Outlook can automatically empty the Deleted Items folder each time you exit Outlook. [Objective 2.6]

T F 5. When looking at e-mail icons in the Folder pane, there is a difference between Reply and Reply All. [Objectives 2.3, 2.5]

Multiple Choice Questions

1. Which of the following is *not* a type of e-mail account available in Outlook? [Objective 2.1]
   a. HTTP
   b. Exchange
   c. HTML
   d. POP3

2. To create a new e-mail message: [Objective 2.3]
   a. Click on the Mail button in the Navigation pane.
   b. Click on the Send button.
   c. Press Ctrl+N
   d. All the above.

3. When responding to an e-mail, which of the following options are *not* available? [Objective 2.3]
   a. Forward
   b. Reply All
   c. Reply
   d. Forward to All

4. The following Inbox icon indicates? 🛎 [Objective 2.5]
    a. Attachment
    b. High importance
    c. Reminder
    d. Flag

5. Which is true of an e-mail with an attachment? [Objective 2.4]
    a. The attachment is automatically saved.
    b. When forwarding the e-mail, the attachment is included.
    c. When replying to the e-mail, the attachment is included.
    d. All the above.

Short Answer Questions

1. Describe the type of information you need to provide Outlook to set up a new e-mail account. [Objective 2.2]

2. Explain how to save an attachment received in an e-mail. [Objective 2.4]

3. Explain how to set up Outlook to automatically empty the Deleted Items folder each time you exit Outlook. [Objective 2.6]

Putting Outlook to Work

Exercise 2.1 [Guided Practice]

Set up an e-mail account in Outlook. *(Note: Student accounts might already be set up if using an Exchange account.)* **[Objectives 2.1, 2.2]**

1. Click on the **File** tab. The *BackStage* window will open.

2. Click on the **Add Account** button. The *Add New Account* dialog box will open.

3. Select the **E-mail Account** radio button.

4. Enter **Your Name** (this will be the name that recipients will see when they receive an e-mail from you).

5. Enter the **E-mail Address, Password,** and **Retype Password** for the e-mail account you are setting up in Outlook.

6. Click **Next.**
    a. Outlook will confirm your e-mail address and validate it with your password.
    b. Once this is complete, your e-mail account is set up, and you can begin using this e-mail account through Outlook.
    c. This setup process only needs to be completed once; Outlook will save your account settings.
    d. If this is the first account you set up in Outlook, this will be your default account in Outlook. If you have multiple accounts in Outlook, you will specify which account you want to be your default account.

7. Click **Finish.**

Exercise 2.2 [Guided Practice]

Create and send an e-mail message through Outlook. [Objective 2.3]

1. Click on the **Mail** button in the *Navigation* pane.
2. Click on the **New E-mail** button in the *New* group on the *Home* ribbon (or press **Ctrl+N**). A new e-mail message will open.
3. Type in your professor's e-mail address in the *To* field.
4. Type your e-mail address in the *Cc* field.
   a. This will send a copy of this message to your Inbox.
5. Type `[your first name]'s first e-mail` in the *Subject* line.
6. Press **Tab** or click in the body of the e-mail.
   a. Notice the Subject of the e-mail is now the title of the message at the top of the new message window.
7. Type your name and e-mail address in the body of the message.
8. Change the font and size of the text in the body.
   a. Be careful about using too small or too large of a font in the body of an e-mail. Also, be aware that some colors and fonts are more difficult to read.
9. Click **Send.**

Exercise 2.3 [Guided Practice]

Create and send an e-mail message with an attachment. [Objectives 2.3, 2.4]

1. Open a new e-mail message (**Ctrl+N** or **New E-mail** button).
2. Click on the **To** button. The *Select Names* dialog box opens.
3. Select the e-mail addresses for your classmates. (Note: These will be in the Global Address List if you are on an Exchange server.)
   a. You can select a range of names (e-mail addresses) by clicking and dragging over the names you wish to include. You can also select a range by clicking on the first item in a list, holding down the **Shift** key, and selecting the last item in the list.
   b. To select nonadjacent names, hold down the **Ctrl** key and click on the names you want to add.
4. Click on the **To** button at the bottom of the *Select Names* dialog box. This will populate the *To* field with the names selected.
5. Select your professor's e-mail address.
6. Click on the **Bcc** button at the bottom of the *Select Names* dialog box. This will send a blind computer copy to your professor.
   a. When the other students receive this e-mail, they will be able to see the other recipients in the To field, but they will not be able to see your professor's e-mail in the Bcc field.
7. Click **OK** to close the *Select Names* dialog box.
   a. Notice the *Bcc* line appears. This line appears only when you have a recipient in the *Bcc* field.
   b. On a new message, the *Bcc* field can be made visible by clicking on the **Options** tab, and clicking on **Show Bcc** in the *Show Fields* group.

8. Type **E-mail with attachment** in the **Subject** field.
9. In the body type **Check out this picture** and include **your name.**
10. On the *Message* ribbon in the *Include* group click on the **Attach File** button. The *Insert File* dialog box will open.
    a. Browse to the *Pictures* folder on your computer and select a picture. (Note: This will vary on some computers.)
    b. Click **Insert** or **double-click** on the file.
    c. Notice the *Attached* field appears below the *Bcc* line.
11. Check to make sure your recipient e-mail addresses are in the *To* field, your professor's e-mail address is in the *Bcc* field, and the attachment is in the *Attached* field.
12. Click **Send.**

Exercise 2.4 [Guided Practice]

Open and reply to an e-mail message. [Objectives 2.3, 2.5]

1. Click on your **Inbox** folder in the *Navigation* pane. The list of received e-mails appears in the *Folder* pane.
2. Click on one of the **[classmate's first name] first e-mail** messages.
    a. Notice the message contents appear in the *Reading* pane (turn on the *Reading* pane if it is off).
3. Double-click on the selected message in the *Folder* pane to open it in a new window.
4. In the *Respond* group you have three options: *Reply, Reply All,* and *Forward.*
5. Click on the **Reply** button.
    a. A new reply message is opened.
    b. Notice the name/e-mail address of the originator of the message is in the *To* field.
    c. An "RE:" has been placed in front of the subject in the *Subject* field. This indicates to the recipient that this e-mail is a reply.
    d. Notice the body of the message has been moved down, and there is a space provided at the top of the body for you to type in a message.
6. Type **Thanks for your e-mail** and your name in the body.
7. Click on the **Send** button.
    a. In the *Folder* pane, notice the icon for Reply appears next to the message. This lets you know visually that you have replied to this e-mail.

Exercise 2.5 [Guided Practice]

Forward an e-mail message with an attachment. [Objectives 2.3–2.5]

1. Click on the **Inbox folder** in the *Navigation* pane. The list of received e-mails appears in the *Folder* pane.
2. Open (double-click) one of the **E-mail with attachment** messages.

3. Click once on the attachment.

a. Notice a preview of the attachment appears in the body of the message.

4. Click on the **Show Message** button on the *Attachments* ribbon to return to the message and close the attachment preview.

5. Click on the **Forward** button in the *Reply* group.

a. Notice the "FW:" before the subject. This indicates to the recipient that the message was forwarded to him or her.

b. Notice the attachment is included in this message to be forwarded.

c. If you reply to an e-mail with an attachment, the attachment will automatically be removed from the reply by Outlook.

6. Click on the **To** button. The *Select Names* dialog box will open.

7. Select two classmates, and click on the **To** button at the bottom.

8. Select your professor, and click on the **Cc** button at the bottom.

9. Click **OK** to close the *Select Names* dialog box.

10. Type a brief message in the body and include your name.

11. Click **Send.**

a. In the *Folder* pane, notice the icon for Forward appears next to the message. This lets you know visually that you have forwarded this e-mail.

b. In the *Folder* pane, notice how related items are grouped by conversation.

Exercise 2.6 [Guided Practice]

Recall a previously sent e-mail message. (Note: Recall will only work with Exchange accounts.) [Objective 2.3]

1. Create a new e-mail message.

2. Use `[your name]'s Recall` as the subject.

3. Type your name and e-mail address in the body.

4. Address the e-mail to all your classmates and your professor.

5. Click **Send.**

6. Go to your *Sent Items* folder in the *Navigation* pane.

7. From the *Folder* pane, open (double-click) the message you just sent.

8. Click on the **Actions** button in the *Move* group on the *Message* ribbon.

9. Choose **Recall This Message.** A *Recall This Message* dialog box will appear.

a. You have two Recall options: *Delete unread copies of this message* and *Delete unread copies and replace with a new message.*

b. There is also a check box that will track if the recall succeeds or fails for each recipient. We will get into tracking in Chapter 3.

10. Select **Delete unread copies of this message.**

11. Click **OK.**

a. The unread copies of the e-mail will be deleted from the recipients' inboxes.

12. Close the open e-mail message.

Exercise 2.7 [Independent Practice]

Create, send, and resend an e-mail message. [Objective 2.3]

1. Create a new e-mail message.
   a. Address the message to your professor.
   b. Use **Recalling a message** as the subject.
   c. In the body, briefly describe the steps to recall a previously sent message.
   d. Include your name.

2. **Send** the message.

3. Go to your *Sent Items* folder and open the e-mail you just sent.

4. Resend this message to all your classmates.

Exercise 2.8 [Independent Practice]

Reply to all and include an attachment. Recall an e-mail message, and use the Clean Up Conversation feature. (Note: Recall will only work with Exchange accounts.) [Objectives 2.3–2.5]

1. Open one of the **"Recalling a message"** e-mails in your *Inbox.*

2. **Reply All.**
   a. In the body type a brief message thanking the sender for the helpful tips.
   b. Include your name.
   c. Include your professor in the Cc line. (Note: If your professor is listed in the To field, delete him or her from that field and add him or her to the Cc field.)

3. Add an **attachment** to the e-mail.
   a. Use a picture from your computer.

4. **Send.**

5. Recall this message, and replace it with a new message without the attachment.
   a. This message will be in your *Sent Items* folder.

6. Go to your Inbox and use the **Clean Up Conversation** feature on the **"Recalling a message"** e-mail conversation to delete redundant e-mail messages.

Exercise 2.9 [Independent Practice]

Forward an e-mail message as an attachment. Ignore a conversation. Delete all messages in your Inbox, and set up Outlook to automatically empty the Deleted Items folder. [Objectives 2.3–2.6]

1. Open one of the **"E-mail with attachment"** e-mails in your *Inbox.*

2. Forward this e-mail as an attachment to your professor.
   a. Don't just forward the e-mail, but rather forward the entire e-mail as an attachment.
   b. Include a brief message and your name.

3. Select one of the **"E-mail with attachment"** e-mails in your *Inbox.*

4. **Ignore** this conversation.

   a. All the e-mails in this conversation should be moved to your *Deleted Items* folder.

5. Manually empty the *Deleted Items* folder.

6. Select all the e-mails in your *Inbox* and delete them.

   a. Hint: **Ctrl+A** is the shortcut for Select All.

7. Set up your Outlook to automatically empty the *Deleted Items* folder each time you exit Outlook.

8. Exit Outlook.

   a. You should be prompted to confirm that you want to empty the Deleted Items folder.

Chapter 3
E-mail Special Features

OBJECTIVES   *After completing this chapter, you will be able to:*

3.1   Differentiate between the types of e-mail formats.

3.2   Customize your e-mail using the different types of e-mail options available in Outlook.

3.3   Use e-mail voting buttons to get responses from recipients and to automatically track responses.

3.4   Customize your e-mails by using signatures, themes, and desktop alerts.

CHAPTER FLYOVER   *This chapter will cover many of the special e-mail features available in Microsoft Outlook.*

- Types of e-mail message formats
- Changing e-mail formats
- Message options
- Properties dialog box
- Voting buttons
- Using preset voting buttons
- Customizing voting buttons
- Reply using voting buttons

- Tracking voting responses
- Customizing your e-mail
- Creating and using signatures
- Setting default signatures
- Using themes
- Setting a default theme and fonts
- Desktop Alerts
- Outlook Social Connector

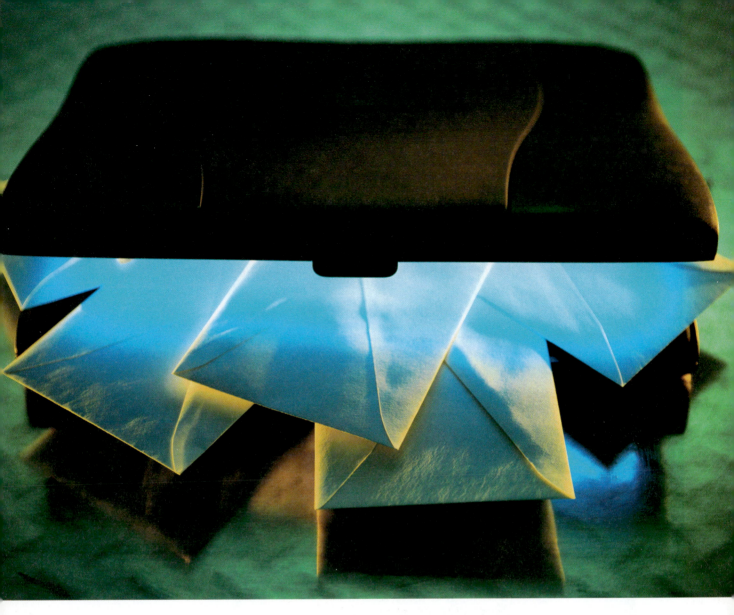

Making Outlook Work for You

Chapter 2 covered the basics of creating, sending, editing, and responding to e-mail. You were also introduced to the different icons used in Outlook to help you identify different aspects of each e-mail message. This chapter will delve into some of the more special e-mail features available in Outlook.

One of the benefits of using Outlook to handle your e-mail accounts is the vast array of features available to customize your messages and the Outlook environment. As your understanding of Outlook increases, you will want to customize your e-mail messages and change some of the default settings in Outlook to more fully meet your needs and preferences.

This chapter will prepare you to customize your e-mail by using some of the different e-mail options available in Outlook. These include marking an e-mail as important, using delivery and read receipts, delaying the delivery of an e-mail, flagging an e-mail for recipients, and many more. You will also learn how to use voting buttons and change the look of your e-mail by using stationery, themes, and signatures. After completing Chapter 2 and this chapter, you will be able to customize Outlook and use e-mail options to meet your personal and professional needs.

Types of E-mail Format

Not all e-mail accounts operate on the same mail format. Outlook provides flexibility in the type of e-mail messages that are available for different situations. The message format you choose determines the types of formatting features you can use such as fonts, formatted text, colors, styles, bullets, numbering, line spacing, and indents. It is important to note that just because you can and do use some of these advanced formatting features in the body of your e-mail does not mean that the recipient of your e-mail will be able to see them.

There are three different types of mail formats available in Outlook: plain text, Rich Text Format, and Hypertext Markup Language.

Plain Text

All e-mail applications support this type of mail format because it does not include most text formatting features. *Plain text* format does not support bold, italic, or any of the other advanced text formatting features. Pictures cannot be displayed in the body of the message when using plain text format; although, pictures can still be attached to the message and sent.

Outlook Rich Text Format (RTF)

Rich Text Format is unique to Outlook users and is supported in an Exchange environment. This format allows users to use the different formatting features available in Outlook. When using RTF, Outlook automatically converts these messages to Hypertext Markup Language (HTML) by default when you send them to an Internet recipient so that the message formatting is maintained and attachments are received. It is probably best to use HTML format if you are sending messages outside of an Exchange environment.

Hypertext Markup Language (HTML)

HTML message format is the default format in Outlook. HTML format lets you format the body of your e-mail message similar to a Microsoft Word document. HTML is the most commonly used message format and will allow your recipients to receive the message in the same format as you sent it unless the recipient's e-mail application supports only plain text formatting.

Setting Default and Changing Message Format

As mentioned previously, HTML message format is the default setting in Outlook. The default message format can be changed, and the message format for an individual e-mail can also be changed.

If you change the default message setting, then all new e-mails will have the new default message format.

STEP-BY-STEP

1. Click on the **File** tab. The *BackStage* window will open.
2. Click on the **Options** button at the left. The *Outlook Options* dialog box will open.

3. Click on the **Mail** button. The mail options will be displayed.

4. Select the default message desired in the *Compose messages* area.

5. Click **OK** to close the *Outlook Options* dialog box.

Default message
format in Outlook
Options

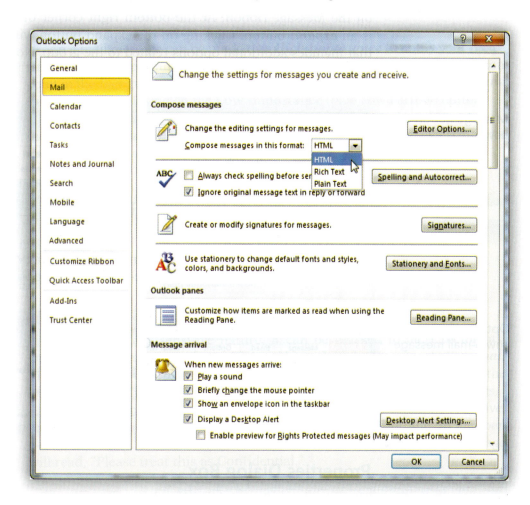

If you are sending a message to recipients whose e-mail application supports only plain text format, you can change the setting on an individual e-mail rather than changing the default setting.

STEP-BY-STEP

1. Open a **New** e-mail message.

2. Click on the **Format Text** tab.

3. In the *Format* group, choose the desired message format.

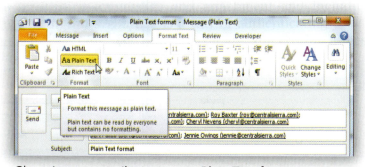

Changing an e-mail message to Plain Text format

attachment scrambles the contents of the message to add a layer of security. The sender uses a ***private key*** to encrypt a message, and the recipient of an encrypted message must have a ***public key*** to view the contents of the message and attachment.

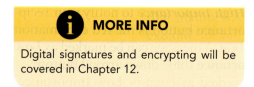

MORE INFO

Digital signatures and encrypting will be covered in Chapter 12.

Security Properties dialog box

Delivery and Read Receipts

Have you ever sent out an e-mail and wondered if the recipients received or read the e-mail? When using Outlook in conjunction with Exchange, ***delivery*** and ***read receipts*** can be used to provide you, the sender, with an electronic receipt that an e-mail has been delivered to or opened by its intended recipients. When a delivery or read receipt has been requested, the sender will receive an e-mail confirmation that the e-mail has been delivered and/or opened by each recipient.

Delivery and Read Receipt options

When a recipient receives a message that has a delivery receipt, Outlook automatically generates a receipt that is sent to the sender. If an e-mail has a read receipt request, the recipient receives a notification that a read receipt has been requested. The recipient is given the option of sending or declining to send a read receipt.

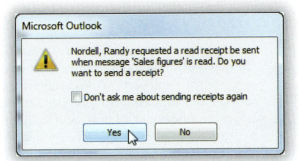

Recipient notification of a Read Receipt

Requesting a delivery or read receipt can be done from the *Tracking* group on the *Options* ribbon or from the *Properties* dialog box.

NETIQUETTE

When a sender requests a read receipt, it is good e-mail etiquette to send a receipt, even though Outlook provides you with an option to not send a receipt.

Receipt options in the Properties dialog box

Outlook uses ***tracking*** to record this information. Tracking is unique to Exchange and provides the sender with a summary of the receipts received. Once a delivery or read receipt has been received, a *Tracking* button will be available on the original e-mail (usually in the *Sent Items* folder).

MORE INFO

Don't solely rely on these receipts because read and delivery receipts work only with Microsoft Exchange. This means that you will not receive these notifications from users not using Exchange. Also, just because a recipient opens an e-mail does not necessarily ensure that he or she will read the e-mail.

Changing the default tracking options for receipts will be covered in Chapter 8 on page 225.

STEP-BY-STEP

1. Click on the **Sent Items** folder in the *Navigation* pane.
2. Open the sent e-mail that had a delivery or read receipt.
3. Click on the **Tracking** button in the *Show* group to view a summary of receipts. The tracking will be displayed in the body of the e-mail.

FACTOID

Depending on the size of the e-mail window (or Outlook window) that is open, the buttons and groups might appear differently on the ribbons.

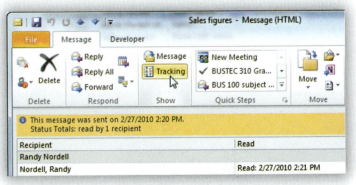

Tracking displayed on a sent e-mail

4. Click on the **Message** button in the *Show* group to return to the text of the message.

Delivery Options

Suppose you are leaving town tomorrow but need to send out an e-mail on Friday, and since you'll be gone, you want to have replies sent to a coworker in your office. Outlook provides users with customized delivery options. The delivery options include having replies sent to other users, delaying delivery, setting an expiration date and time, and saving the sent e-mail in a different location.

Sent e-mail messages are by default saved in the *Sent Items* folder. This location can be changed for an individual e-mail by clicking on the **Save Sent Item To** button in the *More Options* group on the *Options* ribbon. You can choose a folder from the Folder list as the location to save this e-mail, use the default folder, or choose to not save the message. This option applies only to the current message.

Save Sent items options

Delay Delivery is an option that allows you to specify the date and time when an e-mail is to be sent. When this feature is used, an e-mail can be created and sent, and it will stay in your Outbox folder until the scheduled delivery date and time. When you click on the **Delay Delivery** button, the *Properties* dialog box will open.

Delay Delivery button

STEP-BY-STEP

1. In a new e-mail message, click on the **Options** ribbon.
2. Click on the **Delay Delivery** button. The *Properties* dialog box will open.
3. Check the **Do not deliver before** box.
4. Set the day and time the e-mail is to be delivered.

> **ⓘ MORE INFO**
>
> A rule can also be created to delay the delivery of all e-mails you send. Rules will be covered in Chapter 7.

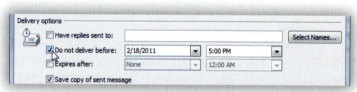

Do not deliver before option in the Properties dialog box

5. Click **Close** to close the *Properties* dialog box.
6. Click **Send.** The message will be stored in your Outbox folder until the specified time to be delivered.

Direct Replies To button

There are times when it is beneficial to have other users receive a reply to an e-mail. When the *Direct Replies To* option is selected, you can select individuals from your contacts to receive replies from an e-mail you've sent.

STEP-BY-STEP

1. In a new e-mail message, click on the **Options** tab.
2. Click on the **Direct Replies To** button. The *Properties* dialog box will open.
3. Click on the **Select Names** button. The *Have Replies Sent To* dialog box will open.

> **↺ ANOTHER WAY**
>
> The **Delay Delivery** and **Direct Replies To** options can be directly accessed from the *Properties* dialog box.

Have replies sent to option in the Properties dialog box

4. Select recipients from the contact list and press **OK** to close the *Have Replies Sent To* dialog box.

5. Click **Close** to close the *Properties* dialog box.

Some e-mails are time sensitive and are no longer relevant to the recipient after a certain time. The ***Expires after*** feature lets you set a time for when an e-mail is to expire. When an e-mail has expired, it still remains visible and can be opened from the recipient's Inbox, but it is marked with a strikethrough.

Expired e-mail displayed in the Folder pane

STEP-BY-STEP

1. In a new message, click on the **expand** button at the bottom right of the *Tags* group on the *Message* ribbon. The *Properties* dialog box will open.

Expand button in the Tags group

2. Check **Expires after.**

3. Set the date and time the e-mail is to expire.

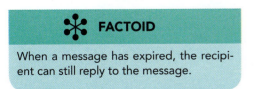

FACTOID

When a message has expired, the recipient can still reply to the message.

Expires after option in the Properties dialog box

4. Click **Close** to close the *Properties* dialog box.

Follow Up Flag

Flagging an item for ***Follow Up*** marks an e-mail with a flag and automatically lists this e-mail as a ***To-Do*** item. This is typically done on an e-mail you have received in your Inbox and serves as a reminder that you have to follow up with some action on this e-mail.

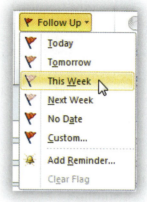

Follow Up flags

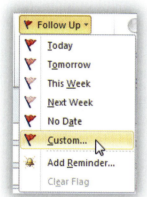

Custom flag to create a Flag for Recipients

An e-mail can be marked for follow up by clicking on the **Follow Up** button in the *Tags* group on the *Message* ribbon and choosing a flag. E-mail messages marked with a flag will display a flag icon in the Folder pane.

Flag for Recipients

A ***Custom*** flag can be used to create a ***Flag for Recipients***. A Flag for Recipients attaches a flag and message to an e-mail and gives you the option of including a reminder date and time. Outlook provides preset ***Flag to*** messages from which to choose, or you can create your own custom message. If a reminder is set (optional), recipients will receive an Outlook reminder that will open on their computer screen at the designated date and time.

STEP-BY-STEP

1. In a new e-mail, click on the **Follow Up** button in the *Tags* group.
2. Select **Custom.** The *Custom* dialog box will open.
3. Deselect the **Flag for Me** check box.
4. Check the **Flag for Recipients** check box.
5. Select a **Flag to** message, or type in your own custom message.
6. If you want the recipients to receive a reminder message, check the **Reminder** box and set a date and time.
7. Click **OK** to close the *Custom* dialog box.

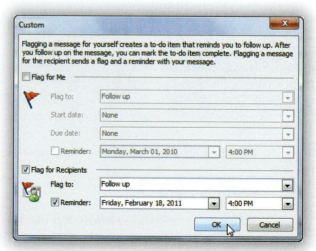

Flag for Recipients in the Custom dialog box

When an e-mail has a Flag for Recipients, there will be a notification in the InfoBar (above the *From:* line on an open e-mail message) visible to both the sender and receiver of the message.

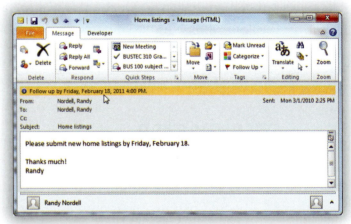

E-mail message with Flag for Recipients

Permission options

Permission

The **Permission** option in the *Permission* group on the *Options* ribbon helps to ensure that sensitive information is not forwarded, printed, or copied. For the permission feature to function properly, your company must enable the **Information Rights Management** (IRM). If IRM is not enabled for your company, you will receive an error message if you select either **Do Not Forward** or **Manage Credentials.**

If the IRM is enabled, the permission can be set to **Do Not Forward** or a custom configuration. When the Do Not Forward permission is selected, recipients will receive a notification in the InfoBar informing them of the restrictions.

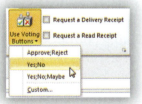

> ✱ **FACTOID**
>
> Voting buttons and tracking responses will only work in an Exchange environment.

Voting Buttons

Voting buttons are a useful way of gathering responses to a question sent via e-mail. The advantage of using voting buttons rather than having respondents reply to an e-mailed question is that you can specify the response choices and Outlook will automatically track and tally the voting responses received. The tracking feature also lets you, the sender of the message, see who has and hasn't voted. You can also export the voting results to Excel.

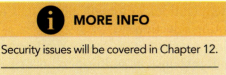

Preset Voting buttons

Preset Voting Buttons

A question can be typed into the body of an e-mail or in the subject line. The voting button feature is located on the Options ribbon of a new message. Outlook provides you with preset voting buttons. The preset voting buttons include: **Approve;Reject, Yes;No,** and **Yes;No;Maybe.**

> ℹ️ **MORE INFO**
>
> Security issues will be covered in Chapter 12.
>
> ──────────
>
> When voting buttons are used, you will see a message in the InfoBar stating, "You have added voting buttons to this message."

STEP-BY-STEP

1. In a new e-mail message, click on the **Options** ribbon.
2. Click on the **Use Voting Buttons** button.
3. Choose from one of the three preset options.
4. Type and send the e-mail.

Custom Voting buttons

Customize Voting Buttons

What if you wanted to use the voting buttons to determine your coworkers' preferences for lunch on Friday? The preset buttons would not be effective in this case. Outlook provides you the option of creating custom voting buttons. Custom voting buttons could be used to find the day of the week that works best for a team meeting or the choice of restaurant for a Friday lunch. As the sender of the message and question, you can create your own custom voting buttons in the *Properties* dialog box by typing each voting option separated by a semicolon.

STEP-BY-STEP

1. In a new e-mail message, click on the **Options** tab.
2. Click on the **Use Voting Buttons** button.
3. Choose **Custom.** The *Properties* dialog box opens.
4. Check **Use voting buttons.**
5. Select and delete the preset voting buttons (Accept;Reject).
6. Type in your voting choices. Separate each choice with a **semicolon.**

Custom voting buttons in the Properties dialog box

7. Click **Close** to close the *Properties* dialog box. The *InfoBar* will inform you that you are using voting buttons on this message.
8. Type and send the e-mail.

Reply Using Voting Buttons

When a recipient receives an e-mail with voting buttons, there is a Vote button to the left of the Reply button in the Respond group. Also, in the InfoBar is a message alerting the recipient to vote by using the Voting button.

When the Vote button is clicked, the voting choices appear in a list below the button. The recipient can make his or her selection from the list of choices.

After the selection is made, the recipient can choose one of the following two options: **Send the response now** or **Edit the response before sending.** If **Send the response now** is selected, Outlook automatically replies to the e-mail and includes the recipient's voting selection.

If **Edit the response before sending** is selected, a reply e-mail opens allowing the recipient to include an e-mail response in addition to his or her voting selection. After typing a response in the body, the recipient must send the response.

STEP-BY-STEP

1. Open the e-mail message that has voting buttons.
2. Click on the **Vote** button and make a selection.

Vote button on a received e-mail message

3. Choose either **Send the response now** or **Edit the response before sending.** If you choose **Send the response now,** click **OK** and you are finished and your voting selection has been sent.
4. If you choose **Edit the response before sending** and click **OK,** a reply e-mail will automatically open.
5. Type any additional information you would like to include in the body of the e-mail.
6. Click **Send.**
7. Close the original e-mail.

Voting response options

Tracking Voting Responses

When recipients respond to an e-mail with voting buttons, the sender of the message will receive the responses. The responses received will include the recipient's voting selection in front of the original subject. Also, Outlook uses tracking to record the responses received.

STEP-BY-STEP

1. Open a voting response you received. The voting response is displayed in both the subject line and the *InfoBar*.

2. Click on the **InfoBar,** and then click on **View voting responses.** The original e-mail message will open. A summary of the voting responses will be displayed in the *InfoBar,* and the individual voting response will be displayed in the body of the message.

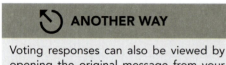

ANOTHER WAY

Voting responses can also be viewed by opening the original message from your *Sent Items* folder. Any sent message that has tracking will be marked with a tracking icon rather than a message icon.

FACTOID

Results of the voting can be copied and pasted into Excel.

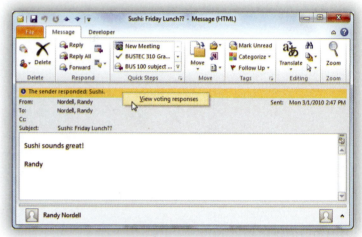

Voting response received

3. After you are finished, close both of the open e-mail messages.

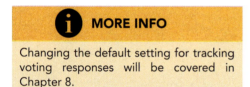

MORE INFO

Changing the default setting for tracking voting responses will be covered in Chapter 8.

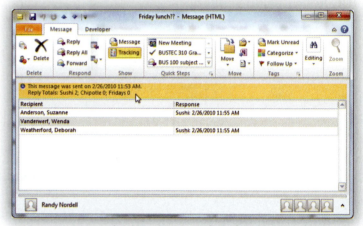

Voting responses displayed in the InfoBar and body of message

Customize Your E-mail

Have you ever received an e-mail where the body of the message had nice fonts, colors, and background graphics? Most likely, the sender did not spend a huge amount of time customizing the design of the e-mail specifically for you.

As covered in Chapter 2, users have much control over how to format the body of an e-mail message. But Outlook also provides users with many features to customize the look of e-mails by using *signatures, stationery,* and *themes.* The *default settings* can be changed so that each new e-mail created will have a consistent and customized look.

Signatures

A *signature* is a saved group of information that can be inserted into the body of an e-mail. Typically, a signature can include the sender's name, title, company, address, and contact information. Signatures can also include logos and graphics. Signatures save time by storing this information so you don't have to type all of it each time you create an e-mail. Signatures can be manually or automatically inserted at the bottom of each new e-mail you create. You can create and save multiple signatures.

STEP-BY-STEP

1. Click on the **File** tab to open the *BackStage*.
2. Click on **Options** at the left. The *Outlook Options* dialog box will open.
3. Click on the **Mail** button at the left.
4. Click on **Signatures.** The *Signatures and Stationery* dialog box will open.

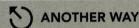

Outlook Options dialog box

5. Click on **New.** The *New Signature* dialog box will open.

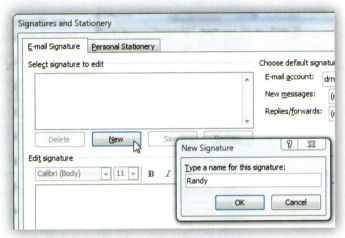

Creating and naming a new signature

6. Type the name for your signature and press **OK** to close the *New Signature* dialog box.
7. In the *Edit signature* section of the dialog box, type your signature information. You can use different fonts, sizes, styles, colors, and alignments to customize your signature.
8. When you are satisfied with your signature, press **Save.**

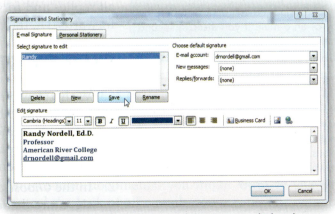

Signature in the Signatures and Stationery dialog box

settings can be changed to include a theme, consisting of fonts, colors, and background graphics, on all new e-mails. If you are not using a theme, you can change the default settings on the font, size, style, and color used on all new e-mails, replies, and forwards.

 MORE INFO

When a default theme is selected, you have the following choices: **Use the theme's font, Use my font when replying and forwarding messages,** or **Always use my fonts.**

✷ **FACTOID**

When using a theme on an e-mail message, not all users will see the same themes fonts, colors, and graphics. This will depend on the type of e-mail account the recipient is using.

STEP-BY-STEP

1. Click on the **File** tab to open the *BackStage* window.
2. Click on the **Options** button at the left. The *Outlook Options* dialog box will open.
3. Click on the **Mail** button.
4. Click on the **Stationery and Fonts** button. The *Signatures and Stationery* dialog box will open.
5. Click on the **Personal Stationery** tab (if it is not already displayed).
6. Set your default preferences for **Theme, New mail messages,** and/or **Replying or forwarding messages.**

Signature and Stationery dialog box

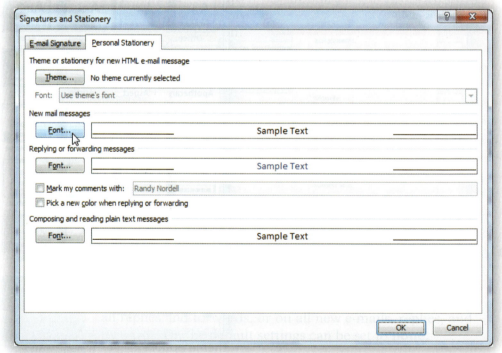

7. Click **OK** to close the *Signatures and Stationery* dialog box.
8. Click **OK** to close the *Outlook Options* dialog box.

Desktop Alerts

A ***Desktop Alert*** is a notification you receive when a new e-mail arrives in your Inbox. The desktop alert appears from the system tray at the bottom right corner of your computer screen and remains there for a few seconds.

By default, desktop alerts are turned on. They will also appear when you receive a Meeting Request or Task Request.

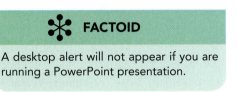

FACTOID

A desktop alert will not appear if you are running a PowerPoint presentation.

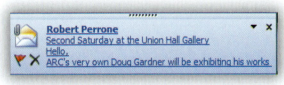

Desktop alert

MORE INFO

Meeting Requests will be covered in Chapter 5, and Task Requests will be covered in Chapter 6.

Desktop alerts only appear for items received in your Inbox. A rule can be created to have desktop alerts appear when an e-mail is received in other folders. Rules will be covered in Chapter 7.

Changing the default settings for desktop alerts will be covered in Chapter 8 on page 221.

The desktop alert notifies you of the name of the sender, the subject, and a portion of the body of the message. Outlook allows you to perform some actions on an e-mail when a desktop alert is displayed. When a desktop alert appears, you can open the e-mail message by clicking on the desktop alert. You can also flag or delete the message from the desktop alert.

People Pane and Outlook Social Connector

The *People pane* appears at the bottom of each e-mail message and consolidates other Outlook items associated with an individual. The People pane will display e-mail messages, meetings, task requests, attachments, and social network activity as links. Clicking on a link displayed in the People pane will open that Outlook item. The People pane can also be collapsed or expanded by clicking on the small arrow in the upper right of the pane.

E-mail with People pane expanded

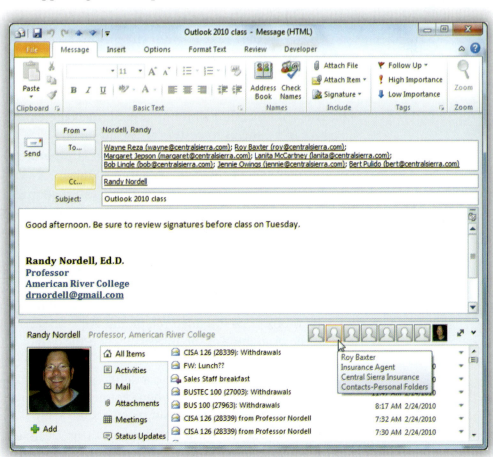

MORE INFO

The People pane and Outlook Social Connector will also be discussed in Chapter 4.

If there are multiple recipients of an e-mail, the People pane can display items related to each of them. Clicking on one of the picture icons at the top right of the People pane will allow you to switch between individuals to be displayed in the People pane.

The **Outlook Social Connector** (OSC) works in conjunction with the People pane and can be used to keep track of social network activity of your personal and business contacts. If your organization is using SharePoint 2010, the OSC can connect with SharePoint to display the activity of your contacts. The OSC can also be used to connect with other social networking sites. To connect to these sites, you will have to download and install an add-in from these sites.

Connect to a social network of a contact using Outlook Social Connector

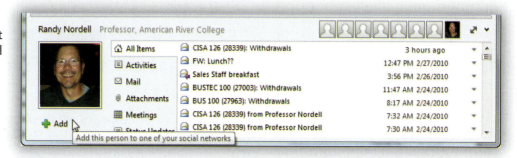

Chapter Highlights

- ▶ Outlook provides three different types of e-mail formats: **plain text, Outlook Rich Text Format** (RTF), and **Hypertext Markup Language** (HTML).

- ▶ By default, Outlook uses HTML format, which is the most common format used for e-mail.

- ▶ Outlook has many different e-mail **Message Options** to customize your e-mail messages to better meet your needs.

- ▶ E-mail messages can be marked with **High** or **Low Importance** to alert the recipient of the message's importance.

- ▶ You can use a **sensitivity** notation to alert your recipients about the handling of the e-mail. Messages can be marked as **Personal, Private,** or **Confidential.** Recipients will receive a notation regarding the message's sensitivity in the InfoBar of the e-mail.

- ▶ An e-mail message can be made more secure by either **encrypting** the message or using a **digital signature.**

- ▶ A **delivery receipt** can be used on an e-mail to ensure it reached the Inbox of its intended recipients. An e-mail confirmation is sent to the originator of the message when the e-mail is delivered to the recipients.

- ▶ A **read receipt** is similar to a delivery receipt except the receipt (confirmation) message is sent when recipients open the e-mail. Recipients will be asked if they want a read receipt to be sent.

- ▶ Outlook uses **tracking** to record and store read and delivery receipts.

▸ There are three types of **delivery options** available in Outlook. **Delay Delivery** delays the delivery of an e-mail until a date and time specified by the message writer. **Direct Replies To** is an option that will automatically send replies to another recipient. **Expires After** is used for time-sensitive e-mail.

▸ **Follow Up flags** are used to mark an e-mail for follow-up and will list the e-mail as a **To-Do** item.

▸ **Flags for Recipients** can be used to alert recipients and provide additional details.

▸ Outlook provides you with the option of setting **Permission** on an e-mail to ensure that it is not printed, forwarded, or copied.

▸ **Voting buttons** can be used on an e-mail to elicit a response from recipients. Preset voting buttons are included in Outlook, or you can customize voting buttons to meet your specific needs.

▸ When voting buttons are used, recipients will receive an e-mail with a **Vote** button next to the Reply button. Outlook will automatically track the voting responses to the question.

▸ A **Signature** is a saved group of information that can be automatically or manually inserted in the body of an e-mail message. Signatures are commonly used to insert your name and company information in an e-mail.

▸ **Themes** control the **font, color, background,** and **fill effect** in the body of an e-mail. You can choose a preset theme to use as the default for all new e-mails you create, or you can customize a theme.

▸ A **Desktop Alert** is a notification you receive when a new e-mail arrives in your Inbox.

▸ The **People pane** displays Outlook items related to an individual. The People pane is displayed at the bottom of an e-mail message.

▸ The **Outlook Social Connector** allows you to connect Outlook 2010 with your personal and business social networks.

What Do You Know About Outlook?

True/False Questions

T F   1. When an e-mail message has been marked for sensitivity, the recipient receives the e-mail with the sensitivity notification in the InfoBar above the sender's name. [Objective 3.2]

T F   2. A read receipt can be used to ensure the recipient reads the e-mail. [Objective 3.2]

T F   3. When a message has expired, the recipient can no longer open or reply to the e-mail. [Objective 3.2]

T F   4. Any item in your Inbox marked with a Follow Up flag will also appear in your To-Do list. [Objective 3.2]

T F   5. Signatures can be used to store sentences and paragraphs of information as well as logos and graphics. [Objective 3.4]

Multiple Choice Questions

1. Which of the following is the default message format in Outlook?
   [Objective 3.1]
   a. Plain text
   b. HTTP
   c. Outlook Rich Text Format
   d. HTML

2. Which of the following e-mail options would be best for time-sensitive information? [Objective 3.2]
   a. Direct Replies to
   b. Sensitivity
   c. Expiration
   d. Importance

3. Which of the following is true of signatures? [Objective 3.4]
   a. Signatures can be set to be inserted automatically in all replies and forwards.
   b. Signatures have to be manually inserted into an e-mail message.
   c. Signatures are used only with new e-mail messages.
   d. All the above.

4. Which of the following is *not* controlled by selecting a theme?
   [Objective 3.4]
   a. Color
   b. Signature
   c. Font
   d. Background

5. Which of the following occurs when you use a read receipt?
   [Objective 3.2]
   a. A receipt is sent when the recipient receives the e-mail.
   b. The recipient has the option of whether or not to send a read receipt.
   c. A receipt is sent when the recipient reads the e-mail.
   d. None of the above.

Short Answer Questions

1. Describe how to use custom voting buttons. [Objective 3.3]

2. Explain how to create a new signature. [Objective 3.4]

3. Explain the difference between Follow Up flags and Flag for Recipients. [Objective 3.2]

Putting Outlook to Work

Exercise 3.1 [Guided Practice]

Create and send an e-mail using e-mail options and plain text format. [Objectives 3.1, 3.2]

1. Create a new e-mail message.
2. Address it to all of your classmates and a copy to your professor.

3. Use **`Types of message formats`** as the subject line.

4. Briefly describe the three types of message formats in the body.

5. Include your name and e-mail address below the body text.

6. Click on the **Format Text** tab, and, in the *Format* group, change the format of the message to plain text.

   a. Notice how "(Plain Text)" appears next to "Message" in the message title at the top of the window.

7. Mark this message as **High Importance.**

   a. This can be done by clicking on the **red exclamation point** in the *Tags* group on the *Message* ribbon.

   b. You can also open the *Properties* dialog box by clicking the **expand** button in the bottom right corner of the *Tags* group and choosing **High Importance.**

8. Request a delivery receipt by clicking on the **Options** tab and checking the **Request a Delivery Receipt** box in the *Tracking* group.

   a. You can also open the *Properties* dialog box and check the box for **Request a delivery receipt for this message.**

9. **Send.**

   a. You will begin to receive delivery receipts in your Inbox.

Exercise 3.2 [Guided Practice]

Create a new signature, and send an e-mail with a signature. [Objective 3.4]

1. Click on the **File** tab to open the *BackStage* window.

2. Choose **Options** at the left. The *Outlook Options* dialog box will open.

3. Click on the **Mail** button.

4. Click on **Signatures.** The *Signatures and Stationery* dialog box opens.

5. Click on **New.** The *New Signature* dialog box will open.

   a. Use your name as the name for the signature.
   b. Click **OK** to close the *New Signature* dialog box.

6. In the *Edit Signature* area of this dialog box, type your full name and **`Outlook Student`** as the title below your name.

7. Change the font, size, and color of your name and title.

   a. Make sure you select the text you want changed before making the formatting changes.

8. When finished making formatting changes, click on the **Save** button.

   a. This signature is now saved and can be inserted into an e-mail message.
   b. When you create a new signature, Outlook will use it as the default setting for all new e-mails.

9. Click **OK** to close the *Signatures and Stationery* dialog box.

10. Click **OK** to close the *Outlook Options* dialog box.

11. Create a new e-mail message.

   a. Notice your signature appears a couple of lines below the top of the body.

8. Click **OK.**

   a. A new reply message will open.
   b. Notice the subject line includes your voting response.
   c. Type a brief message in the body.
   d. **Insert your signature** by clicking on the **Signature** button in the *Include* group and choosing your signature.
   e. **Send** the message.

9. Open and vote on six more of the "**Meeting**" messages in your *Inbox*.

   a. On three of them, choose **Edit the response before sending.**
   b. On three of them, choose **Send the response now.**

Exercise 3.6 [Independent Practice]

Create a new signature, set default signature options, and use e-mail options. Track voting responses. Note: This exercise uses e-mails received from Exercises 3.5. [Objectives 3.2, 3.4]

1. Create a new signature.

   a. Name it *[your name]* 2.
   b. Include your college and e-mail address below your name.
   c. Customize the font, size, and color.
   d. Save the signature.

2. Change the default signature setting to **None** for both *New messages* and *Replies/forwards*.

3. Create a new e-mail message.

   a. Address it to all your classmates and a copy to your professor.
   b. Use **Tracking voting responses** as the subject.
   c. Briefly describe how to track voting responses you have received.
   d. Manually insert your new signature.

4. Include a read receipt.

5. Use **Personal** as the sensitivity notation.

6. **Send.**

7. Open one of the "**Meeting**" response e-mails in your Inbox.

   a. The subject line will include the voting response preceding the subject.
   b. Using the **InfoBar,** track the responses received.

8. Close any open e-mails.

Exercise 3.7 [Independent Practice]

Using custom voting buttons, signature, and e-mail options. [Objectives 3.2–3.4]

1. Create a new e-mail message.

   a. Address it to all your classmates.
   b. Use **"Lunch??"** as the subject.
   c. Include a brief message in the body asking for recipients to vote on where they would like to go for lunch on Wednesday.
   d. Manually insert your new signature.

2. Create custom voting buttons with choices for three restaurants.

   a. Be sure to separate each choice with a semicolon.

3. Have replies sent to both yourself and your professor.

4. Set the message to expire at 8 a.m. on Wednesday.

5. Mark as **High Importance.**

6. Include a flag for recipients with the custom message, `Lunch at 12:30 p.m.`

   a. Include a reminder for Wednesday at 11:30 a.m.

7. **Send.**

Exercise 3.8 [Independent Practice]

Responding to voting buttons, and using signature and e-mail options. Note: This exercise uses e-mails received from Exercises 3.7. [Objectives 3.2–3.4]

1. Open one of the "**Lunch??**" e-mails in your *Inbox*.

   a. Remember the voting response will precede the subject.

2. Vote using the voting buttons.

3. Edit the response to include a brief message and your signature.

4. **Delay delivery** of this message for five minutes.

   a. Set the date for today and the time five minutes from now.

5. **Send.**

   a. Notice the e-mail will remain in your *Outbox* for five minutes.

6. Repeat this process on five other "**Lunch??**" reply e-mails in your *Inbox*.

Chapter 4
Contacts

OBJECTIVES *After completing this chapter, you will be able to:*

4.1 Differentiate between the Contacts folder and the Global Address List.

4.2 Create a contact record from different sources.

4.3 Enhance contact records by editing contact information and fields.

4.4 Use and modify the different contact views.

4.5 Create a contact group, and produce e-mail from a contact or contact group.

CHAPTER FLYOVER

- Contacts
- Database lingo
- Contacts versus Global Address List
- Creating a new contact
- Creating a contact from the same company
- Creating a contact from an e-mail received
- Creating a contact from an electronic business card
- Creating a contact from the Global Address List
- Duplicate contacts
- Editing contact information
- Multiple e-mail addresses

- Changing contact record fields
- Adding a picture to a contact
- Using the map feature
- Using the People pane
- Using the Outlook Social Connector
- Deleting contacts
- Different contact views
- Sending an e-mail to a contact
- Sending a business card
- Creating a contact group
- Using a contact group
- Modifying a contact group

Making Outlook Work for You

Before various electronic means to store contact information, a physical paper address book was where we kept information about family, friends, neighbors, and business acquaintances. Typically included were names, addresses, and phone numbers; you might have also included birthdays and anniversaries. Microsoft Outlook provides users with a place to electronically store information for e-mailing, calling, faxing, or sending letters to individuals.

The Outlook **Contacts** feature gives you the same benefits of a paper address book, but it also has some unique advantages. In addition to standard personal information, contacts can include company information, a picture, and additional notes. Contacts are stored electronically and integrate seamlessly with other Microsoft Office products so you can create envelopes, labels, and letters. Contacts can easily be shared with other Outlook users. Additionally, Outlook Contacts can be synched with cells phones and other electronic devices.

What Is a Contact?

A **contact** is a set of related information about an individual or organization. This could be as simple as a name and e-mail address with the option of storing additional useful information. Outlook Contacts functions similarly to a database, but you do not need to have database knowledge to effectively take advantage of the benefits of Outlook Contacts. Since the Contacts folder is similar to a database, it is important to understand some basic database terminology.

Database Lingo

An Outlook contact is commonly referred to as a **record** or **contact record.** A record is a group of related information about an individual or organization. Each individual piece of information in a record is called a **field.** For example, Full Name, Company, Job Title, and E-mail address are all fields in a contact record. A group of related records is called a **file.** In Outlook, a group of related records can be saved in a Contact folder. Folders can be created in Contacts to store a group of related contact records.

Contacts folder in the Navigation pane

Contacts Versus Global Address List

If you are using Outlook in a home environment (as a stand-alone program rather than on an Exchange server), your contacts will, by default, be saved in the *Contacts* folder. You can choose e-mail recipients from your Contacts, and you can also create, edit, and delete records in this list of contacts. When you click on the **To** button on a new e-mail, your **Contacts address book** will open. This address book lists the names and e-mail addresses of those in your Contacts.

If you are using Outlook in an Exchange environment, in addition to your Contacts address book, you will also have a **Global Address List.** This address book contains the contacts for all the individuals in your organization. Your Exchange server administrator will maintain the Global Address List. You cannot add contacts to this folder, but you can save contacts from the Global Address List to your Contacts folder.

MORE INFO

See page 17 in Chapter 1 for the differences between Outlook as a stand-alone program and Outlook using an Exchange server.

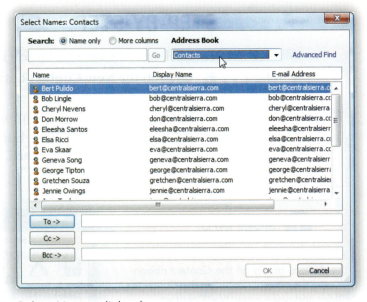

Select Names dialog box

Creating Contacts

As with most Microsoft products there are numerous methods of accomplishing the same task. Adding contact records to your Contacts folder can be accomplished in a number of ways. You can create a new contact from scratch, from the same company as an existing contact, from an e-mail you received, from an electronic business card you received, or from the Global Address List.

New Contact

To create a new contact, make sure you have selected the **Contacts** button in the *Navigation* pane. When you click on the **New Contact** button on the *Home* ribbon, a new contact record will open. This new contact will be a blank record, and you will be able to add the contact information desired.

 SHORTCUT

Ctrl+N will open a new contact record when you are in Outlook Contacts.
Ctrl+Shift+C will open a new contact record anywhere in Outlook.
Ctrl+S will save an open contact.

 ANOTHER WAY

You can save a contact record by clicking on the **Save** button on the *Quick Access toolbar* or by clicking on the **File** tab and choosing **Save.**

New contact record

Address

In addition to storing a contact's address, Outlook contact record addresses can be used to generate mailing lists, envelopes, and/or labels. The address field lets you type the address directly into the text box, or an address field dialog box can be opened and the address can be typed into the dialog box. Each contact record can store up to three different addresses. You have the options of business, home, or other addresses.

 MORE INFO

If Outlook does not recognize the format in which you type an address, a *Check Address* dialog box will open. This will allow you to edit the address.

If you type an e-mail address in a format that Outlook doesn't recognize, a *Check Names* dialog box will open.

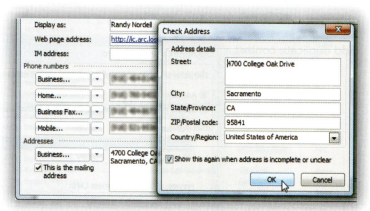

Check Address dialog box

ANOTHER WAY

Any of the field names that are displayed as a button can be clicked on and a dialog box will appear. The information for that field can be typed directly into the dialog box.

Click on the **E-mail** button on a contact record; the *Select Names* dialog box will open and allow you to choose an e-mail address from your *Global Address List*.

Multiple E-mail Addresses

Do you have more than one e-mail account? Well, most of us do. Outlook will let you store up to three e-mail addresses per contact record. Each e-mail address is added to the Outlook Address Book. The main e-mail address is labeled *E-mail,* and the additional e-mail address fields are labeled *E-mail 2* and *E-mail 3.*

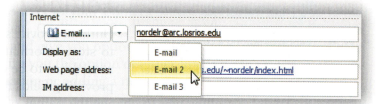

Add multiple e-mail addresses to a contact record

Picture

To further customize a contact record, you can add a contact's picture. The picture will appear on the contact record when it is open. Also, if you have a picture saved in a contact record and you receive an e-mail from that contact, his or her picture will appear on the e-mail message.

STEP-BY-STEP

1. With a contact record open, click on the **picture icon.** The *Add Contact Picture* dialog box will open.
2. Find and select the picture you want on the contact record.
3. Click **OK** to close the dialog box.
4. Click on **Save & Close** to close the contact record.

Picture button

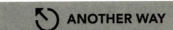
ANOTHER WAY

You can right-click on the picture on the contact record and choose either **Change Picture** or **Remove Picture.**

Picture added to contact record

If you decide that you do not want the picture on the contact record or would like a different picture, you can easily change or delete it.

FACTOID

If you use your cell phone to sync with Outlook (not all cell phones will do this), you will have the option of syncing your Outlook Contacts. If you receive a phone call from a recipient whose contact record has a picture, the picture will be displayed on the cell phone screen during the incoming call.

STEP-BY-STEP

1. Open the contact record.
2. Click on the **Picture** button in the *Options* group on the *Contacts* ribbon.
3. Click on either **Change Picture** or **Remove Picture.**
4. If you select **Change Picture,** the *Add Contact Picture* dialog box will open and you can select a new picture. If you select **Remove Picture,** the picture will be removed from the contact record. (Note: The picture will only be deleted from the contact record, not from your computer.)

Remove picture from contact record

Map

How many times have you used the Internet to get a map or driving directions to a location? You had to go to the Web site and type in the address to find the desired information. Microsoft Outlook provides users with a *map* feature that will link an address from a contact record to an interactive Internet map. So, rather than you having to go to a different Web site and type in an address, Outlook will open Bing Maps from an address in a contact record with the click of a button.

Add members to a contact group

4. Select the contacts to add to your contact group from your *Contacts* folder or the *Global Address List*.

5. Click on the **Members** button.

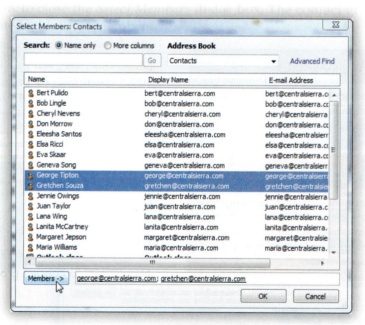

Select members to add to a contact group

6. Click **OK.** The *Select Members* dialog box will close, and the new members are now included in your contact group.

7. Click **Save & Close** to save the updated contact group.

Members can also be easily removed from your contact group.

STEP-BY-STEP

1. Click on the **Contacts** button in the *Navigation* pane.

2. Open the contact group to be modified.

3. In the body of the contact group, select the members to be removed.

4. Click on the **Remove Member** button in the *Members* group.

 **MORE INFO**

When removing members from a contact group, *do not* click on the **Delete Group** button in the *Actions* group. This will delete the entire contact group rather than the members selected to be removed.

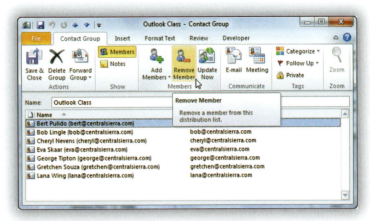

Remove members from a contact group

5. Click on **Save & Close** to save the updated contact group.

The *New E-mail Contact* option is used to add a member to the contact group who is not currently in your Contacts folder.

STEP-BY-STEP

1. Click on the **Contacts** button in the *Navigation* pane.
2. Open the contact group to be modified.
3. Click on the **Add Members** button in the *Members* group, and choose **New E-mail Contact.** The *Add New Member* dialog box will open.

Add new member to contact group

4. Type in the contact's information. Check the **Add to Contacts** check box, and Outlook will add this contact to your *Contacts* folder.
5. Click **OK** to add the new member to the contact group and to close the *Add New Member* dialog box.

Add New Member dialog box

6. Click on **Save & Close** to save the updated contact group.

There will be times when you make changes to a contact in your Contacts folder. If this contact is included in a contact group, the changes will not automatically be updated in the contact group. The *Update Now* button in the *Members* group will update the members in your contact group to match their contact information in your Contacts folder.

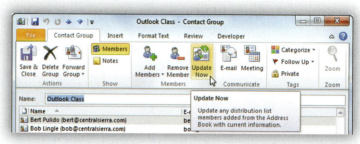

Update a contact group

Chapter Highlights

▶ A **contact** is a set of related information and functions similarly to a database.

▶ A **contact** is referred to as a **record** or **contact record.** A **record** is a group of related **fields.** A **field** is one piece of information about an individual or company.

▶ Outlook stores your contacts in the **Contacts folder.**

▶ If you are using Outlook on an Exchange Server, you will also have a **Global Address List.** The Global Address List contains contact records and contact groups for those within your organization.

▶ In Outlook you can create a contact record in many different ways. You can create a **new contact** from scratch, a **new contact from the same company** as an existing contact, from a **received e-mail,** from an **electronic business card,** and from a Global Address List.

▶ Outlook will alert you if you are saving a **duplicate** contact record and give you the option of adding the new contact record or updating the existing contact record.

▶ Contact records can be customized to better meet your needs. The **field names** of many of the fields in a contact record can be changed.

▶ Contact records can include **addresses,** which can be used to create mailing lists, labels, and envelopes. Multiple addresses can be saved in a contact record.

▶ Multiple e-mail addresses and a picture can be stored in a contact record.

▶ There is a **Map** feature in Contacts that will automatically generate an online map of the address on the contact record.

▶ The **People pane** appears at the bottom of the contact record and provides you with a list of Outlook items associated with a contact.

▶ The **Outlook Social Connector** (OSC) can be used to connect to a social network Web site. Activities and posts from people with whom you are connected will be displayed in the People pane.

▸ Contact records can be **deleted** and are stored in the **Deleted Items** folder until that folder is emptied.

▸ Outlook provides you with different **preset views** in the Contacts folder. Each of these different views can be customized to better meet your needs.

▸ Contacts can be used to populate the recipient list of an e-mail.

▸ A **business card** containing your contact record information can be attached to an e-mail and sent to other Outlook users.

▸ A **contact group** is a saved group of contact records. Contact groups can be used to populate a recipient list in an e-mail message just like a contact record.

▸ Contact groups can be edited to add members, remove members, add a new contact record, or update contact information.

What Do You Know About Outlook?

True/False Questions

T F 1. A contact record must include an individual's name. [Objective 4.2]

T F 2. Some of the field names in a contact record can be changed. [Objective 4.3]

T F 3. The preset views in the Contacts folder can be customized to better meet your needs. [Objective 4.4]

T F 4. Contacts that are deleted are stored in the Deleted Contacts folder. [Objective 4.3]

T F 5. When you are in the Contacts folder, the contact views are listed in the Navigation pane. [Objective 4.4]

Multiple Choice Questions

1. In a contact record, **E-mail** is which of the following? [Objective 4.1]
   a. A file
   b. A record
   c. A field
   d. A contact

2. Which of the following is *not* a preset view in the Contacts folder? [Objective 4.4]
   a. By Company
   b. Phone List
   c. Business Card
   d. By Category

3. Which of the following is true of contacts? [Objectives 4.1, 4.3, 4.5]
   a. Contacts in the Global Address List cannot be saved in your Contacts folder.
   b. Only one e-mail address can be stored in a contact record.
   c. Contact records can be used to populate an e-mail recipient list.
   d. All the above.

4. Which of the following is a method used to create a new contact record? [Objective 4.2]
   a. From an e-mail received
   b. From a new contact from the same company
   c. From an electronic business card
   d. All the above

5. Which of the following is *not* true of a contact group? [Objective 4.5]
   a. A contact group can be used to populate the recipient list of an e-mail.
   b. You can remove members of a contact group.
   c. You can create a new e-mail from a contact group.
   d. You can create a contact group from a contact record.

Short Answer Questions

1. Explain the difference between the Contacts folder and the Global Address List. [Objective 4.1]

2. Describe how to create a contact group. [Objective 4.5]

3. Explain how to add a new contact record of a sender from whom you have received an e-mail. [Objective 4.2]

Putting Outlook to Work

You need to start getting your Contacts folder set up on Outlook. In these exercises you will be creating and editing contacts, saving contacts, sending a contact, creating and modifying a contact group, and sending to a contact group. (*Note: You will need to have access to your professor's and classmates' e-mail addresses. If you are set up on an Exchange server, you most likely have access to these e-mail addresses. If not, your instructor will have to provide them for you.*)

Exercise 4.1 [Guided Practice]

Create a new contact record containing your information.
[Objectives 4.1, 4.2]

1. Click on **Contacts** in the *Navigation* pane.

2. In Contacts create a new contact record.
   a. You can click on the **New Contact** button or press **Ctrl+N**.

3. Type in your full name.
   a. Use **Tab** to move from field to field or **Shift+Tab** to move back one field.
   b. Notice that after you type your name and press **Tab,** the *File As* field is automatically filled in.

4. Use your school name as the **Company.**

5. Use **Student** for the **Title.**
   a. Notice how the business card in the upper right corner of the contact is automatically being filled in as you add information to your contact record.

6. Make sure the **File As** field is last name, first name.

7. For **E-mail,** use the e-mail you are using for this course.

   a. If you are using an Exchange account, you can click on the **E-mail** button and select your e-mail from the *Select Names* dialog box.

   b. If you are not using an Exchange account, type in your e-mail address.

8. In the **Display As** field, make sure your name appears without the e-mail address. You might need to type in your full name (first and last).

9. Enter the school's phone number in the **Business** phone field.

   a. The first time you enter a phone number you will be prompted to enter your area code and set this as your location.

10. Enter a **Mobile** phone number. You can use a fictitious number.

11. Use the school address for the **Business** address.

12. Click on the **Picture** button, and find a picture on the computer to insert.

    a. This does not have to be a picture of you; you can use any picture on your computer.

13. Click on **Save & Close.** Your new contact will be saved in the *Contacts* folder.

Exercise 4.2 [Guided Practice]

Create a new contact record from the same company. [Objectives 4.1, 4.2]

1. Open the contact you created in Exercise 4.1.

2. Click on the arrow to the right of the **Save and New** button in the *Actions* group on the *Contact* ribbon.

3. Click on **Contact from Same Company.**

   a. A new contact record will open with some of the company information already filled in.

4. Type your professor's name in the **Full Name** field.

5. Click on **Save & Close.**

   a. You do not need to put in an e-mail address at this point.

Exercise 4.3 [Guided Practice]

Create a new contact record from a received e-mail, and update a contact record. [Objectives 4.2, 4.3]

1. Click on the **Mail** button in the *Navigation* pane.

2. Open an e-mail from your professor.

   a. You should have an e-mail in your *Inbox* from your professor.

3. Put your mouse pointer on your professor's name next to the *From* field. A communicate window will open.

4. Click on the **+** button on the open menu, and choose **Add to Outlook Contacts.** A new contact record with your professor's information will open.

   a. Fill in any additional information needed.

Exercise 4.7 [Independent Practice]

Use different contact views, edit a contact record, and use the Map feature. [Objectives 4.1, 4.3–4.5]

1. In *Contacts,* look at the different contact views available by clicking on the different view buttons in the *Current View* group on the *Home* ribbon.

   a. Go through each one of the different views, and notice how the contact records are displayed and grouped in the *Folder* pane.

2. Open your contact record, and change the name of the **Mobile** phone field to **Primary.**

3. Add a second e-mail address to your contact record.

   a. Use *[your_name]*@outlook_class.com

4. Use the **Map** feature to open an online map of the address on your contact record.

5. Close the map.

6. Save and close your contact record.

Exercise 4.8 [Independent Practice]

Edit a contact group, and send an e-mail using a contact group. [Objective 4.5]

1. Open the **Outlook Class** contact group.

2. Update the contact group.

   a. The changes you made to your contact record will be updated in the contact group.

3. Remove your name from the contact group.

4. Save and close the contact group.

5. Create a new e-mail, and use the **Outlook Class** contact group as the recipient.

6. Use **E-mail netiquette** as the subject.

7. Mark the e-mail as **High importance.**

8. Include a **Flag for Recipients.**

   a. Use **For Your Information,** and do not include a reminder.

9. Request a **delivery receipt.**

10. In the body, use bulleted format and list at least three netiquette rules you have learned in this class.

11. Include your signature.

12. **Send.**

Exercise 4.9 [Independent Practice]

Create a new contact group, send your contact record as an Outlook contact, and send an e-mail to a contact group. [Objectives 4.4, 4.5]

1. Create a new contact group, and name it **Outlook Class w/o professor.**

2. Include all your classmates as members, but do not include yourself or your professor.

3. Save and close the contact group.

4. Forward your contact record as an Outlook contact.

5. Send the new e-mail to the **Outlook Class w/o professor** contact group and a copy to yourself and your professor.

6. Use `Forwarding an Outlook contact` as the subject.

7. In the body, list the steps in numbered format to send an Outlook contact as an attachment.

8. Include your signature.

9. Mark the e-mail as **High importance.**

10. Include a **read receipt.**

11. Set the message to **expire** tomorrow at 8 a.m.

12. **Send.**

Chapter 5
Calendar

OBJECTIVES *After completing this chapter, you will be able to:*

5.1 Appraise the benefits of an Outlook calendar.

5.2 Contrast the different types of calendar items.

5.3 Differentiate between Outlook Calendar views.

5.4 Use Outlook to create and edit calendar items.

5.5 Incorporate meeting requests into your Outlook calendar.

CHAPTER FLYOVER

- Benefits of an Outlook calendar
- Calendar items
- Appointments
- Events
- Meeting requests
- Navigating calendar views
- Day, Week, Month, and Schedule views
- Other calendar views
- Creating and editing calendar items
- New appointment and event reminders
- Recurring appointments and events
- Moving and copying calendar items
- Deleting calendar items
- Creating and sending a meeting request
- Responding to meeting requests
- Proposing a new time for a meeting request
- Tracking meeting request respondents
- Changing and updating a meeting request
- Deleting a scheduled meeting

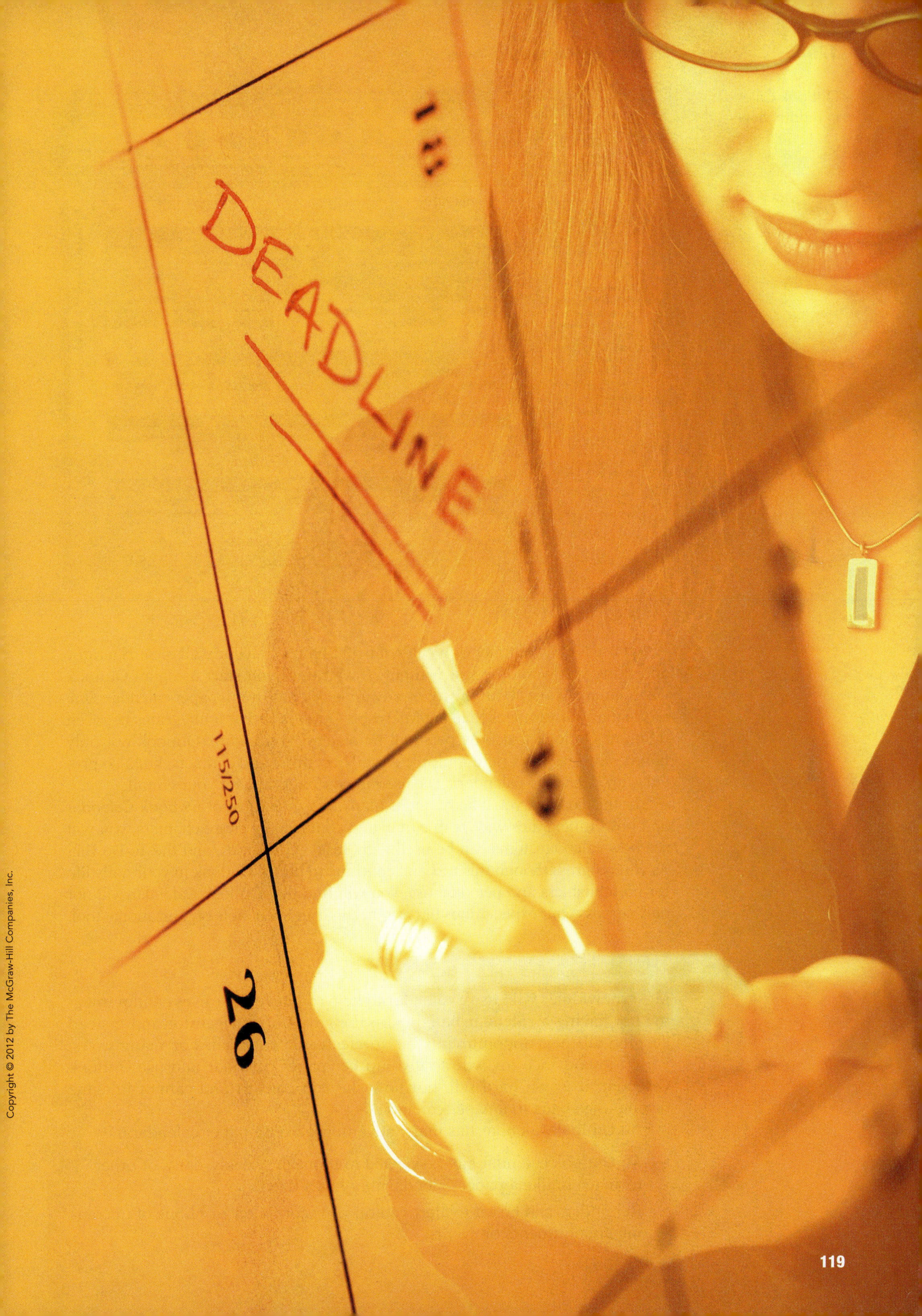
DEADLINE
115/250
26

Outlook Calendar
in month view

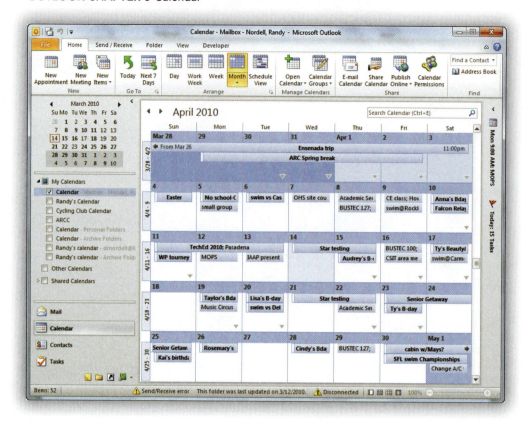

Making Outlook Work for You

If you use a daily planner or a calendar that hangs on your wall or refrigerator and think you would be lost without it, wait until you start using an Outlook calendar and learn about the many advantages it has over a paper calendar. One of the many advantages to using Microsoft Outlook is that it integrates between different Outlook tasks. As personal management software, Outlook not only handles your e-mails (and multiple e-mail accounts) and contacts, but also provides an electronic calendar to be used in conjunction with your e-mail.

In this chapter, you'll learn about many of the features of **Outlook Calendar** and how it integrates with both e-mail and contacts. In future chapters, you will see how calendar items can be used with Tasks, Categories, and the To-Do Bar. As you progress though this text and continue to utilize Outlook in your daily life for both business and personal use, you will find that Outlook Calendar will not only surpass your expectations but also become an invaluable organizational tool.

Benefits of an Outlook Calendar

Most individuals who use a calendar to help organize their lives cannot imagine not having a calendar hanging on their wall or refrigerator and instead keeping all their appointments on an electronic calendar. For many years, I tried to convince my wife to give up her paper calendar and use Outlook Calendar. It was a hard sell, but now she is a convert and cannot imagine having to go back to a paper calendar.

An Outlook calendar has many advantages over a paper calendar.

- An Outlook calendar can be viewed in monthly, weekly, daily, or other formats, unlike a paper calendar that has a fixed view.

- Reminders can be set to alert you on your computer or phone of upcoming appointments or events.

> ### ⓘ MORE INFO
>
> Categories will be covered in Chapter 7 on page 191, and attaching files and Outlook items to a calendar item will be covered in Chapter 10.

- Calendar items can easily be moved, copied, deleted, or set to recur at specific intervals.
- Categories can be used to group calendar items and color them for visual recognition.
- Additional information and details can be included in the body, and items such as contacts and Word documents can be attached to a calendar item.
- Calendar items can be set to recur on a specific interval (daily, weekly, monthly, or yearly).
- Meeting requests can be used to create a meeting on your calendar, invite others to the meeting, and track responses of those attending the meeting.
- Calendars can be synchronized with many of the new cell phones that have a calendar feature.

As you begin using your Outlook calendar, you will most likely realize additional advantages over a paper calendar that are not listed here.

Calendar Items

There are three main types of calendar items: ***appointments, events,*** and ***meeting requests.*** Each of these different items has a distinct purpose and use, but all these items are created in a similar fashion, and you can use the same new calendar item to create each of these different calendar items. For example, an appointment can easily be changed to an event by changing the duration of the calendar item. This consistency makes it easy to learn how to use Outlook Calendar.

Appointments

An ***appointment*** is a calendar item that has a duration of less than 24 hours, for example, a sales meeting, your child's water polo game, or a date with your significant other. This is the most common type of calendar item and can be used for storing all types of appointments or for scheduling blocks of time that are less than a day in length.

Calendar appointment

Events

Events are those calendar items that last for 24 hours or more, like vacations, conferences, birthdays, or long holidays.

Calendar event

When a new appointment is open, it can easily be converted to an event by clicking on the **All day event** check box to the right of the Start and End times. Conversely, an event can be converted to an appointment by deselecting the **All day** event check box and setting the specific time of the appointment.

Meeting Requests

A *meeting request* is used to create a calendar item and invite others to this meeting. It looks similar to both an appointment and event, but the meeting request includes a *To* line used to invite attendees and a *Send* button. A meeting request looks like a combination of a calendar item and a new e-mail and can be either an appointment or event.

Meeting request

An appointment or event can easily be converted to a meeting request by clicking on the **Invite Attendees** button in the *Attendees* group on the *Appointment* or *Events* ribbon (the tab name will vary depending on whether the calendar item is an appointment or event).

Invite Attendees
button

Navigating the Calendar Views

As mentioned previously, one of the advantages of using an Outlook calendar is being able to view the calendar in different formats. There are four main calendar views: *Day, Week, Month,* and *Schedule.* And, there are other views available that list calendar items according to specific criteria. You have to experiment with the different views to find the view or views that work best for you. My preference is the Month view.

When **Calendar** is selected in the *Navigation* pane, it is displayed in the *Folder* pane. The way the calendar is displayed in the Folder pane is dependent upon the calendar view you have selected. The buttons for **Day, Week, Month,** and **Schedule** views are in the *Arrange* group on the *Home* ribbon. Also, displayed in the *Navigation* pane are the ***date navigator*** (a thumbnail of a monthly calendar) and the different calendars available (you can have multiple calendars).

Day View

Day view displays the calendar one day at a time with the calendar broken into half-hour segments. Events are displayed at the top of the daily calendar, while appointments appear on the calendar at their scheduled time.

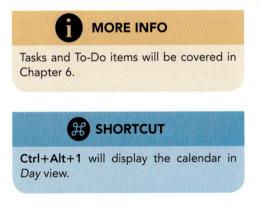

ⓘ MORE INFO

Tasks and To-Do items will be covered in Chapter 6.

⌘ SHORTCUT

Ctrl+Alt+1 will display the calendar in *Day* view.

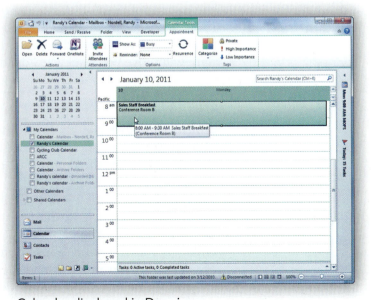

Calendar displayed in Day view

The date is listed at the top of the calendar, and you can move backward or forward one day at a time on the calendar by clicking on the **left** or **right arrow** to the left of the date. You can move to a specific date on the calendar by clicking on the date in the thumbnail calendar provided at the top of the Navigation pane.

A *Daily Task List* is provided at the bottom of the calendar in Day view. It can also be minimized or turned off.

Week View

Week view has two different display options: *Work Week* or *Week.* Work Week view displays a Monday–Friday workweek, while Week view displays a Sunday–Saturday week.

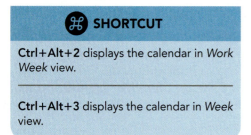

MORE INFO

Changing workweek options, calendar color, and other advanced calendar topics will be covered in Chapter 10.

⌘ SHORTCUT

Ctrl+Alt+2 displays the calendar in *Work Week* view.

Ctrl+Alt+3 displays the calendar in *Week* view.

Calendar displayed in Work Week view

As with Day view, Week view displays events at the top of the calendar and appointments appear at their set time. The Daily Task List is located at the bottom of the Folder pane and can either be minimized or turned off.

The date is displayed at the top of the calendar in the Folder pane showing the date range for the week. The left and right arrows to the left of the date will move you backward or forward one week at a time.

Month View

Month view displays an entire month of the calendar. You are given three different options (Show Low Detail, Show Medium Detail, and Show High Detail) regarding the amount of detail to display on the calendar for each calendar item.

Both events and appointments are displayed on the dates on which they occur. Events appear at the top of the date cell, and appointments appear below the events. You can see more detail about any of the items on the calendar by moving your mouse pointer over the item. Depending on the size of your computer monitor and the Outlook window, Month view will display three of four calendar items on each day. If there are more events or appointments on a certain date than will fit on the calendar, a small arrow will appear

 **SHORTCUT**

Ctrl+Alt+4 displays the calendar in *Month* view.

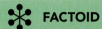 **FACTOID**

The **Today** button in the *Go To* group on the *Home* ribbon will always take you to the current day. Also, you can move to a specific day by clicking on the **date navigator** in the *Navigation* pane.

Calendar displayed in Month view with high details

at the bottom right corner of the date. By clicking on this arrow, you will be taken to Day view to see more appointments and events for that day.

The month is listed at the top of the Folder pane, and the left and right arrows to the left of the month will move you backward or forward one month at a time.

The Daily Task List is not available in Month view, but the To-Do bar can be used to view tasks and To-Do items.

Schedule View

Schedule view is new to Outlook 2010. Schedule view displays your calendar in timeline view in the Folder pane. The timeline is displayed horizontally rather than vertically (Day and Week views). In Schedule view you can type a new appointment directly on the calendar, double-click on a time slot to open a new appointment, or click on the **New Appointment** button on the *Home* ribbon.

 **SHORTCUT**

Ctrl+N opens a new calendar appointment when your calendar is selected.

Ctrl+Alt+5 displays the calendar in *Schedule* view.

 MORE INFO

Sharing and opening shared calendars will be covered in Chapter 10.

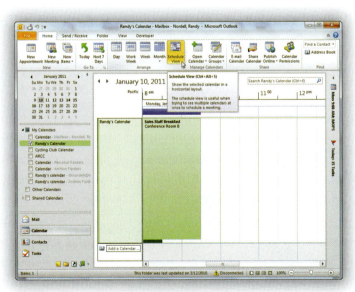

Calendar displayed in Schedule view

One of the distinct advantages of using the Schedule view is the ability to view multiple calendars in the Folder pane. When using Outlook in an Exchange environment, it is common to share your calendar with others in your organization. When others have shared their calendars with you, you can select one or more of these shared calendars to be displayed in Schedule view, which will help facilitate scheduling meetings, appointments, and events.

Other Views

In addition to the four main calendar views, Outlook also has other preset views available. These different views show calendar items in a list rather than Day, Week, or Month view. The different preset views are:

- By category (List view)
- Calendar (Calendar view)
- Preview (Calendar view)
- List (List view)
- Active (List view)

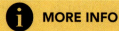
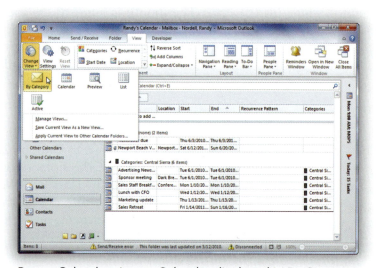

Preset Calendar views—Calendar displayed in By Category view

These other views can be accessed by going to the **View** ribbon, clicking on **Change View,** and choosing the view you want. You can return to Calendar view by following the same steps and choosing **Calendar.**

Creating and Editing Calendar Items

Creating a calendar item varies depending on the calendar view. In all the calendar views, you can type an appointment directly on the calendar. In Day and Week views, you can adjust the duration of an appointment by clicking and dragging on the top or bottom edge of the appointment.

Usually the best way to create a calendar item is to open a new calendar item. This will give you more fields to enter detailed information about the appointment or event.

New Appointment

When you are in your calendar (it doesn't matter which view), a new appointment can be created by clicking on the **New Appointment** button on the *Home* ribbon. The new appointment will open, and the date will be the date you were on in the calendar. The date and time can easily be changed.

STEP-BY-STEP

1. In your calendar, click the **New Appointment** button on the *Home* ribbon. A new appointment will open.
2. Fill in the **Subject** and **Location** of the appointment.
3. Set the **Start time** and **End time** dates and times for this appointment.
4. Additional information about this appointment can be entered in the body of the new appointment.
5. Click **Save & Close.** The appointment will appear on your calendar.

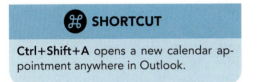

SHORTCUT

Ctrl+Shift+A opens a new calendar appointment anywhere in Outlook.

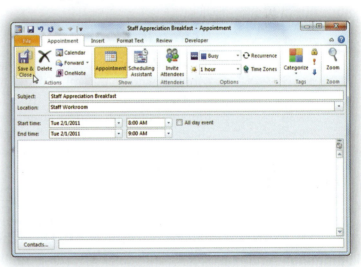

New calendar appointment

New Event

Creating a new event will vary depending on the calendar view. When you are in Day or Week view, a new event can be created by double-clicking on the event area at the top of the calendar in the Folder pane. In Month view, you can create a new event by double-clicking on the date of the event (or the first day of the event).

An appointment can always be converted to an event by clicking the **All day event** check box to the right of the date and time.

STEP-BY-STEP

1. Click on the **New Appointment** button on the *Home* ribbon or press **Ctrl+N.** A new appointment will open.
2. Fill in the **Subject** and **Location** of the event.
3. Click on the **All day event** check box.

New calendar event

4. Set the **Start time** and **End time** dates for this event.
5. Additional information about this event can be entered in the body of the new event.
6. Click **Save & Close.** The event will appear on your calendar.

Reminders

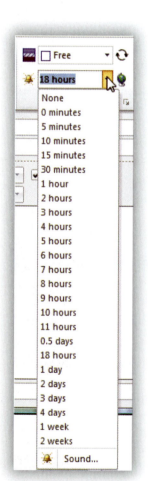

Reminder options

A *reminder* can be set on all calendar items. This reminder will open on your computer screen to remind you of an upcoming appointment, event, or meeting.

The *default* reminder time for an appointment is *15 minutes* before the appointment, and an event is *18 hours* before the event. You can easily change the reminder time by clicking on the **Reminder** pull-down menu in the *Options* group on the *Appointment* or *Event* ribbon. You can also choose to set a specific sound for the reminder. The reminder can also be set to **None.**

When the reminder for an appointment or event comes due, it is displayed on your computer screen. The reminder displays the subject of the calendar item, the start date and time, and the location. You are given the options of **Dismiss All, Open Item, Dismiss,** and **Snooze.** If you choose Snooze, you can choose to be reminded again in a certain amount of time by clicking on the **Snooze** pull-down menu.

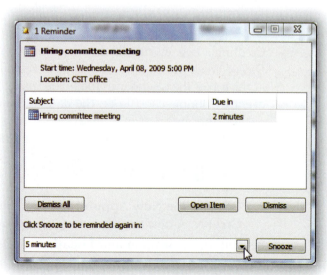

Reminder window

Moving and Copying Calendar Items

One of the distinct advantages of using an Outlook calendar is the ability to easily move and replicate calendar items. Many times an appointment is rescheduled, and when using an Outlook calendar, you can move the item to a new date or time.

To *move* a calendar item, you can open the item from the calendar and change the date and/or time of the item. When you save and close the item, it will be moved to its new date and time on the calendar. If an appointment has been moved to another day and has the same time, you can simply drag and drop the calendar item to the new date on the calendar.

Suppose you have jury duty three days in a row and you don't want to create three separate calendar appointments. To *copy* an existing appointment to another date, you can select the appointment on the calendar, hold down the **Ctrl** key, and drag and drop the appointment on the new date. As you are dragging the calendar item you will see a small plus sign by the mouse pointer to indicate that you are copying a calendar item rather than moving it. The appointment will be copied to the new date.

 SHORTCUT

Ctrl+C copies a selected calendar item.
Ctrl+X cuts a selected calendar item.
Ctrl+V pastes a copied or cut calendar item to a new location.

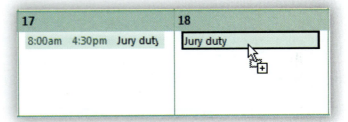

Copy calendar item

Recurring Appointments and Events

When a calendar item has a recurring pattern, it is better to set up the item as a *recurring appointment* or *event* rather than just copying the item to another location. A recurring appointment or event is typically used for appointments or events that occur on a regular basis such as weekly sales meetings, monthly lunch socials, birthdays, or anniversaries.

A calendar item can be set to recur daily, weekly, monthly or yearly. The recurring calendar item can be set to end after a certain number of occurrences, end on a certain date, or have no end date.

STEP-BY-STEP

1. Create a new calendar appointment.
2. Fill in the **Subject, Location, Start time, End time,** and any other needed details in the body.
3. Click on the **Recurrence** button in the *Options* group. A *Recurrence* dialog box will open.

Recurrence button

4. Confirm the correct start and end times in the *Appointment time* section.
5. Set the desired **Recurrence pattern.**
6. Select the *Range of recurrence* for **Start** and **End.**
7. Click **OK** to close the dialog box.

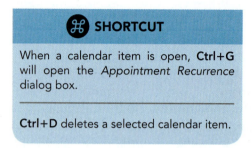

SHORTCUT

When a calendar item is open, **Ctrl+G** will open the *Appointment Recurrence* dialog box.

Ctrl+D deletes a selected calendar item.

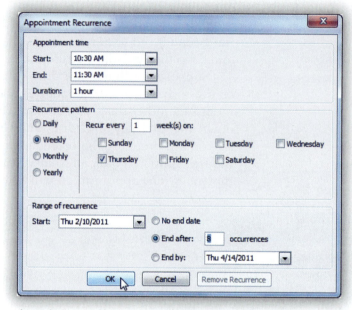

Appointment Recurrence dialog box

Open Recurring Item dialog box

8. Click **Save & Close** to close the recurring appointment.

Recurring items can be edited. When you open a recurring item, Outlook will give you two options. ***Open this occurrence*** will allow you to edit that specific calendar item without changing all the recurring items or the recurrence pattern. ***Open the series*** will allow you to edit the entire series of recurring calendar items.

Deleting Calendar Items

You can delete calendar items by selecting the items to be removed from the calendar and either pressing the **Delete** key on your keyboard, clicking on the **Delete** button on the *Appointment* ribbon, or right-clicking on the calendar item and selecting **Delete.**

Delete recurring calendar item

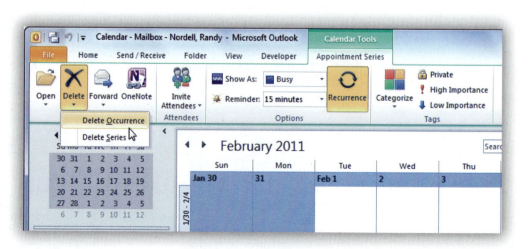

When deleting a recurring item, you are given the options to either **Delete Occurrence** or **Delete Series.** Delete Occurrence will delete an individual calendar item within a series, and Delete Series will delete an entire series.

Deleted calendar items are stored in the Deleted Items folder and remain there until this folder is permanently emptied. If you delete a calendar item by mistake, you can open the **Deleted Items** folder and drag the calendar item from the *Deleted Items* folder to the *Calendar* button in the *Navigation* pane. The calendar item will be restored to its correct location on the calendar.

Create a Calendar Item from an E-mail

There may be times when you receive an e-mail and would like to create a calendar item based on the information in that e-mail. Rather than retyping all the information in the e-mail, you can easily convert to a calendar item.

ANOTHER WAY

Select or open an e-mail, click on the **Move** button in the *Move* group, and choose **Calendar.** A new calendar appointment will open. When you save and close the appointment, the original e-mail message will be moved to your *Deleted Items* folder.

STEP-BY-STEP

1. Click on the e-mail to be converted to a calendar item (do not open the e-mail).

2. **Drag and drop** the e-mail on the *Calendar* button in the *Navigation* pane.

3. A new calendar appointment will open. The subject will be the same as the e-mail subject, and the date will be the current date. The body of the new calendar item will contain the information from the body of the e-mail.

4. Edit the calendar item **Start and End dates and times.**

5. Edit the body of the calendar item.

6. **Save & Close** the calendar item.

Creating and Using Meeting Requests

Suppose you are organizing a meeting within your company, and you want to keep track of those who will be attending and those who are not able to make it to the meeting. Outlook provides you with a calendar feature that not only creates a calendar appointment, but also sends this appointment to others via e-mail and tracks whether or not they will be attending the meeting.

FACTOID

Tracking responses for meeting requests only works when used in an Exchange environment.

Meeting requests are used to invite others to a meeting. It can be either an appointment or event. The advantage of using a meeting request over an e-mail to invite attendees to a meeting is that the recipients receive a meeting invitation and are given the options of **Accept, Tentative, Decline,** or **Propose New Time.** When the recipient accepts the meeting request, the meeting is automatically added to the recipient's Outlook calendar and a response is sent to the sender of the meeting request. The meeting request will automatically keep track of attendees' responses.

Creating and Sending a Meeting Request

A meeting request can be created by clicking on the **New Meeting** button on the *Home* ribbon, or by selecting or opening an existing calendar item and clicking on the **Invite Attendees** button in the *Attendees* group.

STEP-BY-STEP

Invite Attendees
button

1. Create a new meeting request by clicking on the **New Meeting** button in the *New* group on the *Home* ribbon. An existing appointment or event can be converted to a meeting by clicking on the **Invite Attendees** button in the *Attendees* group.

2. Click on the **To** button to invite attendees. The *Select Attendees and Resources* dialog box will open.

3. Select attendees from your contacts. Attendees can be either **Required** or **Optional** to attend the meeting.

NETIQUETTE

When sending a meeting request, provide a brief message and your name in the body.

SHORTCUT

Ctrl+Shift+Q opens a new meeting request.

FACTOID

When you open a new meeting request, it will always be an appointment. The meeting request can be changed to an event by clicking on the **All day event** check box.

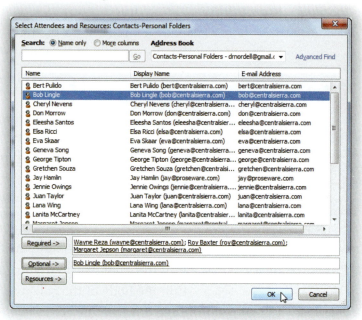

Select Attendees and Resources dialog box

4. Click **OK** to close the dialog box.

5. Fill in the **Subject, Location, Start and End times** (date and time), and any additional information needed in the body.

6. Click **Send** to send the meeting request.

Meeting Request

SHORTCUT

Ctrl+Alt+R creates a new meeting from an existing e-mail message.

A meeting can also be created directly from a received e-mail. When you receive an e-mail and need to create a meeting based upon the information in that e-mail, you do not have to go to your calendar to create a new meeting. A new meeting can be created from this e-mail by clicking on the **Reply with Meeting** button (or **Meeting** button) in the *Respond* group on the *Message* ribbon. The contents of the e-mail message are included in the body of the new meeting. You can add attendees and make any other necessary changes before sending the meeting request.

NETIQUETTE

When creating a meeting from an e-mail message, it is a good idea to clean up the body of the meeting to enhance the appearance of this calendar item.

Reply with a Meeting

Responding to Meeting Requests

When you receive a meeting request, it will come to your Inbox like other e-mails you receive. The Inbox icon for a meeting request will look different than an e-mail icon.

When you open the meeting request, it will look similar to an e-mail, but in the Respond group you are given four additional options: **Accept, Tentative, Decline,** or **Propose New Time.** When one of these responses is selected, a dialog box is opened and you are given the following options: **Edit the Response Before Sending, Send the Response Now,** or **Do Not Send a Response.**

If you choose Accept, Tentative, or Propose New Time, the meeting request is removed from your Inbox and added to your calendar and a response e-mail is sent to the meeting organizer. If you choose Decline, the meeting request is moved from your Inbox to the Deleted Items folder and a response is sent to the meeting organizer.

New to Outlook 2010 is the *Calendar Preview* feature. Previously when you received a meeting request, you had to switch to your calendar to view your existing appointments, events, and meetings to determine your availability. Calendar Preview inserts a snapshot of your calendar in the body of the meeting request so you can view existing calendar items on the day of the new meeting request. Double-clicking on the calendar preview will take you to your calendar.

STEP-BY-STEP

1. Open the meeting request from your *Inbox*.
2. Click on one of the responses in the *Respond* group.

3. Choose **Edit the Response Before Sending** or **Send the Response Now.** If you choose **Edit the Response Before Sending,** the e-mail will open and you will be able to enter a response in the body of the e-mail before sending. If you choose **Send the Response Now,** the response will automatically be sent to the meeting organizer.

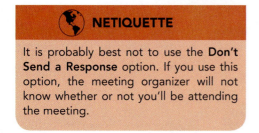

NETIQUETTE

It is probably best not to use the **Don't Send a Response** option. If you use this option, the meeting organizer will not know whether or not you'll be attending the meeting.

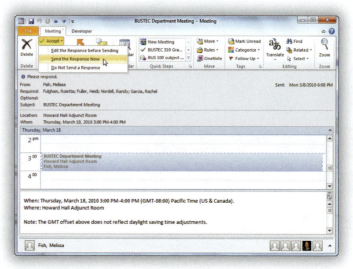

Received meeting request

4. Click **OK** to close the dialog box.

5. Click on **Send** if necessary. If you chose **Accept** or **Tentative,** the response is sent and the meeting request is removed from your Inbox and placed on your calendar.

Proposing a New Time to a Meeting Request

If you can't make a requested meeting at a particular date and time, you have the option of proposing a new time. When you click on **Propose New Time** in the *Respond* group, you are given two options: **Tentative and Propose New Time** and **Decline and Propose New Time.** The *Propose New Time* dialog box will open. You can propose a new time by either dragging the meeting to a new time slot on the date and time timeline or enter a new date and time in the Meeting start and Meeting end time boxes.

STEP-BY-STEP

1. Open the meeting request from your *Inbox.*

2. Click on **Propose New Time,** and choose either **Tentative and Propose New Time** or **Decline and Propose New Time.** The *Propose New Time* dialog box will open.

Propose New Time option on a meeting request

3. Make changes to the date and/or time.

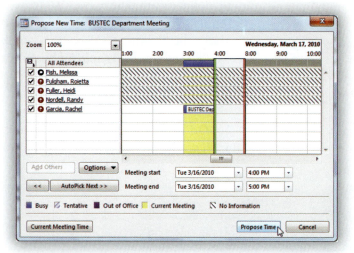

Propose New Time dialog box

4. Click on **Propose Time.** A *New Time Proposed* meeting request response will open. Notice the proposed changes below the subject line.

New Time Proposed e-mail

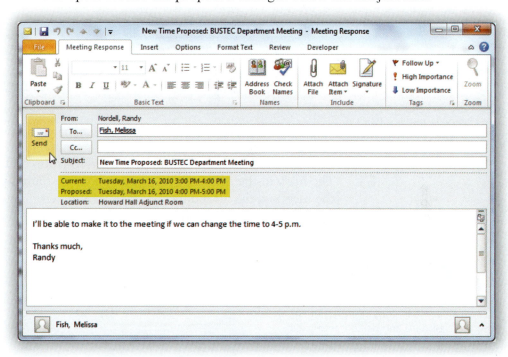

5. Type a brief message in the body.
6. Click on **Send.** The response is sent, and the meeting request is removed from your *Inbox* and placed on your calendar.

Tracking Meeting Request Respondents

When you organize a meeting and send out a meeting request, you will receive meeting request responses in your Inbox. The responses will inform you on the attendance status for each individual.

Meeting request response in Inbox

Outlook will track the responses of those individuals who have responded to your meeting request. When you open from the calendar the meeting request you created, Outlook displays a summary of responses in the *InfoBar* above the *To* button. Also, you can obtain more detailed tracking information by clicking on the **Tracking** button in the *Show* group on the *Meeting* ribbon.

STEP-BY-STEP

1. On your calendar, open the meeting request you created.
2. The summary of responses received is displayed in the *InfoBar*.

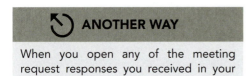

ANOTHER WAY

When you open any of the meeting request responses you received in your Inbox, a summary of responses will be displayed above the body of the message.

Meeting with response summary displayed in the InfoBar

3. Click on the **Tracking** button in the *Show* group on the *Meeting* ribbon. The body of the meeting request displays the names of those invited to the meeting, the attendance status (Meeting Organizer, Required Attendance, or Optional Attendance), and the response of each individual.

MORE INFO

When viewing the tracking of a meeting request, you can copy the tracking status to the clipboard and paste it into Excel.

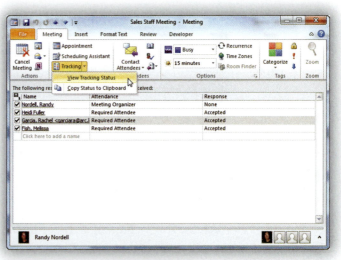

Meeting with tracking displayed

4. Click on the **Appointment** button in the *Show* group to close the tracking and return to the meeting request.
5. Click the **X** in the upper left to close the meeting request.

MORE INFO

If new attendees are added to or deleted from an existing meeting, you will be given the options of **Send updates to only added or deleted attendees** or **Send update to all attendees.**

Changing and Updating a Meeting Request

It is not uncommon for a meeting to have to be rescheduled to a different day, time, or location. Also, there might be the need to invite other attendees to a previously scheduled meeting. The meeting organizer can make changes to the meeting and add attendees. When this is done, a *meeting update* must be sent to attendees. Attendees will again be given the option of accepting or declining the changes to the meeting.

STEP-BY-STEP

1. On your calendar, open the meeting request you created.

2. Make changes to the meeting date and time or location if necessary.

3. The **Contact Attendees** button in the *Attendees* group on the *Meeting* ribbon provides you with the options to add or remove attendees, send a new e-mail message, or send a reply message.

4. After making any necessary changes, click on **Send Update.** Changes will be saved to the meeting on your calendar.

Send Update for changed meeting

 MORE INFO

When you are the meeting organizer (creator), Outlook will not allow you to delete that meeting without sending a meeting cancellation e-mail.

Deleting a Scheduled Meeting

Only the meeting organizer can cancel a meeting. When a meeting is canceled, all the attendees will receive a meeting cancellation e-mail. The meeting will be removed from your calendar, and the attendees will have the option of removing the meeting from their calendars.

Cancel Meeting
button

STEP-BY-STEP

1. On your calendar, open the meeting request you created.
2. Click on the **Cancel Meeting** button in the *Actions* group. The *Send Update* button becomes a *Send Cancellation* button, and there is a message in the *InfoBar*.
3. Click on the **Send Cancellation** button. The meeting request will be removed from your calendar, and all those invited to the meeting will receive an e-mail notifying them of the meeting cancellation.

Send meeting cancellation

Chapter Highlights

▶ An Outlook calendar is an electronic calendar that integrates with other features of Outlook. It can replace your paper calendar and provide you with many distinct advantages over a paper calendar.

▶ The three types of calendar items include: appointments, events, and meeting requests.

▶ **Appointments** are those calendar items that occur within a day—less than 24 hours in duration.

▶ **Events** are full-day or multiday calendar items.

▶ **Meeting requests** are used to create a calendar item, either an appointment or event, and invite others to this meeting. A meeting request is similar to both a calendar item and an e-mail.

▶ When a new calendar item is opened, it can easily be converted to any of the other calendar items (e.g., an appointment can be converted to either an event or meeting request).

▶ The Outlook calendar can be viewed in **Day, Week, Month,** or **Schedule** view. The **Daily Task List** is shown at the bottom of the Folder pane in Day and Week views. The calendar can also be viewed as a list showing all calendar items, listing calendar items by category, and other list views.

▶ You can create a calendar item by typing directly on the calendar, clicking on the **New Appointment** button, or double-clicking on the date and time on the calendar.

▶ On each calendar item, you can provide details about the **subject, location, start** and **end dates** and **times,** and additional details in the body.

▶ A **reminder** can be set on each calendar to electronically remind you of an upcoming appointment, event, or meeting. A reminder will open on your computer screen at the set time.

▶ One of the advantages of the Outlook calendar is the ease of **copying** and **moving** calendar items.

▶ Appointments or events that occur on a regular scheduled interval can be set up as a **recurring** appointment or event. Calendar items can be set up to recur **daily, weekly, monthly,** or **yearly.**

▶ Calendar items can easily be edited or deleted.

▶ You can convert an e-mail to a calendar item by dragging the e-mail from your Inbox to the Calendar button in the Navigation pane. You can also move an e-mail to the Calendar to create an appointment using **Move.**

▶ When a **meeting request** is received in the recipient's Inbox, the recipient has four options: **Accept, Decline, Tentative,** or **Propose New Time.**

▶ **Calendar Preview** is a snapshot of your calendar that is now included in the body of a received meeting request.

▶ The originator of the meeting request will receive responses about the meeting from recipients. Outlook will automatically **track** and summarize these responses for easy viewing.

▶ The originator of the meeting request can **update** or **cancel** a scheduled meeting.

What Do You Know About Outlook?

True/False Questions

T F   1. In Month view the Daily Task List is displayed at the bottom of the calendar. [Objective 5.3]

T F   2. A Word document can be attached to a calendar appointment. [Objectives 5.1, 5.2]

T F   3. An existing appointment can be changed to an event.
       [Objectives 5.2, 5.4]

T F   4. To create an appointment in Day view, type the subject directly
       on the calendar. [Objectives 5.3, 5.4]

T F   5. When a calendar is viewed by Category, calendar items are categorized
       in Month view. [Objective 5.3]

Multiple Choice Questions

1. Which of the following is a method to create a meeting request?
   [Objectives 5.2, 5.5]
   a. Open an existing appointment and click Invite Attendees.
   b. Press Ctrl+Shift+M.
   c. Click on the New button.
   d. All the above.

2. Which view displays an entire seven-day week on your calendar?
   [Objective 5.3]
   a. Day view
   b. Work Week view
   c. Calendar thumbnail in the Navigation pane
   d. None of the above

3. How is an e-mail converted to a calendar item? [Objectives 5.2, 5.4]
   a. Open the e-mail, and click on the Calendar button in the Actions
      group.
   b. Drag the e-mail to the Calendar button in the Navigation
      pane.
   c. Right-click on the e-mail, and choose Convert to Appointment.
   d. All the above.

4. When you receive a meeting request, which of the following is *not* a
   response option? [Objective 5.5]
   a. Accept
   b. Decline
   c. Cancel Meeting
   d. Propose New Time

5. Which of the following is *not* a recurring item option? [Objective 5.4]
   a. Weekly
   b. Daily
   c. Yearly
   d. Bi-monthly

Short Answer Questions

1. Explain three benefits of using an Outlook calendar. [Objective 5.1]

2. Describe how to copy a calendar item to another location on your
   calendar. [Objective 5.4]

3. Explain how to view the attendees' responses to a meeting request.
   [Objective 5.5]

Putting Outlook to Work

In these practice exercises, you will begin to use your Outlook calendar for both business and personal calendar items. You will be creating and editing appointments, events, and recurring calendar items. In addition, you will be creating and responding to meeting requests.

Exercise 5.1 [Guided Practice]

Create a new appointment, and use different calendar views. [Objectives 5.1–5.4]

1. Click on the **Calendar** button in the *Navigation* pane.
2. Click on the **Day** view.
3. Click the **right arrow** next to today's date to go to tomorrow.
4. Click on the **8 a.m.** time slot, type in **Staff Appreciation Breakfast,** and press **Enter.**
   a. Notice a new appointment is created from 8:00–8:30 a.m.
5. Click on the **bottom border** of this appointment, and drag down so the appointment ends at **9 a.m.** rather than 8:30 a.m.
6. Double-click on this appointment to open it.
7. Set the location as **Staff Workroom.**
8. Click on the **Reminder** pull-down menu in the *Options* group, and set the reminder for **1 hour.**
9. Click on **Save & Close.**
10. Click on **Work Week** view.
    a. Notice how the appointment is displayed in this view.
11. Click on **Week** view.
    a. Notice how the appointment is displayed in this view.
12. Click on **Month** view.
    a. Notice how the appointment is displayed in this view.
13. Click on **Schedule View.**
    a. Notice how the appointment is displayed in this view.
14. Click on **Day** view.

Exercise 5.2 [Guided Practice]

Create a new event. [Objectives 5.1–5.4]

1. Click on the **Calendar** button in the *Navigation* pane.
2. Click on **Month** view.
3. Double-click on **Saturday** of the current week. A new event opens.
4. In the *Subject* field, type **Cycling with family.**
5. Type **American River bike trail** as the location.
6. Click on the **Reminder** pull-down menu in the *Options* group and select **None.**

7. In the body, type a note to yourself to remember to bring helmets, water, and food.

8. Click on **Save & Close.**

9. Click on **Day** view.

10. Go to **Saturday** to view this event.

11. Click on **Week** view to view this event.

Exercise 5.3 [Guided Practice]

Create a new meeting request, and invite attendees.
[Objectives 5.1–5.3, 5.5]

1. Click on the **Calendar** button in the *Navigation* pane.

2. Click on **Month** view.

3. Click on the **New Meeting** button in the *New* group on the *Home* ribbon.

   a. You can also press **Ctrl+Shift+Q** to open a new meeting request.

4. In the *Subject* field, type in `[your first name]`'s New Client Meeting.

5. In the *Location* field, type `Conference Room A.`

6. Set the date and time for **Monday** at **2–3 p.m.**

7. Set a reminder to **30 minutes.**

8. In the body type a brief message about this important meeting with our new client, and include your signature.

9. Click on the **To** button to invite attendees. The *Select Attendees and Resources* dialog box will open.

10. Select all your classmates, and click on the **Required** button.

    a. If you have your **Outlook Class w/o professor** distribution list, you can select that rather than individually selecting all your classmates.

11. Select your professor, and click **Optional** button.

12. Click **OK** to close the dialog box.

13. Click **Send** to send the meeting request.

    a. Notice how the meeting request appears on your calendar in *Month* view.

14. Click on **Work Week** view to view this meeting request.

    a. Notice how the meeting request appears on your calendar in *Week* view.

Exercise 5.4 [Guided Practice]

Create a new recurring event for your birthday. [Objectives 5.1–5.4]

1. Click on the **Calendar** button in the *Navigation* pane.

2. Click on **Month** view.

3. Using the **thumbnail calendar** in the *Navigation* pane, find your next birthday.

4. Click on the **date of your birthday.**

   a. You will be taken to your birthday in *Day* view.

5. Double-click in the **events area** near the top of the calendar in the *Folder* pane. A new event will open.

   a. Make sure the **All day event** box is checked and the date is correct.

6. In the *Subject* field, type **[Your Name]'s Birthday.**

7. Set the reminder to **None.**

8. Click on the **Recurrence** button in the *Options* group. The *Appointment Recurrence* dialog box will open.

9. Click on **Yearly** in the *Recurrence pattern* section of the dialog box.

10. Make sure the **Every *[your birth date]*** is selected.

    a. Notice the different options available for Yearly recurrence.

11. In the *Range of recurrence* section, select **No end date** if it is not already selected.

    a. Selecting *No end date* will set this appointment to recur every year.

12. Click **OK** to close the dialog box.

    a. Notice the recurrence pattern appears between the location field and the body.

13. Click **Save & Close.**

14. Click on **Month** view.

15. Using the **right arrow** next to the month, move to your birthday month for this year, and then next year to confirm that your birthday event appears for the next two years.

16. Click on the **Today** button in the *Go To* group on the *Home* ribbon to take you back to today's date on the calendar.

Exercise 5.5 [Guided Practice]

Respond to meeting requests received in your Inbox.
[Objectives 5.1–5.3, 5.5]

1. Click on the **Mail** button in the *Navigation* pane.

2. Click on the **Inbox** folder in the *Navigation* pane.

3. Open one of the ***[name]*'s New Client Meeting** meeting request e-mails in your *Inbox.*

4. Click on the **Accept** button in the *Respond* group.

   a. You will be given three options: *Edit the response before sending, Send the response now,* and *Don't send a response.*

5. Click on **Edit the response before sending.**

6. Click **OK.** The meeting request e-mail will look like a reply e-mail.

7. Click in the body, and type in a brief message and include your signature.

8. Click on the **Send** button.

   a. Notice that the meeting request e-mail is no longer in your *Inbox* but has been moved to your calendar.

9. Click on the **Calendar** button in the *Navigation* pane.

10. Locate and view the meeting request on your calendar.

11. Click on the **Mail** button in the *Navigation* pane.

12. Repeat the preceding process on three more of the meeting request e-mails in your *Inbox*.

    a. Choose **Accept** for one, **Decline** for one, and **Tentative** for the other.

    b. Choose **Send the response now** on all these meeting request responses.

Exercise 5.6 [Independent Practice]

Edit an existing appointment to change it to a meeting request. Invite attendees to this meeting. [Objectives 5.1–5.5]

1. Go to your calendar.

2. Open the **Staff Appreciation Breakfast** appointment (created in Exercise 5.1).

3. Convert this appointment to a meeting request.

4. Invite all your classmates and professor as required.

5. Include a brief message in the body and include your signature.

6. **Send** the meeting request.

Exercise 5.7 [Independent Practice]

Create a recurring appointment. [Objectives 5.1–5.4]

1. Create an appointment for a weekly sales meeting next **Thursday** from **10:30–11:30 a.m.** in `Conference Room B.` Use `Weekly Sales Meeting` as the subject.

2. Set a **2-hour reminder.**

3. Set this appointment to **recur weekly** for **eight occurrences.**

4. Include a brief note in the body to remind you to prepare for this meeting.

5. **Save** this recurring appointment.

6. View your calendar to confirm this appointment recurs for the next eight weeks.

Exercise 5.8 [Independent Practice]

Propose a new time for meeting requests. [Objectives 5.1–5.3, 5.5]

1. Open one of the *[name]*'s **New Client Meeting** meeting request e-mails in your *Inbox*.

2. **Propose a new time** for this meeting.

3. Include a brief message and your signature in the body.

4. **Send** the response.

5. Repeat this process on three other meeting requests.

Exercise 5.9 [Independent Practice]

Make changes to a meeting request and send an update. [Objectives 5.1– 5.3, 5.5]

1. Open the **Staff Appreciation Breakfast** meeting request you created in Exercise 5.6.
2. Change the **time** and **location** of the breakfast.
3. Change the attendees to include your professor as **Optional** rather than **Required.**
4. **Send** the update.

Chapter 6
Tasks and To-Do Items

OBJECTIVES   *After completing this chapter, you will be able to:*

6.1   Distinguish between tasks and To-Do items.

6.2   Create and use tasks in Outlook.

6.3   Understand and customize the Tasks views and the To-Do bar.

6.4   Assign tasks to and accept tasks from other Outlook users.

CHAPTER FLYOVER

- Differences between tasks and To-Do items
- Tasks
- Flagged items
- To-Do List
- To-Do bar
- Creating a task
- Editing a task
- Attaching a file or Outlook item
- Marking a task as complete
- Recurring tasks
- Creating a task from an e-mail

- Creating a task from a calendar item
- Task views
- Reading pane
- Tasks in calendar views
- Customizing the To-Do bar
- Managing tasks
- Assigning tasks
- Accepting tasks
- Task status report
- Completing tasks
- Task options

Making Outlook Work for You

So far in this text we have covered the Outlook working environment, and three of the four major components of Outlook: E-mail, Contacts, and Calendar. The fourth major component of Outlook is Tasks.

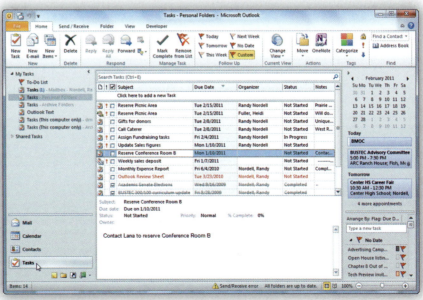

Outlook Tasks

I'm a list person. I usually have a list of tasks to accomplish on any given day or week, and I enjoy the satisfaction of crossing off tasks that I have completed. Outlook provides a tool that can be used to keep track of your daily tasks. The ***Tasks*** feature in Outlook provides you with a place to keep a running list of tasks to be completed. As with calendar items and contacts, Outlook Tasks provides users with many electronic benefits not available on a paper list of tasks, such as electronic reminders, categories, and recurrence.

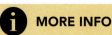 **MORE INFO**

Follow Up flags and Flags for Recipient were introduced in Chapter 3. Using Follow Up flags will be covered in Chapter 7 on page 195.

Understanding Task and To-Do Items

Tasks and ***To-Do items*** are closely related, yet there are some distinct differences. Tasks are those individual items that are kept in the Tasks area of Outlook and also appear in the list of To-Do items.

To-Do items are a much broader category of Outlook items. Any e-mail or contact that has a Flag for Recipient or includes a Follow Up flag will also appear in the ***To-Do List*** and ***To-Do bar.*** So, To-Do items are the broader umbrella category under which tasks are included.

Tasks

A task in Outlook can be created to remind you to make a follow-up phone call for an upcoming fundraiser event or to order theater tickets for "Wicked" when they go on sale Wednesday. When a task is created, Outlook automatically marks the task with a Follow Up flag and the task appears in both the Task List and the To-Do List.

Flagged Items

There might be times when you need to take additional action on an e-mail you received or with a client in your Contacts. In addition to a task, which is automatically flagged in Outlook, e-mails and contacts can also be flagged for follow up. This feature in Outlook provides you with the option of flagging these Outlook items as an additional reminder. When an item is flagged, it will appear as a To-Do item.

Task List

The ***Task List*** is a list of the tasks you have created in Outlook. This list appears in the *Folder* pane when you select **Tasks** in the *My Tasks* area of the *Navigation* pane. The Task List includes only tasks and does not include other flagged items in Outlook.

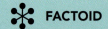 **FACTOID**

Depending on the types of e-mail accounts you have set up, you might have more than one Task List in the My Tasks area of the Navigation pane. Also, you can create additional task folders.

Task list displayed in the Folder pane

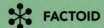 **FACTOID**

The icon for each item in the To-Do List shows you what type of Outlook item it is.

To-Do List

As mentioned previously, the **To-Do List** is a broader list of items than the Task List. The To-Do List includes all Outlook items that have been marked with a flag, which includes tasks, e-mails, and contacts. The To-Do List is available in the My Tasks area in the Navigation pane of Tasks. When the **To-Do List** is selected, the list of *To-Do* items appears at the right in the *Folder* pane.

 MORE INFO

When you click on the **Tasks** button on the *Navigation* pane, by default the *To-Do List* is selected in the *My Tasks* area of the *Navigation* pane and this list will appear in the *Folder* pane. To access *Tasks*, click on the **Tasks** folder in the *My Tasks* area of the *Navigation* pane.

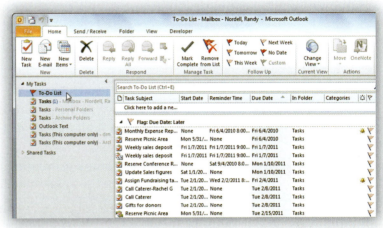

To-Do List displayed in the Folder pane

To-Do Bar

Outlook To-Do Bar

The **To-Do bar** is the area of Outlook to the right of the Folder pane in Outlook and can be displayed in all the Outlook windows (e.g., Mail, Calendar, Contacts, Tasks, Notes, and Journal). The To-Do bar provides you with a date navigator (calendar thumbnail), upcoming calendar items, and To-Do items. The To-Do bar can be customized to show different amounts of information and can be minimized at the right or turned off (*View* ribbon, *Layout* group, *To-Do Bar* button).

Creating Tasks

Creating a task is similar to creating a new e-mail or calendar item and can be accomplished in a couple of different ways. Some of the benefits of Outlook tasks, in comparison to a paper list of tasks, are the ability to include additional details with the task, start and due dates, reminders, and recurrence.

Tasks can also be created from existing information in Outlook. If you receive an e-mail about an upcoming fundraiser for which you are involved, you can create a task from the information included in the e-mail. This can also be done from a calendar item.

New Task

The quickest way to create a new task is to simply type the subject of the task in the **Click here to add a new Task** area above the list of tasks in the *Folder* pane.

STEP-BY-STEP

1. Click on the **Tasks** button in the *Navigation* pane.
2. Click on the **Tasks** folder in the *My Tasks* area of the *Navigation* pane.
3. Click on the **Click here to add a new Task** area above the *Task List* in the *Folder* pane.

Add new tasks by typing directly into Task list

4. Type the subject of the task.

5. Press **Tab** to move to the next field. **Shift+Tab** will move you back one field at a time. Not all task fields are available for editing in the *Task List*.

6. Press **Enter** to complete creating the new task. The task will be listed in the *Task List* in the *Folder* pane.

Another way to create a new task is by clicking on the **New Task** button on the *Home* ribbon, which will open a new task in a new window. When the new task opens, you can type in a subject and any additional information you desire.

STEP-BY-STEP

1. Click on the **Tasks** button in the *Navigation* pane.
2. Click on the **Tasks** folder in the *My Tasks* area of the *Navigation* pane.
3. Click on the **New Task** button in the *New* group on the *Home* ribbon.
4. Type the subject of the task.

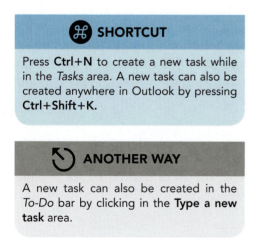

SHORTCUT

Press **Ctrl+N** to create a new task while in the *Tasks* area. A new task can also be created anywhere in Outlook by pressing **Ctrl+Shift+K**.

ANOTHER WAY

A new task can also be created in the *To-Do* bar by clicking in the **Type a new task** area.

New task

5. Press **Tab** to move to the next field to add the **Start** and **Due** dates and additional information as desired.

Select Start and Due dates

6. Press **Save & Close** on the *Task* ribbon to complete creating the new task. The task will be listed in the *Task List* in the *Folder* pane.

Edit Task

A task can be edited to include additional information while creating a new task, or an existing task can be opened (by double-clicking on a task in the *Task List* in the *Folder* pane) to add additional information or edit existing information.

A task can include a start date and due date. These dates can be typed in or you can click on the **pull-down arrow** to the right of *Start Date* or *Due Date* and select from the calendar thumbnail.

The **Status** of the task can be set to **Not Started, In Progress, Completed, Waiting on someone else,** or **Deferred.** By default a new task status is set at **Not Started.**

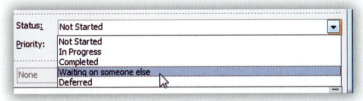

Task status

The **Priority** of a task can be set to **High, Normal,** or **Low.** The priority setting in a task is similar to the **Importance** settings in an e-mail or a calendar item. The default priority setting on a new task is **Normal.**

Priority level

An electronic **Reminder** can be set to automatically remind you when a task is coming due. The reminder date can be either typed in or selected from the thumbnail calendar when you click on the pull-down arrow to the right of the date field. A specific time can also be set.

Task reminder

This reminder will open a reminder window on your computer screen at the date and time you set. You are given the options of **Dismiss All, Open Item, Dismiss,** or **Snooze.** The Dismiss button can be used to dismiss the reminder, or the Dismiss All can be used to dismiss the reminder for all items if there is more than one reminder in the reminder list. The task can be opened to view the task specifics, or you can snooze the task for a certain amount of time, after which, the reminder will pop up again on your computer screen.

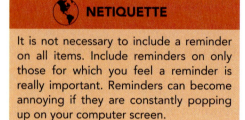

NETIQUETTE

It is not necessary to include a reminder on all items. Include reminders on only those for which you feel a reminder is really important. Reminders can become annoying if they are constantly popping up on your computer screen.

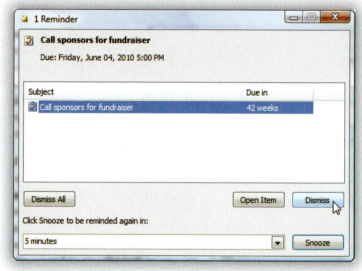

Reminder window

Also within a task, there are other task options available in the Tags group on the Task ribbon.

By default a **_Follow Up flag_** is set for each new task created based upon the due date of the task. This flag can be changed and a different flag selected from the preset flags, or a custom flag can be created and set for a task. These custom flags are similar to those used for e-mails.

MORE INFO

Categories were briefly introduced in Chapter 2 and will be covered more thoroughly in Chapter 7 on page 191.

Delegates will be covered in Chapter 12 on page 344.

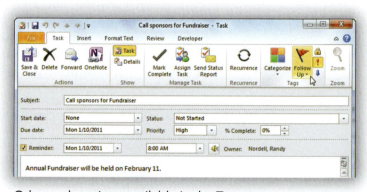

Other task options available in the Tags group

Categories can be used to group tasks (or other Outlook items) by a common category. If you have a list of tasks to be completed for an upcoming fundraiser, a "Fundraiser" category can be created and all tasks pertaining to this fundraiser can be assigned to this category. Tasks can then be viewed by category to show all the tasks grouped and listed by their category.

A task can also be marked as *Private.* This marking does not change any aspect of this task for you, the owner of the task, but rather this feature is important when using Delegates in Outlook. *Delegates* are those individuals with whom you share or give permission to some of the areas of your Outlook, such as Calendar or Tasks.

Attach File or Outlook Item

Another distinct advantage of Outlook Tasks as compared to a paper list of tasks is the ability to attach or include additional resources with a task. If you were creating a task for an upcoming fundraising event, you might want to attach a contact record, an Excel spreadsheet, or an e-mail as a reference and additional information for this task that is to be completed.

In addition to being able to type additional information in the body of the task, you can also use *Attach File,* which could include attachments such as Word or Excel documents, pictures, or most any other type of attachments you could include in an e-mail. You can also attach an *Outlook Item* or a *Business Card,* which could include other Outlook items such as a contact record, an e-mail, or a calendar item.

STEP-BY-STEP

Attach item to a task

1. Open an existing task.
2. Click on the **Insert** tab.
3. In the *Include* group, click on either **Attach File, Outlook Item,** or **Business Card.** An *Insert* dialog box will open.
4. Browse to the file or Outlook item to be attached or included in the task.
5. Select the files or Outlook items.
6. Click **OK** (for Other Outlook Item or Business Card) or **Insert** (for Attach File). The files or items will be attached to the task.

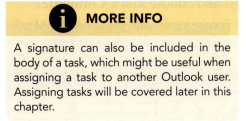

> ℹ **MORE INFO**
>
> A signature can also be included in the body of a task, which might be useful when assigning a task to another Outlook user. Assigning tasks will be covered later in this chapter.

Insert Item dialog box

7. Click **Save & Close** to save and close the task.

Mark a Task as Complete

Being a list person, I get much satisfaction by crossing items off my to-do list. Outlook gives you that same satisfaction by crossing items off your Task List when they are marked as complete. When a task is marked as complete, it remains in your Task List, but a line is drawn through it and it is grayed out.

2. Click on the **Mark Complete** button in the *Manage Task* group on the *Task* ribbon. The open task will automatically close and regenerate itself in the *Task List* in the *Folder* pane.

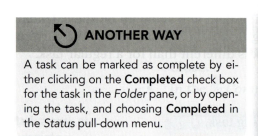

ANOTHER WAY

A task can be marked as complete by either clicking on the **Completed** check box for the task in the *Folder* pane, or by opening the task, and choosing **Completed** in the *Status* pull-down menu.

Recurring task marked as complete and a regenerated task

Creating a Task from an E-mail

There are many times when I receive an e-mail that has some information or job upon which I must take some action. An e-mail can easily be converted to a task by dragging the e-mail from the list of e-mails in the *Folder* pane to the *Tasks* button in the *Navigation* pane. The original e-mail will remain in your Inbox.

When this is done, a new task is opened. The subject of the task is the same as the subject of the e-mail, and the body of the e-mail is included in the body of the task. The body of the task also includes the header information (From, Sent, To, etc.) at the top of the body of the new task.

The body of the e-mail can be edited to include only the pertinent information, and you can also edit the task to include any additional options such as Start date, Due date, or Reminder.

STEP-BY-STEP

1. Click on the **Mail** button in the *Navigation* pane.

2. In the list of e-mails in the *Folder* pane, click on the e-mail to be converted to a task.

3. Drag it to the *Tasks* button in the *Navigation* pane (a small box will appear below the mouse pointer when dragging the e-mail to the *Tasks* button), and release the mouse button. A new task will open.

Drag e-mail from Folder pane to Tasks button in the Navigation pane

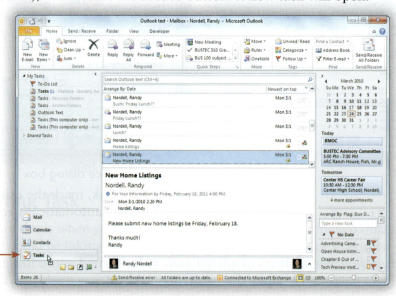

drag to Tasks button

4. Make any necessary editing changes to the new task.

5. Click on **Save & Close.**

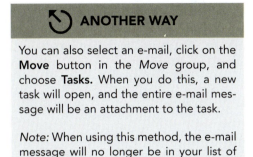

Task created from an e-mail

Creating a Task from a Calendar Item

There are times when you may need to complete a task prior to an upcoming appointment or event on your calendar. A task can be created from an existing calendar item in a similar fashion as creating a task from an e-mail.

Similar to when an e-mail is converted to a task, the subject of the e-mail will be the subject of the new task. The date of the calendar item will be the due date of the task, and the body of the task will include information from the calendar item.

Task created from a calendar appointment

Viewing Tasks and To-Do Items

Another advantage to using Outlook Tasks as opposed to using a paper list of to-do items is that tasks can be grouped and viewed in a variety of ways. Outlook provides you with many different preset views for grouping and viewing tasks in the Folder pane.

 **MORE INFO**

Preset views throughout Outlook can be customized, and new views can be created. This topic will be covered in Chapter 12 on page 368.

Task Views

The different task views are available on both the Home and View ribbons, and you can easily change from one view to another by selecting a view with the **Change View** button on the *Home* ribbon, or with the **Change View** button in the *Current View* group on the *View* ribbon. The preset Task views include:

- By Category
- Detailed
- Simple List
- To-Do List
- Prioritized
- Active

- Completed
- Today
- Next 7 Days
- Overdue
- Assigned
- Server Tasks

Preset Task views available in the Current View group

Reading Pane

Just as for e-mail, Outlook provides a Reading pane for Tasks, which displays the contents of the selected task. The Reading pane can be displayed to the right or at the bottom of the Folder pane, or it can be turned off.

The size of the Reading pane can be adjusted by clicking and dragging on the right or left edge of the pane when it is displayed at the right. When the Reading pane is displayed at the bottom, the size can be adjusted by dragging the top edge up or down.

Reading pane views in Tasks

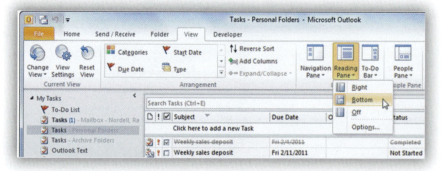

Tasks in Calendar Views

One of the many advantages of using Outlook is the interconnectedness of the different components in Outlook. An example of this is how tasks are connected to the calendar.

When you are using your calendar in Outlook, the current tasks are displayed at the bottom of the Day and Week views in the ***Daily Task List,*** but not in Month view.

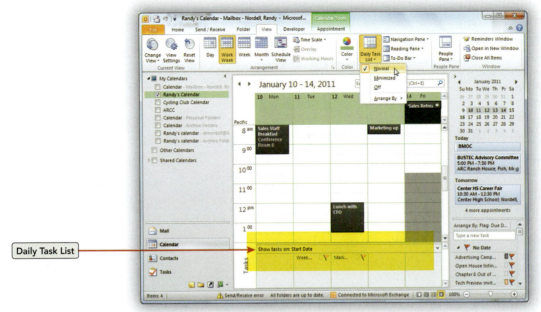

Daily Task List displayed at the bottom of the calendar

Customizing the To-Do Bar

The To-Do bar provides you with a summary of both your calendar and flagged items in Outlook. It is displayed at the right of the Outlook working environment. The To-Do bar has three components: **_Date Navigator,_** **_Appointments,_** and **_Task List._** The Task List includes tasks and flagged items but does not include completed items.

> ### ⓘ MORE INFO
>
> Click on the small arrows at the top of the To-Do bar to minimize or expand it.

In the Layout group on the View ribbon, you are given three different display options for the To-Do bar: Normal, Minimized, and Off. In minimized view, you are shown just one appointment and a summary of upcoming task items. Drag the left edge of the To-Do bar to the right or left to adjust its width.

To-Do Bar displayed
in Normal view

To-Do Bar displayed
in Minimized view

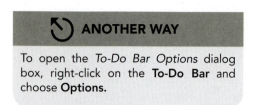

To open the *To-Do Bar Options* dialog box, right-click on the **To-Do Bar** and choose **Options.**

You can customize the To-Do bar by removing any of the existing components (Date Navigator, Appointments, Task List) or adjusting the amount of content to be shown. You can also change the number of calendar month thumbnails to be displayed, and the number of displayed appointments.

STEP-BY-STEP

1. In *Tasks,* click on the **View** tab.
2. Click on the **To-Do bar** button in the *Layout* group.
3. Choose **Options.** The *To-Do Bar Options* dialog box opens.
4. Make the desired changes.
5. Click **OK.**

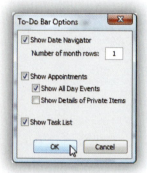

To-Do Bar Options dialog box

Managing Tasks

If you were planning an upcoming event, most likely there would be many tasks to be accomplished prior to the event to ensure success. Each of these jobs could be set up as individual tasks. It is common that others would be responsible to complete some of the different tasks that need to be accomplished.

Another advantage of Outlook Tasks is its ability to assign tasks to others and track the progress and completion of these tasks.

Assigning Tasks

When a task is assigned to another Outlook user, the task request becomes similar to an e-mail. In addition to the other task fields, To and Send buttons appear on the task request. The To button is used to add an Outlook recipient, and the Send button is used to send the task request as an e-mail.

STEP-BY-STEP

1. Create a new task, or open an existing task.
2. Click on the **Assign Task** button in the *Manage Task* group on the *Task* ribbon. A *task request* e-mail will open.

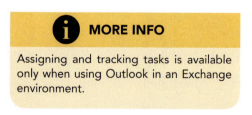

MORE INFO

Assigning and tracking tasks is available only when using Outlook in an Exchange environment.

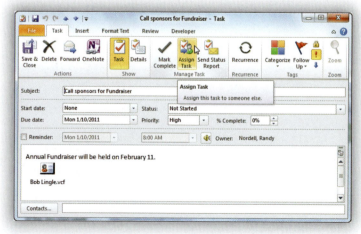

Assign Task button

3. Click on the **To** button, and choose a recipient.

4. Include a brief message in the body of the task request.
5. Click **Send.**

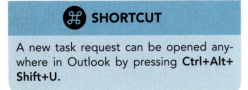

SHORTCUT

A new task request can be opened anywhere in Outlook by pressing **Ctrl+Alt+ Shift+U.**

NETIQUETTE

Assign a task request to only one recipient to ensure responsibility that a task is completed. If multiple individuals are to be assigned a task, think about how you can break the task into smaller parts to assign individually. Also, always include a brief message in the body of the task request.

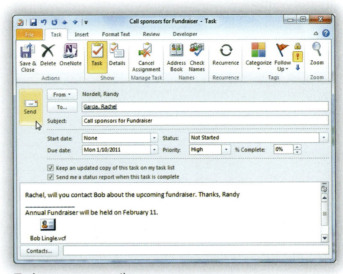

Task request e-mail

Accepting Tasks

When a task is assigned to another Outlook user, it is received in the user's Inbox and looks similar to an e-mail. When the recipient opens the task request, he or she has the option to either accept or decline the task request.

When the task request is either accepted or declined, the recipient again has two options: **Edit the response before sending** or **Send the response now.** If **Edit the response before sending** is chosen, the task request recipient will be able to type a message to the task originator before sending the response. If **Send the response now** is chosen, the response to the task request is automatically sent.

When the task request has been accepted and the response has been sent, the task request is removed from the recipient's Inbox and placed in his or her Task List. The person accepting the task request is now the owner of this task.

STEP-BY-STEP

1. Click on the **Mail** button in the *Navigation* pane.
2. In your *Inbox,* open the **task request** message.

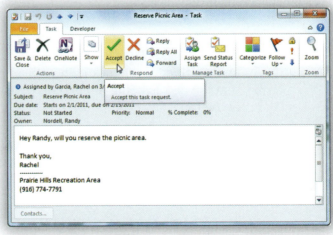

Received Task request

Response options in the Accepting Task dialog box

Send task request acceptance

3. Choose **Accept.** An *Accepting Task* dialog box opens.
4. Select **Edit the response before sending.**
5. Press **OK** to close the dialog box. The task request response opens, and you can type a response in the body.
6. Press **Send.** The task request is removed from your *Inbox* and moved to your *Task List.* The originator of the task will receive a *Task Accepted* message from you.

Task Icons

Different icons are used to help you distinguish between tasks, tasks assigned, and tasks accepted. These icons will be displayed on your task request e-mails in your Inbox and in the Task List displayed in the Folder pane of Tasks.

INBOX ICONS

 Task Request. The task request will be in the recipient's Inbox, and it will have the task icon with a hand at the bottom indicating that the task is being handed off or assigned and an envelope icon at the top.

 Task Accepted. When a task recipient accepts a task from you, you receive a task-accepted message in your Inbox. The icon has the task pad with a hand at the bottom and a check at the top.

TASK LIST ICONS

 Assigned Task. There is a hand at the bottom of the task indicating that this task has been handed off or assigned to someone.

Accepted Task. When you accept a task request from someone, there is a hand at both the top and bottom of the task icon indicating that the task has been handed off or assigned and accepted.

Task Status Report

A status report can be sent to the originator of the task and others to give an update on the progress of this task. The ***Status*** and ***% Complete*** on the task can be specified to give the originator a status update.

The ***Details*** section of an open task can be used to provide a more detailed task status to the originator of the task. The Details section of the task is available by clicking on the **Details** button in the *Show* group on the *Task* ribbon.

Accepted task
request in task list

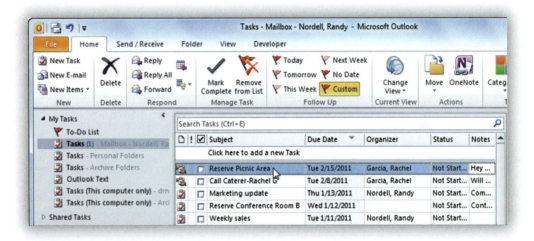

STEP-BY-STEP

1. Click the **Tasks** button in the *Navigation* pane.
2. Open the accepted task in your *Task List*.
3. Click on the **Details** button in the *Show* group on the *Task* ribbon.
4. Fill in details for this task.

Task details

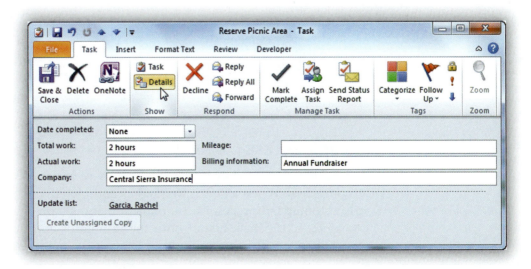

5. Click on the **Task** button in the *Show* group.
6. Fill in the **Status** and **% Complete.**

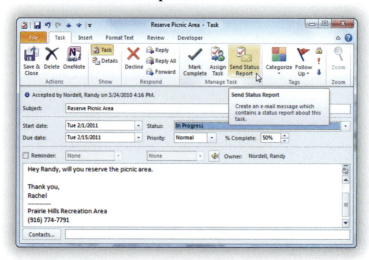

Task Status and % Complete updated

7. Click the **Send Status Report** button in the *Manage Task* group on the *Task* ribbon. A *Task Status Report* e-mail is opened. This message contains detailed status report information for the recipients.
8. Include a brief message in the body.
9. Select other recipients if necessary. The originator of the task will automatically be a recipient.
10. Click **Send.** The recipients will receive a *Task Status Report* e-mail in their Inbox.

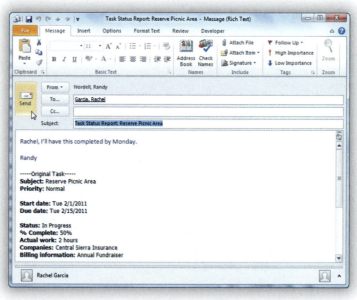

Send status report e-mail to originator of task

Complete Task

As mentioned previously in this chapter, there are many ways to mark a task as completed. When a task is marked as completed, the originator of the task will automatically receive an e-mail informing him or her that the task is complete. In the Task List of both the originator and owner of the task, the task will have a line through it to indicate it is a completed task.

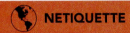

ANOTHER WAY

A task can also be marked as complete by selecting the task in the *Folder* pane and clicking on the **check box** on the task, clicking on the **Mark Complete** button in the *Manage Task* group, or right-clicking on the task and choosing **Mark Complete**.

NETIQUETTE

When you accept a task, make sure you follow through on completing the task. Periodically send a status report to the originator so he or she knows you are working on this task. Be sure to mark the task as complete when finished.

Mark task as complete

Task Options

Outlook provides you with the flexibility of customizing some of the default settings for all task items. The ***Task options*** are available in the *Outlook Options* dialog box.

By default Outlook does not include a reminder on a new task with a due date. You can change the default setting to include a reminder on all new tasks with a due date. When a reminder is used, the default reminder setting is 8 a.m. This default time can be changed to better meet your needs.

The next two check boxes pertain to assigning tasks. The first default setting is to keep a copy of an assigned task in your Task List. It is a good idea to keep this selected so you have a copy of the task that was assigned to someone else. By default Outlook will send a status report to the creator of the task when an assigned task is marked as complete. If you have created a task and assigned it to someone else, it is usually important to get acknowledgment when the task is completed.

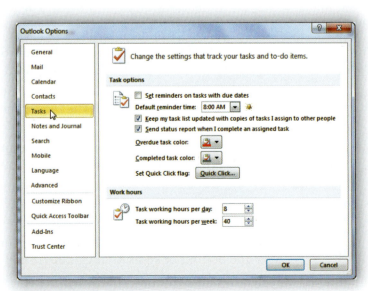

Task option in the Outlook Options dialog box

The color of overdue and completed tasks can be changed. The default setting is red for overdue tasks and gray for completed tasks. You can set a **Quick Click** Follow Up flag that will mark a task with the specified flag when it is clicked.

STEP-BY-STEP

1. Click on the **File** tab. The *BackStage* window is displayed.
2. Choose **Options** at the left. The *Outlook Options* dialog box will open.
3. Click on **Tasks** to change task default settings. The *Task Options* window box opens.
4. Make the desired Task option changes.
5. Click **OK** to close the *Task Options* dialog box.
6. Click **OK** to close the *Outlook Options* dialog box.

Chapter Highlights

▶ The **Tasks** feature in Outlook provides you with a place to keep a running list of tasks to be completed and is one of the four major components of Outlook.

▶ The **Task List** is accessed from the Navigation pane in Tasks and is displayed in the Folder pane.

▶ While the **Task List** and the **To-Do List** are similar, the To-Do List not only includes tasks, but also includes any flagged items including e-mail and contacts.

▶ The **To-Do bar** is displayed throughout Outlook at the right side of the Outlook window. This bar displays a **date navigator,** upcoming **calendar items,** and **To-Do items.**

▶ Tasks can be edited to include start and due dates, status, priority, a reminder, attachments, category, a follow-up flag, and additional details in the body.

▶ When a task is completed, it can be **marked as completed** and will be displayed with a line drawn through it.

▶ Similar to recurring appointments or events, a task can be set up to **recur** on a regular interval. The recurring task will **regenerate** to a new task when the current task has been marked as complete.

▶ Tasks can be created from an existing **e-mail** or **calendar item** by dragging one of these items to the Tasks button in the Navigation pane.

▶ There are numerous **preset task views.** These views are listed in the **Current View** group on the **Home** ribbon.

▶ Tasks can be displayed in the **Reading** pane. This pane can be displayed at the bottom or right, or it can be turned off.

▶ The **Daily Task List** appears at the bottom of the Day, Work Week, and Week calendar views.

- The **To-Do bar** can be displayed in expanded or minimized view. This bar can also be customized to change the items displayed and the amount of content.
- One of the many advantages of using Outlook Tasks is its ability to assign tasks to others. A **task request** gives you the ability to assign a task to another Outlook user.
- When a task is assigned to another Outlook user, the task can be accepted or declined.
- The originator of the task can receive **status updates** and will receive a notification when the task is marked as completed.
- Outlook uses specific icons in the Inbox and Task List to help you easily identify the status of the task.
- Outlook provides you the ability to customize default task features including **reminders, reminder time, overdue task color,** and **completed task color.**

What Do You Know About Outlook?

True/False Questions

T F 1. The Task List includes both tasks and other Outlook items that have been flagged for follow up. [Objectives 6.1, 6.3]

T F 2. A Task request should be assigned to only one person. [Objective 6.4]

T F 3. The To-Do bar can be displayed at the bottom of the Outlook window. [Objectives 6.1, 6.3]

T F 4. A task has to be open to be marked as complete. [Objective 6.2]

T F 5. When you click on the Tasks button, the To-Do List is displayed in the Folder pane. [Objective 6.1]

Multiple Choice Questions

1. Where does the Daily Task List appear? [Objective 6.3]
   a. In the Task List.
   b. At the bottom of the calendar in Week view.
   c. At the bottom of the calendar in Month view.
   d. In the To-Do List.

2. Which of the following is *not* a way to create a new task? [Objective 6.2]
   a. Press Ctrl+Shift+T.
   b. Press Ctrl+N when in Tasks.
   c. Type into the Task List in the To-Do bar.
   d. Drag an e-mail to the Tasks button.

3. What occurs after a task request has been accepted by an Outlook user? [Objective 6.4]
   a. The task is by default removed from the originator's Task List.
   b. The person accepting the task becomes the owner of the task.
   c. A status report is automatically generated and sent to the originator.
   d. All the above.

4. A task can be set to recur at which of the following intervals? [Objective 6.2]
   a. Daily
   b. Weekly
   c. Yearly
   d. All the above

5. Which of the following areas of the To-Do bar can be customized? [Objective 6.3]
   a. Calendar view
   b. Number of contacts displayed
   c. Number of appointments displayed
   d. All the above

Short Answer Questions

1. Explain how a recurring task differs from a recurring calendar appointment or event. [Objective 6.2]

2. Describe how to accept a task request you have received. [Objective 6.4]

3. Explain the difference between the Task List and the To-Do List. [Objective 6.1]

Putting Outlook to Work

You are responsible for organizing the annual fundraiser at your company. You'll be creating tasks and assigning some of these tasks to others. You'll also be receiving, accepting, and completing task requests from others in your company (class). (Include your first name in each of the tasks to distinguish them from the task of other students in your class.)

Exercise 6.1 [Guided Practice]

Create three new tasks for the upcoming fundraiser. [Objectives 6.1, 6.2]

1. Click on the **Tasks** button in the *Navigation* pane.
2. Click on **Tasks** in the *My Tasks* area in the *Navigation* pane.
3. Click on the **New Task** button to create a new task (or press **Ctrl+N**).
4. Type **Reserve Picnic Area—*[your first name]*** as the subject.
5. Set the **start date** as today and the **due date** two weeks from today.
6. In the body of the task, include the following information.
   a. **Prairie Hills Recreation Area**
   b. **(916) 774-7791**
7. Click on **Save & Close**.
8. Create another task with the following information.
   a. Subject: **Call Caterer—*[your first name]***
   b. Start date: today
   c. Due date: one week from today
   d. Body: **West Ridge Catering, (916) 762-4483**
9. Click on **Save & Close**.

10. Create another task with the following information.

    a. Subject: `Gifts for donors—[your first name]`
    b. Start date: today
    c. Due date: one week from today
    d. Body: `Unique Treasures, (916) 794-5688`

11. Click on **Save & Close.**

Exercise 6.2 [Guided Practice]

Send e-mail to classmates reminding them of the upcoming fundraiser. [Objective 6.1]

1. Click on the **Mail** button in the *Navigation* pane.

2. Click on **New E-mail** to create a new e-mail message.

3. Click on the **To** button and select all your classmates. Include yourself and your professor in the **Cc** line.

4. Type **Annual Fundraiser—*[your first name]*** in the subject line.

5. Type a brief message letting your recipients know that the annual fundraiser will be the last Friday of next month (put in the date) and will be held at the Prairie Hills Recreation Area. Let them know you will be sending out task requests to get help organizing this event. Include your signature.

6. Include a **Flag for Recipients.**

    a. Use **For Your Information.**
    b. Do not include a reminder.

7. Mark this message as **High Importance.**

8. Click on the **Send** button to send this message.

Exercise 6.3 [Guided Practice]

Create a calendar event for the fundraiser, and view the tasks and To-Do items. [Objectives 6.1, 6.3]

1. Click on the **Calendar** button in the *Navigation* pane.

2. Click **New Appointment** to create a new appointment. Include the following information.

    a. Subject: `Annual Fundraiser`
    b. Location: `Prairie Hills Recreation Area`
    c. Date: last Friday of next month
    d. Time: **4–7 p.m.**
    e. Mark as **High Importance**

3. Click on **Save & Close.**

4. Click on **Tasks** in the *Navigation* pane.

5. Click on **To-Do List** in the *My Tasks* area in the *Navigation* pane.

    a. Notice the list of *To-Do items* in the *Folder* pane.

6. Click on **Tasks** in the *My Tasks* area in the *Navigation* pane.

    a. Notice the list of *Tasks* in the *Folder* pane.

7. Look at the *To-Do bar* to the right of the *Folder* pane.

    a. Notice the calendar items and the *To-Do items* listed.

8. Click on the **small arrow** in the upper left corner of the *To-Do bar* to minimize the bar.

Exercise 6.4 [Guided Practice]

Create a new task for yourself to remind you to assign annual fundraiser tasks to others in your class. [Objective 6.2]

1. Click on the **Tasks** button in the *Navigation* pane.
2. Click on the **New Task** button to create a new task.
3. Use the following information for the new task.

   a. Subject: `Assign Fundraising tasks—[your first name]`
   b. Start date: today
   c. Due date: this Friday
   d. Status: **In Progress**
   e. Priority: **High**
   f. Reminder: **8 a.m.** tomorrow

4. Click on **Save & Close.**

Exercise 6.5 [Guided Practice]

Assign a task to one of your classmates and accept a task from a classmate. [Objectives 6.1–6.4]

1. Click on the **Tasks** button in the *Navigation* pane.
2. Open the **Call Caterer—*[your first name]*** task.
3. Click on the **Assign** button.
4. Click on the **To** button, and select one of your classmates.

   a. You will need to team up with another student in the class.

5. Type a brief message in the body of the task request asking the recipient to call and reserve the caterer for the upcoming fundraiser.

   a. Make sure both the **Keep an updated copy of this task on my task list** and **Send me a status report when this task is complete** are selected.

6. Click **Send.**
7. Click on the **Mail** button in the *Navigation* pane.

   a. You should receive a task request in your *Inbox*.

8. Open the **Call Caterer—*[your classmate's name]*** task request you received in your *Inbox*.
9. Click on the **Accept** button.
10. Choose **Send the response now,** and click **OK.**

    a. Notice the task request is no longer in your *Inbox*.

11. Click on the **small arrow** at the top of the minimized *To-Do bar* to expand it.

    a. Notice the items in your *Task List*.

12. Click on the **Tasks** button in the *Navigation* pane.
13. Click on **Tasks** in the *My Tasks* area in the *Navigation* pane.

    a. Notice the tasks and the different *Task List* icons.

Exercise 6.6 [Independent Practice]

Assign a task to one of your classmates, and accept a task from a classmate. [Objectives 6.2–6.4]

1. In *Tasks,* open the **Reserve Picnic Area—*[your first name]*** task and assign it to a classmate.
2. Include a brief message, and mark it as **High Priority.**
   a. Make sure both **Keep an updated copy of this task on my task list** and **Send me a status report when this task is complete** are selected.
3. **Send** the task request.
4. Open the **Reserve Picnic Area—*[your classmate's name]*** task request in your *Inbox* from your classmate.
5. **Accept** the task request, and include a brief message before sending.
6. In *Tasks,* change the view to **Active.**

Exercise 6.7 [Independent Practice]

Send a Status Report for an accepted task. [Objectives 6.2–6.4]

1. In *Tasks,* open the **Reserve Picnic Area—*[your classmate's name]*.**
2. Update **Status** (change to **In Progress**) and **% Complete** (change to **50%**).
3. Include additional information in the *Details* section of this task.
4. Send the **Status Report** for this task.
5. View the tasks in **To-Do List** view.
6. In your *Inbox,* open and view the status report you received from your partner.
7. Look at the *To-Do bar,* and notice your tasks to be completed.

Exercise 6.8 [Independent Practice]

Mark tasks as complete, and change To-Do bar options. [Objectives 6.1–6.4]

1. In *Tasks,* view your tasks as a **Simple List.**
2. Mark the following tasks as complete. If you don't have one or more of the tasks below, create them and then mark as complete.
   a. **Call Caterer—*[your classmate's name]***
   b. **Reserve Picnic Area—*[your classmate's name]***
   c. **Assign Fundraising Tasks—*[your first name]***
3. In your *Inbox,* view completed task e-mails you received.
4. Look at your *To-Do bar,* and notice your tasks.
5. In *Tasks,* change view to **Completed.**
6. In *Tasks,* change view to **Simple List.**
7. In your *To-Do bar,* change the options to include **two months** in the *Date Navigator* and deselect **Show Details of Private Items.**

Chapter 7

Folders, Rules, Quick Steps, Categories, and Follow Up Flags

OBJECTIVES *After completing this chapter, you will be able to:*

7.1 Create, arrange, and modify Outlook folders.

7.2 Devise, apply, and change Outlook rules and Quick Steps.

7.3 Utilize categories to organize Outlook items.

7.4 Apply and integrate Follow Up flags throughout Outlook.

CHAPTER FLYOVER

- ▸ Creating folders
- ▸ Moving folders
- ▸ Deleting folders
- ▸ Using the Folder List
- ▸ Creating Quick Rules
- ▸ Creating advanced rules
- ▸ Modifying rules
- ▸ Deleting and turning on/off rules
- ▸ Running rules
- ▸ Ordering rules

- ▸ Modifying and using Quick Steps
- ▸ Customizing categories
- ▸ Assigning categories
- ▸ Viewing by categories
- ▸ Setting Quick Click category
- ▸ Using Follow Up flags
- ▸ Flagging items
- ▸ Setting default Follow Up flag
- ▸ Viewing To-Do items

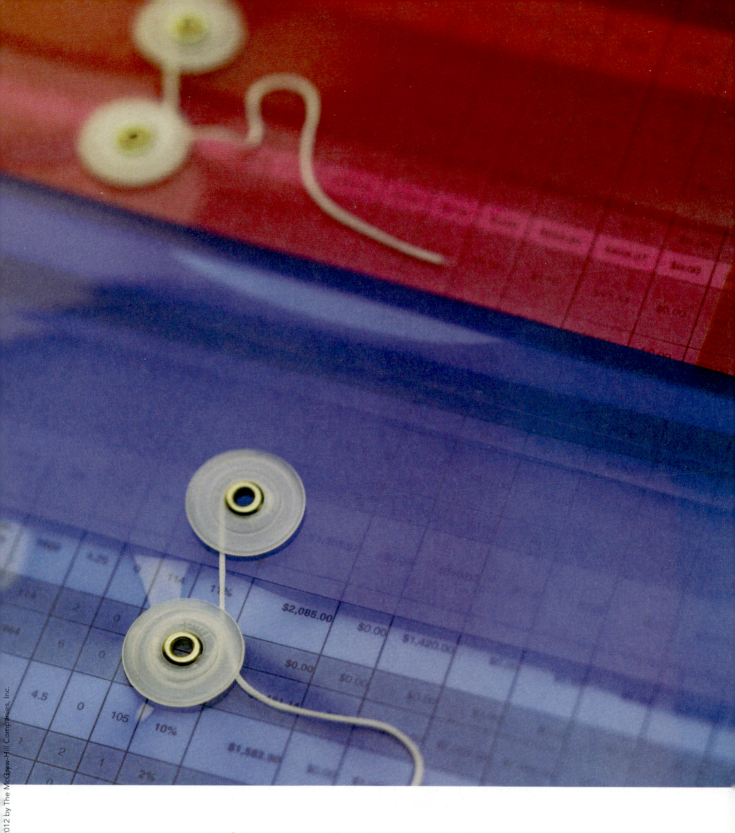

Making Outlook Work for You

After completing the first half of this book, you now have a good understanding of the main components of Outlook—E-mail, Contacts, Calendar, and Tasks. Building on this essential foundation, we will delve into the numerous ways you can customize Outlook to best meet your needs. Outlook provides you with a range of features to help organize, categorize, and prioritize items within Outlook. Using *folders, Quick Steps, rules, categories,* and *Follow Up flags* will help you to become a more efficient and effective Outlook user.

Using Folders

Most of you have some sort of filing system in your home. You might have a filing cabinet with separate folders for bills, insurance, tax papers, investments, and so forth. Can you imagine having just one drawer in your filing cabinet and throwing everything in that drawer? What a mess and how hard it is to find something for which you are looking. (Sorry, to those of you who use this unorganized filing system!)

When using your computer, you create folders to store various files. You might create and use different folders in the Documents folder to store tax information files, Grand Canyon road trip files, recipes, and so forth. These Windows folders are generic folders in that they can store various types of files—Word, Excel, .pdf, pictures, and others.

In Outlook, folders can be used to help organize and group your e-mails, contacts, calendar, tasks, notes, and journals. In contrast to the generic type of folders used in Windows, Outlook folders are specific to the type of Outlook items they store. For example, a Mail folder is used to store e-mail and a Task folder is used to store tasks.

Creating Folders

Creating folders in Outlook is actually very simple. The most important aspect to remember is that each Outlook folder is created to store a specific type of Outlook item. When the ***Create New Folder*** dialog box is opened, it is important to confirm the type of folder you are creating and the location of the file.

In Outlook the following types of folders can be created:

- Calendar Items
- Contact Items
- InfoPath Form Items
- Journal Items
- Mail and Post Items
- Note Items
- Task Items

Follow these steps to create a new ***Mail*** folder. The steps are the same for creating any type of Outlook folder.

New Folder button
on the Folder ribbon

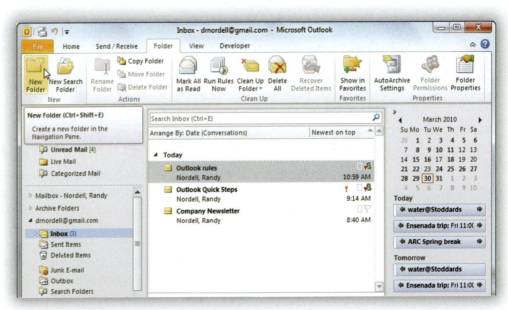

STEP-BY-STEP

1. Click on the **Mail** button in the *Navigation* pane.
2. Click on the **Folder** tab.
3. Click on the **New Folder** button in the *New* group. The *Create New Folder* dialog box will open.

ANOTHER WAY

You can create a new folder by right-clicking on the folder inside which you would like to create a new folder, and then select **New Folder.**

SHORTCUT

Ctrl+Shift+E opens the *Create New Folder* dialog box throughout Outlook.

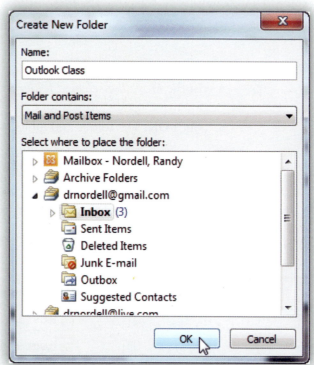

Create New Folder dialog box

4. Type the **name** of the new folder to be created.
5. In the *Folder contains* menu, confirm that the folder type is **Mail and Post Items.**
6. In the *Select where to place the folder* section, specify the location in which to save the new folder.
7. Click **OK.**

Moving Folders

There might be times when you add a new folder in the wrong location, or you might just want to move a folder from one location to another. The easiest way to move a folder to a new location is to click on the folder in the Navigation pane and drag and drop it on the new location. The folder and all its contents will be moved to the new location.

Another way to move a folder is to use the ***Move*** feature.

STEP-BY-STEP

1. In the *Navigation* pane, select the folder to be moved.
2. Click on the **Folder** tab.

3. Click on the **Move Folder** button in the *Actions* group. The *Move Folder* dialog box opens.

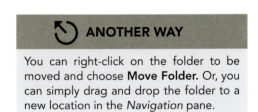

ANOTHER WAY

You can right-click on the folder to be moved and choose **Move Folder.** Or, you can simply drag and drop the folder to a new location in the *Navigation* pane.

Move Folder button

4. In the *Move the selected folder to the folder* section, click on the desired location to move the folder.
5. Click **OK.** The folder and all its contents will be moved to the new location.

Move Folder dialog box

ANOTHER WAY

Right-click on the folder to be deleted and choose **Delete Folder.**

Deleting Folders

Folders are sometimes created to store information temporarily. Folders can be deleted when they are no longer needed. When a folder is deleted, all the items in the folder are deleted as well. The deleted folder is stored in the Deleted Items folder.

STEP-BY-STEP

SHORTCUT

Ctrl+D deletes the selected item. This shortcut will delete a folder or other selected Outlook items.

Ctrl+6 displays the Folder List in the Navigation pane.

1. To delete a folder, select the folder to be deleted in the *Navigation* pane.
2. Click on the **Delete** button in the *Actions* group on the *Folder* ribbon. A warning dialog box opens asking you if you are sure you want to delete the folder and its contents.

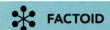

✳ **FACTOID**

In all the areas of Outlook except Mail and Folder List, your folders are not displayed in hierarchical structure. In other words in these other areas, it is hard to know whether or not a folder is located inside of another folder.

Delete Folder button

3. Click **Yes** to delete the folder and all its contents.

Using the Folder List

Folder List displayed in the Navigation pane.

When you are in the Mail, Calendar, Contacts, Tasks, Notes, or Journal areas, only those folders associated with that part of Outlook are displayed in the Navigation pane. The **Folder List** is a useful view to display all your Outlook folders in the Navigation pane.

The Folder List view can be used to view your folder structure in Outlook. This is also a good view to use when you are moving folders from one location to another.

The Folder List can be displayed in the *Navigation* pane by clicking on the **Folder List** button at the bottom of the *Navigation* pane.

Using Rules and Quick Steps

I teach numerous courses at my college and receive a crazy amount of e-mails every day from my students. If all these e-mails ended up in my Inbox, it would be hard to distinguish in which class the student is enrolled, and these e-mails would get intermingled with other e-mails in my Inbox. In my Outlook, I create folders and set up rules to automatically move e-mail from students to the appropriate course folder. I have students use a specific subject line in all e-mails they send me. I create a rule to look at the subject of the e-mail and move it to the appropriate folder. Using rules helps me keep my sanity and makes me more responsive to students in my classes.

Rules might be one of the most useful features in Outlook. They can be used to check incoming or outgoing e-mails and apply some type of action. If you have ever used the IF function in Microsoft Excel, rules operate similar to this if/then logical principle. Most rules have two basic parts: a **condition** and an **action.** There is also an **exception** that can be added to the rule.

- **Condition.** The condition is what Outlook is looking for when an e-mail is received or sent. This could be an e-mail that includes a specific word or words in the subject or body, sent from a specific person, received through a specific e-mail account, or marked as high importance.

- **Action.** The action is what is done with the e-mail when the condition is met. This could include moving the e-mail to another folder, marking the e-mail as high importance, categorizing the e-mail with a specific category, deleting the e-mail, or forwarding the e-mail to someone else.

- **Exception.** An exception can be used to nullify an action. For example, a rule can be set up to look for the word "BUS 310" in the subject line and move it to the BUS 310 folder, except if it comes from the Dean of the CSIT area. Exceptions are not commonly used in rules.

Quick Steps are new to Outlook 2010. They are similar to rules, but do not include a condition. So rather than automatically applying an action to an e-mail when it meets a condition, Quick Steps can be applied to e-mail on an individual basis. For example, a Quick Step can be used to create a meeting request from a received e-mail message.

Creating Quick Rules

A rule can be created quickly based upon an e-mail in your Inbox. These quick rules can be used for many of the common rules used in Outlook. These rules have a limited number of options for the condition and action and do not include options for exceptions.

If an e-mail arrives in your Inbox with the subject "Outlook," and you know that there is going to be an e-mail discussion with others based on this topic, a rule can quickly be created to move all e-mails with the word "Outlook" to an Outlook folder to keep all these related messages together.

The steps to create this rule are as follows:

STEP-BY-STEP

1. In your *Inbox,* open the e-mail for which you would like to create a new rule.
2. Click on the **Rules** button in the *Move* group on the *Message* ribbon.
3. Choose **Create Rule.** The *Create Rule* dialog box opens. The three *conditions* are at the top, and the three *actions* are at the bottom of this dialog box.

MORE INFO

If you forget to create a folder before creating a rule, you can create a new folder in the *Rules and Alerts* dialog box by clicking on the **New** button.

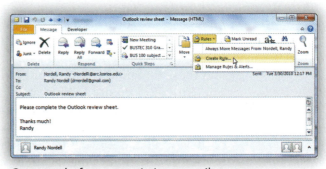

Create rule from an existing e-mail message

4. In the *conditions* area (top half of the dialog box), check **Subject contains** and make sure the word in the subject is correct. If not, correct it.
5. In the *actions* area (bottom half of the dialog box), check **Move the item to folder.** The *Rules and Alerts* dialog box will open.

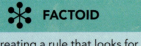

FACTOID

When creating a rule that looks for a word in the subject, Outlook looks for *exactly* what you type. Common errors include misspellings and a space after the word. The word you type is not case sensitive.

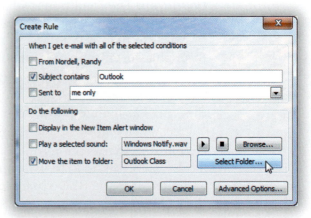

Create Rule dialog box with condition selected

6. Select the desired **folder** from the folder list and press **OK.** The *Create Rule* dialog box will still be open. Confirm that the correct folder was selected. If not, click on the **Select Folder** button and select the correct folder.

Choose a folder in the Rules and Alerts dialog box

ANOTHER WAY

When an e-mail is selected in your *Folder* pane, a quick rule can be created by clicking on the **Rules** button in the *Move* group, or by right-clicking on the message and choosing **Rules** and then **Create Rule.**

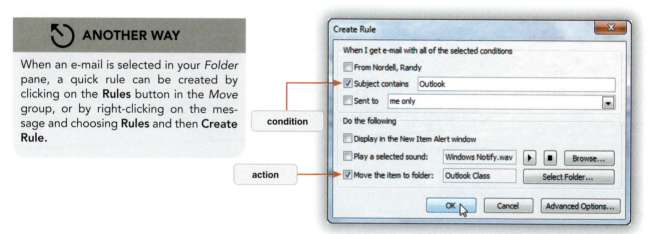

Create Rule dialog box with condition and action selected

7. Click **OK.** A *Success* dialog box will open.
8. Check the **Run this rule now . . .** box.
9. Click **OK.**

Success dialog box and Run this rule now selected.

10. All the e-mails in your *Inbox* with a subject that matches the condition will be moved to the specified folder.

Creating Advanced Rules

Creating a quick rule based upon an e-mail in your Inbox is effective and efficient, but you are limited by the number of conditions and actions from which to select.

To have more customization options for the rules you create, you will need to open the **Rules and Alerts** dialog box (click on the **Home** ribbon, **Rules** button in the *Move* group, and select **Manage Rules & Alerts**). This dialog box lists the rules existing on your computer and allows you to create, modify, delete, and order the existing rules.

When you click on the **New Rule** button, the *Rules Wizard* dialog box will open, which will step you through the creation of your rule. There will be five steps in the Rules Wizard dialog box to create your new rule.

- *Step 1.* Choose to use a rule **template** or create a **blank rule.** This step will also determine whether this rule is to be applied to incoming or outgoing e-mails.
- *Step 2.* Select the **condition** of the rule.
- *Step 3.* Set the **action** Outlook is to perform if the *condition* is met.
- *Step 4.* Specify any **exceptions** to the rule.
- *Step 5.* **Name** and **run** the rule.

There are rule templates created for the most common types of rules used. When one of these is selected, you will be taken to the next step to specify the condition. You can also choose to start creating a rule from a blank rule.

The following steps create a rule to move all e-mails from a specific person (my wife) to a different folder (Kelly).

STEP-BY-STEP

1. Click on the **Mail** button in the *Navigation* pane.
2. Create a **new folder** in your *Inbox.* I created a folder named *Kelly.*
3. Click on the **Rules** button in the *Move* group on the *Home* ribbon, and choose **Manage Rules & Alerts.** The *Rules and Alerts* dialog box will open.

Click on the Manage Rules & Alerts button to open the
Rules and Alerts dialog box

4. Click on the **New Rule** button. The *Rules Wizard* dialog box will open.

Create New Rule
from Rules and
Alerts dialog box

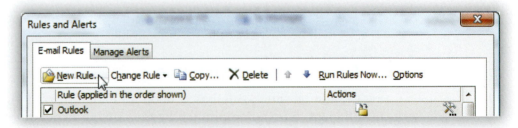

5. Select **Apply rule on messages I receive** in the *Start from a blank rule* section.

Rules Wizard dialog box. Apply rules on messages received

6. Click **Next.** You will be taken to the next step to select a condition for the rule.

7. Check the **from people or public group** box. In the bottom section of this dialog box, the condition is displayed.

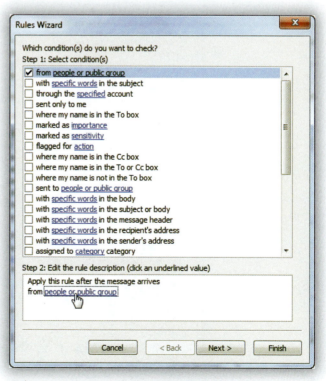

Select condition in Rules Wizard dialog box

8. Click on the **people or public group** link in the bottom section. The *Rule Address* dialog box will open.

9. Select the **name of the individual** for the condition of the rule.

10. Click **From** and **OK.** The *Rule Address* dialog box will close, and you will be taken back to the *Rules Wizard* dialog box. Notice the person's name appears in the bottom section as the condition for which Outlook is looking.

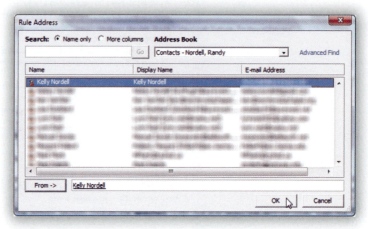

Rule Address dialog box

11. Click **Next.** You will be taken to the *action* step in the *Rules Wizard* dialog box.

12. Check the **move it to the specified folder** box.

13. In the bottom section, click on the **specified** folder link. The *Rules and Alerts* dialog box will open.

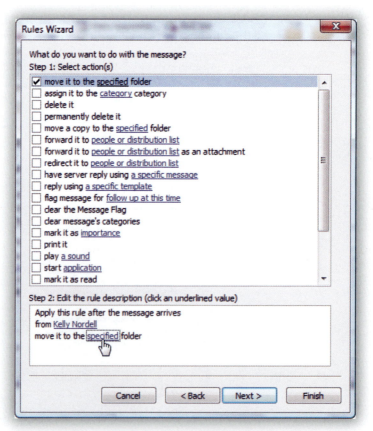

Select action in the Rules Wizard dialog box

14. Click on the desired **folder** and press **OK.** You will be taken back to the *Rules Wizard* dialog box. Always read the rule in the bottom section to make sure the *condition* and *action* are correct.

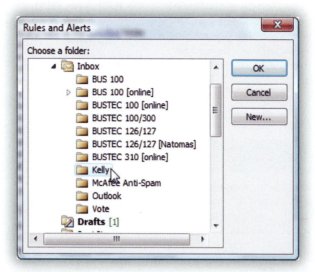

Select destination folder from Rules and Alerts dialog box

15. Click **Next.** You will be taken to the *exceptions* step.

16. Click **Next.** There will be no exceptions to this rule. The *Finish rule setup* step appears.

17. Customize the name of the rule in the *Step 1* area.

18. Check the **Run this rule now . . .** box.

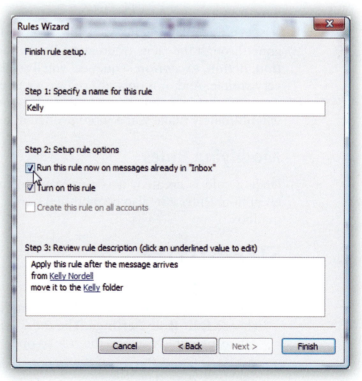

Finish rule setup in the Rules Wizard dialog box

19. Confirm that the **Turn on this rule** box is selected.

MORE INFO

It is best to keep rules simple—one condition and one action (and an exception if necessary). The more conditions and actions you have in one rule, the greater the chance of either diluting the effectiveness of the rule or causing the rule to not function as intended.

FACTOID

When using Outlook in a stand-alone environment, your rules are stored on your computer.

If you are using Outlook in an Exchange environment, your rules are stored on the Exchange server. This means that most rules will run wherever you access Outlook, including Outlook Web Access. Some rules are client-only rules, which means they will only run on the computer on which they were created.

20. In the bottom section, read the rule one last time to confirm that the condition and action are correct.

21. Click **Finish.** The rule will check the condition (from Kelly) on all the e-mails in your *Inbox.* If the condition is met, Outlook will move all e-mails matching the condition to the folder (*Kelly*).

22. You will be taken back to the *Rules and Alerts* dialog box. Notice the new rule is in the list of rules.

23. Click **Apply** and then **OK.**

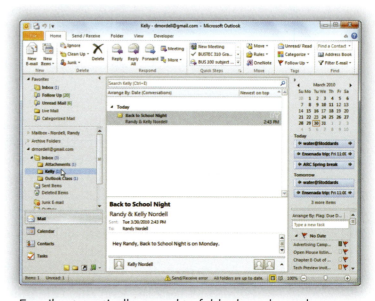

E-mail automatically moved to folder based on rule

Creating rules might seem like a daunting process, but once you have gone through the steps of creating a rule and understand the logical ***condition, action, exception*** sequence, you'll realize that creating rules is actually very simple. And, not only are rules easy to create and use, but they are also very effective in helping you to organize and customize your Inbox, which will ultimately make you a more proficient and productive Outlook user.

Modifying Rules

Once a rule is created, it is very easy to modify the condition, action, or exception. Rules can also be modified to run on different folders within your mailbox.

STEP-BY-STEP

1. Open the **Rules and Alerts** dialog box.

2. Select the rule to be modified, click on the **Change Rule** button, and choose **Edit Rule Settings.** The *Rules Wizard* dialog box will open. You can also double-click on the rule to open the *Rules Wizard* dialog box.

3. You can change the *condition, action, exception, name,* or *folder* on which the rule is to run.

4. If you modify a rule, be sure to check the **Run this rule now . . .** box and click **Finish** to apply the changes and run the rule.

Deleting and Turning On/Off Rules

There will be times when you will no longer need or want a rule that you created previously. A rule can easily be deleted by selecting the rule in the *Rules and Alerts* dialog box and either pressing the **Delete** button or right-clicking on the rule and choosing **Delete.**

Sometimes you might want to turn off a rule, but not delete it because you might use it again sometime in the future. Rules can easily be turned off so that no action will be performed.

STEP-BY-STEP

1. Open the **Rules and Alerts** dialog box.
2. **Deselect** the check box to the left of the rule to turn it off.

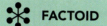

FACTOID

Outlook has a default rule (*Clear categories on mail*) that has been created for you. This rule clears any categories on incoming messages. It is important to keep this rule, as you do not want others' categories conflicting with your categories. Using categories will be covered later in this chapter on page 191.

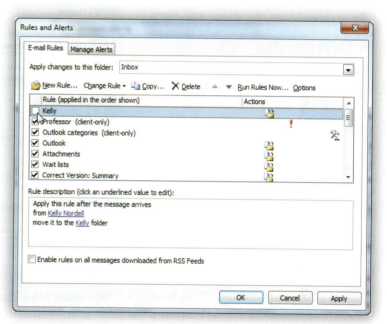

Turn rule off

3. Click **Apply** and then **OK.** The rule is now turned off.

Rules can be turned back on by clicking on the **check box** to the left of the rules in the *Rules and Alerts* dialog box. It is easy to view which rules are *on* or *off* by looking at your list of rules in the *Rules and Alerts* dialog box. A check in the check box indicates that a rule is turned on, and no check in the check box indicates that a rule is turned off.

Running Rules

When a rule that was turned off is turned back on, it is important to run this rule on messages currently in the Inbox. Outlook provides you with a feature to run specific rules without having to step through the Rules Wizard.

You will be given the options of selecting the rules to be run, the folder on which to run each rule, and what type of messages on which to apply each rule (All Messages, Unread Messages, Read Messages). A *Rule Description* is provided in the middle of this dialog box for the selected rule.

STEP-BY-STEP

1. Select the e-mail in the *Folder* pane or open an e-mail on which to apply the Quick Step.

2. In the *Quick Steps* group, click on the **Quick Step** to be applied (*Team E-mail* used in this example). The *Customize Quick Step* (or *First Time Setup*) dialog box will open.

3. Click on the **To** button to select the team members to be included in this Quick Step.

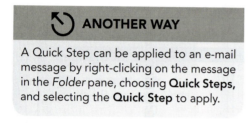

ANOTHER WAY

A Quick Step can be applied to an e-mail message by right-clicking on the message in the *Folder* pane, choosing **Quick Steps,** and selecting the **Quick Step** to apply.

Customize Quick Step dialog box

4. Change the **Name** of the Quick Step if desired.

5. Clicking the **Options** button will open the *[Quick Step's name]* dialog box. You can add additional actions to this Quick Step in this dialog box.

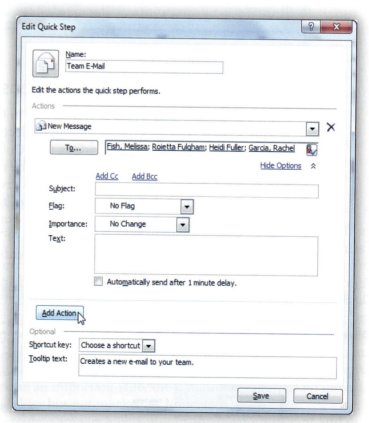

Edit Quick Step dialog box

6. Click on the **Show Options** link to display more options available for this action. The **Hide Options** link will hide these available options.

7. Click **Save** to close this dialog box and return to the *Customize Quick Step* dialog box.

8. Click **Save and Apply** to save this Quick Step and apply it to the selected message.

As you begin using Quick Steps, you will find the need to create your own custom Quick Steps. These new custom Quick Steps will appear in the Quick Steps group on the Home and Message ribbons. Quick Steps are not limited to one action, but can include multiple actions to be performed on a selected e-mail message. For example, you can create a Quick Step to mark an e-mail as high importance, mark it as read, and move it to a folder.

STEP-BY-STEP

1. Click on the **More** button at the bottom right corner of the *Quick Steps* list to expand the list.

2. Click on the **Create New** Quick Step. The *Edit Quick Step* dialog box will open. You can also click on the **New Quick Step** button and select **Custom.**

3. Give the Quick Step a **Name.**

Create New Quick Step

4. Click on the pull-down arrow to display a list of actions that can be performed. Note: The list of actions includes more than are displayed in the figure below.

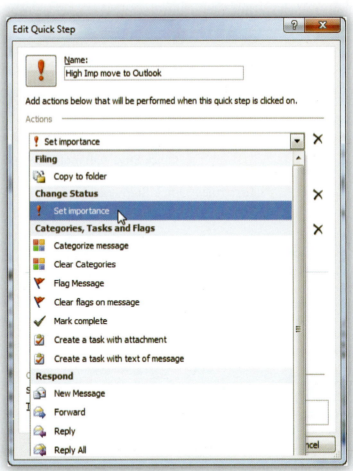

Select action for new Quick Step

5. Select the action to be performed. If additional criteria are available, the *Show Options* link will appear below the action.

6. Click on the **Add Action** button to add another action. An action can be deleted by clicking on the **X** (delete) button to the right of the action.

7. In the *Tooltip text* area, type a description for this Quick Step. This *Tooltip* will appear when your mouse pointer is placed over the Quick Step.

8. When all the actions have been added, click on the **Finish** button to create the new Quick Step. The new Quick Step will be included in the list of *Quick Steps*.

Quick Step with multiple actions

Like rules, Quick Steps can easily be managed. The *Manage Quick Steps* dialog box allows you to create **New** Quick Steps and **Modify, Duplicate** or **Delete**

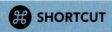 **SHORTCUT**

A shortcut can be added to a Quick Step by selecting a shortcut keystroke combination when creating or editing a Quick Step.

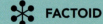 **FACTOID**

The **Reset to Defaults** button in the *Manage Quick Steps* dialog box will restore the Quick Steps to their original settings.

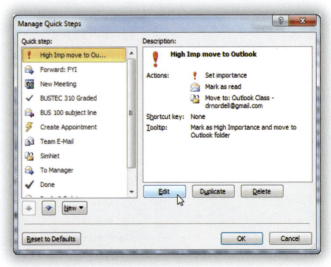

Manage Quick Steps dialog box

existing ones. You can change the display order of Quick Steps, and as you begin to have a lot of them, you can create groups in which to organize Quick Steps.

MORE INFO

Categories were introduced in Chapter 2 on page 47.

Using Categories

There might be times when you want to group together related e-mails, tasks, calendar items, or contacts, but you do not want to create a separate folder in which to store these related items. For example, you might want to group all your cycling buddies' contacts together so they are easy to find or group together tasks and e-mails related to the upcoming fundraiser at work.

The *Category* feature can be used to mark Outlook items into a particular group. One of the useful and unique aspects of categories is that they are global; they can be used throughout Outlook (e-mails, calendars, contacts, tasks, notes, and journals) to mark different types of Outlook items. Whereas folders are useful for grouping specific items together, they only store one type of Outlook item. Categories are yet another method provided by Outlook to help you organize information. Each of the different areas of Outlook lets you view these Outlook items by category.

Customizing Categories

Outlook is set up with default categories for your use. These categories are really not all that useful until you customize them to meet your individual needs. Each category has a color, and the default name is the name of the color.

I use categories extensively in Outlook both for work and personal use. For work I have categories set up for each of my courses so I can use these categories to mark e-mails from students, students' contact records, and calendar items and tasks associated with each course. At home I have a different category for each of us in the family, and one for vacation, church, school, birthdays, anniversaries, and others. Almost all our calendar items are marked with a category, so it is very easy to visually distinguish by color the category of the event or appointment on the calendar.

The default categories in Outlook are labeled by color. ***Customizing*** a category is very easy; pick the color of category and rename it. One of the handy features of categories is that you can ***rename*** or ***create*** a category anywhere in Outlook and it will be available throughout Outlook. Let's start customizing categories.

STEP-BY-STEP

1. Click on the **Calendar** button in the *Navigation* pane.
2. Click on **Month** view.
3. Click on any appointment or event on your calendar. The *Appointment* ribbon will be displayed.

4. Click on the **Categorize** button in the *Tags* group and choose **All Categories,** or right-click on the calendar item and choose **Categorize** and then **All Categories.** The *Color Categories* dialog box will open.

Categorize options

5. Click on the color of the category to be renamed.
6. Click on the **Rename** button.

MORE INFO

The *Color Categories* dialog box can be accessed throughout Outlook. Simply click on an e-mail, calendar item, contact, or task and follow the preceding steps.

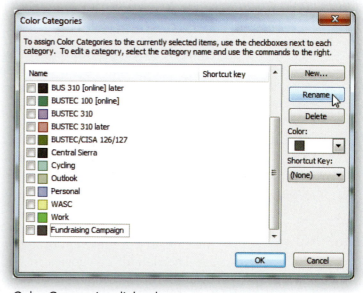

Color Categories dialog box

7. At the left type the **new name** of the category and press **Enter** (you can also click on another category).
8. Continue to rename categories as desired.
9. Press **OK** when finished. Your categories are now set up and ready to use.

New categories can also be created following a similar process and can be done throughout Outlook.

STEP-BY-STEP

1. Click on the **Mail** button in the *Navigation* pane.
2. Click on any e-mail in your *Inbox.*

3. Click on the **Categorize** button in the *Tags* group on the *Home* ribbon and choose **All Categories,** or right-click on the mail item and choose **Categorize** and then **All Categories.** The *Color Categories* dialog box opens.

4. Click on the **New** button. The *Add New Category* dialog box opens.

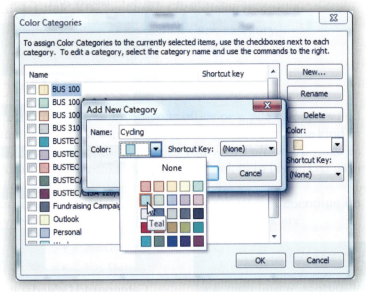

Add New Category dialog box

5. Type the **Name** of the category.

6. Click on the **arrow** to the right of *Color* and select a color.

7. Click **OK.** The new category is added to your list of categories.

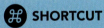

⌘ SHORTCUT

A shortcut key combination can be added to any category by clicking on the **small arrow** to the right of *Shortcut Key* and selecting the desired shortcut. This can be done on the *Add New Category* and *Color Categories* dialog boxes.

Add shortcut to a category

✳ FACTOID

Outlook items can be assigned to more than one category. When viewing items by category, an item that is assigned to multiple categories will appear in both or multiple category sections; although, it is still only one Outlook item.

Assigning Categories

Once your categories are renamed or created, you can assign a category to any Outlook item. You can select or open the item to be categorized, click on the **Categorize** button on the ribbon, and then select the category. You can also right-click on the item in the *Folder* pane, choose **Categorize,** and then select the category.

A category can be removed from an Outlook item by following this same process, but selecting **Clear All Categories.**

4. Close the Outlook item. This marked item is now included in the list of *To-Do* items.

A reminder and/or custom Follow Up flag can be added to an Outlook item. If a reminder is set, an electronic reminder will open on your computer screen providing you with details about the marked item.

A custom Follow Up flag can be set to give more specific follow-up details on an Outlook item. These include a custom message, start date, due date, and reminder. Outlook provides a few default messages for custom flags, or you can type in your own custom flag message.

STEP-BY-STEP

1. Open an Outlook item (e-mail, contact, or task).
2. Click on the **Follow Up** button in the *Tags* group.
3. Select **Custom** or **Add Reminder.** The *Custom* dialog box opens.
4. Enter the desired details in the *Custom* dialog box.
5. Click **OK** to close the dialog box. Details of the follow-up status are included in the *InfoBar* of the Outlook item.

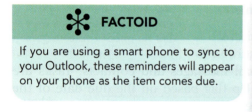

FACTOID

If you are using a smart phone to sync to your Outlook, these reminders will appear on your phone as the item comes due.

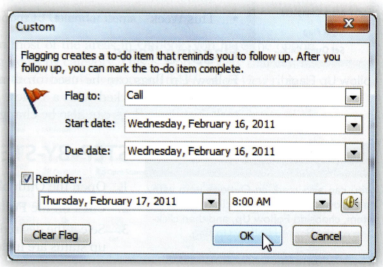

Custom follow up flag dialog box

Setting a Quick Click Follow Up Flag

I like to mark many of the e-mails I receive with a Follow Up flag. At the right side of the list of my e-mail messages in the Folder pane is a column for Follow Up flags. A flag can be added by clicking on this area of the e-mail message without having to select a specific flag.

The **Quick Click** flag can be customized to flag the Outlook item with the flag you use most regularly.

STEP-BY-STEP

1. Click on the **Follow Up** button in the *Tags* group.
2. Choose **Set Quick Click.** The *Set Quick Click* dialog box opens.

Set Quick Click
dialog box

3. Choose the desired **Follow Up flag** for Quick Click from the list of flag options.
4. Press **OK.**

To add a Quick Click flag, simply click on the **Follow Up flag** area of the Outlook item and the Quick Click flag will be set on that item.

View To-Do Items

Outlook items marked with a Follow Up flag will remain in their location in Outlook (i.e., Inbox, Contacts, or Tasks), but they are also consolidated in the *To-Do List.* As mentioned previously, *To-Do items* are all Outlook items marked with a Follow Up flag and can include e-mail, tasks, and contacts. The To-Do items are also listed in the *To-Do* bar.

To-Do List

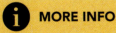

✳ FACTOID

In addition to the To-Do List and the To-Do bar, rules and search folders can be used to group items that have been flagged for follow up.

Rules were covered earlier in this chapter, and search folders will be covered in Chapter 11 on page 323.

ⓘ MORE INFO

You can remove a flag (different than marking it as completed) by selecting the Outlook item, opening the **Follow Up** menu, and choosing **Clear Flag.**

When an Outlook item that has been marked with a Follow Up flag has been completed, you can use *Mark Complete* to indicate the item has been completed and the flag will be replaced with a check mark. Or, if the To-Do List is displayed, the item will be crossed out indicating that it has been marked as complete.

There are numerous ways in Outlook to use Mark Complete for an item that has been flagged.

- Click on the **flag icon** and the *Mark Complete check* will replace the flag.

- Right-click on the item, choose **Follow Up,** and click on **Mark Complete.**

- In the *To-Do List,* click on the **Complete** check box to mark an item as completed.

- Open the item, click on the **Follow Up** button in the *Tags* group, and choose **Mark Complete.**

Chapter Highlights

▶ **Folders** can be created and used in Outlook to help manage e-mails, contacts, tasks, calendar items, notes, and journals.

▶ Outlook folders differ from Windows folders in that each folder is designed for a specific type of Outlook item.

▶ The **Folder List** allows you to view all your Outlook folders in the Navigation pane. Folders are hierarchical, and the Folder List shows the hierarchy of your Outlook folders.

▶ Folders can easily be **moved** from one location to another by using the **Move Folder** button and selecting the new location or by dragging the folder from its location and dropping it on the new location.

▶ Folders can also be easily **deleted.** When you delete a folder, you also delete the contents of the folder.

▶ **Rules** can be created in Outlook and used in conjunction with folders to help you manage e-mails.

▶ Rules have three basic parts: **condition, action,** and **exception.**

▶ Rules can be applied to **incoming** or **outgoing** e-mail.

▶ A **quick rule** can be created based on an e-mail in your Inbox. When creating a quick rule, you are given just a few conditions and actions from which to choose.

▶ More complex rules can be created using the **Rules and Alerts** dialog box. When a new rule is created, the **Rules Wizard** walks you through step by step.

▶ Rules can also be **turned on or off, edited, deleted,** or **prioritized** in the Rules and Alerts dialog box.

▶ The rules in Outlook are **hierarchical,** which means that those at the top of the list run before those at the bottom.

▶ **Quick Steps** are similar to rules, but they do not contain a condition and are not automatically applied. Quick Steps perform actions to a selected e-mail message.

▶ Outlook provides you with preset Quick Steps, which you can customize. You can also create your own custom Quick Steps.

▶ **Categories** can be used to group different types of Outlook items. Categories can be used on e-mails, calendar items, contacts, tasks, notes, and journals.

▶ Outlook items can be viewed by category.

▶ Categories can be edited or added to meet your business or personal needs.

▶ An Outlook item can be assigned to more than one category. When viewing these items by category, the item that is assigned to more than one category will appear in each category to which it is assigned even though it is still one Outlook item.

▶ **Follow Up flags** can be used to mark an Outlook item that needs further attention. Items marked with a flag become a **To-Do Item.**

▸ Follow Up flags can be used on e-mails, contacts, and tasks. Follow Up flags are not used on calendar items because these items are already associated with a date.

▸ **Custom Follow Up flags** can be used, and a **reminder** can be set.

▸ E-mail items can be **flagged for recipient.**

▸ To-Do items include tasks and all items that have been marked with a Follow Up flag.

What Do You Know About Outlook?

True/False Questions

T F 1. A shortcut key can be added to a Follow Up flag. [Objectives 7.3, 7.4]

T F 2. Rules can be used on both incoming and outgoing e-mails. [Objective 7.2]

T F 3. When viewing Outlook items by category, an item assigned to more than one category will only appear in the first category to which it is assigned. [Objective 7.3]

T F 4. When creating a quick rule, you cannot set an exception to the rule. [Objective 7.2]

T F 5. The color of a Follow Up flag changes as the due date approaches. [Objective 7.4]

Multiple Choice Questions

1. A Mail and Post Items folder will store which type of Outlook items? [Objective 7.1]
   a. E-mail
   b. Calendar items
   c. Tasks
   d. All the above

2. Which of the following Outlook items are *not* included in the To-Do List? [Objective 7.4]
   a. Tasks
   b. E-mail
   c. Calendar items
   d. Contacts

3. Outlook Quick Steps apply to which of the following? [Objective 7.2]
   a. Tasks
   b. E-mail
   c. Calendar items
   d. All the above

4. How can a category be assigned? [Objective 7.3]
   a. Applying it to an open Outlook item
   b. Clicking in the category field
   c. Right-clicking on an item and selecting a category
   d. All the above

5. Which of the following is a method to create a new folder anywhere in Outlook?
   a. Ctrl+N
   b. Ctrl+Shift+E
   c. Click on the New button
   d. All the above

Short Answer Questions

1. Explain the three e-mail parts of a rule. [Objective 7.2]

2. Describe how Follow Up flags are related to To-Do items. [Objective 7.4]

3. Describe the Folder List, and explain when it might be helpful to use the Folder List. [Objective 7.1]

Putting Outlook to Work

After spending some time using Outlook at home and work, you have decided to try and organize your Outlook items by using folders, rules, categories, and Follow Up flags. In these exercises, you will be using some of the features previously learned in Outlook, and you will be trying some of the new features learned in this chapter.

Exercise 7.1 [Guided Practice]

Create two new Inbox folders. [Objective 7.1]

1. Click on the **Mail** button in the *Navigation* pane.
2. Click on your **Inbox** in the *Mail Folders* area of the *Navigation* pane.
3. Click on the **Folder** tab, and click on the **New Folder** button in the *New* group. The *Create New Folder* dialog box will open.
4. Name the new folder **Outlook,** and press **OK.**
   a. Notice the new folder appears in your *Inbox*. If the new folder appears in a different location, move or drag it to your *Inbox*.
5. Right-click on your **Inbox** folder, and choose **New Folder.** The *Create New Folder* dialog box will open.
6. Name the new folder **Attachments,** and click **OK.**
   a. Notice the new folder appears in your *Inbox*. If the new folder appears in a different location, move or drag it to your *Inbox*.

Exercise 7.2 [Guided Practice]

Create and send three new e-mails. [Objective 7.4]

1. Create a new e-mail.
   a. Address it to all your classmates and professor.
   b. Use **Outlook Follow Up flags** as the subject.
   c. Include a message briefly describing Follow Up flags.
   d. Include your signature in the body.

2. **Send.**

3. Create another new e-mail.

   a. Address it to all your classmates and instructor.
   b. Use `Company Picnic picture` as the subject.
   c. **Attach** a picture. Use one of the pictures in the *Pictures* folder on your computer.
   d. Include a brief message about the company picnic and your signature in the body.

4. **Send.**

5. Create another new e-mail.

   a. Address it to all your classmates and instructor.
   b. Use `Company Newsletter` as the subject.
   c. Include a brief message stating that articles for the newsletter are due by Friday.
   d. Include your signature in the body.

6. **Send.**

Exercise 7.3 [Guided Practice]

Create three new categories, and assign a category to an e-mail message. Customize and use a Quick Step. [Objectives 7.2, 7.3]

1. Click on an e-mail in your *Inbox*.

2. Click on the **Categorize** button in the *Tags* group on the *Home* ribbon, and select **All Categories.** The *Color Categories* dialog box will open.

3. Create the following three new categories. You can use any colors you want.

   a. `Work`
   b. `Personal`
   c. `Outlook`

4. Make sure that none of the categories have check marks. If any do, deselect them.

5. Click **OK** to close the *Color Categories* dialog box.

6. Select (don't open) one of the **Company Picnic picture** e-mails you have in your *Inbox*.

7. Use one of the methods you have learned to assign the **Work** category to this e-mail.

8. Click on the **Team E-mail** Quick Step. The *Customize Quick Step* dialog box will open. (Note: If this dialog box does not open, click on **Manage Quick Steps,** click on the **Team E-mail** Quick Step, and click on **Edit.**)

   a. Change the name to `Outlook class e-mail.`
   b. Click on the **To** button. The *Address Book* dialog box will open.
   c. Select all your classmates and your professor.
   d. Click **OK** to close the *Address Book* dialog box.
   e. Click on **Save.** The *Customize Quick Step* dialog box will close.

8. Click on one of the **Company Newsletter** e-mails in your *Inbox*, and apply the **Create Meeting** Quick Step.

    a. Add any necessary details to the appointment, and **save** and **close** the appointment.

    b. Confirm that the appointment has been added to your *Calendar*.

Exercise 7.7 [Independent Practice]

Create a new rule to mark all e-mails from your professor as high importance. Edit the Outlook rule, and order rules in the Rules and Alerts dialog box. [Objectives 7.1, 7.2]

1. Click on your **Inbox** in the *Navigation* pane.

2. Create a new rule to mark all e-mails received from your professor as **high importance.**

    a. Name the rule **Professor.**

3. Edit the **Attachments** rule to add an *exception.*

    a. Perform the action of the rule unless the e-mail is from your professor.

    b. This will take effect on all e-mails in your *Inbox* and all new e-mails.

4. **Order** the rules so they appear in the following order in the *Rules and Alerts* dialog box.

    a. Professor

    b. Outlook

    c. Attachments

Exercise 7.8 [Independent Practice]

Turn off a rule. Use a Quick Step to create a new e-mail message. [Objectives 7.1–7.3]

1. In the *Rules and Alerts* dialog box, turn off the *Outlook* rule.

2. Create a new e-mail using the **Outlook class e-mail** Quick Step.

    a. Use **Outlook rules** as the subject.

    b. Include a **No Response Necessary** flag for recipients with no reminder.

    c. In the body, use numbering to create brief steps on how to create a rule in the body.

    d. Include your signature.

3. **Send** the e-mail.

Exercise 7.9 [Independent Practice]

Create a new rule to assign the Outlook category to all e-mails with Outlook in the subject. Order rules in the Rules and Alerts dialog box, turn on a rule, and use the Run Rules Now feature. [Objectives 7.3, 7.4]

1. Click on your **Inbox** in the *Navigation* pane.

2. Create a new rule to assign all e-mails with "**Outlook**" in the subject to the **Outlook category.**

    a. Name this rule **Outlook category.**

    b. Note: This is a client-only rule, and you will get a dialog box informing you of this.

3. Edit the order of rules so this rule appears **second** in the list below the *Professor* rule.

4. Turn on the **Outlook** rule.

   a. This rule was turned off in Exercise 7.8.

5. Use the **Run Rules Now** feature in the *Rules and Alerts* dialog box.

   a. Check all the rules you have created.
   b. Make sure these rules are running on the *Inbox,* and check the **Include subfolders** box.

account. It determines the type of account (Exchange, POP, IMAP, or HTTP) and validates the account settings.

The two pieces of information you will need are your ***username*** or ***e-mail account*** and your ***password.*** Outlook will automatically detect your e-mail account settings and set up your account in Outlook.

STEP-BY-STEP

1. Click on the **File** tab. The *BackStage* will open.
2. Click on **Add Account.** The *Add New Account* dialog box will open.

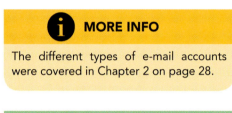

MORE INFO

The different types of e-mail accounts were covered in Chapter 2 on page 28.

FACTOID

For some online e-mail accounts, you must enable POP on the online account for your e-mail to be delivered to Outlook. This is typically done by logging into your account on the Internet and editing the settings to enable POP. This will vary from account to account.

Add New Account from Outlook BackStage

3. Click on the **E-mail Account** radio button.

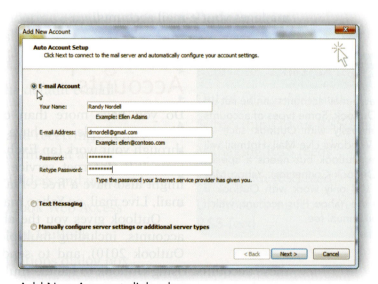

Add New Account dialog box

4. Fill in the following fields: **Your Name, E-mail Address, Password, Retype Password.**
5. Click **Next.** Outlook will automatically configure and test the account settings. If the account was set up properly, you will see three green check marks and a *"Congratulations!"* message.

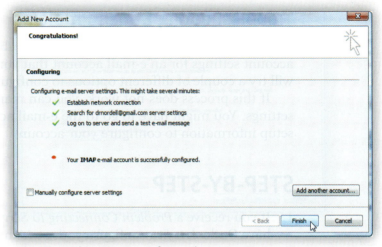

New e-mail account configured

6. Click **Finish.** The *Account Settings* dialog box appears. Notice your new e-mail account is now included in your list of e-mail accounts.

7. Click **Close.**

If you are using Outlook in a stand-alone environment, your e-mail messages will be delivered to your Inbox in your Personal Folders. If you are using Outlook in an Exchange environment, you will have two sets of folders: **Mailbox - [Your Name]** and **Personal Folders.** Your e-mail account through Exchange will be handled in your Mailbox—*[Your Name]* folders, and your personal e-mail accounts will, by default, be handled in your Personal Folders. If you are using an IMAP account such as Gmail, Outlook will set up an additional set of folders for this account.

 **NETIQUETTE**

It is not a good idea to set up all your personal e-mail accounts on your work computer because most employers do not want you to be distracted by personal e-mails while at work.

 MORE INFO

You will also have another set of folders called Archive Folders, which will be covered in Chapter 11 on page 330.

Mail folders in the Navigation pane

you might try using the **Repair** feature provided in Outlook. This automated feature in the *Account Settings* dialog box will walk you through a couple of steps and try to automatically repair an existing e-mail account.

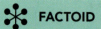

FACTOID

A setting change on the e-mail server end might cause an existing e-mail account in Outlook to stop functioning properly. The **Repair** feature might be able to automatically adjust the account settings to restore this account.

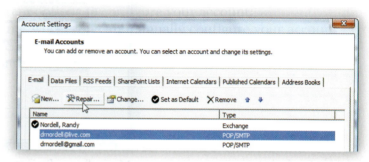

Repair e-mail account

Using Outlook Connector

Outlook easily integrates multiple e-mail accounts of different types. But some free e-mail accounts, such as Live and Hotmail, need an add-in to make them function properly. The **Outlook Connector** is the add-in that allows you to set up a Live or Hotmail account in Outlook and provides two-way synchronization with these accounts.

To set up a Live or Hotmail account, you will follow the same procedures as for setting up an Exchange account or an e-mail account through your ISP. Outlook will prompt you to install the Outlook Connector during the setup process.

STEP-BY-STEP

1. Click on the **File** tab. The *BackStage* will open.
2. Click on **Add Account.** The *Add New Account* dialog box will open.

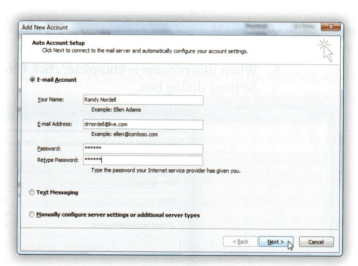

Add New Account dialog box

3. Click on the **E-mail Account** radio button.
4. Fill in the following fields: **Your Name, E-mail Address, Password, Retype Password.**
5. Click **Next.**
6. A dialog box will open prompting you to download and install Outlook Connector.

7. Click **Install Now.**

Install Outlook Connector

8. Check the box to accept the license agreement for the Outlook Connector, and click **Install.** Outlook will install the Outlook Connector and finish configuring your account.

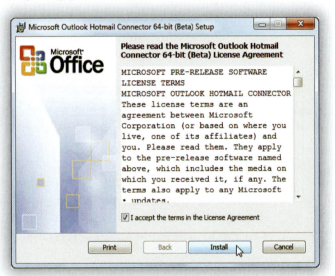

Accept Outlook Connector license agreement

9. Click **Finish** to complete the Outlook Connector installation.

Finish installing the Outlook Connector

10. Click **Finish** to complete the account setup.

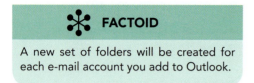

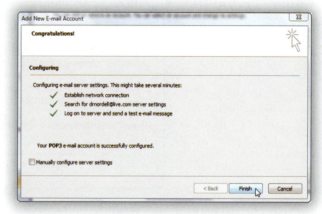

Finish the account setup process

Managing Multiple E-mail Accounts

One of the issues with having multiple e-mail accounts in Outlook is keeping them separate in your mail folders. Managing multiple e-mail accounts can become confusing if e-mails are all being delivered into the same Inbox. Another issue is choosing the account through which you create and send new e-mails and respond to or forward e-mails. Having multiple e-mail accounts somewhat complicates this process, but being deliberate about setting your default e-mail account and having e-mails delivered to different folders can help you to effectively manage multiple e-mail accounts.

Setting the Default Account

The default e-mail account is the account that will, by default, be used to send any new e-mail that is created and sent. This should be the account used most often in Outlook. This will be the first e-mail account you set up in Outlook unless you specify a different account. It is easy to change your default e-mail account.

STEP-BY-STEP

1. Click on the **File** tab to open the *BackStage*.
2. Click on the **Account Settings** button, and choose **Account Settings.** The *Account Settings* dialog box will open, and one of the accounts will be noted with a check mark.

Set an e-mail account as the default account

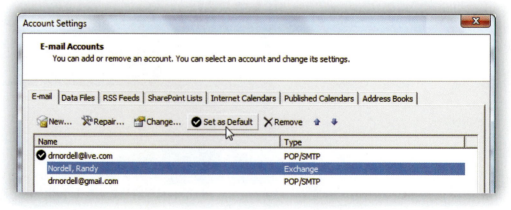

3. Click on the e-mail account you want as your default account.
4. Click on the **Set as Default** button. This account will be moved to the top of the list and will be the default e-mail account.

MORE INFO

When you create a new e-mail, the account being used will be displayed to the right of the *From* button. The e-mail will be sent through the default account unless you choose a different account.

NETIQUETTE

It is probably best to reply to an e-mail using the same account through which the e-mail was received.

Sending E-mail Through a Different Account

As mentioned earlier, when you create and send a new e-mail, it will be sent through your default e-mail account. But if you are replying to or forwarding an e-mail, it will be sent through the account through which it was delivered. For example, if you received an e-mail through your Gmail account (assuming this is not your default account), and you reply to or forward this e-mail, it will be sent through your Gmail account unless you choose a different account through which to send this e-mail.

When you have multiple e-mail accounts set up in Outlook, you can decide through which account the e-mail will be sent. This can be done on new e-mails, replies, or forwards. A **From** button will appear to the right of the *Send* button on all your e-mails when you have multiple accounts set up in Outlook. You can select the account from which to send an e-mail using the **From** button.

STEP-BY-STEP

1. Open an existing e-mail.
2. Click on the **Reply** or **Forward** button.
3. To the right of the *From* button, a message appears informing you of the account that will be used to send the e-mail.
4. Click on the **From** button, and choose a different account. Notice the account displayed to the right.

Select account through which to send an e-mail

5. Click **Send** to send the e-mail through the chosen account.

Changing the E-mail Delivery Folder

On personal e-mail accounts, you can change the folder to which your e-mail is delivered. You do not have this option with an Exchange account. When managing multiple e-mail accounts, it is probably best to have different accounts delivered to different folders. If your default account is being delivered to your Inbox, you might want to create a Gmail folder and have your Gmail always delivered to this folder. You can change the default delivery folder for an e-mail account in the Account Settings dialog box.

STEP-BY-STEP

1. Click on the **File** tab to open the *BackStage*.

2. Click on the **Account Settings** button, and choose **Account Settings.** The *Account Settings* dialog box will open.

3. Click on one of your accounts that is not the default account. Notice the *delivery folder* to the right of the *Change Folder* button.

Change e-mail delivery folder in the Account Settings dialog box

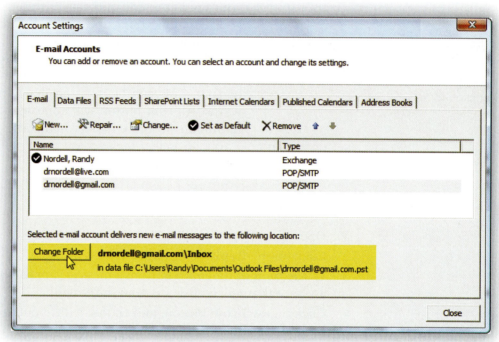

4. Click on the **Change Folder** button. The *New E-mail Delivery Location* dialog box opens.

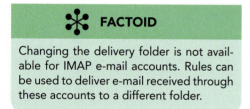

FACTOID

Changing the delivery folder is not available for IMAP e-mail accounts. Rules can be used to deliver e-mail received through these accounts to a different folder.

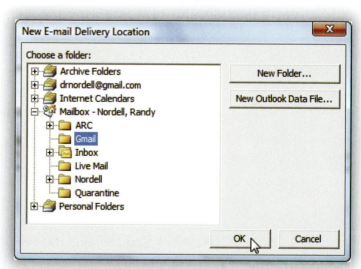

New E-mail Delivery Location dialog box

5. Select the **new delivery folder.** A new folder can also be created by clicking on the **New Folder** button.

6. Click **OK** to close the *New E-mail Delivery Location* dialog box.

7. Click **Close** to close the *Account Settings* dialog box. All e-mails from the chosen account will now be delivered to the folder you chose.

MORE INFO

Rules were covered in Chapter 7 on page 177.

Creating Folders and Using Rules

Rules can also be used to deliver e-mails from specific accounts to a different folder. The **condition** would be looking for e-mails received through a specified account (for example, a Gmail or Live account), and the **action** would be to move it to a specified folder. This rule would do the same thing as changing the default delivery folder, but it could easily be turned off or on.

Using Outlook Web Access

One of the advantages of using e-mail is the ability to access it from any computer that has Internet access. If you have an e-mail account through your Internet service provider (ISP) or a free e-mail account such as Gmail or Yahoo Mail, you can log on to the Internet and access your e-mail account through their website. You need to know your username and password to have access to your online e-mail account.

If you are using Outlook in an Exchange environment, most companies have their Exchange server connected to **Outlook Web Access** (**OWA**). OWA allows you to access your Exchange account through the Internet. You need to know the URL (web location) of your company's OWA and log on with your username and password. OWA provides you not only with e-mail access, but also access to your calendar, contacts, tasks, and notes.

OWA will be displayed differently depending on the Internet browser you're using (for example, Microsoft Internet Explorer, Google Chrome, or Mozilla Firefox). OWA will look different than Outlook on your computer, but you will still have most of the functionality of your Outlook account.

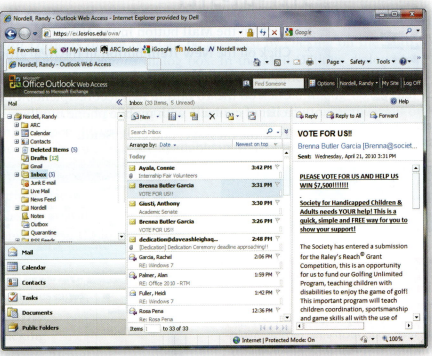

Outlook Web Access (OWA)

Texting from Outlook

OMG . . . you can text from Outlook! In addition to being able to set up multiple e-mail accounts in Outlook, you can also send and receive text messages in Outlook.

The button at the left of each of these areas opens a dialog box with many additional features that you are able to customize.

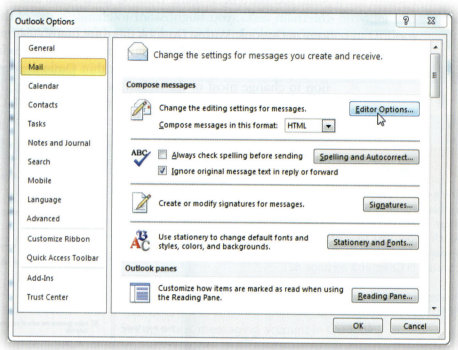

Mail options in the Outlook Options dialog box

The **Editor Options** and **Spelling and Autocorrect** buttons open the *Editor Options* dialog box. In this dialog box you are given many options on the *Proofing* and *Advanced* areas.

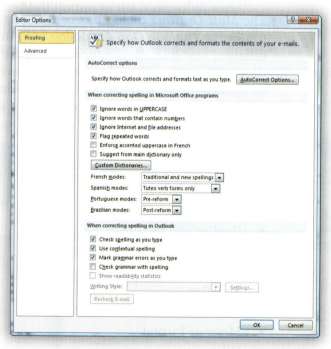

Editor Options dialog box

The **Signatures** and **Stationery and Themes** buttons open the *Signatures and Stationery* dialog box. In this dialog box, you can create and edit signatures, and on the *Personal Stationery* tab you can customize the theme and fonts for e-mails.

Signatures and
Stationery dialog
box

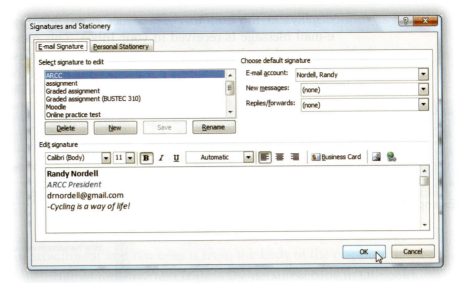

Outlook Panes

The *Outlook panes* section allows you to control how messages displayed in the Reading pane interact with the Folder pane. Messages can be set to be marked as read when they are displayed in the Reading pane or marked as read when the selection in the Folder pane changes. Also, the space bar can be set up and used to move through the text of a message and move to the next message in the Folder pane. This is a handy feature to quickly preview and move through messages in the Reading pane.

Reading Pane dialog
box

Message Arrival

The *Message arrival* section of Mail Options controls what happens in Outlook when a message arrives in your Inbox. By default when a new e-mail message arrives, a sound is played, the mouse pointer briefly changes, an envelope is displayed in the notification area, and a desktop alert is displayed.

Message arrival
section of Mail
Options

This area will also allow you to control how the desktop alerts appear when a new message arrives. Clicking on the **Desktop Alert Settings** button will open the *Desktop Alert Settings* dialog box. The **Duration** and **Transparency** for these alerts can be customized. A **Desktop Alert** is a message that briefly

Typically, a semicolon is used to separate recipients' e-mail addresses in the *To* line of a message, but a comma can also be used to separate recipients. The ***Auto-Complete List*** is used to suggest recently used names when typing names in the *To, Cc,* and *Bcc* lines of an e-mail. This list can be cleared by clicking on the **Empty Auto-Complete List** button.

MailTips

MailTips are new to Outlook 2010 and are used to inform you about when you are sending an e-mail to a large number of recipients, to a recipient who is out of the office, to recipients whose mailbox is full, or to an invalid e-mail address, and about many other e-mail situations. MailTips provide you with real-time information about the status of an e-mail message to be sent. The MailTips information bar appears in the InfoBar area of a message.

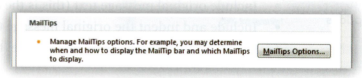

MailTips section of Mail Options

The *MailTips Options* dialog box allows you to customize the settings for how MailTips will appear. The MailTips bar by default will only be displayed when one or more of the MailTips apply. You can change the setting so that the MailTips bar will appear on all e-mail messages.

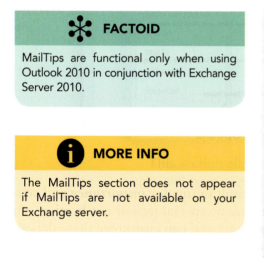

FACTOID

MailTips are functional only when using Outlook 2010 in conjunction with Exchange Server 2010.

MORE INFO

The MailTips section does not appear if MailTips are not available on your Exchange server.

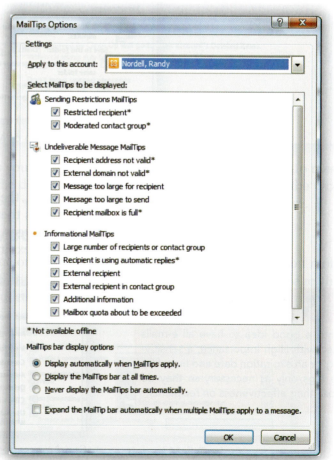

MailTips Options dialog box

Tracking Options

If you are using Outlook in an Exchange environment, Outlook automatically tracks responses when using voting buttons and meeting requests. Outlook will also track receipts received when a read receipt or delivery receipt has been used on an e-mail. The *Tracking Options* dialog box allows you to determine how Outlook tracks and responds to these items.

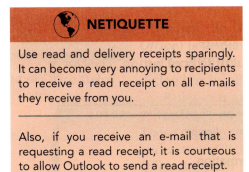

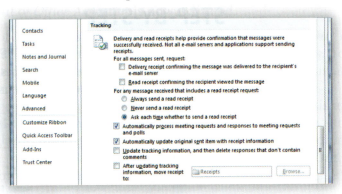

Tracking section of Mail Options

 NETIQUETTE

Use read and delivery receipts sparingly. It can become very annoying to recipients to receive a read receipt on all e-mails they receive from you.

Also, if you receive an e-mail that is requesting a read receipt, it is courteous to allow Outlook to send a read receipt.

(i) MORE INFO

Delivery receipts, read receipts, and voting buttons were covered in Chapter 3. Meeting requests were covered in Chapter 5.

You can customize how voting button and meeting request responses are processed when they arrive in your Inbox. Also, you can change the default settings for read and delivery receipts for outgoing e-mails and how Outlook should handle read receipts on e-mails you receive.

Message Format and Other

The last two sections of the *Mail Options* dialog box include some behind-the-scenes options for formatting your e-mail messages. Outlook allows you to customize some of these not so common e-mail formatting options. It is probably best to leave the default settings in these areas unless you have specific reasons to change them.

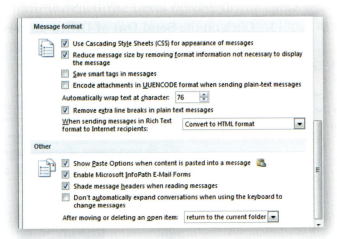

Message format and Other sections of Mail Options

Out of Office Assistant

Most of us have times away from the office or home when you are not able to respond to e-mails for an extended time. You might be on vacation or a business trip and don't want to totally ignore those who send you an e-mail. The ***Out of Office Assistant*** provides you the option of creating an automated response to reply to all e-mails you receive while you are not able to answer e-mail.

of the screen. This news feed is similar to an **RSS** (really simple syndication) *feed* from a website. RSS feeds are headlines of new articles or information on a website. RSS feeds are useful in that when you subscribe to an RSS feed you are automatically sent the new articles from this website to your RSS feed reader. So, rather than having to visit each of your favorite news, sports, recipes, and entertainment websites to search for new information, this new information is automatically sent to you as an RSS feed.

Outlook can manage your RSS feeds like it does your e-mail accounts. When a new item is available on a website, it is delivered to an RSS feed folder. You will receive RSS feeds like an e-mail. These feeds will come with a subject line and a brief summary of the article. There is also usually a link to take you to the website to read the full article if you're interested.

Subscribing to an RSS Feed

Outlook provides you with an RSS feed folder to store the RSS feeds to which you subscribe. Outlook also provides you with a menu of RSS feeds from which to easily subscribe. When you click on the **RSS Feeds** folder in the *Navigation* pane, the **Outlook Syndicated Content (RSS) Directory** appears in the *Folder* pane. You can click on any of these links to subscribe to an RSS feed and automatically add a new folder to your *RSS Feeds* folder.

STEP-BY-STEP

1. Click on the **Mail** button in the *Navigation* pane.
2. Click on the **RSS Feeds** folder in the *Mail Folders* list in the *Navigation* pane. The *Outlook Syndicated Content (RSS) Directory* appears in the *Folder* pane. You can scroll down in the Folder pane to view the different RSS feeds available.

MORE INFO

This RSS Syndicated Directory might not appear in your Outlook. You can find these Office blogs at www.blogs.office.com

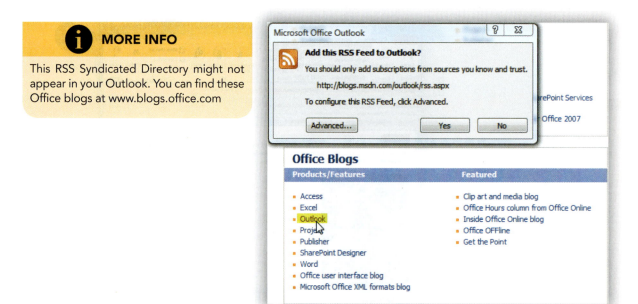

Add Outlook RSS feed to RSS Feeds folder

3. Click on one of the **RSS feed links.** A dialog box will open asking, *Add this RSS Feed to Outlook?*

4. Click **Yes.** Outlook subscribes you to this RSS feed, and a new folder is added in the *RSS Feeds* folder. This folder will contain the current RSS feed articles.

New RSS feed folder added

5. You can click on any of the RSS feed articles to open and read any of the interesting articles.

Although Outlook provides you with many RSS feeds in its RSS Directory, you are not limited to subscribing to only these feeds. Many commercial websites provide you with RSS links that can be subscribed to in Outlook. Many websites will also have the RSS feed icon or link to help you to subscribe to the RSS feed link.

RSS feed icon

To subscribe to an RSS feed from a website, you have to copy the Web address (URL) of the RSS feed and paste it into the *New RSS Feed* dialog box. Follow the steps below to create a new RSS feed.

URL to RSS feed

STEP-BY-STEP

1. Go to the Web page of your choice, and locate the RSS feed icon or link. It may take some searching to find the RSS feed icon or link, and not all websites will have RSS feeds available.

2. Right-click on the **RSS icon,** and choose **Copy link address.** If the RSS link is provided as a URL, select and copy (**Ctrl+C**) the URL.

> **i MORE INFO**
>
> The RSS icon or URL will vary from site to site. If you copy and paste an incorrect URL, Outlook will let you know that it is not a valid RSS feed. You will need to go back to the Web page and find the correct RSS feed link or URL.

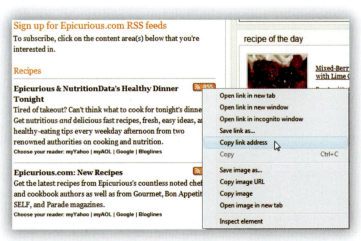

Copy link address for an RSS feed from a website

3. Go back to Outlook and right-click on the **RSS Feeds** folder in the *Navigation* pane.

4. Choose **Add a New RSS Feed.** The *New RSS Feed* dialog box will open.

SHORTCUT

To copy a URL, press **Ctrl+C.** To paste a URL, press **Ctrl+V.**

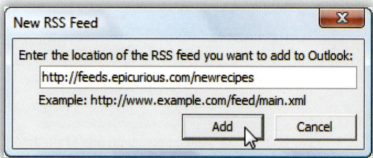

New RSS Feed dialog box

5. Click in the **Enter the location of the RSS feed you want to add to Outlook** box.

6. Press **Ctrl+V** to paste the URL.

7. Click **Add.** A dialog box will open asking you *Add this RSS Feed to Outlook?*

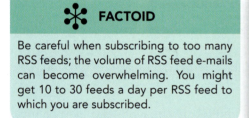

FACTOID

Be careful when subscribing to too many RSS feeds; the volume of RSS feed e-mails can become overwhelming. You might get 10 to 30 feeds a day per RSS feed to which you are subscribed.

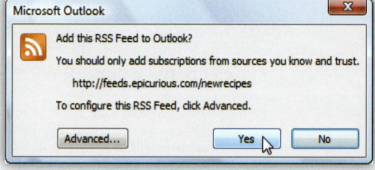

Add RSS feed confirmation dialog box

8. Click **Yes.** The RSS feed is subscribed to, and a new RSS feed folder is added to your *RSS Feeds* folder.

Managing RSS Feeds

After subscribing to RSS feeds, you will have a separate folder for each of your RSS feeds inside the *RSS Feeds* folder. Inside of each of these folders are the RSS feed e-mails.

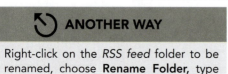

ANOTHER WAY

Right-click on the *RSS feed* folder to be renamed, choose **Rename Folder,** type the new name, and press **Enter.**

Outlook manages RSS feeds in the *Account Settings* dialog box. By opening the **Account Settings** dialog box and clicking on the **RSS Feeds** tab, you can see the RSS feeds to which you are subscribed. You can rename a feed, change the delivery location, and change how information in the feed is downloaded.

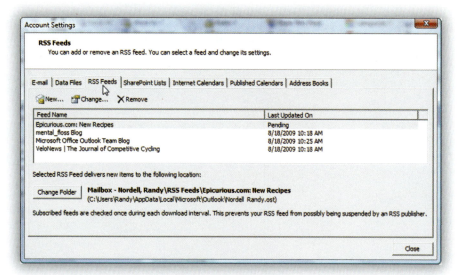

RSS feeds in the Account Settings dialog box

You can also rename the RSS feed folder in the Navigation pane.

STEP-BY-STEP

1. In the *Navigation* pane, click on the RSS feed folder to be renamed.
2. Click on the **Folder** tab at the top of the window.
3. Click on the **Rename Folder** button in the *Actions* group.
4. Type the new name for the RSS feed folder.
5. Press **Enter.** The folder will be renamed.

Sharing an RSS Feed

RSS feeds can easily be shared with other Outlook users. You might want to send them the URL of the RSS feed and have them add this link as a new RSS feed, but Outlook has provided a much easier way to share an RSS feed.

STEP-BY-STEP

1. Click on one of the RSS feed folders in the *Navigation* pane. All the RSS feed e-mails will be displayed in the *Folder* pane.
2. In the *Folder* pane, open one of the RSS feed e-mails.
3. Click on the **Share This Feed** button in the *RSS* group on the *RSS Article* ribbon. A new e-mail will open.

ANOTHER WAY

With an RSS feed e-mail selected in the *Folder* pane, click on the **Share This Feed** button in the *RSS* group on the *Home* ribbon.

Share RSS feed with other Outlook users

4. Click on the **To** button to select recipients and then press **Send.** This RSS feed e-mail will be sent to recipients, and they will be given the option to add this RSS feed to their Outlook.

E-mail sending an RSS feed to another Outlook user

When this feed is shared with other Outlook users, they will receive an e-mail in their *Inbox*. They can subscribe to this RSS feed by opening the e-mail and clicking on the **Add this RSS Feed** button in the upper left of the e-mail.

Add RSS feed from a shared feed

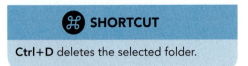

SHORTCUT

Ctrl+D deletes the selected folder.

Unsubscribing from an RSS Feed

There are a couple of different ways to unsubscribe from an RSS feed. If you want to unsubscribe from an RSS feed and remove the RSS feed folder and all the RSS feed e-mails, you can right-click on the RSS feed folder and choose **Delete Folder.** A dialog box will open asking if you want to delete the folder and all its contents.

You can also unsubscribe from an RSS feed using the *RSS Feeds* tab in the *Account Settings* dialog box.

STEP-BY-STEP

1. In the *Account Settings* dialog box, click on the **RSS Feeds** tab.
2. Select the RSS feed to be removed, and click on the **Remove** button.
3. Click **Yes** on the confirmation dialog box.

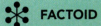 **FACTOID**

When unsubscribing from an RSS feed from the *Account Settings* dialog box, the RSS feed subscription is removed, but the RSS feed folder and previously received RSS feed e-mails are not deleted.

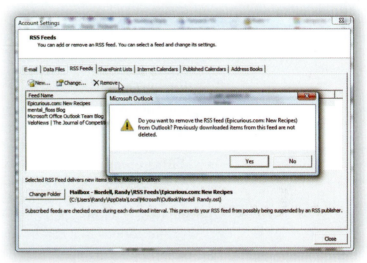

Unsubscribe from an RSS feed in the Account Settings dialog box

4. Click **Close** to close the *Account Settings* dialog box.

Chapter Highlights

▶ In Outlook 2010 you can set up multiple **Exchange, POP3, IMAP,** or **HTTP** e-mail accounts. Previous versions of Outlook only allowed one Exchange account.

▶ The **Auto Account Setup** in Outlook will set up your e-mail account if you provide your **e-mail address** and **password.**

▶ Outlook can troubleshoot e-mail setup problems and can usually detect the correct account settings to make your e-mail account work properly in Outlook. You can also manually configure your e-mail settings.

▶ The **Outlook Connector** is an Outlook add-in that can be used to configure free e-mail accounts such as Live and Hotmail.

▶ If you have multiple e-mail accounts, one of them will be set as your **default** account. New e-mail will by default be sent through this account.

▶ If you have an Exchange account, this will usually be your default account. You can change your default account.

▶ When you have multiple e-mail accounts set up in Outlook, a **From** button will appear above the **To** button on new e-mails, replies, and forwards.

▶ The **From** button can be used to choose which account to use to send an e-mail.

▶ Outlook will always display, to the right of the **From** button, the account through which you are sending an e-mail message.

▶ On **personal e-mail accounts,** you can specify the folder to which your e-mails will be delivered. By default, e-mails from personal accounts will be delivered to your **Inbox** in your **Personal Folders.**

▶ **Outlook Web Access** (OWA) is usually available if you have an **Exchange** e-mail account. OWA allows you to access your e-mail account from any computer with Internet access.

▶ You can use Outlook to send and receive **text messages.** Setting up a text message account is similar to setting up a new e-mail account. A third-party SMS service must be used to handle text messaging through Outlook.

▶ You can customize many e-mail settings in the **Outlook Options** dialog box. These are global settings that will influence e-mail throughout Outlook.

▶ **Mail Options** include **Compose messages, Outlook panes, Message arrival, Conversation Clean Up, Replies and forwards, Save messages, Send messages, MailTips, Tracking, Message format,** and **Other.** Within each of these sections, there are many customizations that can be made.

▶ **Desktop alerts** appear at the bottom right of your computer monitor when a new e-mail arrives.

▶ The **Out of Office Assistant** can automatically send a reply message to all messages you receive when you are out of your office or away from your computer.

▶ You can subscribe to **RSS** (really simple syndication) **feeds** in Outlook. Outlook can manage multiple RSS feeds for you.

▶ RSS feeds are e-mails that are sent to you from websites. These e-mails contain a summary of new articles or information on the website. There is usually a link to take you to the website to read the full article.

▶ RSS feeds can be shared with other Outlook users.

What Do You Know About Outlook?

True/False Questions

T F   1. Only one Exchange e-mail account can be set up in Outlook. [Objective 8.1]

T F   2. When you have multiple e-mail accounts and are sending an e-mail, the account through which the e-mail will be sent is always displayed. [Objective 8.1]

T F   3. Once turned on, the Out of Office Assistant will remain on until you turn it off. [Objective 8.3]

T F 4. RSS feeds are delivered to an RSS feed folder. [Objective 8.4]

T F 5. Outlook can set up your e-mail account automatically if you provide your name, e-mail address, and password. [Objective 8.1]

Multiple Choice Questions

1. When replying to a message, Outlook will do which of the following by default? [Objective 8.3]
   a. Only include your response in the body of the message.
   b. Include the original message below your response.
   c. Include the original message as an attachment.
   d. Change the original message to a different color.

2. A desktop alert will allow you to do which of the following? [Objective 8.3]
   a. Open the message.
   b. Delete the message.
   c. Flag the message.
   d. All the above.

3. What will occur when you use multiple e-mail accounts? [Objective 8.1]
   a. By default a new e-mail message will be sent through the default account.
   b. By default a reply will be sent through the account from which it was received.
   c. New e-mails can be sent through any of your accounts.
   d. All the above.

4. Which is *not* true of an RSS feed? [Objective 8.4]
   a. Most news websites have RSS feeds available.
   b. An RSS feed can be shared with other Outlook users.
   c. Clicking on an RSS feed icon or link on a website will subscribe you to the RSS feed.
   d. An RSS feed e-mail you receive in Outlook usually contains a link to take you to the full article on the website.

5. Which is true when using multiple e-mail accounts? [Objectives 8.1, 8.2]
   a. Rules and folders can be used to direct the delivery of e-mails.
   b. The default delivery folder cannot be changed.
   c. All e-mail will be delivered to your Inbox.
   d. All the above.

Short Answer Questions

1. Explain the default account used when there are multiple e-mail accounts. [Objective 8.2]

2. Describe RSS feeds and how they are handled in Outlook. [Objective 8.4]

3. Explain why it is important to have e-mails delivered to different folders when using multiple e-mail accounts in Outlook. [Objectives 8.1, 8.2]

Putting Outlook to Work

It's time to add an additional e-mail account to Outlook and use some of the advanced e-mail features. You will need to create a Gmail account (http://mail.google.com/mail/) to use for these exercises. Make sure you write down your new e-mail address and password; you'll need this to set up your Gmail account in Outlook. Before setting up your account in Outlook, you will also need to change the settings in your Gmail account to enable POP Download or IMAP Access (Settings, Forwarding and POP/IMAP). *(Note: If you already have a Gmail account that you regularly use, you will still want to create a new Gmail account to use for this class because you will be sending and receiving many e-mails to and from your classmates.)*

Before you begin these exercises, **delete the folders and rules you created in Chapter 7** (do not delete the *Clear categories on mail* rule).

Exercise 8.1 [Guided Practice]

Set up a Gmail account in Outlook. *Note: By default Outlook will set up your Gmail account as an IMAP account. Your professor can help you to set up this account as a POP3 account if desired.* **[Objective 8.1]**

1. Click on the **Mail** button in the *Navigation* pane.
2. Click on the **File** tab to open the *BackStage*.
3. Click the **Account Settings** button, and choose **Add Account.** The *Add New Account* dialog box will open.
4. Type your name in the **Your Name** field.
   a. Type your first and last name, capitalizing the first letter of each name.
5. Type your e-mail address in the **E-mail Address** field.
6. Type your password in the **Password** and **Retype Password** fields.
7. Click **Next.**
   a. Outlook will automatically set up your e-mail account using the information you provided.
   b. You will receive a message stating your account has been successfully set up.
   c. Notice the type of account set up by Outlook.
8. Click **Finish.**
   a. Notice your new e-mail account in the list of e-mail accounts.
   b. Your Gmail account should not be your default account.
   c. By default, you will have a separate set of folders for your Gmail account.

Exercise 8.2 [Guided Practice]

Create a new folder and set up a rule to move all e-mails received through your Gmail account to a different folder. [Objectives 8.1, 8.2]

1. Click on your **Inbox** in the *Navigation* pane.
   a. Use the *Inbox* in either your Exchange or Personal folders depending on your professor's preference.
2. Click on the **Folder** tab.

3. Click on the **New Folder** button in the *New* group.

4. Name the folder **Gmail.**

5. Open the **Rules and Alerts** dialog box.

6. Create a new rule to move all e-mails received through your Gmail account to the *Gmail* folder.

   a. Condition: E-mail received through **Gmail** account
   b. Action: move to **Gmail** folder
   c. Name of rule: **Gmail**

Exercise 8.3 [Guided Practice]

Manage e-mail tracking receipts through the use of folders and e-mail options. [Objectives 8.2, 8.3]

1. Click on your **Inbox** in the *Navigation* pane.

2. Right-click on your **Inbox,** and choose **New Folder.**

3. Name the folder **Receipts.**

4. Click on the **File** tab to open the *BackStage*.

5. Click on **Options.** The *Outlook Options* dialog box will open.

6. Click on **Mail Options.**

   a. The mail options will be displayed in the *Outlook Options* dialog box.

7. Scroll down to the *Tracking* section.

8. Check **After updating tracking information, move receipt to** and click on the **Browse** button. The *Select Folder* dialog box will open.

9. Choose the **Receipts** folder in your *Inbox*.

   a. You might have to click the arrow to the left of the *Inbox* to view all *Inbox* folders.

10. Click **OK** to close the *Select Folder* dialog box.

11. Click **OK** to close the *Outlook Options* dialog box.

Exercise 8.4 [Guided Practice]

Send and receive e-mails through your Gmail account and your default account. Reply to e-mails using your Gmail account. [Objectives 8.2, 8.3]

1. Click on your **Inbox** in the *Navigation* pane.

2. Click on the **New E-mail** button to create a new e-mail.

   a. Address the e-mail to all your classmates and your professor.
   b. Include a **read receipt** on this e-mail.
   c. Use *[your name]*'s **Gmail** as the subject.
   d. Include a brief message letting recipients know your new Gmail address.
   e. Include your **signature.**
   f. Click on the **From** button above the *To* button, and choose your **Gmail** account.

3. Click **Send.**

   a. You should begin receiving *[student's name]*'s **Gmail** e-mail messages in your *Inbox*.

4. Open one of the *[student's name]*'s **Gmail** e-mail messages from your *Inbox.*

   a. Send a **read receipt** as requested by the sender.

5. **Reply** to the message.

   a. Include a brief message in the body thanking them for sending their e-mail address.
   b. Include your signature.
   c. Click on the **From** button, and choose your **Gmail** account.

6. Click **Send.**

7. Repeat the preceding steps for each of the *[student's name]*'s **Gmail** e-mail messages from your *Inbox.*

   a. You will begin to receive e-mail messages in your *Gmail* folder.

Exercise 8.5 [Guided Practice]

Subscribe to an RSS feed. [Objectives 8.2, 8.4]

1. Click on the **RSS Feeds** folder in the *Navigation* pane.

   a. The *Outlook Syndicated Content (RSS) Directory* is displayed in the *Folder* pane.
   b. If this directory is not available, go to the www.blogs.office.com website.

2. Scroll down to the *Office Blogs* area, and click on **Outlook.**

   a. A dialog box will open asking you, *Add this RSS Feed to Outlook?*

3. Click **Yes.**

   a. A new RSS feed folder will be added to your *RSS Feeds* folder, and you will receive RSS feed e-mails in this folder.

4. Open one RSS feed e-mail.

5. To view the entire article, click on the **InfoBar** and choose **View in Browser,** or click on the **View article** link at the bottom of the information in the body of the message.

   a. An Internet browser window will open, and you will be taken to the website where the full article will be displayed.

6. Close the browser window, and the open RSS feed message.

7. Click on the new RSS feed folder.

8. Click on the **Folder** tab to display the *Folder* ribbon.

9. Click on the **Rename Folder** button in the *Actions* group.

10. Name the folder `Outlook blog`, and press **Enter.**

Exercise 8.6 [Independent Practice]

Create a new signature to be used with your Gmail account. Change desktop alert options, and turn on the Out of Office Assistant. [Objectives 8.1, 8.4]

1. Create a new signature, and name it `[your name]'s Gmail`.

2. Include your name and Gmail address.

3. For the **E-mail Account,** choose your **Gmail** account.

4. Set this signature as the **default** for new messages and replies and forwards.

5. Change the desktop alert setting so the **duration is 10 seconds** and the **transparency is 30%.**

6. Turn on the **Out of Office Assistant,** and set the date range from **today until 6 a.m. Monday.**

7. Create a message to those both inside and outside your organization informing them you will be out of town until Monday.

   a. This will be different if you are not using an Exchange account.

Exercise 8.7 [Independent Practice]

Edit a rule, and send an e-mail through your Gmail account.
[Objectives 8.1, 8.4]

1. Edit the **Gmail** rule to include an exception; except if from your professor.

2. Send an e-mail to your classmates and your professor using your **Gmail** account.

   a. Inform them that you will be out of town until Monday and use *[your name]*'s Vacation as the subject.
   b. Mark this e-mail as **high importance** and include a **read receipt.**
   c. Have this message **expire** on Monday at 6 a.m.

3. Send the message.

   a. Notice you will begin receiving *Out of Office* messages in your *Gmail* folder from your classmates.

4. Open and reply to at least five of the *[student's name]*'s Vacation e-mail messages using your **Gmail** account. Send a read receipt as requested by the sender.

Exercise 8.8 [Independent Practice]

Turn off the Out of Office Assistant. Subscribe to an RSS feed from a website, and share this feed. Subscribe to an RSS feed from a shared feed.
[Objectives 8.1–8.4]

1. Turn off the **Out of Office Assistant.**

2. Open your Internet browser, and find an RSS feed from a website you frequently visit. Remember, not all websites have RSS feeds. If you can't find any RSS feeds, you can either search for them in a search engine or subscribe to one of the CNN RSS feeds (www.cnn.com/services/rss/).

3. After subscribing to the RSS feed, **rename** the new RSS feed folder.

4. Open one of the new RSS feed e-mails, and share this feed with your classmates and professor.

   a. You should begin receiving these shared RSS feed e-mails from your classmates.

5. Browse these RSS feed e-mails, and subscribe to two or three of them.

Chapter 9
Advanced Contacts

OBJECTIVES *After completing this chapter, you will be able to:*

9.1 Integrate Outlook contacts with folders, categories, and activities.

9.2 Create and utilize electronic business cards.

9.3 Share contact information by importing to and exporting from Outlook.

9.4 Use Outlook Contacts with other Microsoft Office programs.

CHAPTER FLYOVER

- ▶ Changing the default address book
- ▶ Using folders
- ▶ Using categories
- ▶ Tracking contact activities
- ▶ Updating contacts
- ▶ Customizing contact options
- ▶ Sending electronic business cards

- ▶ Customizing your business card
- ▶ Importing contacts
- ▶ Exporting contacts
- ▶ Exporting and Importing an Outlook Data File
- ▶ Using contacts with other Microsoft Office programs
- ▶ Using contacts to create mailing labels

Making Outlook Work for You

Contacts are an essential part of Outlook and are used when e-mailing, assigning tasks, and creating meeting requests. The longer you use Outlook, the more you will find that your Contacts list will grow and that you are using this stored contact information on a regular basis. You will also realize how your stored contacts integrate with Outlook and other Microsoft Office 2010 programs.

As you become more familiar with the different features available in Outlook, you will want to customize how contacts appear, where they are stored, and how they are categorized. Outlook also provides you with the ability to share contacts with other users or between different programs. Importing and exporting contacts, and merging contacts with other programs can save you a huge amount of time.

 MORE INFO

Contacts were covered in Chapter 4.

Creating and using folders and categories were covered in Chapter 7.

Managing Contacts

As your list of contacts increases and you are using your contacts in Outlook on a more regular basis, you will want to customize your default address book, create folders in which to store contacts, and assign a category to a contact. Using folders and categories will help you to manage an ever-growing list of contacts, and tracking contacts' activities will make you more effective in your use of Outlook.

Changing the Default Address Book

When you create a new e-mail (or meeting or task request) and click on the **To** button, your default address book will open allowing you to select recipients. If you are using Outlook as a stand-alone program, by default this address book will be your *Contacts* folder.

When you are using Outlook in an Exchange environment, your default address book will be the *Global Address List.* If you work for a medium or large company, this list of contacts could number in the hundreds or thousands. Your most frequently used contacts should be saved in your Contacts folder.

You can easily change the default address book so your contacts appear first when selecting recipients. This does not mean that you will not have access to your Global Address List or other contact folders, but it will save you time and frustration by not having to search through different address books to find your recipients.

STEP-BY-STEP

1. Click on the **Contacts** button in the *Navigation* pane.
2. Click on the **Address Book** button in the *Find* group on the *Home* ribbon. The *Address Book* dialog box will open.

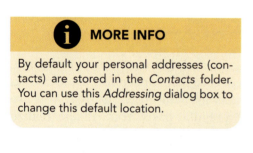

MORE INFO

By default your personal addresses (contacts) are stored in the *Contacts* folder. You can use this *Addressing* dialog box to change this default location.

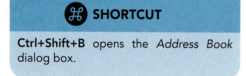

SHORTCUT

Ctrl+Shift+B opens the *Address Book* dialog box.

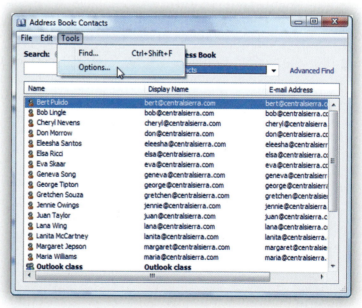

Address Book dialog box

3. Click on the **Tools** menu, and choose **Options.** The *Addressing* dialog box opens.

Addressing dialog box

4. In the *When opening the address book, show this address list first* field, choose the address book to be the default.

5. Click **OK.**

6. Close the *Address Book* dialog box.

Using Folders

Because I use my Outlook at both work and home and don't want all my contacts in the **Contacts** folder, I use folders to help organize my contact records. I use a separate folder for student contacts for each of my courses

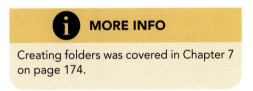

MORE INFO

Creating folders was covered in Chapter 7 on page 174.

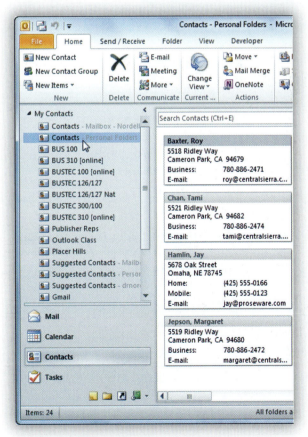

Contact folder in the Navigation pane
and contacts displayed in the Folder pane

and a separate folder for publisher representatives. By using folders, it helps to keep contacts organized and it's much easier to locate contact information. Creating a folder in Contacts is similar to creating an e-mail folder.

STEP-BY-STEP

1. Click on the **Contacts** button in the *Navigation* pane.
2. Click on the **Contacts** folder in the *My Contacts* area of the *Navigation* pane.
3. Click on the **Folder** tab.
4. Click on the **New Folder** button in the *New* group. A *Create New Folder* dialog box opens.

 **SHORTCUT**

Ctrl+Shift+E opens the *Create New Folder* dialog box. Be sure the *Contacts* folder is selected before using this shortcut.

 ANOTHER WAY

Right-click on the **Contacts** folder, and choose **New Folder.**

FACTOID

Contact folders displayed in the My Contacts area are not displayed in hierarchical format; although, by viewing your Folder List, you can see the hierarchy of folders.

Create New Folder dialog box

5. Type the name of the new folder. Confirm that **Contact Items** is selected in the *Folder contains* area and that the **Contacts** folder is selected in the *Select where to place the folder* area.
6. Click **OK.** The new folder will appear in the list of *Contacts* folders (*My Contacts*).

Once the new folder is created, you can drag and drop contacts from your Contacts folder or other contact folders to the new folder. When you click on any of the **Contacts** folders, the contents of the folder are displayed in the *Folder* pane.

ANOTHER WAY

You can assign a category to an open contact by clicking on the **Categorize** button in the *Tags* group on the *Contact* ribbon.

Using Categories

If you are working on a project and have a team of individuals with whom you're working, you might want to group these contacts together, but not necessarily move them to a different Contacts folder. Grouping these contacts by a category would be an effective use of categories to mark and group contact records. Contacts can be viewed ***By Category*** (one of the preset Contacts views).

To assign a contact to a category, you can either use an existing category or create a new category.

STEP-BY-STEP

1. Click on the **Contacts** button in the *Navigation* pane.
2. Click on **Contacts** in the *My Contacts* area.
3. Select the contacts to be categorized.

Categorize selected contacts

4. Click on the **Categorize** button in the *Tags* group on the *Home* ribbon, and select the desired **category.**
5. Click on **By Category** in the *Current View* section of the *Navigation* pane. Your contacts will be displayed in list format and grouped *By Category* in the *Folder* pane.

ℹ MORE INFO

Creating categories was covered in Chapter 7 on page 191.

A contact record can be assigned to more than one category. When viewed with By Category, this contact will appear in the list in each of the categories for which it is assigned.

Contacts viewed by category

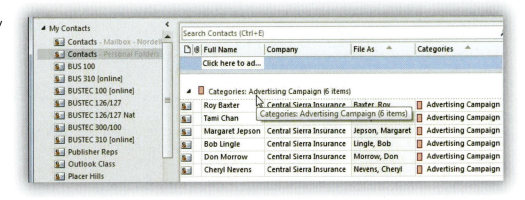

When a contact record is open and if it has been assigned to a category, the category will be displayed in the *InfoBar* of the contact record. To clear this category or add another category, you can right-click on the **InfoBar** for the different category option available.

Edit categories from the InfoBar

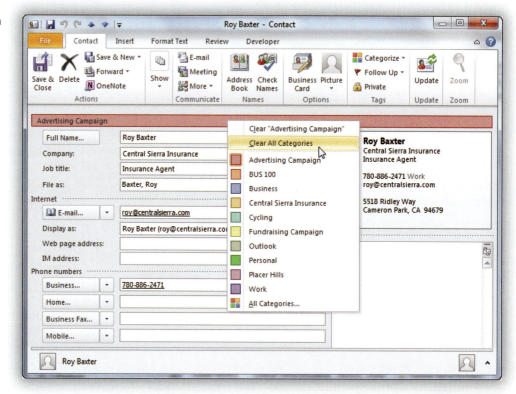

Tracking Contact Activities

As you have seen throughout this text, many of the Outlook items are inter-related: Such as, a contact might be associated with e-mails in your Inbox, a task in your To-Do List, or a calendar item.

Outlook provides a useful feature to track *Activities* for which a contact is associated. The **Activities** button on a contact record will display the Outlook items (e-mails, calendar items, contacts, tasks, and journals) related to a specific contact.

STEP-BY-STEP

1. Open the contact record.

2. Click on the **Activities** button in the *Show* group on the *Contact* ribbon. All the Outlook items for which this contact is associated will be displayed in the body of the contact record. You can open an item in the list by double-clicking on it.

Activities associated with a contact record

3. Click on the **General** button in the *Show* group to return to the contact record.

Updating Contacts

Outlook can automatically *update* information on your contact records using information from your company's global address list when using Outlook in conjunction with an Exchange server.

To update a contact, click on the **Update** button in the *Update* group on the *Contact* ribbon. Any changes made to the contact will be displayed in the Notes area of the contact record.

Update contact button

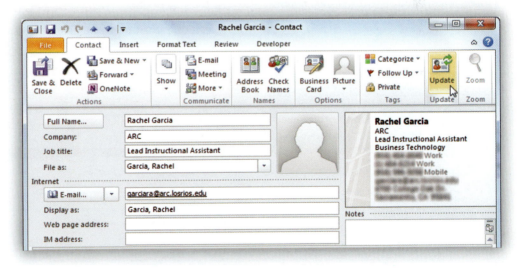

Customizing Contact Options

In Chapter 8, we went over how to customize many of the different options available for e-mails. Outlook also allows you to customize some of the options in Contacts.

The Contacts customization options are available by opening the **Outlook Options** dialog box (**File** tab, **Options**), and selecting the **Contacts** button at the left.

You can customize the order you want Outlook to use for new names and the setting for how Outlook saves new contacts.

Contact options in the Outlook Options dialog box

FACTOID

Contact linking is a very important and useful feature in Outlook. You should turn this feature on if it is not on already.

Contact *linking* enables Outlook to link contacts to other items such as e-mails, calendar items, tasks, journals, and other contacts. When the **Linking** button is checked, a *Contacts* field will appear on other Outlook items. This will allow you to select a contact to be associated with these items.

SHORTCUT

Ctrl+Shift+V opens the *Move Items* dialog box.

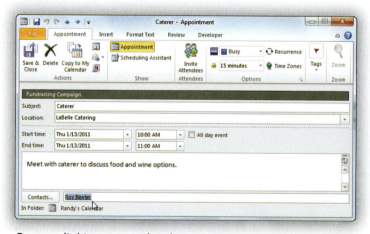

Contact linking on a calendar appointment

Outlook created contacts is new to Outlook 2010. If this option is turned on, Outlook will automatically generate a list of ***Suggested Contacts*** who do not appear in any of your Contacts folders. Outlook creates a *Suggested Contacts* folder for each set of mail folders you have in Outlook. These suggested contacts can be moved to another *Contacts* folder by either using the **Move** button or dragging and dropping to a new folder.

Suggested Contacts folders in the Navigation pane

✳ FACTOID

In Outlook, the terms *business card* and *electronic business card* are used synonymously. Contact records can be sent as business cards, and since they are in electronic format, they are in essence electronic business cards.

Business Cards

Have you ever been asked to send your contact information to someone via e-mail? This is a very common request, and many times can be done by inserting an existing signature containing this information. But, if you are sending this information to other Outlook users, they will still have to type this information into a new contact record, which is a waste of time.

Outlook allows you to send a contact record (or more than one) as an attachment to an e-mail. You can also add an electronic business card to a signature or customize your business card.

Sending Electronic Business Cards

Sending electronic business cards in an e-mail is a similar process to attaching a file to an e-mail. The difference is you will be attaching an Outlook item rather than a different type of file such as a Word document or picture.

STEP-BY-STEP

1. Open a new e-mail.
2. Select recipients, include a subject, and type a brief message.

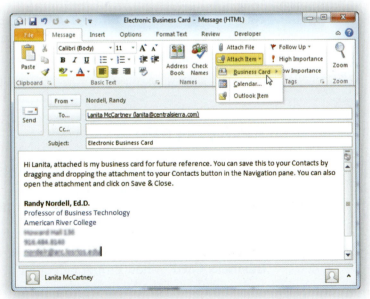

Attach business card to an e-mail message

3. Click on the **Attach Item** button in the *Include* group on the *Message* ribbon, choose **Business Card,** and then choose **Other Business Cards.** The *Insert Business Card* dialog box will open. The **Insert Business Card** button is also in the *Include* group on the *Insert* ribbon.

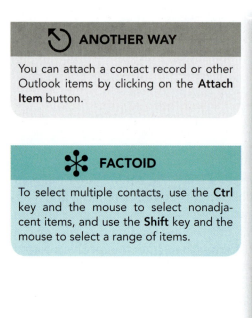

ANOTHER WAY

You can attach a contact record or other Outlook items by clicking on the **Attach Item** button.

FACTOID

To select multiple contacts, use the **Ctrl** key and the mouse to select nonadjacent items, and use the **Shift** key and the mouse to select a range of items.

Insert Business Card dialog box

4. Select the **Contacts** folder in the *Look in* area.
5. Select the contacts to be attached.
6. Click **OK** to close the *Insert Business Card* dialog box. The selected contacts will be attached to the e-mail, and a graphic of the business card will be inserted in the body of the message.
7. Press the **Send** button to send the e-mail.

You can also send a contact as a business card from the Contacts area.

STEP-BY-STEP

1. Click on the **Contacts** button in the *Navigation* pane.
2. Select the **Contacts** folder in *My Contacts.* The contact records will be displayed in the *Folder* pane.
3. Select the contacts to whom you want to send a business card.
4. Right-click on the contact, choose **Forward Contact,** and select **As a Business Card.** A new e-mail will open with the business card attached and a graphic of the business card in the body of the message.

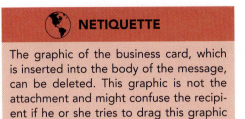

NETIQUETTE

The graphic of the business card, which is inserted into the body of the message, can be deleted. This graphic is not the attachment and might confuse the recipient if he or she tries to drag this graphic to the Contacts button.

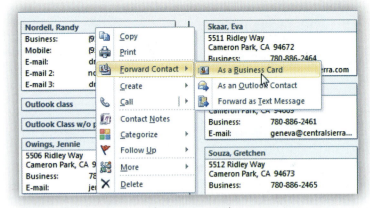

Forward a contact as a business card

5. Select recipients, include a subject, and type a brief message.

E-mail with business card attached

6. Click **Send.**

Include Your Business Card in Your Signature

Another way to include your business card in an e-mail message is to attach it to your signature. You can set up multiple signatures in Outlook, and you might want to create a signature that includes your business card. This will save you from having to manually attach or forward a business card.

When you insert a signature that has a business card attached, the business card will automatically be included as an attachment to the e-mail.

STEP-BY-STEP

1. Open the **Signatures and Stationery** dialog box (**File** tab, **Options, Mail, Signatures** button).
2. Click on **New.** A *New Signature* dialog box opens.
3. Type the name of the signature, and press **OK.**
4. Type the information to be included in the signature in the *Edit signature* area.

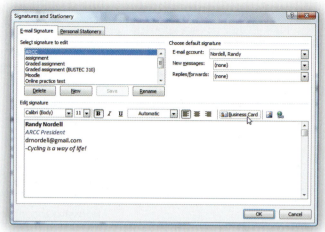

Signatures and Stationery dialog box

5. Click on the **Business Card** button. The *Insert Business Card* dialog box will open.

6. Select the contact to be included as a business card.

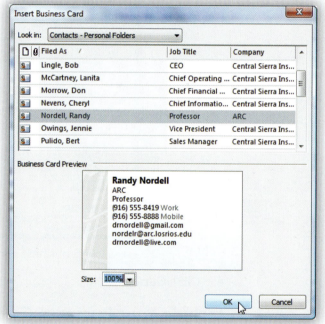

Insert Business Card dialog box

7. Press **OK**. The business card graphic will be included with your signature.

8. Click **Save** to save your signature.

9. Click **OK** to close the *Signatures and Stationery* dialog box.

10. Click **OK** to close the *Outlook Options* dialog box.

When you insert this signature into an e-mail, the signature and graphic of the business card will be inserted into the body of the e-mail. The graphic of the business card can be deleted without removing the attachment.

Customizing Your Business Card

When you create a contact record, a business card is automatically generated. Outlook provides much flexibility in customizing the layout, colors, styles, and information of a business card.

Business Card button
on a contact record

To edit a business card, click on the **Business Card** button in the *Options* group on the *Contact* ribbon. The Edit Business Card dialog box opens, and you can customize a business card to meet your needs.

Edit Business Card dialog box

A graphic of the business card is displayed in the upper left of this dialog box. The changes made to the business card will be made to this graphic so you can see what your business card looks like with the changes made.

In the *Card Design* area, you can change the layout of the card, background color, image, image area, and image alignment.

In the *Fields* area, you can add or remove the fields included on the business card. In the *Edit* area, you can change the font size, style, alignment, and color. A label for each field can be included or omitted.

There are also many ***online templates*** you can use to customize your business card. A business card template controls the layout, graphics, colors, fonts, styles, and fields included. You can do an Internet search to find these templates. Microsoft's website has these templates available.

Once a template has been selected and downloaded, you can customize it in the same manner as customizing a business card as just described.

Online e-mail business card templates

STEP-BY-STEP

1. Open an Internet browser window and go to www.office.microsoft.com. Search the templates for e-mail business cards.

2. Select the business card template of your choice, and follow the steps to download it. The template will be saved in a temporary location until it is edited and saved in your *Contacts* folder.

3. Enter your contact information. The card will, by default, be filled in with example information.

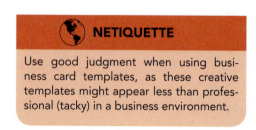

NETIQUETTE

Use good judgment when using business card templates, as these creative templates might appear less than professional (tacky) in a business environment.

Custom business card using an online template

4. You can click on the **Business Card** button in the *Options* group to further edit the business card.

5. Click **Save & Close.**

Importing and Exporting

MORE INFO

Remember a *Field* is one piece of information about a contact such as First Name, Last Name, Phone, or E-mail. A *Record* (contact record) is a group of related fields. It is important to make this distinction when working with database information.

By now you have created new contacts in Outlook. There are many ways to do this: from scratch, from a received e-mail, from a contact from the same company, and from a contact record sent to you as a business card. What if you had to enter 30, 50, 100, or 1000 new contacts from a database or spreadsheet? This would take a huge amount of time.

Outlook provides *Import* and *Export* features that enable you to both import and export records without spending a good portion of a day manually creating them in Outlook. Outlook can import and export many different types of file formats such as Access, Excel, comma-separated values, and tab-separated values. One of the great advantages of using Outlook for this process is that you do not need any knowledge of these different types of files or the programs with which they are associated to be able to import and export.

Importing and Exporting is one of the more complex tasks in Outlook, but Outlook walks you through this process with a step-by-step wizard. After going through the importing and exporting process a couple of times, you'll be amazed at the time that will be saved by using this feature.

Importing Contacts

The following is an overview of the steps you will take to import contact records. If you are importing from a different type of file, these steps will still work.

- Create a Contacts folder in which to import the records.
- Choose the process—Import.
- Choose the type of file to import.
- Choose the file to import.
- Choose the location to which to save the imported records.
- Map fields—this is the process to make sure that the fields from the contacts being imported are mapped (matched) with the fields in the Outlook contact record.
- Import.

The following steps walk you through the process of importing contact records from a Microsoft Access database file (Placer Hills Real Estate).

STEP-BY-STEP

Create new contacts folder

1. Click on the **Contacts** button in the *Navigation* pane.
2. Create a new *Contacts* folder in which to save the new contacts. Name this folder **Placer Hills.**
3. Click on the **File** tab to open the *BackStage.*

4. Click on **Open,** and choose **Import.** The *Import and Export Wizard* dialog box will open.

Import button on the BackStage

5. Click on **Import from another program or file.**

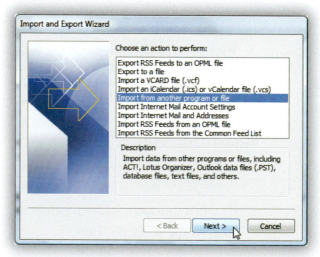

Import and Export dialog box—choose action to perform

6. Click **Next.** The *Import a File* dialog box will open.
7. Click on **Microsoft Access** as the type of file to import from.

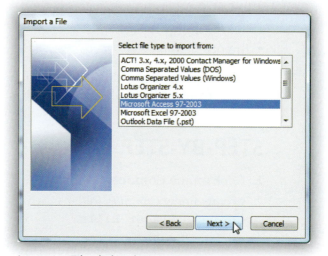

Import a File dialog box

8. Click **Next.** The next *Import a File* dialog box will open.

9. Click on the **Browse** button to locate the file on your computer to import. Note: You will be importing the Placer Hills Real Estate database when you complete Exercise 9.4 at the end of this chapter.

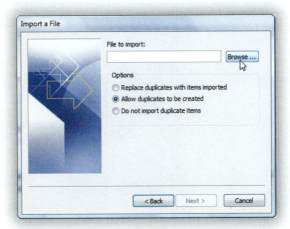

Click on the Browse button to select the file
to import

10. Select the file to import, and press **OK.**

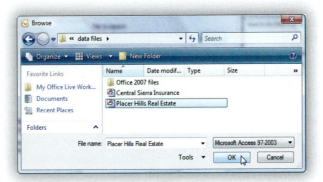

Select file to import from the Browse dialog box

11. The path to the file appears in the *File to import* box.

12. The *Options* area gives you choices about what action Outlook should perform if duplicate contact records are detected. Because you are importing into a new folder with no contact records, these options are irrelevant.

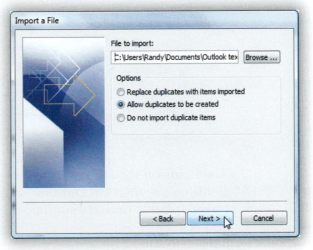

Import file selected and import options

13. Click **Next.** The next *Import a File* dialog box will open.

14. Choose **Placer Hills** as the *destination folder;* the folder into which the new contact records will be imported.

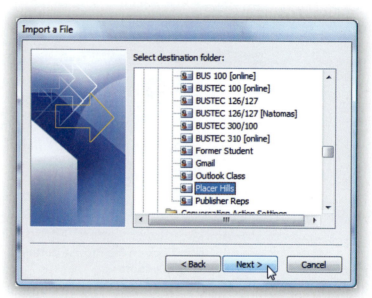

Select a destination folder for the import

15. Click **Next.**

16. Click on the **Map Custom Fields** button. The *Map Custom Fields* dialog box opens. The fields from the Access database (Placer Hills Real Estate) are listed on the left, and the fields available in the Outlook contact record are listed on the right.

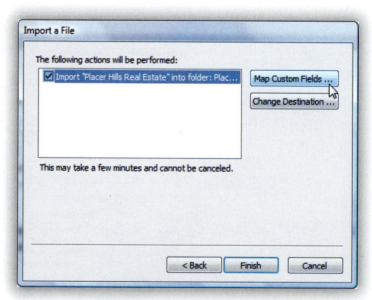

Map Custom Fields button

17. The fields on the *left* (from Access) need to be mapped to the fields on the *right* (to Outlook contact record). Outlook makes a guess at fields that are similar; this does not ensure that they are correct.

18. Click on the **Clear Map** button. This clears the *Mapped from* fields on the right.

19. Drag each field from the left (Access) to the corresponding field on the right (Outlook contact). *Don't drag a field from the left to a field on the right with a plus by it (e.g., Name).* Open (click on the plus) this field category to see the individual fields. Use the following table to map fields.

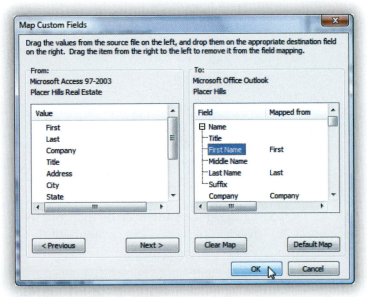

Map Custom Fields dialog box

From Access	To Outlook Contact
First	First Name
Last	Last Name
Company	Company
Title	Job Title
Address	Business Street
City	Business City
State	Business State
Zip	Business Postal
E-mail	E-mail Address
Phone	Business Phone

20. Once you have mapped each of the fields, click the **Next** button to see the first Access record displayed at both the left and right. The actual field contents will be displayed next to their corresponding Outlook contact fields.

21. Click **OK** when you have confirmed that all the fields are mapped correctly.

22. Click **Finish** to import the records from Access to Outlook.

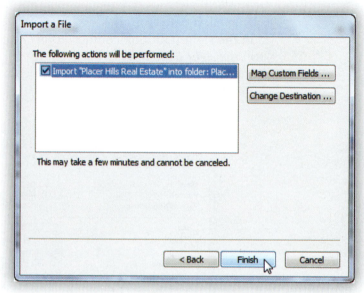

Finish the import

23. Click on the **Placer Hills** folder in the *My Contacts* area of the *Navigation* pane. The contents of this folder will be displayed in the *Folder* pane.

 **MORE INFO**

Usually if a mistake is made, it is in mapping fields. If you find a mistake, it is usually quicker to delete the contact records from the contact folder and redo the import.

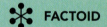 **FACTOID**

If you use an online e-mail account such as Gmail, Yahoo Mail, or Windows Live Mail, you can import or export contacts. The comma separated value (CSV) file format can be used for importing and exporting in Outlook as well as most online e-mail accounts.

Imported records displayed in the Folder pane

Congratulations on your first import! Once you go through this process a couple of times, you'll be able to perform an import in about the time it would take to type in one contact record.

Exporting Contacts

Exporting is a similar process to importing, but it is a little easier. Rather than mapping the fields, you just have to drag over the fields from the contact that you want included in the export. Not all of the Outlook contact fields will be exported because many of the fields in a contact record are blank.

In the steps that follow, you will be exporting the contents of a contact folder (Placer Hills) to a Microsoft Excel file.

STEP-BY-STEP

1. Click on the **Placer Hills** folder in the *My Contacts* area in the *Navigation* pane.
2. Click on the **File** tab, and click on the **Options** button. The *Outlook Options* dialog box will open.

Export button on the BackStage

3. Click on the **Advanced** button.
4. Click on the **Export** button. The *Import and Export Wizard* will open.
5. Click on **Export to a file.**

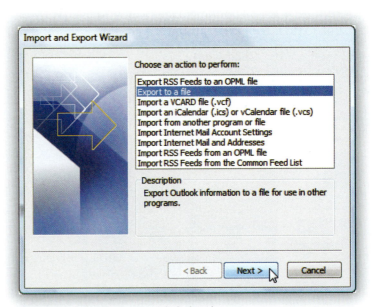

Import and Export Wizard dialog box

6. Click on **Next.** The *Export to File* dialog box opens.

7. Choose **Microsoft Excel** as the type of file to create.

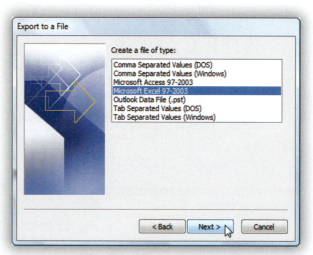

Export to a File dialog box

8. Click **Next.**

9. Select the **Placer Hills** folder as the contact folder from which to export.

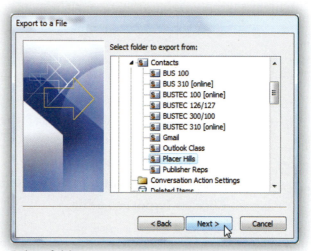

Select folder to export

10. Click **Next.**

11. Click on **Browse.** The *Browse* dialog box will open.

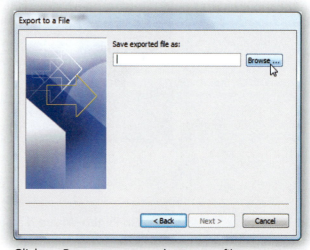

Click on Browse to name the export file

12. Select the location on your computer where you want to save the export file.

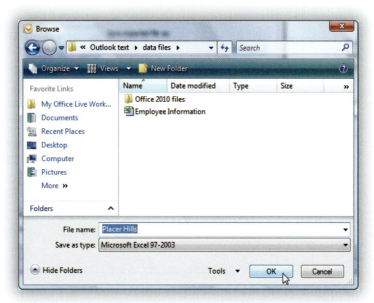

Select save location and name export file in the Browse dialog box

13. In the *File name* box, type **Placer Hills** as the name of the file. Confirm that you are saving as a **Microsoft Excel** file in the *Save as type* box.

14. Click **OK,** and then click **Next.**

15. Click the **Map Custom Fields** button. The *Map Custom Fields* dialog box opens.

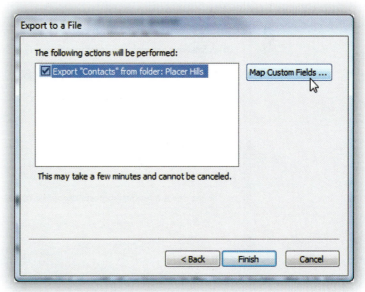

Map Custom Fields button

16. The fields from the Outlook contact are listed on the left, and the fields to be exported to Excel are listed on the right. You don't want all the fields to be exported because you will have many blank fields in the exported spreadsheet if you do.

17. Click **Clear Map.** This clears the fields to be exported.

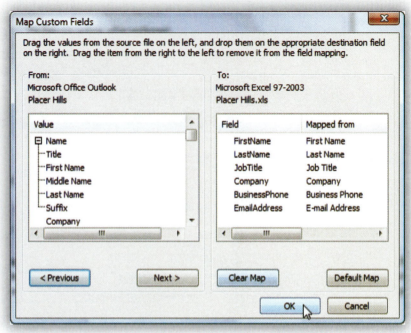

Map Custom Fields dialog box

18. Drag the following fields from the *left* side (Outlook contact) to the *right* side (Excel export): **First Name, Last Name, Job Title, Company, Business Phone, E-mail Address.**

19. Click **OK** to close the *Map Custom Fields* dialog box.

20. Click **Finish.** The Excel file is now created with the exported contacts.

Finish export

21. Open the **Placer Hills** Excel file to confirm that the records were exported correctly.

FACTOID

An Excel file can be saved as a comma separated value (CSV) or tab delimited file. Both of these types of files can be used for importing and exporting from various programs.

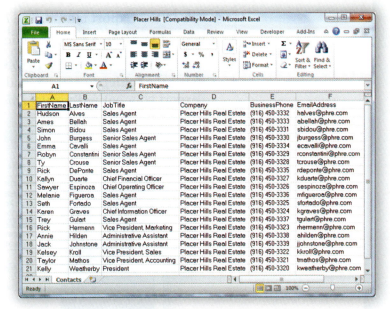

Contact records exported to an Excel file

This exported file can now be sent to others as an attachment, and they can use this file to import these contact records into Outlook or use it with other programs.

Exporting and Importing an Outlook Data File

I enjoy getting a new computer, but I always dread the amount of time it is going to take me to set up all the software and copy all the files. If you're like me, you might wonder how you are going to get all your information from Outlook on your existing computer to the new computer.

FACTOID

If you are using Outlook in a stand-alone environment, it is a good idea to occasionally back up (export) your Outlook Data File and save this file in a location other than your computer.

If you're working in an Exchange environment, all this information is stored on the Exchange server, so setting up Outlook and retrieving all your information is done when you set up your Exchange account in Outlook on the new computer. But what if you are getting a new home computer and want to transfer all your existing Outlook information to the new computer? Or, what if your computer crashes?

Outlook has provided you with a way to transfer and backup your files with ease. Outlook stores all your information in an ***Outlook Data File,*** which is a ***.pst*** file. This file resides on your computer and contains all your Outlook information.

If you are changing from one computer to another, Outlook helps you to export your Outlook Data File and save it as a file. Then this file, which contains all your Outlook information, can be imported into Outlook on the new computer.

This process is similar to the importing and exporting process described previously, but does not take as long. The following is a summary of the Outlook Data File export process.

STEP-BY-STEP

1. Click on the **File** tab, and click on the **Options** button. The *Outlook Options* dialog box will open.

2. Click on the **Advanced** button.

Using Contacts with Other Office 2010 Programs

An advantage of using Microsoft Office products is the ability to share information between programs. You can easily use your Outlook Contacts to create mailing labels, envelopes, and business letters. Contacts can also be used in conjunction with Excel and Access without having to recreate all this stored information.

Using Contacts to Create Mailing Labels in Word

Outlook 2010 has streamlined the process of using information in your contact records in a *Mail Merge.* Outlook works in conjunction with Microsoft Word to create labels, envelopes, or form letters. You can use all the contacts in a folder, or you can choose the contacts to be included in the merge. You don't have to be an expert in Word to create mailing labels; you can use the Mail Merge feature, which will walk you through this process.

The following example will walk you through the process of creating mailing labels from all the contacts you imported into the Placer Hills contacts folder.

STEP-BY-STEP

1. In the *Navigation* pane, select the contacts folder to be used in the merge.

2. Click on the **Mail Merge** button in the *Actions* group on the *Home* ribbon. The *Mail Merge Contacts* dialog box will open.

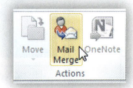

Mail Merge button

3. In the *Mail Merge Contacts* dialog box, select **All contacts in current view** and select the *Document file* to be a **New document.**

4. In the *Merge options* section, select **Mailing Labels** and merge to **New Document.**

Mail Merge Contacts dialog box

5. Click **OK.** Microsoft Word will open, and a dialog box will open informing you to set up your mailing labels.

6. Click **OK.** The *Mail Merge Helper* dialog box will open.

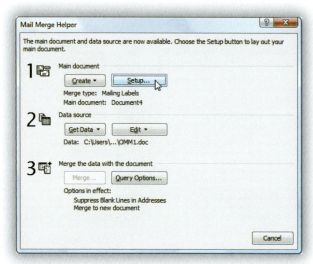

Mail Merge Helper dialog box

7. Click on **Setup.** The *Label Options* dialog box will open.

8. Select your **label brand and type** (Avery 5160 is a standard label type), and press **OK.**

Label Options dialog box

Mail Merge Wizard
dialog box

9. Close the **Mail Merge Helper** dialog box.

10. On the open Word document, click on the **Mailings** tab.

11. Click on the **Start Mail Merge** button, and choose **Step by Step Mail Merge Wizard.** The *Mail Merge wizard* opens to the right of the document.

12. You will be on *Step 3 of 6;* click **Next.**

13. *Step 4 of 6:* Click on the **Address Block** link. The *Insert Address Block* dialog box opens.

14. Select how you want your address block to appear, and click **OK.**

15. Click the **Update all labels** button, and click **Next.**

16. *Step 5 of 6:* Your labels will appear in the document. Click **Next.**

17. Select the entire document (**Ctrl+A**), and change the paragraph spacing to **0 pt. before** and **after,** and change the line spacing to **Single.**

18. *Step 6 of 6:* You can either select **Print** or **Edit individual labels.**

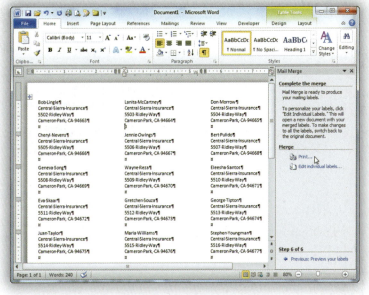

ANOTHER WAY

Using Mail Merge can be done directly from Word. The *Mail Merge Wizard* in Word will walk you through the mail merge process. Outlook contacts can be selected as a data source.

Outlook contacts merged into labels in Word

Chapter Highlights

▶ The address book can be changed so that **Contacts,** rather than the Global Address List, is the **default address book.**

▶ **Folders** can be created to group and store contacts.

▶ Contacts can be assigned to a **category.** Contacts can be viewed **by category.**

▶ Outlook tracks **activities** associated with a contact record and can display these associated activities in the body of a contact record.

▶ The **Update** button can be used to automatically update contact information to match your company's address list.

▶ You can customize **filing options** in the Contact Options dialog box. You can also enable **Contact Linking,** which allows you to link contacts to other Outlook items.

▶ A contact record can be sent to others via e-mail as an **electronic business card.** You can attach your electronic business card to your signature.

▶ You can **customize** the design, color, image, and fields included in your electronic business card.

▶ There are also custom **online business card templates** that can be used to create an electronic business card.

▶ Outlook can **import** contact record information from many different file formats such as Microsoft Access, Microsoft Excel, comma-separated values, and tab-separated values.

▶ Outlook can also **export** contact records to many different file formats. These exported contact records can then be used with other software programs and shared with others.

▶ The **Outlook Data File** (a **.pst** file) contains all your Outlook information when using Outlook in a stand-alone environment. A backup of your Outlook Data File can be made by exporting this file.

▶ You can import your Outlook Data File to a new computer.

▶ Outlook can integrate with other Microsoft Office programs. You can create mailing labels, envelopes, or form letters in Microsoft Word using contacts from Outlook.

What Do You Know About Outlook?

True/False Questions

T F 1. When an electronic business card is attached to a signature, the business card is automatically attached to the e-mail when the signature is inserted. [Objective 9.2]

T F 2. Information in Outlook can be used in other Microsoft Office programs such as Word, Excel, and Access. [Objective 9.4]

T F 3. An Outlook Contacts folder can contain contacts, categories, e-mails, and tasks. [Objective 9.1]

T F 4. Electronic business card templates can be downloaded from the Internet and customized with your contact information. [Objective 9.2]

T F 5. Mailing labels can be created in Microsoft Word from Outlook contact records only after the contact records have been exported to another type of file such as Access or Excel. [Objective 9.4]

Multiple Choice Questions

1. Which is true when exporting contacts from Outlook? [Objective 9.3]
   a. Clear the export map, and include only those fields to be exported.
   b. Outlook can export to Access, Excel, and comma-separated value formats.
   c. Any of the Contacts folders can be exported.
   d. All the above.

2. To attach a contact record to an e-mail message, click on which button? [Objective 9.2]
   a. Attach File
   b. Insert File
   c. Address Book
   d. Attach Item

3. Which is true when using categories with contacts? [Objective 9.1]
   a. When a contact record is assigned to a category, the category is displayed in the InfoBar.
   b. Only existing categories can be used.
   c. The By Category view displays contact records as business cards.
   d. All the above.

4. When importing contacts from another file, you must do which of the following? [Objective 9.3]
   a. Import into a folder other than Contacts.
   b. Specify the type of file to be imported.
   c. Replace existing contacts.
   d. Allow duplicates to be created.

5. When using Outlook in an Exchange environment, what is your default address book? [Objective 9.1]
   a. Contacts
   b. Global Address List
   c. The most recent Contacts folder created
   d. None of the above

Short Answer Questions

1. What is the purpose of the Outlook Data File in Outlook? Explain how this file can be used to set up Outlook on a new computer. [Objective 9.3]

2. Describe how to track contact activities and how this feature can be useful in Outlook. [Objective 9.1]

3. Explain why mapping fields is important when importing contact records into Outlook. [Objective 9.3]

Putting Outlook to Work

In these exercises you will be organizing and using some of the advanced Contacts features in Outlook. You will be importing and exporting contacts to and from Outlook. In Chapter 8, you set up a Gmail account in your Outlook. You will be using this Gmail account for some of these exercises.

Exercise 9.1 [Guided Practice]

Create a new Gmail folder for contacts, and create a new contact record containing your Gmail account information. [Objectives 9.1, 9.2]

1. Click on the **Contacts** button in the *Navigation* pane.
2. Click on the **Contacts** folder in the *My Contacts* list of contacts folders.
3. Click on the **Folder** tab and then on the **New Folder** button in the *New* group. The *Create New Folder* dialog box will open.
   a. Confirm that the folder will be created in the **Contacts** folder and the folder contains **Contact Items.**
4. Type `Gmail` as the name of the folder, and press **OK.**
   a. The *Gmail* folder will appear below your *Contacts* folder.
5. Click on the **Gmail** folder in the *My Contacts* list.
6. Click on the **New** button to create a new contact. A new blank contact record will open.
7. Create a new contact record using your information. Fill in the following contact information.
   a. **Full Name**
   b. **Company** (use your school)

c. **Title** (type **Student**)
d. **E-mail** (your Gmail e-mail address)
e. Notice the *Display as* field will automatically be filled in when you press **Tab** after filling in your e-mail address.

8. Click **Save & Close.**

a. Notice your new contact record will be saved in your *Gmail* folder. If it was saved in the *Contacts* folder or a different folder, drag your new contact record to the *Gmail* folder.

Exercise 9.2 [Guided Practice]

Create a new signature with your business card attached to it. Send an e-mail to your classmates with your new signature and business card attached. [Objectives 9.1, 9.2]

1. Click on the **Mail** button in the *Navigation* pane.
2. Open the **Signatures and Stationery** dialog box.
3. Click **New,** and name the new signature **Gmail with business card.**
4. Type your **name, college,** and **Gmail address** in the body of the signature. Change formatting as desired.

a. Press **Enter** after the last line of your signature.

5. Click on the **Business Card** button. The *Insert Business Card* dialog box will open.
6. In the *Look in* area, choose the **Gmail** folder.
7. Select your contact record, and press **OK.**

a. Your contact record will be inserted below your signature.

8. In the *Choose default signature* area, choose your **Gmail** account.
9. Set both new messages and replies/forwards default settings to **None.**
10. Click on the **Save** button to save your signature.
11. Click **OK** to close the *Signatures and Stationery* dialog box.
12. Create a new e-mail.

a. Address it to all your classmates and your professor.
b. Use **[*your name*]'s Gmail contact record** as the subject.
c. Insert your **Gmail with business card** signature into the body of the e-mail.
d. Your business card should be inserted as an attachment.
e. **Delete** the business card graphic in the body of the e-mail message.

13. **Send** this e-mail through your class e-mail account (or other account as directed by your professor).

Exercise 9.3 [Guided Practice]

Save business cards in your Gmail folder. [Objectives 9.1, 9.2]

1. Click on the **Mail** button in the *Navigation* pane.
2. Click on your **Inbox** folder.

a. You should begin receiving *[student's name]'s* Gmail contact record e-mails in your *Inbox*.

3. Open one of the received *[student's name]'s* Gmail contact record e-mails.

9. Type **Placer Hills export** as the **File name,** and click **OK.**

10. Click **Next.**

11. Click on the **Map Custom Fields** button. The *Map Custom Fields* dialog box will open.

    a. The fields from the Placer Hills Outlook contacts are listed at the left, and the Microsoft Excel export fields are listed at the right.

12. Click on the **Clear Map** button.

    a. This clears all the fields on the right side.

13. Drag the following fields from the left side (Outlook contact) to the right side (Excel export).

    a. **First Name, Last Name, Job Title, Company, Business Phone, E-mail Address.**

14. Click **OK** to close the *Map Custom Fields* dialog box.

15. Click **Finish.** The Excel file is created with the exported contacts and saved to your desktop.

16. Minimize Outlook and open the **Placer Hills export** Excel file from your desktop to confirm that the records were exported correctly.

17. Close the open Excel file.

Exercise 9.6 [Independent Practice]

Categorize contact records, and view contacts by category. Create a new contact group, and send an e-mail to a contact group. View activities for a contact record. [Objectives 9.1, 9.2]

1. Select all the contacts in the *Gmail* contacts folder.

   a. Hint: Use **Ctrl+A** to select all contacts.

2. Assign all the selected contacts to the **Outlook** category.

3. Click on the **By Category** button in the *Current View* group on the *Home* ribbon to view contacts by category.

4. Create a new contact group.

5. Name the contact group **Gmail Contacts,** and add your classmates and professor as members.

   a. Be sure you are adding their Gmail contact records.

6. Save and close the **Gmail Contacts** contact group.

7. Create a new e-mail, and use the **Gmail Contacts** contact group as the recipient.

8. Use **Importing Contacts** as the subject, and briefly describe the importing process in the body of the message.

9. **Send** through your Gmail account.

   a. You should begin receiving these e-mails in your *Gmail* folder if your Gmail rule from Chapter 8 is still turned on.

10. Open one of your Gmail contacts, and click on the **Activities** button to view Outlook items related to this contact. Close the contact when finished.

Exercise 9.7 [Independent Practice]

Import contacts from a Microsoft Access database, and assign a category to contacts. For this exercise you will be importing from the Central Sierra Insurance database, which is located in your student data files for this text. It would be best to save this file to your desktop. [Objectives 9.1, 9.3, 9.4]

1. Create a new contacts folder, and name it `Central Sierra Insurance.`

2. Import the **Central Sierra Insurance** database to your **Central Sierra Insurance** contacts folder.

   a. This file is included with your student data files for this text.
   b. Be sure to click on the **Clear Map** button before mapping the fields from the database to the contact records.

3. View the imported contacts in Outlook to confirm that the contacts were imported correctly.

4. Assign all contacts in both the **Central Sierra Insurance** and **Placer Hills** folders to the **Work** category.

Exercise 9.8 [Independent Practice]

Export Outlook contacts to a comma-separated values file, and send this file as an attachment. [Objectives 9.3, 9.4]

1. Export your **Gmail** contacts as a **comma-separated values (Windows)** file.

2. Save the exported file to your desktop, and name it `Gmail export.`

3. Include the following fields in the export: **First Name, Last Name, Company, Job Title,** and **E-mail Address.**

   a. Be sure to click on the **Clear Map** button before selecting the fields to be exported.

4. After the export is completed, open the **Gmail export** file from your desktop.

   a. This file will most likely open in Microsoft Excel.

5. Create a new e-mail, and use your **Gmail contacts** contact group as the recipient.

6. Use `Gmail Export` as the subject, and briefly describe the exporting process in the body of the message.

7. Attach the **Gmail export** file from your desktop.

8. Include a read receipt and have the message expire at 6 a.m. next Monday.

9. Include a **For Your Information** flag for recipients. Do not include a reminder date.

10. **Send** the message.

Chapter 10
Advanced Calendars

OBJECTIVES   *After completing this chapter, you will be able to:*

10.1 Create and use multiple Outlook calendars.

10.2 Customize your Outlook calendar using calendar options.

10.3 Incorporate printing and sharing with your Outlook calendar.

10.4 Utilize advanced calendar features.

CHAPTER FLYOVER

▸ Create a new calendar

▸ View multiple calendars

▸ Work time options

▸ Calendar options

▸ Display options

▸ Time zones

▸ Scheduling Assistant

▸ Resource scheduling

▸ Print an Outlook calendar

▸ Forwarding a calendar item

▸ Share a calendar

▸ Send a calendar via e-mail

▸ Publish a calendar

▸ Viewing shared calendars

▸ Use categories with calendar items

▸ Attaching items to a calendar item

▸ Private calendar items

▸ Create a recurring meeting

▸ Use the Scheduling Assistant

▸ AutoPick meeting times

Making Outlook Work for You

Hopefully, after learning about the Outlook calendar earlier in this text, you have been using your Outlook calendar to create appointments, events, and meeting requests. You might have found the Outlook calendar to be such a useful tool that you are no longer using your paper calendar.

Now that you are comfortable using an electronic calendar to help organize your daily life, you are ready to incorporate some of the additional Outlook calendar features. In this chapter, you will learn how to create and use multiple calendars, incorporate advanced calendar features, customize the default calendar options, and print and share calendars.

Using Multiple Calendars

Up to this point, you probably have been keeping all your calendar items on the default Outlook calendar. But, what if you wanted to keep all your personal calendar items on one calendar and all your business-related calendar items on a separate calendar? Or, you might be involved in a professional organization, club, or charity organization and would like to have a separate calendar for each of these activities.

Outlook provides you with the option of having multiple calendars, which can help keep you organized by having a separate calendar for different personal and business areas of your life.

Create New Calendar

Creating a new calendar is similar to creating a new Inbox or Contacts folder. When you create a new calendar, it will appear in the *My Calendars* list in the *Navigation* pane.

STEP-BY-STEP

1. Click on the **Calendar** button in the *Navigation* pane.

2. Click on **Calendar** in the *My Calendars* list in the *Navigation* pane.

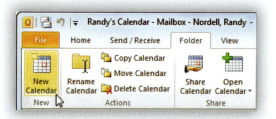

New Calendar button on the Folder ribbon

3. Click on the **Folder** tab and then on the **New Calendar** button in the *New* group. The *Create New Folder* dialog box will open.

4. Type the **Name** of the new calendar. Confirm that the folder contains **Calendar Items,** and the new calendar will be placed in the **Calendar** folder.

5. Click **OK.** The new calendar will be created and will appear in your *My Calendars* area in the *Navigation* pane.

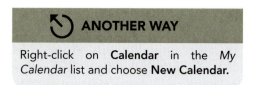

ANOTHER WAY

Right-click on **Calendar** in the *My Calendar* list and choose **New Calendar.**

Create New Folder dialog box

Ctrl+D deletes the selected calendar.

You can delete a calendar by selecting the calendar and clicking on the **Delete Calendar** button in the *Actions* group on the *Folder* ribbon. The default Outlook calendar cannot be deleted.

View Multiple Calendars

By default, your main calendar (Calendar) will be displayed in the Folder pane. The check box to the left of the calendars listed in the My Calendars area indicates which calendars will be displayed in the Folder pane.

An additional or different calendar can be displayed in the *Folder* pane by checking the box to the left of the calendar name in the *My Calendars* area in the *Navigation* pane.

When multiple calendars are displayed in the Folder pane, they can be viewed in **side-by-side mode** or in **overlay mode.** When calendars are viewed in side-by-side mode, the items on each of the calendars are smaller and more difficult to read. The overlay mode allows you to easily switch between calendars in the Folder pane. Each calendar will appear in a different color.

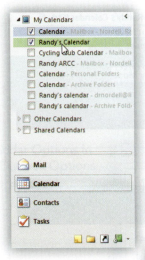

My Calendars in the Navigation pane

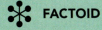

Calendars displayed in Overlay mode

FACTOID

At least one calendar must be selected at all times; Outlook will not allow you to deselect all the calendars in the list of calendars.

The tab at the top of each calendar displays the name of the calendar. When you are in overlay mode, click on a tab to display the selected calendar on top of the other calendar.

times and the default response when proposing a new time for a meeting. When you set up a meeting request, attendees will have the option to propose a new time for the meeting. If you do not want this option to be available, you can deselect this option in the *Calendar Options* dialog box.

Free/Busy Options are used in conjunction with an Exchange server to allow the meeting organizer to see free and busy time on your calendar. There are different types of calendars used throughout the world. Outlook will allow you to set up an alternate calendar. Also, by default when you send a meeting request outside of your organization, Outlook uses an ***iCalendar*** format, which enables other e-mail users to view the meeting information.

Outlook can automatically add ***holidays*** to your Outlook calendar, and you can choose the country or countries from which to add holidays.

STEP-BY-STEP

1. Click on the **File** tab, and choose **Options.** The *Outlook Options* dialog box will open.

2. Click on the **Calendar** button. The *Calendar Options* dialog box will open.

3. Click on the **Add Holidays** button. The *Add Holidays to Calendar* dialog box will open.

FACTOID

Most countries have a lot of holidays. Be careful not to add too many countries' holidays, so as not to clutter up your calendar.

Add Holidays to Calendar dialog box

4. Select the country or countries of your choice.

5. Click **OK.** The holidays will be added to your calendar.

6. Click **OK** to close the *Calendar Options* dialog box.

7. Click **OK** to close the *Outlook Options* dialog box.

Display Options

The color of the default Outlook calendar can be changed. When you view multiple calendars in the Folder pane, Outlook will automatically select a different color for each calendar displayed in the Folder pane. You have the option of making all the displayed calendars the same color by checking the **Use this color on all calendars** box. It is probably best to have each calendar be a different color to help you distinguish between calendar items.

Display options area of Calendar Options

By default, a ***Click to add prompt*** appears when you put your mouse pointer over a blank area on your calendar (this is true in any of the calendar views). This default setting can be changed so that this prompt does not appear.

Week numbers (1–52) can be added so they will be displayed in Month view and in the *Date Navigator*. By default, Outlook does not display week numbers.

Schedule view is new to Outlook 2010. Schedule view displays a single calendar or multiple calendars in the timeline view to assist you in scheduling appointments and meetings. The last three check boxes allow you to control how calendars and free appointments are viewed when using Schedule view. By default, free appointments are not displayed in Schedule view.

Time Zones

What if you regularly do business with a company or individual from a different time zone? Outlook will allow you to change the time zone on your calendar or add an additional time zone to your calendar. If you add an

Time zones area of Calendar Options

additional time zone to your calendar, both time zones will be displayed when you view your calendar in Day or Week view. You can also add labels to each of the time zones, which will be displayed on the calendar in Day and Week views.

Multiple time zones displayed in Day view

Time zones

Scheduling Assistant

The **Scheduling Assistant** can be used when creating meetings, appointments, or events on your calendar. It displays your calendar in timeline view in the body of a new calendar item to assist you in selecting a day and time for the calendar item. By default calendar details are displayed in both ScreenTips and the scheduling grid.

Scheduling assistant and Resource scheduling areas of Calendar Options

MORE INFO

Sharing calendars will be covered later in this chapter.

Resource Scheduling

When shared calendars are being used in conjunction with an Exchange server, resources such as rooms can be viewed to determine availability when scheduling meetings, events, or appointments.

Resource Scheduling dialog box

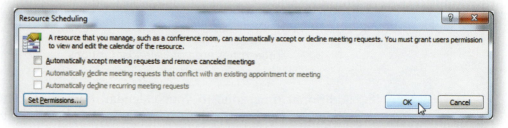

MORE INFO

Recurring meeting requests will be covered later in this chapter.

Outlook also gives you the option of automatically accepting meeting requests and removing cancelled meetings. You can also change the default settings to control how Outlook handles meeting requests that conflict with other calendar items and how Outlook handles recurring meeting requests.

Printing and Sharing an Outlook Calendar

It's great being able to keep all your appointments and events on your calendar, but there might be times when you need a hard copy of your calendar or you want to share your calendar with others. Outlook provides you with a variety of ways to both print and share your Outlook calendar.

Print an Outlook Calendar

There are times when you might be away from your computer, but you would like to have your calendar available. Outlook will allow you to print your calendar in various formats. You can print your calendar in the following styles:

- Daily Style
- Weekly Style
- Monthly Style
- Tri-fold Style
- Calendar Details Style

STEP-BY-STEP

1. Click on the **File** tab to open the *BackStage*.
2. Click on the **Print** button to display the print options on the *BackStage*.

Print settings and options on the BackStage

3. Select the style of calendar to print in the *Settings* area. A preview of the selected calendar style will be displayed to the right.

4. Click on the **Print Options** button to open the *Print* dialog box. The *Print* dialog box will allow you to specify the style of calendar and the date range to print.

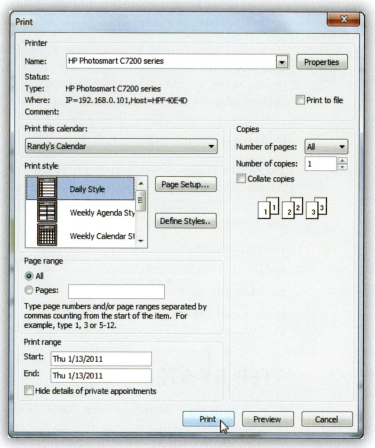

Print dialog box

5. Click on **Print** to print the calendar.

Forwarding an Appointment

When you create and send a meeting request, the meeting is automatically placed on the recipient's Outlook calendar. There might be times when a meeting request is not needed or not appropriate but you still want to send a calendar item to another Outlook user. You can easily forward a calendar item as an attachment to an e-mail to other Outlook users.

STEP-BY-STEP

1. Open an item on your calendar.

2. Click on the **Forward** button in the *Actions* group on the *Appointment* (or *Event*) ribbon. A new e-mail will open with the calendar item as an attachment.

Forward a calendar appointment as an attachment

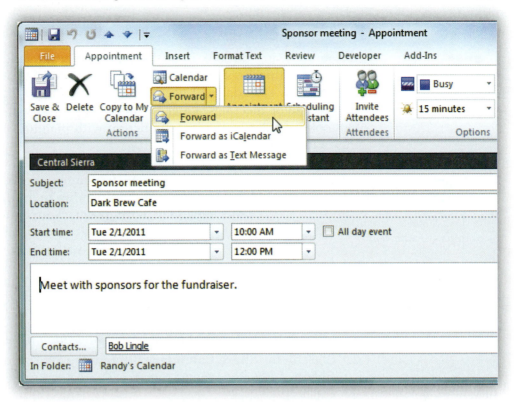

3. Select the recipients, and include any necessary information in the body.
4. **Send.**

ANOTHER WAY

You can also right-click on a calendar item and choose **Forward.** A new e-mail will open with the calendar item attached.

⌘ SHORTCUT

Ctrl+F will forward a calendar item when the item is selected on your calendar.

🌎 NETIQUETTE

If you are sending a calendar item to recipients who are not using Outlook, it is probably best to forward it as an iCalendar so they can view the details of the calendar item.

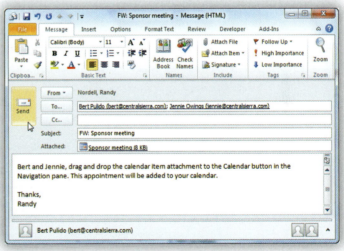

Calendar item attached to an e-mail

When a calendar item is received as an attachment to an e-mail, it can be added to the recipient's calendar by dragging and dropping the attachment on the **Calendar** button in the *Navigation* pane, or opening the attached calendar item and clicking on **Save & Close.** The calendar item will automatically be placed on the correct date on the calendar.

Share a Calendar

If you are using Outlook in an Exchange environment, you can share your calendar with others on the same Exchange server. This will enable them to view your calendar and use it to facilitate scheduling of events, appointments, and/or meetings. Later in this chapter you will see how sharing an Outlook calendar works in conjunction with planning a meeting and Auto-Pick a meeting time.

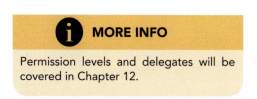

MORE INFO

Permission levels and delegates will be covered in Chapter 12.

When you share your calendar with other Outlook users on the same Exchange server, an e-mail will be sent to those users informing them that you have shared your calendar with them. You can request that they share their calendar with you also. Those with whom you share your calendar will only have Reviewer (read-only) permission when viewing your calendar.

STEP-BY-STEP

Share Calendar button

1. Click on the **Calendar** button in the *Navigation* pane.
2. Click on the **Share Calendar** button in the *Share* group on the *Home* ribbon. A Sharing request e-mail will open.
3. Select recipients.
4. Check **Request permission to view recipient's Calendar** to gain access to your recipients' calendars.
5. Make sure **Allow recipient to view your Calendar** is checked.
6. Add any necessary information in the body.

Sharing Request e-mail to share a calendar with others

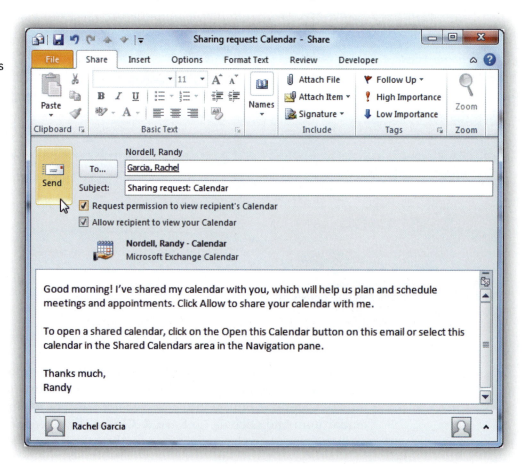

7. Click **Send.** A dialog box will open asking you to confirm that you want to share your calendar.

8. Click **Yes** to send the sharing request e-mail.

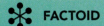
FACTOID

By default, Outlook will share your main calendar. You can share other calendars you have created by right-clicking on the calendar, choosing **Sharing,** and selecting **Share Calendar.**

Confirm Sharing Request

When your calendar has been shared with others, they will receive an e-mail message informing them they now have access to your calendar. The **Allow** button will share the recipient's calendar with the sender (as requested). The **Open this Calendar** button will open the sender's calendar. Shared calendars will appear in the *Shared Calendars* area in the *Navigation* pane.

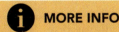
MORE INFO

The **Calendar Permissions** button in the *Share* group on the *Home* ribbon will provide you with a summary of those with whom you have shared your calendar.

FACTOID

If you try to share your Outlook calendar with a recipient who is not on your Exchange system, a dialog box will open informing you of this and giving you the option of sending the calendar through e-mail.

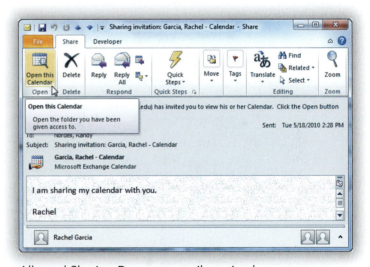

Allowed Sharing Request e-mail received

Send a Calendar via E-mail

What if you want to send your calendar to someone outside your Exchange environment or to someone who does not even use Outlook? Outlook will allow you to send a calendar via e-mail. You can specify the calendar to send, the date range to send, the details to be included, and the layout of the e-mail.

This feature creates a type of ***Internet calendar*** to be attached to the e-mail and a ***Calendar Snapshot,*** which displays the calendar information in the body of the e-mail. Recipients can view your calendar in the body of the e-mail they receive. If they are Outlook users, they will be able to open your calendar from the attached Internet calendar.

STEP-BY-STEP

1. Click on the **E-mail Calendar** button in the *Share* group on the *Home* ribbon. The *Send a Calendar via E-mail* dialog box will open.

E-mail Calendar button

2. Choose the **Calendar** to send.

3. Choose a **Date Range.** Your options are: **Today, Tomorrow, Next 7 days, Next 30 days, Whole calendar,** and **Specify dates.**

4. Choose a **Detail.** Calendar details to be included in the e-mail are: **Availability only, Limited details,** and **Full details.**

5. Click on the **Show** button in the *Advanced* area to display other detail options.

6. Your options are **Include details of items marked private** and **Include attachments with calendar item.**

7. Choose an **E-mail Layout.** Your options are **Daily schedule** or **List of events.**

8. Click **OK** to close the *Send a Calendar via E-mail* dialog box.

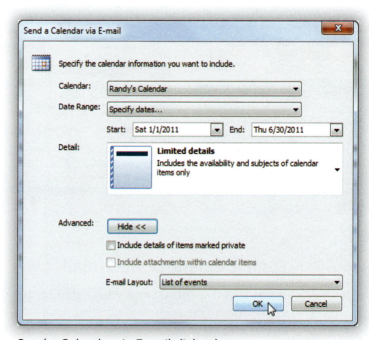

Send a Calendar via E-mail dialog box

9. Click **Send.**

Recipients will receive an e-mail with your Internet calendar attached and the Calendar Snapshot in the body of the message. The Internet calendar can be opened from the attachment.

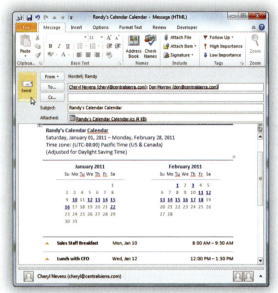

E-mail with Internet Calendar attached and
Calendar Snaphot in the body

Publish a Calendar

Suppose you belong to a cycling club and keep a separate Outlook calendar
for all the club rides, events, and activities. If this calendar is updated regularly, you don't want to have to send out a new Internet Calendar through
e-mail each time there is an update. A much more effective method would be
to publish your calendar online.

An Outlook calendar can be published on the *Microsoft Office Online
Calendar Sharing Service.* This service allows you to publish your calendar
and then invite others to subscribe to and view your calendar. A published
calendar will be synchronized on a regular basis so that those viewing
the calendar will be seeing current calendar information. To publish your
Outlook calendar, you must have a *Windows Live ID account.*

STEP-BY-STEP

1. Select the calendar to be published in the *My Calendars* list in the
   Navigation pane.

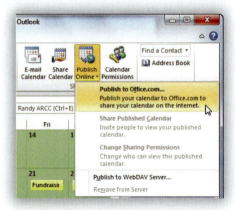

Publish Calendar button

2. Click on the **Publish Online** button in the *Share* group on the *Home*
   ribbon, and choose **Publish to Office.com.** The *Publish Calendar to
   Office.com* dialog box will open.

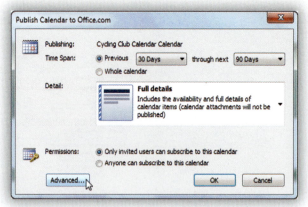

Publish Calendar to Microsoft Office Online
dialog box

3. Select the **Time Span** to publish.

4. Select the **Details** to publish. Your options are **Availability only, Limited details,** and **Full details.**

5. Select the **Permissions** setting. You can allow anyone to subscribe to the published calendar or allow only invited users.

6. Click on the **Advanced** button. The *Published Calendar Settings* dialog box will open.

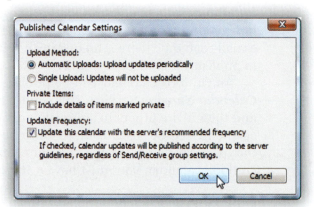

Publish Calendar Settings dialog box

7. Choose settings for **Update Method, Private Items,** and **Update Frequency.**

8. Click **OK** to close the *Published Calendar Settings* dialog box.

9. Click **OK.** The *Windows Security* dialog box will open.

Sign into Windows Live ID

10. You will be prompted to sign in to your *Windows Live ID* account. If you already have an account, you can sign in, or if not, you will be prompted to sign up for a *Windows Live ID.*

11. Provide your **Windows Live ID username** and **password.**

12. Click **OK.** Outlook will publish your calendar to Microsoft Office Online.

13. The *Send a Sharing Invitation* dialog box will open.

Send a Sharing Invitation dialog box

14. Click **Yes** to create an e-mail sharing invitation. A sharing invitation e-mail will open.

15. Select recipients, and include any details in the body of the message.

16. Click **Send.**

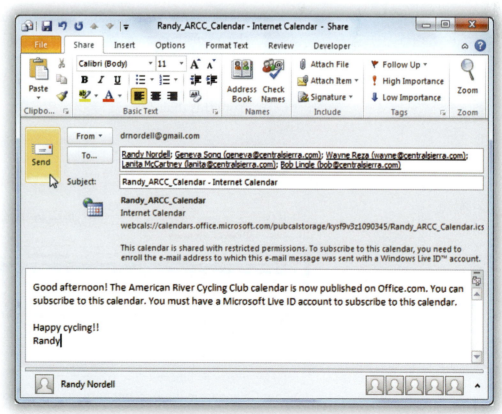

E-mail message with published calendar information

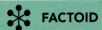
Recipients will receive an e-mail message informing them of the availability of this online calendar. They will be given the option to **Subscribe to this Calendar.**

If a recipient chooses **Subscribe to this Calendar,** the calendar will be available in the *Other Calendars* list in the *Navigation* pane. Outlook will periodically check online for updates to this calendar and synchronize it with the published calendar.

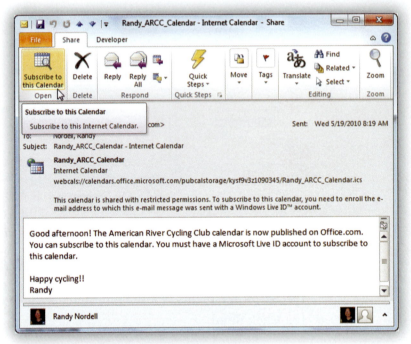

Subscribe to published Internet Calendar

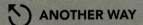
In addition to being listed in the *Other Calendars* area in the *Navigation* pane, all the Internet calendars to which you are subscribed will be listed in the *Account Setting* dialog box under the *Internet Calendars* tab. You can delete a subscription to an Internet Calendar by deleting the calendar from this dialog box.

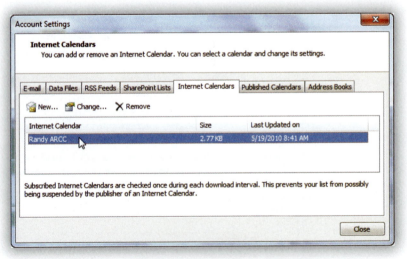

Internet Calendars in the Account Settings dialog box

Other Calendars in
the Navigation pane

Viewing Shared Calendars

When others have shared their Outlook calendar with you, these calendars will appear in the *Shared Calendars* area in the *Navigation* pane. When you have subscribed to Internet calendars, these calendars will appear in the *Other Calendars* area of the *Navigation* pane.

To view a shared calendar or one you have subscribed to, check the box to the left of the calendar name. The calendar will be displayed in the *Folder* pane. When you deselect the calendar check box, the calendar will no longer be displayed in the *Folder* pane.

To remove any of the calendars from the *Shared Calendars* list, right-click on the calendar and choose **Delete Calendar.** This will remove the calendar from the *Shared Calendars* list, but it will not remove your permission to view this calendar. Only the owner of the calendar can change the permission settings.

To open a calendar (shared or subscribed to) that does not appear in one of the calendar lists, click on the **Open Calendar** button in the *Manage Calendars* group on the *Home* ribbon and select the type of calendar to open.

Open Shared Calendar

Advanced Calendar Features

Outlook provides you with many advanced calendar features to help you organize your calendar items and schedule meetings. Calendar items can be assigned to a category. Files and other Outlook items, such as an e-mail or contact, can be attached to a calendar item. Calendar items can be marked as private so others with whom your calendar is shared cannot see the details of an event or appointment. Outlook can also work in conjunction with shared calendars to assist you in scheduling meetings.

Using Categories

Just as with e-mails, contacts, and tasks, *categories* can be used to group calendar items. A category can be assigned to a calendar item by selecting the calendar item, clicking on the **Categorize** button in the *Tags* group, and selecting the category. Also, with a calendar item open, you can assign it to a category by clicking on the **Categorize** button in the *Tags* group on the *Event* or *Appointment* ribbon.

STEP-BY-STEP

1. Click on the **File** tab to open the *BackStage*.
2. Click on the **Print** button.
3. Click on the **Print Options** button. The *Print* dialog box will open.
4. Check the **Hide details of private appointments** check box in the *Print Range* area.

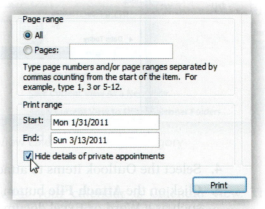

Hide details of calendar item when printing

MORE INFO

Creating recurring appointments and events was covered in Chapter 5 on page 121.

Creating meeting requests was covered in Chapter 5 on page 122.

Recurring Meetings

If you have a weekly brainstorming meeting, you can create a meeting request that recurs on a scheduled interval. Creating a recurring meeting request is similar to creating a recurring appointment or event. This recurring meeting will appear on your calendar for each date and time in which it is to recur.

STEP-BY-STEP

1. Create a new appointment.
2. Enter **Subject, Location, Start time,** and **End time.**
3. Click on **Invite Attendees** in the *Attendees* group.
4. Click on the **To** button, select attendees, and click **OK.**
5. Click on the **Recurrence** button in the *Options* group. The *Appointment Recurrence* dialog box will open.
6. Confirm the appointment start and end times and duration.

Recurrence button in the Options group

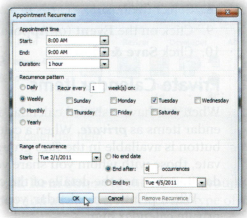

Appointment Recurrence dialog box

7. Set a **Recurrence pattern.**
8. Set the **Range of recurrence.**

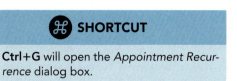

SHORTCUT

Ctrl+G will open the *Appointment Recurrence* dialog box.

9. Click **OK** to close the *Appointment Recurrence* dialog box.
10. Click **Send.**

When a recipient accepts a meeting request, the recurring meeting request will be saved on his or her calendar.

Using the Scheduling Assistant

When creating an appointment or meeting request, you will sometimes have to check your calendar for other calendar items on that date. Rather than having to switch between Outlook windows, you can use the **Scheduling Assistant** to show you existing appointments, events, or meetings currently on your calendar.

Scheduling Assistant information displayed in the body of the appointment

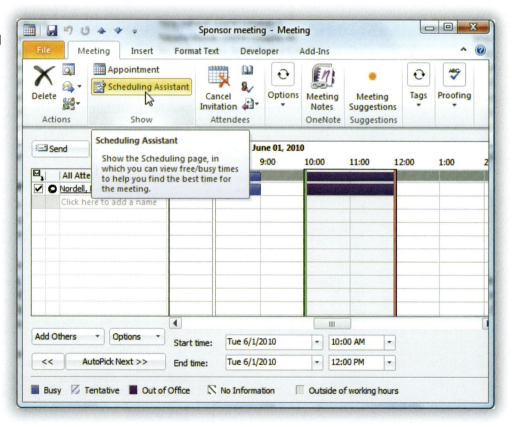

MORE INFO

The Scheduling Assistant is available when using Outlook in both an Exchange and stand-alone environment. But, displaying others' calendars is only available when using Outlook on an Exchange server.

To use the Scheduling Assistant, click on the **Scheduling Assistant** button in the *Show* group. The Scheduling Assistant will display your calendar items in timeline format in the body section of the new appointment. You can adjust the date and/or time of the appointment based on your other calendar items.

The Scheduling Assistant can be particularly helpful when you are creating a meeting request. Attendees will appear in the list at the left of the body. If the Attendees have shared their calendar with you, their appointments and events will be displayed in timeline format below your calendar items, which will facilitate selecting a meeting date and time.

AutoPick Meeting Times

There are times when a scheduled meeting needs to be changed. If you have already sent out a meeting request and others have responded to it, you can make changes to the meeting request and send an update to attendees.

Outlook has an *AutoPick* feature that can automatically pick a new time for the meeting based upon the shared calendars of others. To use this feature, you must be working on an Exchange server and the attendees must also be on the same Exchange server. Clicking on the **AutoPick Next** button will pick the next time available for those to whom the meeting request was sent.

STEP-BY-STEP

1. From your calendar, open the meeting to be rescheduled.
2. Click on the **Scheduling Assistant** button in the *Show* group. The list of attendees will appear at the left, and if attendees have shared their calendar with you, they will appear in timeline view in the body of the meeting request.

AutoPick Next button in the Scheduling Assistant

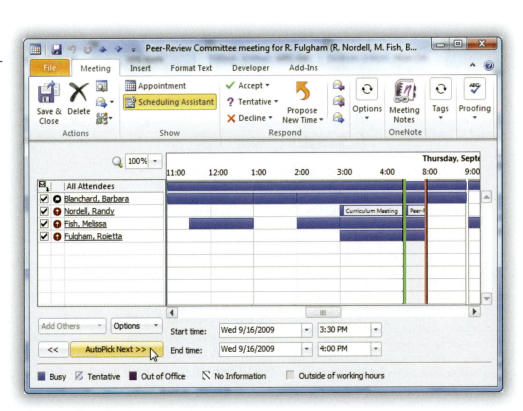

3. Click on the **AutoPick Next** button to choose the next available time for attendees. The left-pointing arrows to the left of the *AutoPick Next* button allow you to pick an earlier time available for attendees.

4. The **Options** button will allow you to choose between a few options regarding the displayed calendars and *AutoPick* options.

5. Click on the **Appointment** button to return to the meeting request.

6. Click on **Send Update.** An update will be sent to all the recipients of the original meeting request.

Chapter Highlights

▶ Additional calendars can be added in Outlook. All your calendars will be displayed in the **My Calendars** area of the Navigation pane.

▶ The calendars selected in the My Calendars area will display in the Folder pane. **Multiple calendars** can be viewed at the same time in the Folder pane.

▶ When you are viewing multiple calendars in the Folder pane, they can be viewed in **side-by-side mode** or **overlay mode.**

▶ When viewing in overlay mode, the items on the nondisplayed calendar will appear on the displayed calendar.

▶ The **default reminder** setting for appointments can be changed in the **Options** dialog box.

▶ The **Calendar Options** dialog box gives you the option of customizing your work week and time.

▶ You can change the **color** of your calendar. When you are viewing multiple calendars, each calendar will, by default, be displayed in a different color.

▶ Outlook can automatically add **holidays** to your calendar, and you can change or add a **time zone** to your calendar.

▶ A calendar can be printed in **Daily, Weekly, Monthly, Tri-Fold,** and **Calendar Details** styles. The calendar can be printed for a specific **date range.**

▶ A calendar item can be **forwarded** as an attachment to an e-mail message. Others receiving this forwarded calendar item can save it on their Outlook calendar.

▶ When your are using Outlook in an Exchange environment, your calendar can be **shared** with and viewed by others. Recipients of a shared calendar will receive an e-mail informing them of the shared calendar.

▶ Calendars that have been shared with you will appear in the **Shared Calendars** area of the Navigation pane.

▶ To share your calendar with others who are not on your Exchange system or those who are not using Outlook, you can send a calendar via e-mail.

▸ A calendar sent by e-mail will contain a **Calendar Snapshot** in the body of the e-mail, and the calendar will be attached to the e-mail.

▸ You can also publish your calendar on the **Microsoft Office Online Calendar Sharing Service.** This service will allow others to preview or subscribe to a published calendar. A **Windows Live ID** is needed to publish, preview, or subscribe to an online calendar.

▸ Published calendars to which you subscribe will be displayed in the **Other Calendars** area in the Navigation pane.

▸ A calendar can be assigned to a **category** (or multiple categories), and calendar items can be viewed by category.

▸ Other Outlook items, such as an e-mail, contact, or task, can be attached to a calendar item. Other files, such as a Word document or a picture, can be attached to a calendar item.

▸ A calendar item can be marked as **private,** which prevents others with whom your calendar is shared from viewing the details of a calendar item.

▸ You can set up a **recurring meeting request.** A recurring meeting will recur at the interval you specify.

▸ The **Scheduling Assistant** will display your calendar in timeline view in the body of a calendar item. You can view multiple shared calendars in timeline view using the Scheduling Assistant.

▸ When using Outlook in conjunction with an Exchange server, **AutoPick** meeting times will find the next available time on participants' calendars to schedule a meeting.

What Do You Know About Outlook?

True/False Questions

T F 1. You can customize your calendar work week to set Wednesday as the first day of the week. [Objective 10.2]

T F 2. When using the Microsoft Office Online Calendar Sharing Service, others can preview your calendar without a Windows Live ID account. [Objective 10.3]

T F 3. When using the Scheduling Assistant with a meeting request, the calendars of all attendees will be displayed in timeline format. [Objective 10.4]

T F 4. When multiple calendars are displayed in the Folder pane, the name of each calendar is always displayed on the tab at the top of the calendar. [Objective 10.1]

T F 5. Items attached to a calendar item will be included when the calendar item is forwarded. [Objective 10.4]

Multiple Choice Questions

1. Which of the following is the default reminder setting for an event? [Objective 10.2]
   a. 15 minutes
   b. 12 hours
   c. 18 hours
   d. 1 day

2. Which is true when multiple calendars are selected in the Navigation pane? [Objective 10.1]
   a. Calendar items appear only on the calendar in which they reside.
   b. Calendars in the Folder pane are by default displayed in different colors.
   c. Only two calendars can be displayed in the Navigation pane at one time.
   d. All the above.

3. Which is true of a shared calendar? [Objective 10.3]
   a. The default permission setting for a shared calendar is "Reviewer."
   b. A calendar that has been shared with you will be displayed in the My Calendars list.
   c. Private items will not be displayed on a shared calendar.
   d. All the above.

4. Which is true when using categories with calendar items? [Objective 10.4]
   a. The category is displayed in the item's InfoBar.
   b. The calendar items can be displayed By Category.
   c. A calendar item can be assigned to multiple categories.
   d. All the above.

5. Which calendar view displays calendar items from one calendar on another calendar?
   a. Side-by-side mode
   b. Overlay mode
   c. By Category view
   d. All the above

Short Answer Questions

1. Explain how your Outlook calendar can be shared with others not on your Exchange system. [Objectives 10.1, 10.3]

2. Describe how a private appointment is used in conjunction with a shared calendar. [Objectives 10.3, 10.4]

3. Explain how the Scheduling Assistant can help in scheduling appointments, events, and meetings. [Objectives 10.1, 10.3, 10.4]

Putting Outlook to Work

In these exercises, you will be setting up a new Outlook calendar for the American River Cycling Club (ARCC). You will be using many of the advanced calendar features covered in this chapter to help keep your club organized, in shape, and cycling!

Exercise 10.1 [Guided Practice]

Create a new calendar, and create appointments.
[Objectives 10.1, 10.4]

1. Click on the **Calendar** button in the *Navigation* pane.

2. Right-click on **Calendar** in the *My Calendars* area.

3. Click on the **Folder** tab and then on the **New Calendar** button.
   The *Create New Folder* dialog box will open.

4. Name the new calendar *[your first name]'s* ARCC.

   a. Confirm that the folder contains **Calendar Items** and will be saved
      in the **Calendar** folder.

5. Click **OK.**

   a. The *[your first name] ARCC* calendar will appear in the *My Calendars*
      area of the *Navigation* pane.

6. Select the ***[your first name]* ARCC** calendar so it appears in the
   Folder pane.

7. View the two calendars in **Side-By-Side** mode.

8. On the *[your first name] ARCC* calendar, create a new recurring
   appointment.

   a. Name the appointment **River Ride.**
   b. The location is **American River trailhead.**
   c. Set the date for this **Saturday** from **8–11 a.m.**
   d. In the body type: **Fairly flat 50-mile ride. All riders
      welcome.**
   e. Set the appointment to recur **weekly** with **no end date.**
   f. Click **Save & Close** to save the recurring appointment.

9. Create a new appointment on the *[your first name] ARCC*
   calendar.

   a. Name the appointment **Fundraising meeting.**
   b. The location is **Starbucks.**
   c. Set the date for this **Friday** from **8–9 a.m.**
   d. In the body type: **Meet with potential donors for Italy
      trip.**
   e. Click on the **Private** button in the *Tags* group.
   f. Click **Save & Close** to save the appointment.

Exercise 10.2 [Guided Practice]

Change calendar options on your main calendar.
[Objectives 10.1, 10.2]

1. Click on the **Calendar** button in the *Navigation* pane.

   a. Both your *Calendar* and the *[your first name] ARCC* calendar should
      appear in the *Folder* pane.

2. Click on the **arrow** to the left of the *[your first name] ARCC* calendar
   name to display the calendars in **Overlay** mode.

3. Click on the **Calendar** tab in the *Folder* pane.

   a. Your *Calendar* will be displayed on top of the *[your first name] ARCC* calendar.

4. Click on the **File** tab, and choose **Options.** The *Outlook Options* dialog box will open.

5. Click on the **Calendar** button at the left. The *Calendar Options* dialog box will open.

6. Change the **color** of the calendar to one of your choice.

7. Click on the **Add Holidays** button. The *Add Holidays to Calendar* dialog box will open.

8. Select **Italy** and **United States.**

9. Click **OK** to add these holidays to your calendar.

10. Click **OK** to close the *Outlook Options* dialog box.

Exercise 10.3 [Guided Practice]

Create a new signature and a recurring meeting request. Use the Scheduling Assistant, and attach a file to a calendar item. [Objectives 10.1, 10.2, 10.4]

1. Create a new signature to be used for ARCC e-mails.

   a. Name the signature `ARCC`.
   b. Include your **name, `ARCC President`** as your title, and **e-mail address.**
   c. Save the new signature, and close any open dialog boxes.

2. Click on the **Calendar** button in the *Navigation* pane.

3. Deselect the **Calendar** in the *My Calendars* area.

   a. Only the *[your first name] ARCC* calendar should be displayed in the *Folder* pane.

4. Create a recurring meeting request.

   a. Invite all your classmates and your professor. *(Use Exchange accounts if available.)*
   b. Name the meeting **[your name]'s `Italy meeting`.**
   c. The location is **`Conference Room`.**
   d. Click on the **Insert** tab and then the **Attach File** button.
   e. Attach the **Italy Tour Itinerary** document (from your data files) to the meeting request.
   f. Click on the **Meeting** tab.
   g. Click on the **Scheduling Assistant** button to help you pick a date and time.
   h. Choose a **date** and **time** in the next week, and make the duration of the meeting **2 hours.**
   i. In the body type: **`Meeting for Italy Tour riders`.**
   j. Insert your **ARCC** signature.
   k. Click on the **Recurrence** button in the *Options* group on the *Meeting* ribbon.
   l. Set the meeting to recur **monthly** for **3 months.**
   m. Click **Send** to send the meeting request.

Exercise 10.4 [Guided Practice]

Share your main calendar with others. Open and view shared calendars. *Note: If you are not on an Exchange server, skip this exercise.* **[Objectives 10.1, 10.3]**

1. Click on the **Calendar** button in the *Navigation* pane.

2. Select the **Calendar** in the *My Calendars* area.

3. Deselect the *[your first name]* **ARCC** calendar.

4. Click on the **Share Calendar** button in the *Share* group. A *Sharing invitation* e-mail will open.

   a. Select your classmates and your professor as recipients.
   b. Make sure the **Allow recipient to view your Calendar** check box is checked.
   c. Type a brief message in the body informing the recipients that you have shared your calendar with them.
   d. Insert your **ARCC** signature.
   e. Click **Send** to send the invitation.
   f. Click **Yes** to share your calendar if another dialog box opens.

5. You will begin receiving *Sharing invitation* e-mails in your *Inbox*.

6. Click on the **Mail** button in the *Navigation* pane.

7. Open one of the **Sharing invitation** e-mails in your *Inbox*.

8. Click on the **Open this Calendar** button.

   a. The shared calendar will be displayed in the *Folder* pane.
   b. Notice the calendar also appears in the *Shared Calendars* list in the *Navigation* pane.

9. Close the **Sharing invitation** e-mail.

10. Repeat this process to open two more of the **Sharing invitation** e-mails.

11. Click on the **Open Calendar** button in the *Manage Calendars* group on the *Home* ribbon, and choose **Open Shared Calendar.** The *Open a Shared Calendar* dialog box will open.

12. Click on the **Name** button. The *Select Names* dialog box will open.

13. Select from your list of contacts one of your classmates who has shared his or her calendar with you.

14. Click **OK** to close the *Select Names* dialog box.

15. Click **OK** to close the *Open a Shared Calendar* dialog box.

   a. The shared calendar should appear in the *Shared Calendars* list in the *Navigation* pane.

16. Repeat this process to open two more shared calendars.

17. Deselect all calendars except **Calendar** and *[your first name]* **ARCC.**

   a. The shared calendars will remain in your *Shared Calendars* list even though they are not displayed in the *Folder* pane.

Exercise 10.5 [Guided Practice]

Send an Internet calendar via e-mail, and view calendars received via e-mail. [Objectives 10.1, 10.3]

1. Click on the **Calendar** button in the *Navigation* pane.
2. Deselect **Calendar** from the *My Calendars* area in the *Navigation* pane.

   a. Only the *[your first name] ARCC* should be displayed in the *Folder* pane.

3. Click on the **E-mail Calendar** button in the *Share* group on the *Home* ribbon.

   a. A blank e-mail message will open, and the *Send a Calendar via E-mail* dialog box will open.

4. Make sure the ***[your first name]* ARCC** calendar is selected.
5. Select **Next 30 days** for the *Date Range*.
6. Select **Full details** in the *Details* section.
7. Click on the **Show** button in the *Advanced* area.
8. Choose **Include attachments with calendar items.**
9. Confirm that **List of events** is selected for the *E-mail Layout***.**
10. Click **OK** to close the *Send a Calendar via E-mail* dialog box.

    a. Notice the attached Internet calendar and the information in the body of the e-mail message.

11. Include a brief message in the body and your **ARCC** signature.
12. Use the **Gmail Contacts** distribution list as the recipient.
13. **Send** through your **Gmail** account.
14. You will begin receiving *[student's name] ARCC Calendar* e-mails in your *Inbox* (if your Gmail rule is on, you will receive these in your *Gmail* folder).
15. Click on the **Mail** button in the *Navigation* pane.
16. Open one of the ***[student's name]* ARCC Calendar** e-mails.

    a. Notice the calendar information in the body of the e-mail.

17. Click on the **Open this Calendar** button in the *Open* group on the *Message* ribbon.

    a. A dialog box will open warning you to only open a calendar from those whom you trust.

    b. The attached calendar will open.

    c. View the calendar items on the calendar.

18. Close the calendar you opened and any open e-mails.

Exercise 10.6 [Independent Practice]

Create a new category, and assign calendar items to this category. Create a new calendar appointment, and respond to meeting requests. [Objectives 10.1, 10.3, 10.4]

1. Click on the **Calendar** button in the *Navigation* pane.
2. Select the ***[your first name]* ARCC** calendar.

3. Create a new category named `ARCC`.

4. Assign all the calendar items on the *[your first name]* ARCC calendar to the **ARCC** category.

5. Add a new calendar appointment for an upcoming ride.

    a. Use `Dusk ride` as the subject.
    b. The location is the `Auburn Confluence`.
    c. Set the date for next **Wednesday** and the time for **6–8 p.m.**
    d. Include a brief description and categorize it as **ARCC**.
    e. Click on **Save & Close** to save the appointment.

6. Go to your *Inbox*.

7. Open and respond to three of the *[student's name]* Italy meeting request e-mails (from Exercise 10.3).

    a. **Accept** one.
    b. **Decline** one.
    c. Choose **Tentative** on one, and propose a new time.

Exercise 10.7 [Independent Practice]

Create a Windows Live ID account, and publish your calendar.
[Objectives 10.1, 10.3]

1. Click on the **Calendar** button in the *Navigation* pane.

2. Select the *[your first name]* **ARCC** calendar in the *Navigation* pane.

    a. Make sure it is the only calendar displayed in the *Folder* pane.

3. Click on the **Publish Online** button in the *Share* group on the *Home* ribbon, and choose **Publish to Office.com.**

    a. If needed, follow the steps to create a **Windows Live ID** account.
    b. Use your **Gmail** address when creating your Live ID account.

4. Publish the whole *[your first name]* **ARCC** calendar to Microsoft Office Online.

5. Invite your classmates and professor to view your published calendar.

    a. Use your **Gmail Contacts** distribution list as the recipients to invite.

Exercise 10.8 [Independent Practice]

Preview and subscribe to a published calendar.
[Objectives 10.1, 10.3, 10.4]

1. Open one of the *[student's name]* **ARCC_Calendar-Internet Calendar** e-mails in your *Inbox*.

2. Subscribe to the published Internet calendar.

    a. Notice it will be in the *Other Calendars* area in the *Navigation* pane.

3. Repeat this process to subscribe to two more published Internet calendars.

4. Open the **Account Settings** dialog box, and view your published calendar and Internet calendar to which you are subscribed.

5. Remove one of the Internet calendars to which you are subscribed.

6. Display one of the **Other Calendars** in your *Folder* pane.

Exercise 10.9 [Independent Practice]

Use AutoPick to select a new time for an upcoming meeting. *Note: If you are not on an Exchange server, skip this exercise.* **[Objectives 10.1, 10.3, 10.4]**

1. Open the *[your name's]* **Italy meeting** request on your *[your first name] ARCC* calendar.

   a. Make sure you open the meeting request you created, not one you have accepted.
   b. Open this occurrence, not the series.

2. Display the **Scheduling Assistant.**

3. Use the **AutoPick Next** button to select the next meeting time that fits into the calendar for attendees.

4. Click on **Send Update** to update the meeting.

Chapter 11

Notes, Journal, Search Folders, Shortcuts, and Archiving

OBJECTIVES *After completing this chapter, you will be able to:*

11.1 Create and use Notes in Outlook.

11.2 Integrate the Outlook Journal with Outlook items and Microsoft Office documents.

11.3 Utilize search folders to find e-mail messages.

11.4 Incorporate shortcuts in Outlook.

11.5 Use archiving to store Outlook items.

CHAPTER FLYOVER

- Creating notes
- Editing notes
- Categorizing notes
- Note views
- Forwarding notes
- Changing default settings on notes
- Manually record a journal entry
- Automatically record a journal entry

- Journal views
- Using existing search folders
- Creating new search folders
- Customizing search folders
- Deleting search folders
- Creating a new shortcut
- Creating a new group
- Editing a shortcut or group
- AutoArchive settings
- Custom AutoArchive settings

Making Outlook Work for You

Just when you think that we've covered just about everything Outlook has to offer, there are still more Outlook tasks and features available to help keep you organized. Outlook **Notes** store information that might not fit neatly into a task or calendar item. Outlook **Journal** can be used to track the time spent on Outlook items and other Microsoft Office documents.

Earlier in this text we covered rules, and in this chapter you will be introduced to **search folders,** which are closely related to rules. **Shortcuts** can be incorporated into Outlook to quickly move you to areas regularly used in Outlook. Finally, you'll be introduced to the **Archive** feature. Archiving your Outlook data creates a different set of folders to store older information.

Using Notes

Do you have sticky notes stuck to your computer monitor, bathroom mirror, or refrigerator? If you're like most people, you use these sticky notes to write down reminders or random pieces of information. Outlook provides you with a feature similar to paper sticky notes. These notes can be used to store information that does not necessarily fit as a task or calendar item. These items can be used to store a book wish list, a username to a website, a grocery list, a mileage rate for travel reimbursement, or other miscellaneous pieces of information.

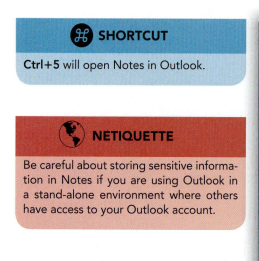

SHORTCUT

Ctrl+5 will open Notes in Outlook.

NETIQUETTE

Be careful about storing sensitive information in Notes if you are using Outlook in a stand-alone environment where others have access to your Outlook account.

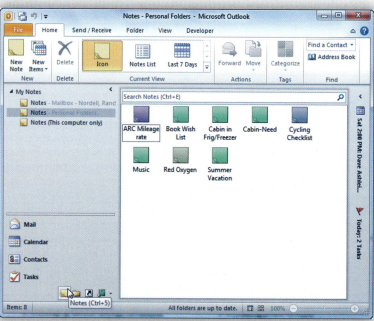

Notes button at the bottom of the Navigation pane and notes displayed in the Folder pane

Creating Notes

The Notes button is located at the bottom of the *Navigation* pane. By clicking on the **Notes** button, the *Notes* folders are displayed in the *My Notes* list in the *Navigation* pane, and your notes are displayed in the *Folder* pane.

STEP-BY-STEP

1. Click on the **Notes** button in the *Navigation* pane.
2. Click on the **New Note** button. A new note will be displayed.

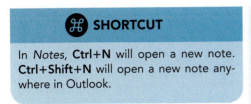

In *Notes*, **Ctrl+N** will open a new note. **Ctrl+Shift+N** will open a new note anywhere in Outlook.

New Note button and note displayed

3. Type the information to be included in the note.
4. Click on the **X** in the upper right corner to save and close the note. The first line of the note will be the name of the note that will be displayed in the *Folder* pane.

Editing Notes

Notes are very basic; you do not have as many formatting options available for notes that you have when customizing an e-mail, task, signature, or calendar item. To edit a note, simply double-click on the note to be edited in the *Folder* pane. The note will open, appearing similar to a sticky note on your computer screen, and you will be able to change the contents of the note. To save and close the note, click on the **X** in the upper right corner.

Categorizing Notes

As with other Outlook items, notes can be assigned to a category. When a note is assigned to a category, the color of the note changes to the color of the category to which it was assigned.

STEP-BY-STEP

1. Select the notes to be categorized.

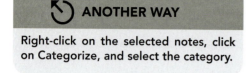

ANOTHER WAY

Right-click on the selected notes, click on Categorize, and select the category.

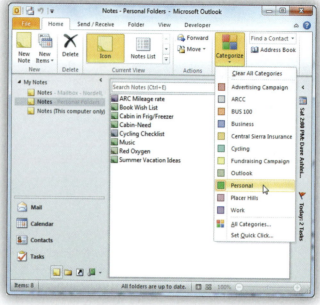

Categorize notes

2. Click on the **Categorize** button in the *Tags* group on the *Home* ribbon.

3. Click on the **selected category.** The notes will change to the color of the assigned category.

Note Views

Notes can be displayed in a variety of ways. The different views are available in the **Current View** area in the *Navigation* pane. The default view is **Icon.** Other note views include **Notes List** and **Last 7 Days.**

Different note views

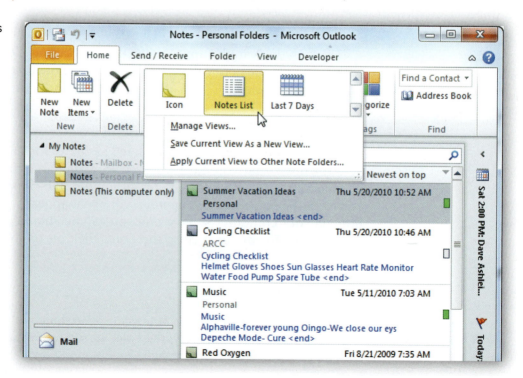

Notes can also be displayed on your computer desktop (just like putting a sticky note on your computer screen). To display a note on your desktop, drag the note from the *Folder* pane and drop it on the *desktop*. A copy of the note is placed on the desktop.

Within the *Icon* view, the notes can be displayed as large icons, small icons, or as a list. Click on the **View** tab to display the different options in the *Arrangement* group.

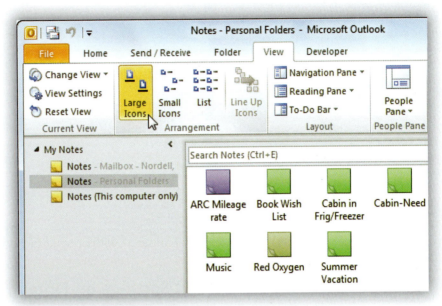

Notes displayed as large icons

Forwarding Notes

Notes can be forwarded as an attachment via e-mail to other Outlook users. When a recipient receives a forwarded note, he or she can drag the attached note to the **Notes** button and the note will be saved in his or her *Notes* folder.

STEP-BY-STEP

1. Select the notes to be forwarded.
2. Click on the **Forward** button in the *Actions* group on the *Home* ribbon. A new e-mail will open with the notes attached.

Forward notes as attachments to an e-mail message

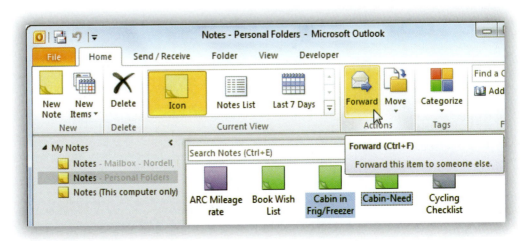

3. Select recipients, type a subject, and include necessary information in the body.

4. Click **Send** to send the notes.

⌘ SHORTCUT

Ctrl+F can be used to forward selected notes. A new e-mail message will open with the selected notes.

↺ ANOTHER WAY

Right-click on the selected notes, and choose **Forward**.

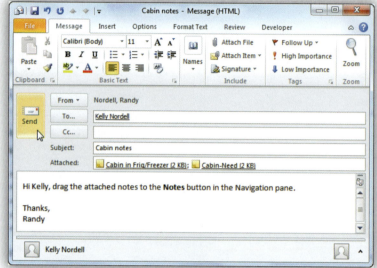

E-mail message with notes attached

Changing Default Settings on Notes

If you don't like the default color, size, or font of your Outlook Notes, you can customize these settings in the *Notes Options* dialog box. You are also given the option of whether or not to display the date and time the note was last modified.

STEP-BY-STEP

1. Click on the **File** tab, and choose **Options.** The *Outlook Options* dialog box will open.

2. Click on the **Notes and Journal** button. The *Notes Options* will be displayed.

Notes and Journal options

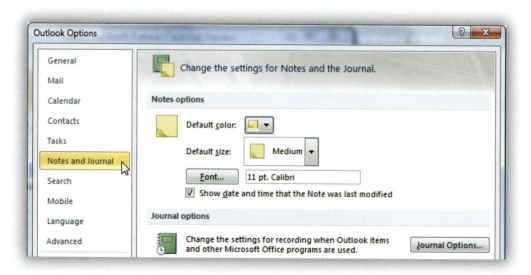

3. Make the desired changes to create new defaults for the **Color, Size, and/or Font.**

4. Click **OK** to close the *Outlook Options* dialog box.

Using the Journal

Outlook *Journal* is a feature used to track the amount of time you have spent working on a particular document or task. You can also use a journal to track activities related to a particular contact. An Outlook journal can be particularly useful if you or your company charges customers based on the time spent working on activities for them. A journal entry can be manually created and tracked, or you can have Outlook automatically create and track certain types of documents or specific contacts.

By default the Journal button is not displayed in Outlook. To access the journal feature, you have to set Outlook to display the Journal button in the Navigation pane.

STEP-BY-STEP

1. Click on the **Configure buttons** button at the bottom of the *Navigation* pane, and choose **Navigation Pane Options.** The *Navigation Pane Options* dialog box will open.

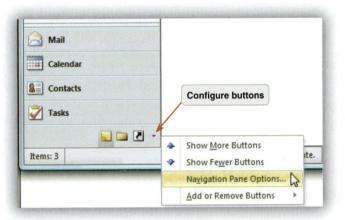

Configure buttons and Navigation Pane Options

2. Check **Journal.**

Navigation Pane Options dialog box

3. Click **OK** to close the *Navigation Pane Options* dialog box.

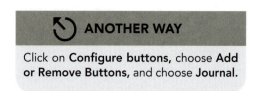

ANOTHER WAY

Click on **Configure buttons,** choose **Add or Remove Buttons,** and choose **Journal.**

⌘ SHORTCUT

Ctrl+8 opens the Journal.

The Journal button will be displayed as a small icon at the bottom of the Navigation pane. Click on this icon to open the Outlook Journal.

Journal button in the Navigation pane

Manually Record a Journal Entry

A journal entry can be created to track the amount of time spent on numerous Outlook and other activities. The different activities that can be tracked with a journal entry are: Conversation, Document, E-mail message, Fax, Letter, Meeting, Meeting cancellation, Meeting request, Meeting response, Microsoft Office Access, Microsoft Office Excel, Microsoft PowerPoint, Microsoft Word, Note, Phone call, Remote session, Task, Task request, and Task response.

 MORE INFO

The first time you click on the Journal button, a dialog box will open asking if you want the Journal to automatically track Microsoft Office documents. If this dialog box opens, choose **No** for now.

When you manually create a journal entry, you can record the **Subject, Entry type, Company, Start time,** and **Duration.** You can use the **Start Timer** button to automatically record the amount of time you spent on a journal entry, or you can manually enter the time into the journal.

STEP-BY-STEP

1. Click on the **Journal** button in the *Navigation* pane.
2. Click on the **Journal Entry** button. A new journal entry will open.
3. Fill in the **Subject.**
4. Select the **Entry type.**
5. Select the **Start time** or click on the **Start Timer** button.

New Journal Entry button

⌘ SHORTCUT

When you are in *Journal,* **Ctrl+N** will open a new journal entry. **Ctrl+Shift+J** will open a new journal entry anywhere in Outlook.

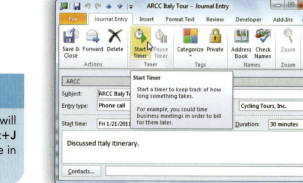

A manually created new journal entry

6. If not using the timer, select the **Duration** for the journal entry.

7. Add any details to the body.

8. Click on **Save & Close.**

Automatically Record a Journal Entry

Outlook can automatically track Outlook items and Microsoft Office documents related to a specific contact. It can also automatically track all the time you spend working on Microsoft Office documents. For example, it will track the amount of time you spent working on a report in Microsoft Word for a specific contact.

When automatic tracking is turned on in the journal, a journal entry is automatically created based on the settings you chose in the Journal Options dialog box. If automatic tracking in the journal has not been turned on and you click on the **Journal** button, a dialog box will open asking if you want to turn the Journal on. If you click **Yes,** the *Journal Options* dialog box will open.

STEP-BY-STEP

1. Click on the **Journal** button in the *Navigation* pane. A dialog box will open asking, "*Do you want to turn the Journal on?*"

Turn on Journal automatic tracking

2. Click **Yes** if this dialog box appears. The *Journal Options* dialog box will open. You can also open the *Journal Options* dialog box by clicking on the **File** tab, clicking on **Options,** clicking on the **Notes and Journal** button, and clicking on the **Journal Options** button.

Journal Options dialog box

3. Select the type of Outlook items to record in the *Automatically record these items* area.

4. Select the type of Microsoft Office document to record in the *Also record files from* area.

5. Select the contacts to record in the *For these contacts* area.

6. Click **OK** to close the *Journal Options* dialog box.

The automatic journal entries will appear in your list of journal entries. When you open a journal entry, you can edit the subject and/or other details of the journal entry. If the journal entry is associated with a particular Microsoft Office document, the document will be attached to the journal entry and you can open it from the open journal entry by double-clicking on the attachment.

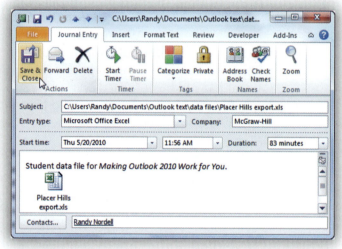

Automatically created journal entry

Journal Views

Outlook has numerous preset views by which to see your journal entries in the Folder pane. Some of the views display your journal entries in timeline

Journal entries displayed in By Category timeline view

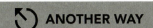

> ↻ **ANOTHER WAY**
>
> You can also change the scale of the timeline (Day, Week, Month) by right-clicking on the timeline in the *Folder* pane and selecting either **Day, Week,** or **Month.**

format, while others display them in list format. The preset journal views are:

- By Category (timeline view)
- Timeline (timeline view)
- Entry List (list view)
- Phone Calls (list view)
- Last 7 Days (list view)

Journal entries in the timeline view can be displayed in a Day, Week, or Month arrangement. These different arrangement options are provided in the *Arrangement* group on the *Home* ribbon.

Using Search Folders

Search folders are somewhat related to rules in that they look for a specific condition or criterion in e-mail messages, and if the condition is met, the message will be displayed in the search folder. Search folders differ from rules in that the message is not physically moved to a different location.

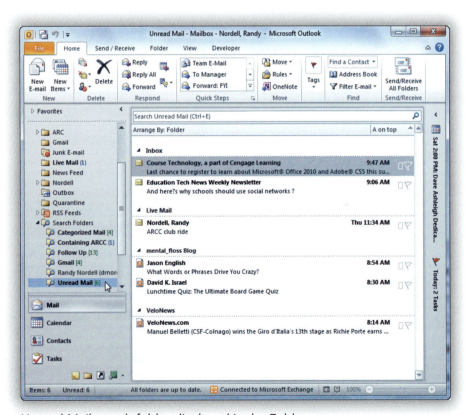

Unread Mail search folder displayed in the Folder pane

> ℹ **MORE INFO**
>
> Rules were covered in Chapter 7 on page 177.

Search folders are virtual folders; they don't actually contain any messages, but rather display e-mail items that are located in other folders that meet a certain condition. For example, Outlook has a default search folder for ***Unread Mail.*** Any e-mail message in your mailbox that is unread will be displayed in the *Folder* pane when you click on the **Unread Mail** search folder in the *Navigation* pane.

Using Existing Search Folders

Outlook provides you with three default search folders: *For Follow Up,* *Large Mail,* and *Unread Mail.* The *For Follow Up* search folder displays all e-mails marked with a Follow Up flag. The *Large Mail* search folder displays all e-mails that are larger than 100 KB in file size. And the *Unread Mail* search folder displays all unread (or marked as unread) e-mails.

These default search folders look for e-mail messages in all your mailbox folders (or personal folders) and display them in the search folder. When a search folder is selected in the *Navigation* pane, the e-mail messages that meet the criterion of the selected search folder will be displayed in the *Folder* pane. In the *Folder* pane, each message and the location of that message (e.g., Inbox, RSS Feeds) are displayed.

Creating New Search Folders

Suppose you wanted to create a search folder that looks for all the e-mails from your professor, but you do not want to create a rule to physically move these messages to a separate folder. A search folder can be created to find and display all the messages from your professor.

Search folders are very easy to create, customize, and delete. Use the following steps to create a search folder to display e-mail from a specific person.

STEP-BY-STEP

1. Click on the **Mail** button in the *Navigation* pane.

New Search Folder button

2. Click on the **Folder** tab and then on the **New Search Folder** button in the *New* group. The *New Search Folder* dialog box will open.

3. Select **Mail from specific people** as the condition.

New Search Folder dialog box

4. Click on **Choose** to select a contact. The *Select Names* dialog box will open.

5. Select the name of the contact for the condition of the search folder. Click on the **From** button to add the contacts or double-click on the contacts.

6. Click **OK** to close the *Select Names* dialog box.

7. Click **OK** to close the *New Search Folder* dialog box. The new search folder will appear in your list of search folders in the Navigation pane.

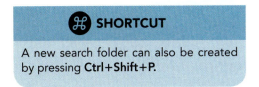

SHORTCUT

A new search folder can also be created by pressing **Ctrl+Shift+P.**

New search folder added
to Search Folders

When creating a new search folder, there are many different criteria options available from which to choose. You can also choose **Create a custom Search Folder** for more customization options.

Customizing Search Folders

You can customize search folders by changing the name of the folder, the criteria for the search, and/or the mailbox folders to be included in the search. When you create a new search folder, by default, all the mailbox folders (or personal folders) are included in the search for mail messages meeting the criterion.

STEP-BY-STEP

1. Click on the **Mail** button in the *Navigation* pane.

2. Click on the search folder to be customized.

Customize This Search Folder button

3. Click on the **Folder** tab and then on the **Customize This Search Folder** button in the *Actions* group. The *Customize* dialog box will open.

4. You can change the **Name** of the search folder, select the **Criteria,** or indicate which folders to include in the *Mail from these folders will be included in the Search Folder* selection box.

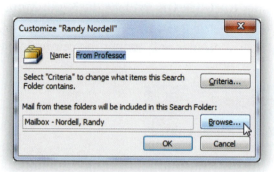

Customize dialog box

5. Click on the **Browse** button to change the folders to be included in the search. The *Select Folder(s)* dialog box will open.

6. Select the folders to be included in the search for this search folder. Notice the *Search subfolders* option at the bottom of the dialog box.

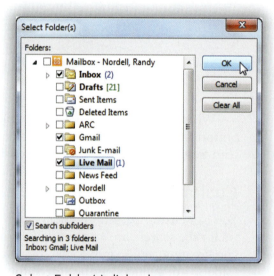

Select Folder(s) dialog box

MORE INFO

There is also a **Rename Folder** button in the *Actions* group on the *Folder* ribbon, which can be used to rename a search folder.

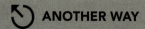

ANOTHER WAY

Right-click on the search folder, and choose **Customize This Search Folder.**

7. Click **OK** to close the *Select Folder(s)* dialog box.

8. Click **OK** to close the *Customize* dialog box.

Search folders can also be customized to show either the total number of items in the folder or the number of unread items in the folder.

STEP-BY-STEP

1. Click on one of the search folders.

2. Click on the **Folder** tab.

3. Click on the **Folder Properties** button in the *Properties* group. The *[Folder's Name] Properties* dialog box will open.

4. Click on either **Show number of unread items** or **Show total number of items.**

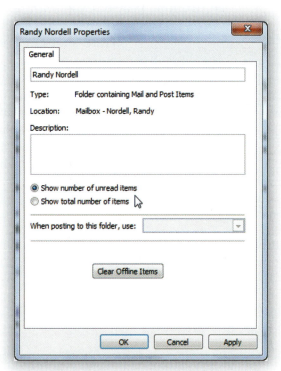

Search folder Properties dialog box

5. Click **Apply** and then **OK.**

Deleting Search Folders

Because search folders are virtual folders, they don't physically contain any e-mail messages. When a search folder is deleted, none of the messages that were displayed in the search folder are deleted.

To delete a search folder, click on the search folder in the *Navigation* pane and click on the **Delete** button in the *Actions* group on the *Folder* ribbon or press **Delete** on your keyboard. You can also right-click on the search folder and choose **Delete Folder.** When deleting a search folder, a dialog box will open asking if you want to delete the search folder and informing you that the items contained in the search folder will not be deleted. Press **Yes** to delete the search folder.

Confirm deletion
dialog box

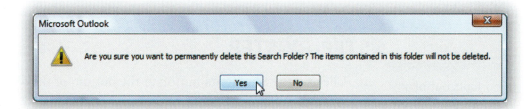

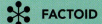

Using Shortcuts

In addition to Mail, Calendar, Contacts, Tasks, Notes, Folder List, and Journal, Outlook provides you with another Navigation pane view. The ***Shortcuts*** view in the Navigation pane gives you the ability to create shortcut links to Outlook folders, other computer folders, programs on your computer, specific documents on your computer, or a website. ***Groups*** can be created in the Shortcuts area to group related shortcuts. If the link in the Shortcuts area is to an Outlook folder, the Outlook folder will be displayed in the Folder pane when the link is clicked. If the link in the Shortcuts area is to a program or file, the program or file will open in a new window when you click on the shortcut.

SHORTCUT

Ctrl+7 opens the *Shortcuts* view in Outlook.

Shortcuts and groups in the Navigation pane and selected shortcut displayed in the Folder pane

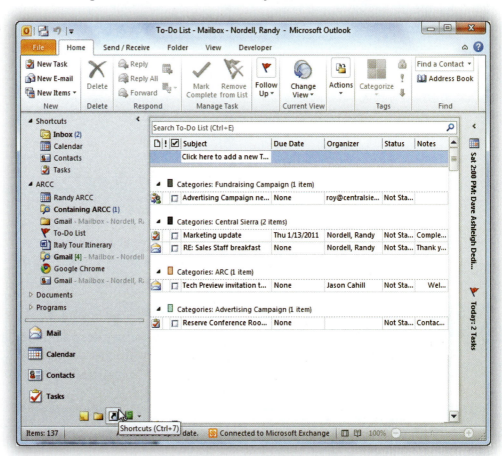

Creating a New Shortcut

Shortcuts can be created to quickly take you to a folder, program, or document you regularly use. For example, a shortcut can be created in Outlook to open an Outlook folder you regularly use, to quickly access a Microsoft Word document, or to launch an Internet browser window.

To access the *Shortcuts* area, click on the **Shortcuts** button at the bottom of the *Navigation* pane.

Shortcuts button in the Navigation pane

STEP-BY-STEP

1. Click on the **Shortcuts** button at the bottom of the *Navigation* pane.
2. Click on the **Folder** tab.

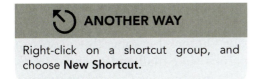

ANOTHER WAY

Right-click on a shortcut group, and choose **New Shortcut.**

New Shortcut button on the Folder ribbon

3. Click on the **New Shortcut** button in the *New* group. The *Add to Navigation Pane* dialog box will open and will display all your Outlook folders.

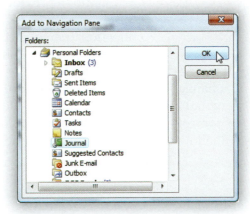

Add to Navigation Pane dialog box

4. Select an Outlook folder to be added as a shortcut.

5. Click **OK** to add the shortcut to the *Navigation* pane.

6. The shortcut will appear in the *Navigation* pane. When the shortcut is clicked, the folder will appear in the *Folder* pane.

A document (such as a Microsoft Word document), a folder of documents, or a program can also be added to the Shortcuts area in Outlook. To add a link to any of these in the Shortcuts area of Outlook, drag and drop the document, folder, or program to a shortcuts group heading in the *Navigation* pane.

Creating a New Group

Groups can be created within the Shortcuts area to group related items. To create a new group, right-click in the **Shortcuts** area in the *Navigation* pane and select **New Shortcut Group.** A new group will be created in the *Navigation* pane, and you will need to type the name of the new group.

FACTOID

When you delete a shortcut, the actual item is not deleted; just the shortcut to the item is deleted.

Editing a Shortcut or Group

Shortcuts and shortcut groups can be rearranged by dragging the shortcut up or down in the list of shortcuts or right-clicking on the shortcut and choosing **Move Up** or **Move Down.** Shortcuts can also be renamed by right-clicking on the shortcut, choosing **Rename Shortcut,** and typing the new shortcut name. Groups can be rearranged or renamed similarly to how a shortcut link is rearranged or renamed.

You can delete shortcuts and groups by right-clicking on the shortcut or group and choosing **Delete Shortcut** or **Delete Group.** If you remove a group, all the shortcuts within that group will be deleted.

FACTOID

Contacts are not archived because they are not time sensitive like e-mails, calendar items, tasks, notes, and journals.

 MORE INFO

If you archive items on your local computer, you will not be able to retrieve them from OWA as the items have been removed from the Exchange server and are only available locally.

Archiving Outlook Folders

After you have been using Outlook for some time, you will find that you have numerous old e-mail and calendar items taking up storage space. If you are using Outlook in a stand-alone environment, space is typically not a problem, but if you are on an Exchange server, you only have a limited amount of space on the server to store all your Outlook data. If you like to keep all your old e-mail and calendar items, you might receive an e-mail message warning you that you are close to or over your allotted space on the server.

Outlook provides you with a solution to this space limitation. ***Archiving*** is moving older Outlook items from their location (personal folders or mailbox folders) to a set of ***archive folders.*** When ***AutoArchive*** runs, a set of archive folders is created and stored locally on your computer rather than on the Exchange server. This set of folders mirrors the folders in your mailbox or personal folders and contains the older archived Outlook items. This helps to control the amount of space you are using on the Exchange server while still allowing you to save and have access to these older Outlook items.

Archive folders

AutoArchive can be set to run periodically and will automatically move older Outlook items to your archive folders. You can customize the AutoArchive settings to move older mail, calendar, tasks, notes, and journals to the archive folders. You can also customize the archive settings for individual Outlook folders.

AutoArchive Settings

AutoArchive is, by default, turned on in Outlook. The AutoArchive dialog box has many settings that you can customize. AutoArchive can be set to run automatically at a regular interval (e.g., every 14 days), and you can be prompted before AutoArchive runs. If you choose **Prompt before AutoArchive runs,** a dialog box will open asking you if you want to run AutoArchive. If this option is not selected, AutoArchive will run automatically on the set schedule.

In the *AutoArchive* dialog box, you have the option to either delete older Outlook items or move (archive) them to another set of folders. The default setting is to move older items to the archive folders, which are stored locally on your computer rather than on the Exchange server. In the *Clean out items older than* area, you can specify when you want your older items archived. This setting can be set from 1 day to 60 months. AutoArchive can also be set to delete expired e-mail items. You can specify the location on your computer where you want archive folders saved. This set of folders is saved as an Outlook Data File (.pst).

The settings made in the AutoArchive dialog box are global and can be applied to all Outlook folders by clicking on the **Apply these settings to all folders now** button.

STEP-BY-STEP

1.   Click on the **File** tab, and choose **Options.** The *Outlook Options* dialog box will open.

2.   Click on the **Advanced** button.

AutoArchive Setting button in the Outlook Options dialog box

3.   Click on the **AutoArchive Settings** button in the *AutoArchive* area. The *AutoArchive* dialog box will open.

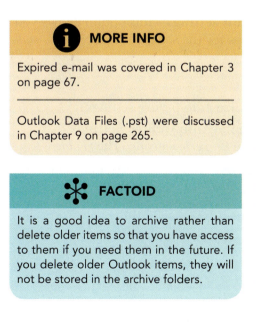

ⓘ MORE INFO

Expired e-mail was covered in Chapter 3 on page 67.

Outlook Data Files (.pst) were discussed in Chapter 9 on page 265.

✳ FACTOID

It is a good idea to archive rather than delete older items so that you have access to them if you need them in the future. If you delete older Outlook items, they will not be stored in the archive folders.

AutoArchive dialog box

4.   Make the desired changes to the *AutoArchive* settings.

5.   Click **OK** to close the *AutoArchive* dialog box.

6.   Click **OK** to close the *Outlook Options* dialog box.

Custom AutoArchive Settings

There might be some folders in Outlook that you do not want to archive or you want to archive at different AutoArchive settings than the default ones. For example, you might not want to archive your Inbox and Tasks, but you might want to archive your calendar more or less frequently than your current default (global) AutoArchive settings. Outlook allows you to customize the archive settings on individual folders.

When customizing AutoArchive settings for individual folders, you are given three options.

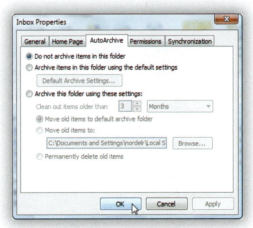

Custom AutoArchive settings in the
Inbox Properties dialog box

- **Do not archive items in the folder**—this option turns off AutoArchive on the selected folder.
- **Archive items in this folder using the default settings**—this option uses the default AutoArchive settings for the selected folder.
- **Archive this folder using the default settings**—this option allows you to customize the AutoArchive settings for the selected folder.

STEP-BY-STEP

1. Select the folder on which to customize *AutoArchive* settings.
2. Click on the **Folder** tab and then on the **AutoArchive Settings** (or **Folder Properties**) button in the *Properties* group. The *[Folder name] Properties* dialog box opens.

ANOTHER WAY

You can right-click on any Outlook folder and choose **Properties** to open the *Properties* dialog box. You will then need to click on the **AutoArchive** tab.

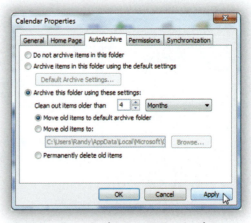

Custom AutoArchive settings in the
Calendar Properties dialog box

3. Select one of the three custom **AutoArchive** options and make any desired changes to the **AutoArchive** settings.
4. Click **Apply.**
5. Click **OK** to close the dialog box.

These custom settings will now be the AutoArchive settings for this folder and will override the default AutoArchive settings in Outlook. You can customize the AutoArchive settings on any of your folders that will be archived in Outlook.

Outlook allows further customization regarding the archiving of specific items in Outlook. Individual Outlook items can be set so they are not archived even if they are in a folder that will be archived.

STEP-BY-STEP

1. Open the Outlook item you wish not to be archived.
2. Click on the **File** tab to open the *BackStage.*

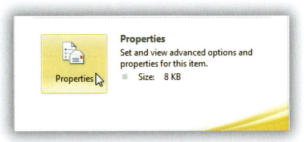

Properties button on the BackStage

3. Click on the **Properties** button. The *Properties* dialog box will open.
4. Check the **Do not AutoArchive this item** check box.

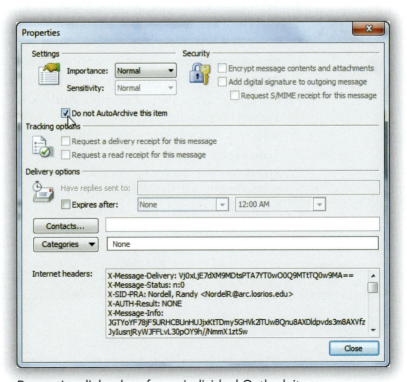

Properties dialog box for an individual Outlook item

5. **Close** the *Properties* dialog box.

Chapter Highlights

▶ Outlook **Notes** can be used to store information that would not necessarily be stored as a task or calendar item.

▶ Notes can be grouped by category, displayed in different views, forwarded to others via e-mail, and displayed on your computer desktop.

▶ Outlook **Journal** can be used to track the amount of time you spend working on Outlook items, Microsoft Office documents, and activities associated with a specific contact.

▶ Journals can also be used to track the time you spend on phone calls, conversations, meetings, and remote sessions.

▶ Journals can be created **manually,** or you can set up Outlook to **automatically** track specific contacts, Outlook items, or Microsoft Office documents.

▶ **Search folders** can be used to display e-mail messages that meet specific criteria.

▶ Search folders are similar to rules, but the e-mail messages are not physically moved to a different folder.

▶ Search folders are **virtual folders** that do not actually contain any e-mail messages, but rather display e-mail messages that meet the search criterion or condition in the search folder.

▶ Outlook provides you with some default search folders, and you can create, edit, and delete search folders.

▶ The **Shortcuts** area in Outlook allows you to create links to Outlook items, documents, programs, or folders you use regularly.

▶ **Groups** can be created in the Shortcuts area to group related links.

▶ **Archiving** is backing up older Outlook items and storing these items in a file on your computer. Archiving allows you to reduce the amount of space you are using on your Exchange server.

▶ **AutoArchive** automatically archives older Outlook items on a regular basis. You can customize the AutoArchive settings in Outlook.

▶ Outlook creates a set of **archive folders** to store archived Outlook items. The archive folders mirror the folders in your Outlook mailbox and/or personal folders and contain the older archived items.

▶ **AutoArchive** is turned on by default in Outlook. You can customize the AutoArchive settings for individual folders to either turn off AutoArchive or use settings different than the default settings.

▶ Individual Outlook items can be set so they are not archived according to default or folder AutoArchive settings.

What Do You Know About Outlook?

True/False Questions

T F   1. A reminder and due date can be set for an Outlook note. [Objective 11.1]

T F   2. When you click on a shortcut link, the object of the shortcut link will always be displayed in the Folder pane. [Objective 11.4]

T F   3. Notes can be forwarded to other Outlook users. [Objective 11.1]

T F   4. When a search folder is deleted, the items in the search folder are also deleted. [Objective 11.3]

T F   5. When a group is deleted in the Shortcuts area, the items in the group are also deleted. [Objective 11.4]

Multiple Choice Questions

1. Which of the following items are *not* archived in Outlook? [Objective 11.5]
   a. Mail folders
   b. Contacts
   c. Journal entries
   d. Calendar

2. Shortcuts can be created for which of the following? [Objective 11.4]
   a. Microsoft Word
   b. Picture folder on your computer
   c. Sent Items in Outlook
   d. All the above

3. A journal entry can be automatically created for which of the following items? [Objective 11.2]
   a. Task request from a contact
   b. Phone call from contact
   c. Fax from a contact
   d. All the above

4. Which of the following is true of search folders? [Objective 11.3]
   a. The action of the search folder can be changed.
   b. The condition or criterion of the search folder can be changed.
   c. E-mail messages that meet the criterion are moved to the search folder.
   d. None of the above.

5. When customizing the AutoArchive settings on a specific Outlook folder, which of the following is true? [Objective 11.5]
   a. AutoArchive can be turned off.
   b. Older items can be deleted.
   c. The default AutoArchive settings can be used.
   d. All the above.

Short Answer Questions

1. Explain the difference between a journal entry that is manually recorded and one that is automatically recorded. [Objective 11.2]

2. Compare and contrast search folders and rules. [Objective 11.3]

3. Why might you customize AutoArchive settings for a specific folder rather than using the default AutoArchive settings? [Objective 11.5]

Putting Outlook to Work

In these exercises, you will be using notes, journals, search folders, shortcuts, and AutoArchive to help you organize your leadership of and communication within the American River Cycling Club and further customize your Outlook.

Before beginning these exercises, turn off all rules except for **Gmail** (e-mail received through your Gmail account delivered to your Gmail folder) and **Clear categories on mail.** In the *Calendar* area, make sure your calendar (main calendar) is the only one selected.

Exercise 11.1 [Guided Practice]

Create two new search folders, and send an e-mail. [Objective 11.3]

1. Click on the **Mail** button in the *Navigation* pane.
2. Click on the **Folder** tab and then on the **New Search Folder** button in the *New* group. The *New Search Folder* dialog box will open. **Ctrl+Shift+P** will also open the *New Search Folder* dialog box.
3. Click on **Mail with specific words** in the *Organizing Mail* area.
4. Click on the **Choose** button. The *Search Text* dialog box opens.
   a. Type **ARCC,** and click **Add.**
   b. Click **OK** to close the *Search Text* dialog box.
5. Click **OK** to close the *New Search Folder* dialog box.
   a. Notice the *Containing ARCC* search folder appears in the search folders list.
6. Create another new search folder to find all the e-mails from your professor. Follow the steps 2–5, but use **Mail from specific people** as the criterion or condition.
   a. Select your professor's e-mail address (if there is more than one, select all).
   b. Close the dialog boxes, and notice the new search folder in the list.
7. Create a new e-mail.
   a. Address it to your classmates and professor.
   b. Use **ARCC club ride** as the subject.
   c. Include a brief message about the club ride this Saturday and your **ARCC** signature.
   d. Mark the message as **high importance.**
   e. **Send** the message. Notice that both the sent message and the incoming messages will appear in your *Containing ARCC* search folder.

Exercise 11.2 [Guided Practice]

Create new notes, categorize notes, and send an e-mail with an attachment. [Objective 11.1]

1. Click on the **Notes** button in the *Navigation* pane.
2. Click on the **New Note** button to create a new note. A new note will open. **Ctrl+N** will also open a new note.
   a. Type **Cycling Checklist** on the first line of the note, and press **Enter** twice.

b. Type the following items on separate lines on the note: `Helmet,`
`Gloves, Shoes, Sunglasses, Heart Rate Monitor, Water,`
`Food, Pump, Spare Tube.`

c. If needed, increase the size of the note by dragging the bottom right
corner down.

d. Click on the **X** in the upper right corner to save and close the note.

3. Create two more new notes using the following information.

a. Type **Book Wish List** as the first line, and then type the titles of
three to five books you'd like to read in the next year.

b. **Close** the note.

c. Type **Summer Vacation Ideas** as the first line, and then type
three to five places you'd like to go for next year's summer vacation.

d. **Close** the note.

4. Assign the **ARCC** category to the **Cycling Checklist** note.

5. Assign the **Personal** category to the other two notes.

6. Create a new e-mail.

a. Send to all your classmates and your professor.

b. Use **ARCC Italy Itinerary** as the subject.

c. Attach the **Italy Tour Itinerary** document. This document is located
in your student data files for this text.

d. In the body type **Are you planning on going to Italy?**
Please vote.

e. Include your **ARCC** signature.

f. Include custom voting buttons: **Definitely!; No; I Hope So.**
Remember to separate the options with a semicolon.

g. Set the message to **expire** this **Friday** at **5 p.m.**

h. **Send** the e-mail.

Exercise 11.3 [Guided Practice]

Create two journal entries, and save an attached document.
[Objectives 11.2, 11.3]

1. Click on the **Journal** button in the *Navigation* pane. Click **No** if a dialog
box opens asking if you want Outlook to automatically track documents.

a. Note: The *Journal* button might not be available in the *Navigation*
pane. Follow steps b–d to display the *Journal* button in the *Naviga-*
tion pane.

b. Click on **Configure buttons** at the bottom of the *Navigation* pane.

c. Choose either **Navigation Pane Options** or **Add or Remove Buttons.**

d. Select **Journal.**

2. Click on the **Journal Entry** button in the *New* group on the *Home*
ribbon, or press **Ctrl+N.** A new journal entry will open.

a. Type **ARCC Italy Tour** as the *Subject.*

b. Choose **Phone call** as the *Entry type.*

c. Type **Cycling Tours, Inc.** as the *Company.*

d. Set the *Start time* as **yesterday** at **9 a.m.**

e. The *Duration* of the call was **30 minutes.**

f. In the body type: **Discussed Italy itinerary.**

g. Assign this journal entry to the **ARCC** category.

h. Click **Save & Close** to save the journal entry.

3. Create a new journal entry.

     a. Subject: **Italy Tour Meeting.**
     b. Entry type: **Meeting.**
     c. Company: **ARCC.**
     d. Start time: **Last Friday, 11 a.m.**
     e. Duration: **2 hours.**
     f. Category: **ARCC.**
     g. Body: **12 people at meeting.**
     h. Click **Save & Close.**

4. Click on the **Phone Calls** button in the *Current View* group on the *Home* ribbon.

     a. Notice how the journal entries are displayed in the *Folder* pane.

5. Click on the **By Category** button in the *Current View* group on the *Home* ribbon.

     a. Notice how the journal entries are displayed in the *Folder* pane.

6. Click on the **Mail** button in the *Navigation* pane.

7. Click on the **Containing ARCC** search folder.

     a. The e-mails are displayed in the *Folder* pane.

8. Open one of the **ARCC Italy Itinerary** e-mails.

9. Save the **Italy Tour Itinerary** document to your desktop.

10. Close the e-mail.

Exercise 11.4 [Guided Practice]

Change Journal options settings, open a Word document, send a meeting request, and accept meeting requests. [Objectives 11.2, 11.3]

1. Click on the **Journal** button in the *Navigation* pane.

2. Click **Yes** if a dialog box opens asking if you want Outlook to automatically track documents. The *Journal Options* dialog box will open. If this dialog box does not open, click on **File** tab, **Options, Notes and Journal,** and **Journal Options.**

     a. In the *Automatically record these items* area select **E-mail message, Meeting request,** and **Task request.**
     b. In the *For these contacts* area, choose your professor's contacts and at least two of your classmates (preferably those sitting on either side of you).
     c. In the *Also record files from* area select **Microsoft Office Excel** and **Microsoft Word.**

3. Click **OK** to close the *Journal Options* dialog box.

4. Click **OK** to close the *Options* dialog box.

5. Open the **Italy Tour Itinerary** document from your desktop. This document should have been saved to your desktop in Exercise 11.3. If it is not on your desktop, open it from your student data files.

6. If you still have the **Placer Hills export** (from Chapter 9, Exercise 9.5) Excel file with exported contacts, open it. If it is not on your desktop, open this document from your student data files.

7. Leave these documents open; they will be used in Exercise 11.7.

8. Create a new meeting request (*use your main Calendar*).

   a. Address it to all your classmates and professor.
   b. Use *[your first name]* `ARCC training ride` as the subject.
   c. Set the date and time to be sometime this weekend.
   d. The location is the **American River bike trail.**
   e. Assign to the **ARCC** category.
   f. Provide a brief message, and include your **ARCC** signature.
   g. **Send.**

9. Click on the **Containing ARCC** search folder in the *Mail* area in the *Navigation* pane. You should begin receiving the *[student's name] ARCC training ride* meeting requests.

10. **Accept** the meeting requests from your professor and the two classmates from whom you are automatically creating journal entries (*from step 2c*).

11. **Decline** the rest of the meeting requests.

Exercise 11.5 [Guided Practice]

Create shortcuts, create a new group, and change default AutoArchive settings. [Objectives 11.4, 11.5]

1. Click on the **Shortcuts** button in the *Navigation* pane.

2. Click on the **Folder** tab and then on the **New Shortcut** button in the *New* group. The *Add to Navigation Pane* dialog box will open.

   a. Click on **Inbox.**
   b. Click **OK** to add this shortcut to the *Navigation* pane.
   c. Notice the shortcut to your *Inbox* in the *Navigation* pane.

3. Click on the **Inbox** shortcut.

   a. Notice the items in your *Inbox* are displayed in the *Folder* pane.

4. Add the following new shortcuts.

   a. **Calendar**
   b. **Tasks**
   c. **To-Do List**

5. Right-click on **Shortcuts** in the *Navigation* pane and choose **New Shortcut Group.**

6. Type **ARCC** as the new group name, and press **Enter.**

7. Right-click on the **ARCC** group heading, and choose **New Shortcut** to add the following shortcuts to the *ARCC* group.

   a. **ARCC** calendar
   b. **Containing ARCC** search folder
   c. **Gmail** mail folder

8. Click on the **File** tab, and select **Options.** The *Outlook Options* dialog box opens.

9. Click on the **Advanced** button and then on the **AutoArchive Settings** button. The *AutoArchive* dialog box opens.

   a. Change or confirm the settings in the dialog box.
   b. Select **Run AutoArchive every 7 days.**
   c. Deselect **Prompt before AutoArchive runs.**

d. Select **Delete expired items.**
e. Select **Archive or delete old items.**
f. Select **Show archive folder in folder list.**
g. Select **Clean out items older than 4 months.**
h. Select **Move old items to,** and accept the default location on your computer.
i. Click on **Apply these settings to all folders now.**
j. Click **OK** to close the *AutoArchive* dialog box.

10. Click **OK** to close the *Options* dialog box.

Exercise 11.6 [Independent Practice]

Create a new search folder, and customize search folders. [Objective 11.3]

1. Create a new search folder to display all e-mails sent to your Gmail account.

   a. Name this search folder **Gmail.**
   b. Hint: Use **Create a custom Search Folder.**
   c. The criterion should be items sent to your **Gmail** account.

2. Select your **Gmail** search folder to customize it.

   a. Click on the **Customize This Search Folder** button in the *Actions* group on the *Folder* ribbon.
   b. Change the settings so this search folder searches only the **Inbox** and **Gmail** folders.
   c. Change the properties of this search folder to display the total number of items in this folder.

3. Customize your **Containing ARCC** search folder.

   a. Change the folder name to **ARCC.**
   b. Change the settings so this search folder searches only the **Inbox** and **Gmail** folders.
   c. Change the properties of this search folder to display the total number of items in this folder.

4. Customize your search folder to look for e-mails from your professor.

   a. Change the name to **From Professor.**
   b. Change the settings so this search folder searches only the **Inbox** and **Gmail** folders.
   c. Change the properties of this search folder to display the total number of items in this folder.

Exercise 11.7 [Independent Practice]

Create a journal entry, view journal items, and forward notes. *Note: This exercise uses documents opened in Exercise 11.4.* **[Objectives 11.1, 11.2]**

1. **Close** the open Word and Excel documents (from Exercise 11.4).
2. View your journals.

   a. Notice the journal entries for the *Italy Tour Itinerary* and *Placer Hills export* documents that were opened in Exercise 11.4. Note the subjects for these journal entries will be the locations and file names of the documents.
   b. View in different views.

3. Create a new journal.
   a. Start the timer.
   b. Attach the **Italy Tour Itinerary** (on your desktop). Hint: Click on the **Insert** tab.
   c. Use `Italy Tour Itinerary` as the subject.
   d. Change the entry type to Microsoft Word.
   e. Leave this journal entry open.

4. In the *Notes* area, forward the two notes in the *Personal* category to your professor and classmates.
   a. Use *[your name]*`'s notes` as the subject.
   b. Include a read receipt.
   c. Include a brief message in the body and signature.

5. Save and close the **Italy Tour Itinerary** journal.

6. View your journals and the duration of the journal entries that were automatically created.

Exercise 11.8 [Independent Practice]

Customize AutoArchive settings, add shortcuts, and delete a shortcuts group. [Objectives 11.4, 11.5]

1. Turn off **AutoArchive** on your *Inbox* and *ARCC* calendar.

2. Change **Calendar** AutoArchive settings.
   a. Archive items older than 12 months.

3. Change **Gmail** folder AutoArchive settings.
   a. Archive items older than 6 months.

4. In the *Shortcuts* area, drag the **To-Do List** from the **Shortcuts** group to the **ARCC** group.

5. Delete the **Shortcuts** group.

6. Add the following shortcuts to your **ARCC** group.
   a. **Italy Tour Itinerary** document. Hint: Drag the document from your desktop to this group.
   b. **Gmail** search folder.
   c. **Internet browser.** Hint: Drag the icon or shortcut of your Internet browser from your desktop to this group.
   d. **Gmail** contacts folder.

Chapter 12
Sharing, Security, Search, and User Interface

OBJECTIVES   *After completing this chapter, you will be able to:*

12.1 Collaborate with other Outlook users' delegates.

12.2 Incorporate security features in Outlook.

12.3 Apply search features to find information in Outlook.

12.4 Customize the user interface in Outlook to better meet your needs.

CHAPTER FLYOVER

- ▶ Understanding delegates and permissions
- ▶ Assigning a delegate
- ▶ Opening another Outlook user's folders
- ▶ Creating Outlook items as a delegate
- ▶ Removing a delegate
- ▶ Outlook Trust Center
- ▶ Trusted Publishers
- ▶ Add-ins
- ▶ DEP settings
- ▶ Privacy options
- ▶ E-mail security
- ▶ Attachment handling
- ▶ Automatic download
- ▶ Macro settings

- ▶ Programmatic access
- ▶ Junk e-mail options
- ▶ Digital signatures
- ▶ Instant search
- ▶ Search options
- ▶ Advanced find
- ▶ Outlook Today
- ▶ Navigation pane options
- ▶ Favorites folders
- ▶ Customize Quick Access toolbar
- ▶ Sorting and Arrangement
- ▶ Add Columns and Field Chooser
- ▶ Show in groups
- ▶ Customizing views
- ▶ Creating a custom view

SSL Level 1

SSL Level 2

SSL Level 3

SSL Level 4

Making Outlook Work for You

We have just a few more topics to discuss, and then we will have covered all the most important aspects of Outlook. After completing this text, you will be the Outlook guru at your workplace or in your neighborhood. You will not only be able to effectively use Outlook to meet your personal and professional needs, but also be able to help others become more proficient in using Outlook.

A distinct advantage of Outlook in an Exchange environment is its ability to share your information with others. Many of you collaborate with others on work projects. The **Delegates** feature in Outlook allows you to give access to certain areas of Outlook to others with whom you work.

Security has become an increasingly important topic when dealing with digital information. Outlook provides many security features to protect your information from viruses and other potential threats.

As you continue to use Outlook to its potential, you will find that you have a huge amount of information stored in Outlook. The *search* features help you to quickly find information. Outlook also allows you to customize the user interface to better meet your needs and preferences.

 **MORE INFO**

Sharing calendars was covered in Chapter 10 on page 287.

Sharing Your Outlook with Others

Earlier in this text we discussed sharing your Outlook calendar with others. Outlook also allows you to share other areas of Outlook with coworkers who are on the same Exchange server. The *Delegate* feature gives you control over who has access to your Outlook information and how much access they have. This feature will only work with those who are on the same Exchange server.

Understanding Delegates and Permissions

A *delegate* is someone to whom you have given access to certain folders of your Outlook. This feature is commonly used with administrative assistants and members of a work team so they have access to the e-mails, calendars, contacts, tasks, notes, and/or journals of others.

The delegate feature gives you more flexibility than simply sharing a calendar. Not only can you specify what areas of Outlook to share, but also the *permissions* of the delegate. The permission is the level of access granted to a delegate. For example, when sharing a calendar with another Outlook user, the default permission they have is a *Reviewer,* which means they can see your calendar but cannot create, delete, or edit an appointment.

The permission settings for a delegate can be customized for each area of Outlook. There are four different permissions that can be granted to a delegate.

- *None*—delegates have access to this area of Outlook.
- *Reviewer*—can read items, but does not have access to create, delete, or edit items.
- *Author*—can read and create items, but does not have access to delete or edit items.
- *Editor*—can read, create, delete, or edit items.

Assigning a Delegate

The advantage of using the delegate feature rather than the sharing feature is that the role for each area of Outlook can be set and customized from one area. It's easy to view or change permissions from this one dialog box.

STEP-BY-STEP

1. Click on the **File** tab, click on the **Account Settings** button, and choose **Delegate Access.** The *Delegates* dialog box will open.

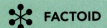

FACTOID

Just like sharing a calendar, you can share other areas of Outlook by clicking on the **Permissions** button in the *Properties* group on the *Folder* ribbon. When you share areas of Outlook with others, the default permission level is Reviewer. The *Delegate* feature gives you more options for customizing the permissions of delegates.

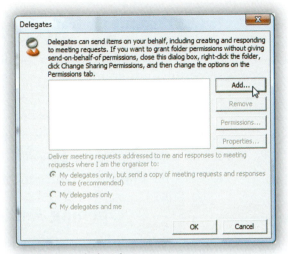

Delegates dialog box

2. Click on the **Add** button. The *Add Users* dialog box will open.

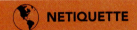

NETIQUETTE

Be careful about granting permission to others, especially if you are granting Editor permission. Delegates with this permission have full control of the area of Outlook for which you assign them the role of Editor.

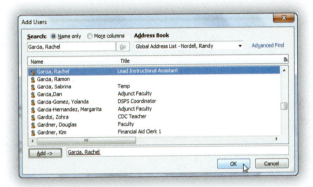

Add Users dialog box

3. Select the names of the delegates to be added. You can select multiple delegates and customize the permission level for each delegate.

4. Click **Add.**

5. Click **OK** to close the *Add Users* dialog box. The *Delegate Permissions* dialog box will open.

6. You can set the permission level for this delegate for each area of Outlook. Different roles can be set for different areas of Outlook.

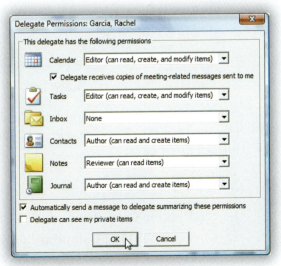

Delegate Permissions dialog box

7. Check the **Automatically send a message to delegate summarizing these permissions** check box. This will automatically generate and send an e-mail message to the delegate informing him or her of the permissions granted.

8. If you want the delegate to see your private items, check the **Delegate can see my private items** box.

9. Click **OK** to close the *Delegate Permissions* dialog box.

10. Click **OK** to close the *Delegates* dialog box.

11. Click the **File** tab to return to Outlook.

> **ⓘ MORE INFO**
>
> You can follow the preceding steps to open another user's calendar to open other areas of Outlook to which you were granted permission.

Opening Another Outlook User's Folders

When an Outlook user on your Exchange server assigns you as a delegate, you will most likely receive an e-mail summarizing your permission levels for the different areas of Outlook.

E-mail summarizing delegate permissions

Once you have been granted permission, you can open that user's folders in your Outlook. For example, you can open the user's calendar and view it in your Outlook.

STEP-BY-STEP

1. Click on the **Calendar** button in the *Navigation* pane.

2. Click on the **Open Calendar** button in the *Manage Calendars* group on the *Home* ribbon and choose **Open a Shared Calendar.** The *Open a Shared Calendar* dialog box will open.

Open a shared calendar

Open a Shared Calendar dialog box

3. Click on the **Name** button to open the *Select Name* dialog box.
4. Select the name of the contact, and click on **OK.** The calendar will appear in the *Shared Calendars* list in the *Navigation* pane.

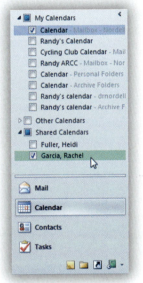

Shared Calendars
list in the Navigation
pane

Creating Outlook Items as a Delegate

If you are assigned the role of Author or Editor, you can create e-mails, calendar items, contacts, tasks, notes, or journal items for those to whom you are a delegate.

Shared Tasks displayed in the Folder pane

For example, to create a task for another user, you must first open his or her **Tasks** folder so you can view it in your Outlook.

When his or her **Tasks** folder is selected from the *Shared Tasks* area in the *Navigation* pane, it is displayed in the *Folder* pane. You can create a task in his or her Tasks folder in the same way you would create a task in your folder. The task that you create as a delegate will appear in his or her Outlook task list.

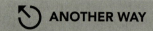

ANOTHER WAY

If you want to restrict access of a delegate without removing him or her as a delegate, you can change the permission settings to **None** in any of the areas you want to restrict.

Removing a Delegate

In the *Delegates* dialog box, you can change the permission settings for a delegate by clicking on the **Permissions** button and making the desired changes.

To delete a delegate, select the delegate to be removed and press the **Remove** button. The delegate will be removed from the delegate list and will no longer have access to your Outlook.

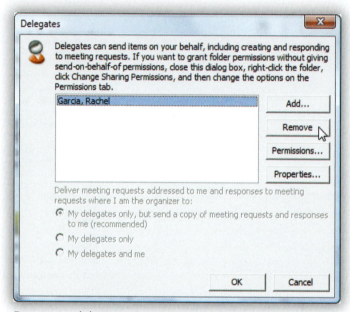

Remove a delegate

Security

As more and more communication is being done through e-mail, security has become an important issue to protect your computer and information from viruses and malicious attacks. Microsoft has provided Office users with a ***Trust Center*** to give you control over many security aspects of online information from one central area. Outlook also provides options for controlling which e-mails are treated as junk mail.

Outlook Trust Center

The Outlook Trust Center allows you to custom tailor your Outlook security in the following areas: Add-ins, Trusted Publishers, Privacy Options, E-mail Security, Attachment Handling, Automatic Download, Macro Security, Programmatic Access.

The Outlook Trust Center can be opened by clicking on the **File** tab, selecting **Options,** and choosing **Add-Ins** or **Trust Center.**

Add-Ins

Add-ins are those programs that add functionality to your Outlook. This could include adding a button on a ribbon such as OneNote or Outlook

Social Connector. The Add-ins are automatically listed in this area when a program or application used in conjunction with Outlook is installed on your computer. This area of the Trust Center lists Active, Inactive, and Disabled Application Add-ins. The area below the Add-ins list gives you the publisher, location (on your computer), and description of the selected Add-in.

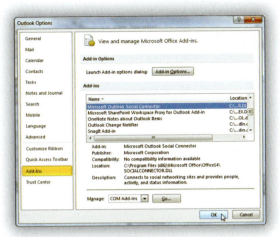

Microsoft Office Add-Ins

Trusted Publishers

Trusted publishers are those organizations that are reputable and have a digital signature assigned to the macro or program that you allow to run on your computer. The Outlook Trust Center stores this information to validate this publisher or developer. If a macro or other code is run on your computer from a source that is not a trusted source, you will receive a warning message prompting you to allow or deny the action.

Trusted Publishers in the Trust Center

DEP Setting

Data Execution Prevention (DEP) is new to the Trust Center in Outlook 2010. It protects your computer from malicious code saved and run on your

DEP Settings in the Trust Center

computer. This setting makes it more difficult for hackers to silently run their programs on your computer. Outlook will detect and shut down code it deems as malicious.

Privacy Options

The *Privacy Options* area of the Trust Center allows you to control what information is sent to and received from Microsoft. These options can provide additional functionality and resources in Outlook, as well as monitoring your Outlook usage to help with product improvement.

In this area, you can also control available translation and research options.

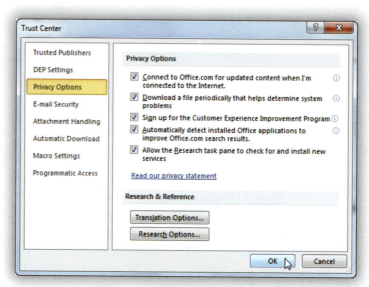

Privacy Options in the Trust Center

E-mail Security

The *E-mail Security* area allows you to control the use of encrypted e-mails and Digital IDs.

ⓘ MORE INFO

Digital signatures will be covered later in this chapter.

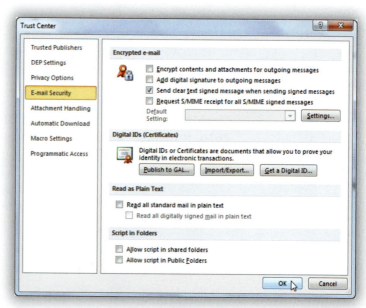

E-mail Security in the Trust Center

Encrypting is a way to add another level of security to the messages and attachments you send. You can also choose to automatically include a *digital signature* to each message you send.

S/MIME (Secure/Multipurpose Internet Mail Extensions) can be used to confirm that an e-mail was sent and received unaltered and provides details about when the e-mail was opened and read.

Digital IDs (certificates) can be used to verify your identity and electronically sign documents of high importance. Digital IDs are used in conjunction with encryption to secure e-mail messages and attachments. To encrypt a document, the sender must have a digital ID and use a *private key* to encrypt the data. The receiver of the encrypted message must have the *public key* that matches the private key of the sender to view the encrypted message.

Attachment Handling

The Trust Center allows you to control how documents attached to an e-mail are handled in Outlook. By default, Outlook blocks some attachments it views as potentially dangerous.

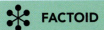

FACTOID

Microsoft Access documents are not allowed as attachments in an Outlook e-mail message. To be able to send an Access file, you must compress or zip the file and attach the compressed or zipped folder.

Attachment Handling in the Trust Center

You can use the *Add properties to attachments to enable Reply with Changes* feature. Most Microsoft Office documents allow you to include comments and changes, but this feature provides this functionality on other documents sent as attachments.

MORE INFO

Previewing attachments was covered in Chapter 2 on page 41.

File Previewing dialog box

Outlook allows you to preview many types of attachments. You can turn off the ***Attachment Preview*** feature or change the settings to control the types of documents to be previewed in Outlook. Click on the **Attachment and Document Previewers** button to open the *File Previewing Options* dialog box.

Automatic Download

Most of you have received an e-mail message with embedded HTML content—pictures and text that look similar to a Web page. By default, Outlook does not download pictures and graphics embedded in these messages.

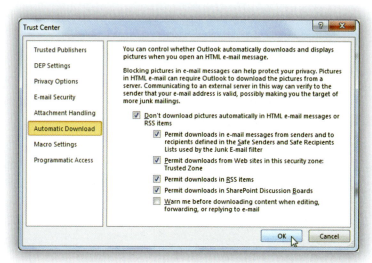

Automatic Download in the Trust Center

When you receive an e-mail with HTML content, Outlook automatically blocks the content. The InfoBar will give you the option of downloading the content of the e-mail. When HTML content is downloaded from a server, the sender of the message knows that your e-mail account is active and you might start receiving more unsolicited e-mails—junk mail. In the ***Automatic Download*** area, you can customize how Outlook handles this type of e-mail.

E-mail with HTML content blocked

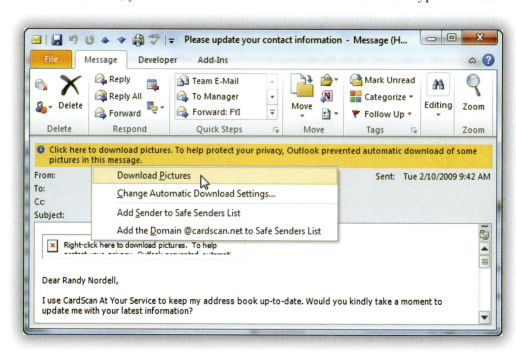

Macro Settings

Macros are simply a set of programming instructions. They are very common in electronic documents, and most perform some necessary actions in a document. But many viruses are spread by the use of macros, so Outlook tries to protect you from these malicious macros by proactively warning you about macros that are detected in e-mail messages or attachments.

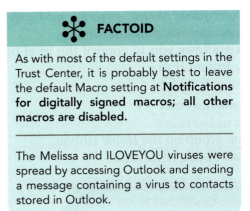

✱ **FACTOID**

As with most of the default settings in the Trust Center, it is probably best to leave the default Macro setting at **Notifications for digitally signed macros; all other macros are disabled.**

The Melissa and ILOVEYOU viruses were spread by accessing Outlook and sending a message containing a virus to contacts stored in Outlook.

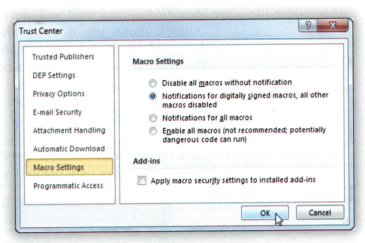

Macro Settings in the Trust Center

Programmatic Access

The *Programmatic Access Security* controls the actions in Outlook when your antivirus software is turned off or not functioning properly. If your antivirus software is functioning properly, it will protect your computer from being accessed by a virus. If your antivirus software is not on or not functioning properly, Outlook will warn you when suspicious activity is detected.

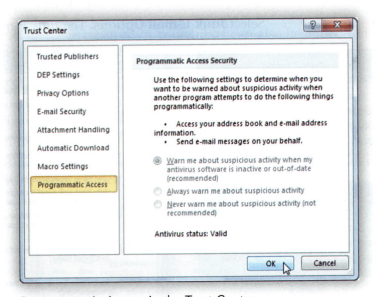

Programmatic Access in the Trust Center

Junk E-mail Options

If you are like most e-mail users, you receive quite a few junk e-mail messages each day. Antivirus software continues to improve and can identify and move potential junk e-mail messages to a different folder. Even online e-mail

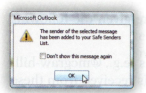

Message confirming
sender will be added
to Safe Sender list

4. If **Block Sender** is selected, the message will be moved to the *Junk E-mail* folder and the sender's e-mail address will be added to the *Blocked Senders* list. Outlook will always move e-mail messages received from this sender to the *Junk E-mail* folder.

5. If **Never Block Sender, Never Block Sender's Domain,** or **Never Block this Group or Mailing List** is selected, the sender's e-mail and/or domain name will be added to the *Safe Senders* list.

Within the *Junk E-mail Options* dialog box, each of these lists can be edited. You can add or remove e-mail addresses or domains from any of the lists, or you can edit entries included in the lists.

If an e-mail is delivered to your *Junk E-mail* folder and it is not a junk e-mail, it can be marked as **Not Junk,** and the sender's e-mail address will be added to the *Safe Senders* list.

STEP-BY-STEP

1. Select or open an e-mail in the *Junk E-mail* folder.

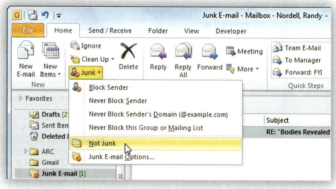

Not Junk button

2. In the *Delete* group, click on the **Junk** button and select **Not Junk.** The *Mark as Not Junk* dialog box will open. You are given the option to always trust e-mail from this sender.

Mark as Not Junk dialog box

3. Click **OK.** The e-mail will be moved to the *Inbox* folder, and the sender's e-mail address will be added to the *Safe Senders* list.

Digital Signatures

Digital signatures are used to verify the authenticity of the sender. Including a digital signature in a message is not the same as including a signature in a message. A digital signature uses a certificate to verify who you are and a public key that can be used by the receiver of the message to access encrypted information. Digital IDs can be obtained through your Exchange administrator; most digital IDs are issued by third-party sources.

If you have a digital ID, you can include a digital signature on all outgoing e-mail by changing the settings in the *E-mail Security* area of the *Trust Center* to **Add digital signature to outgoing messages.**

> ℹ **MORE INFO**
>
> Signatures were covered in Chapter 3 on page 63.

Change default setting to add digital signature to all outgoing messages

You can also add a digital signature individually to an e-mail.

STEP-BY-STEP

1. Open a new e-mail or an e-mail to which you are going to reply.
2. Click on the **expand** button at the bottom right of the *Tags* group on the *Message* ribbon. The *Properties* dialog box opens.
3. Click on the **Security Settings** button. The *Security Properties* dialog box opens.
4. Check **Add digital signature to this message.** In this dialog box, you can encrypt a message or add a digital signature to the message.

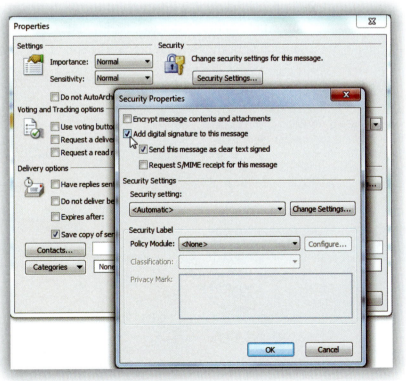

Security Properties dialog box

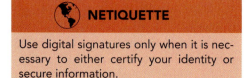

5. Click **OK** to close the *Security Properties* dialog box.
6. Click **OK** to close the *Properties* dialog box.

Searching for Outlook Items

Have you ever tried to find an e-mail item that you sent or received months ago? You might have searched through many different folders looking for a specific e-mail. You might not even remember who sent you the e-mail, the subject of the e-mail, or to whom the e-mail was sent. Even if you don't remember all the specifics about the item for which you are looking, you can use the Instant Search feature to find Outlook items.

Instant Search

The ***Instant Search*** feature in Outlook provides you with a tool to quickly search for Outlook items in a specific folder or all folders. It indexes all Outlook items in your folders and searches for items that match the specific criteria for which you are looking. For example, you can search all your mailbox folders for e-mails from your professor, for all e-mails with the word "Outlook" in the subject or body, or all contacts who work for McGraw-Hill. Outlook will display in the Folder pane all items that match your criteria.

When you click in the **Search** box at the top of the *Folder* pane, the *Search* area expands and the *Search* ribbon is displayed in Outlook. On the *Search* ribbon in the *Scope* group, you can select the folders or areas of Outlook to be searched. The *Refine* group will provide you with options to help locate the information for which you are looking. The *Options* group provides you with a list of recent searches and other advanced search tools.

STEP-BY-STEP

1. Click on the **Mail** button in the *Navigation* pane.
2. Click on the folder to be searched.
3. Click in the **Search** box at the top of the *Folder* pane.

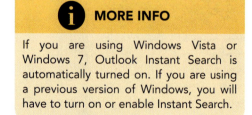

MORE INFO

If you are using Windows Vista or Windows 7, Outlook Instant Search is automatically turned on. If you are using a previous version of Windows, you will have to turn on or enable Instant Search.

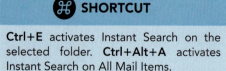

SHORTCUT

Ctrl+E activates Instant Search on the selected folder. **Ctrl+Alt+A** activates Instant Search on All Mail Items.

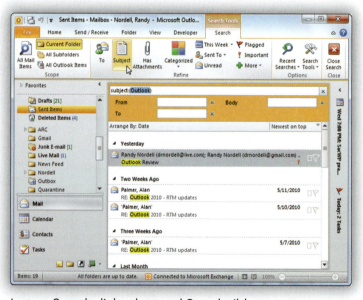

Instant Search dialog box and Search ribbon

4. Type in the words in the fields to be searched. Outlook will display matching e-mails in the *Folder* pane.

5. Additional criteria can be selected from the *Refine* group.

6. The *Scope* group will allow you to specify where Outlook performs the search.

7. Click the **Close Search** button (**X**) to the right of the search field to clear the search and close the *Search* area and ribbon. You can also click on one of your mailbox folders to close *Instant Search*.

When you use Instant Search, Outlook will display the matching items in the Folder pane, highlight the matching criteria, and list the folder in which the item is located. You can open any of these items from the search results by double-clicking on it in the *Folder* pane.

Search Options

You can change the ***search options*** for Instant Search to customize which folders are indexed, how the results are displayed, whether or not the Deleted Items folder is included in the search, and the default folders to be searched.

You can open the *Search Options* dialog box by clicking on the **Search Tools** button in the *Options* group on the *Search* ribbon and selecting **Search Options.**

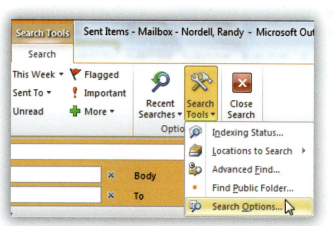

Search Options button

Search Options in the Outlook Options dialog box

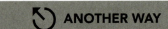

The *Search Options* dialog box can be opened from the Outlook *BackStage*. Click on the **File** tab, choose **Options**, and click on **Search**.

Advanced Find

When you use Instant Search in Mail, Outlook just searches for e-mail items. Outlook also provides you with **Advanced Find** to search for any type of Outlook items rather than being limited to just one type of item. Advanced Find displays Outlook items that match your criteria in the *Advanced Find* dialog box.

STEP-BY-STEP

1. Click in the **Search** box at the top of the *Folder* pane.
2. Click on the **Search Tools** button in the *Options* group on the *Search* ribbon, and select **Advanced Find.** The *Advanced Find* dialog box will open.

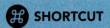 **SHORTCUT**

Ctrl+Shift+F opens the *Advanced Find* dialog box.

Advanced Find dialog box

3. Select the type of item to find in the *Look for* area.
4. Select the location to search in the *In* area. Click the **Browse** button to select the folder to search.
5. Type in the criteria for which to search. You can click on the **From** or **Sent To** buttons to select contacts. You can also click on either the **More Choices** or **Advanced** tabs for more search options.
6. Click on the **Find Now** button to search for items that match your criteria. The matching items will be displayed at the bottom of the dialog box.
7. Click on **New Search** to clear the current search, or click on the **X** in the upper right corner to close the *Advanced Find* dialog box.

Customizing Outlook to Fit Your Needs

Now that you are an advanced Outlook user and regularly use the different tasks and special features offered by Outlook, you might want to customize the user interface. You can customize the look and contents of *Outlook Today,* the *Navigation* pane, *Favorites,* and the *Quick Access* toolbar. There are also many other user interface options you can choose to customize how information is displayed in the Folder pane. You can change which fields are displayed in the Folder pane and how information is sorted and grouped.

Outlook Today

Outlook Today is the opening window that is displayed in the Folder pane when Outlook is started. It gives you a snapshot of your upcoming calendar, task, and message items. By clicking on an item displayed in Outlook Today, you will be taken directly to that item in Outlook.

Outlook Today can be customized to include different amounts of calendar and task items. You can select different mail folders to be displayed, and you can change the overall look and layout of Outlook Today.

 **MORE INFO**

You can access *Outlook Today* by clicking on your **Mailbox** folder in the *Navigation* pane.

STEP-BY-STEP

1. Click on the **Customize Outlook Today** button in the *Folder* pane. The *Customize Outlook Today* screen will be displayed in the *Folder* pane.

Outlook Today displayed in the Folder pane

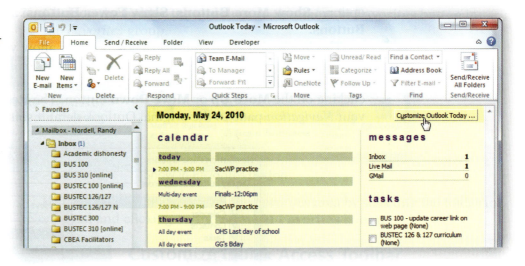

2. Click on the **Startup** check box to have Outlook Today automatically displayed each time you open Outlook.

3. In the *Messages* area, you can choose the folders to be displayed in Outlook Today.

4. In the *Calendar* area, you can select the number of days to display in Outlook Today.

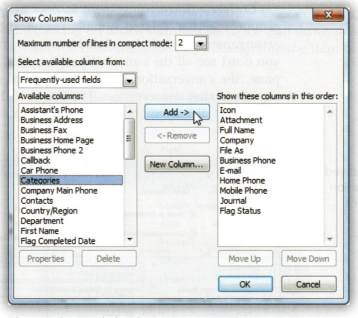

Show Columns dialog box

3. In the *Available* columns area, select the column to be added and click on the **Add** button. Columns can also be removed in this dialog box.

4. You can arrange the display order of columns by clicking on the column at the right and using the **Move Up** or **Move Down** button.

5. Click **OK** to close the *Show Columns* dialog box.

To display the *Field Chooser* dialog box, right-click on any one of the column headings and choose **Field Chooser.** Drag the selected field from the *Field Chooser* dialog box to the desired location in the *Folder* pane. When adding fields to the *Folder* pane, a red arrow will appear in the location where the field will be placed.

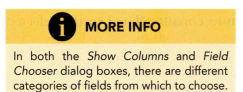

MORE INFO

In both the *Show Columns* and *Field Chooser* dialog boxes, there are different categories of fields from which to choose.

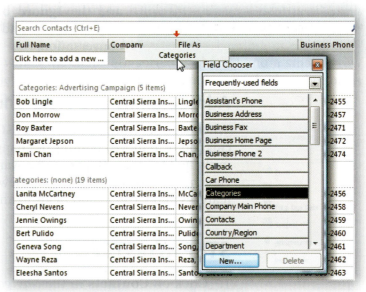

Using the Field Chooser to add a column

You can easily remove a field by dragging and dropping it (column heading) to a different location among the column headings. You can also remove a field by dragging and dropping the field below the column headings area in the Folder pane.

Deleting a field

ANOTHER WAY

You can also remove a field from the *Folder* pane by right-clicking on the column heading and choosing **Remove This Column.**

Show in Groups

When items are shown in a list in the Folder pane, Outlook can group the items by the field by which the items are sorted. For example when items are sorted by date, Outlook will group them by Today, Yesterday, Last Week, Two Weeks Ago, Three Weeks Ago, Last Month, and Older.

STEP-BY-STEP

Show in Groups options in the Arrangement group

1. Click on the **Mail** button in the *Navigation* pane.

2. Click on the **View** tab.

3. In the *Arrangements* group, click on the **More** button to expand the arrangements (or choose **Arrange By**).

4. Click on **Show in Groups.** The items displayed in the *Folder* pane are displayed in groups.

E-mail messages displayed in groups in the Folder pane

You can change the grouping by selecting a different field (column heading) by which to group the items. Click on a column heading to toggle it back and forth between ascending and descending sort order. Clicking on the small triangle to the left of the group name will expand or collapse the group. You can turn off grouping by deselecting **Show in Groups.**

You can also expand or collapse groups by clicking on the **View** tab and selecting **Expand/Collapse.** You will have the options of **Collapse This Group, Expand This Group, Collapse All Groups,** and **Expand All Groups.**

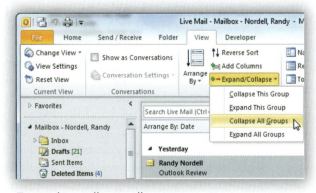

Expand or collapse all groups

Customizing Views

Outlook also provides you with an ***Advanced View Settings*** dialog box to further customize how your items are displayed in the Folder pane. The Advanced View Settings dialog box will allow you to customize the view by which you are currently displaying items in the Folder pane. Click on the **View Settings** button in the *Current View* group on the *View* ribbon.

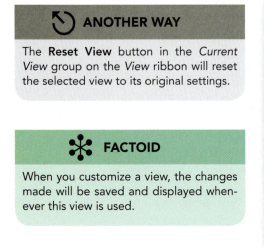

ANOTHER WAY

The **Reset View** button in the *Current View* group on the *View* ribbon will reset the selected view to its original settings.

FACTOID

When you customize a view, the changes made will be saved and displayed whenever this view is used.

Advanced View Settings dialog box

- ***Columns***—you can choose the fields to be displayed.
- ***Group By***—you can group and sort by multiple fields.
- ***Sort***—you can specify the fields and type of sort to be applied.
- ***Filter***—you can create a filter so only certain items are displayed.
- ***Other Settings***—you can customize font, size, gridlines, AutoPreview, and Reading pane options.
- ***Conditional Formatting***—you can customize how specific items are displayed in the Folder pane. The options in this area will vary depending on the type of Outlook items being displayed in the Folder pane.
- ***Format Columns***—you can customize the format, width, and alignment of the fields displayed.
- ***Reset Current View***—you can reset the view to its original default settings.

Creating a Custom View

For each area of Outlook, you are provided with many different preset views. As discussed, you can modify any of these views to meet your individual needs. The ***Manage All Views*** dialog box will allow you to customize preset views or create a new custom view for that area of Outlook. Custom views can be saved and used on different folders in Outlook.

STEP-BY-STEP

1. In any area of Outlook, click on the **View** tab, choose **Change View,** and click on **Manage Views.** The *Manage All Views* dialog box will open.

Manage Views option on the View ribbon

2. Click on the **New** button. The *Create a New View* dialog box will open.

Manage All Views dialog box

3. In the *Name of new view* area, type a name for the view.

4. In the *Type of view* area, select **Table.** This selection will vary depending on the type of view to be created and the area of Outlook for which you are creating this view.

5. In the *Can be used on* area, click on **All Contact folders.** This will enable this view to be used on all *Contact* folders.

6. Click **OK.** The *Advanced View Settings* dialog box will open.

Create a New View dialog box

7. Click on each of the following buttons to customize: **Columns, Group By, Sort, Filter, Other Settings, Conditional Formatting,** and **Format Columns.**

8. When all changes have been made, click **OK** to close the *Advanced View Settings* dialog box.

Advanced View Settings dialog box

9. Click **Apply View** to apply the new view on the current folder.

10. Click **OK** to close the *Manage All Views* dialog box.

This new view will now be available for use on all your contact folders (or whichever type of folders for which you created the new view). You can copy, modify, rename, or delete views from the *Manage All Views* dialog box.

Chapter Highlights

▸ Outlook allows you to customize how your information is shared by using delegates and permissions.

▸ A **delegate** is another Outlook user to whom access is given to specific areas of your Outlook.

▸ **Permissions** are the level of access granted to a delegate. The different delegate permissions include: **Reviewer, Author,** and **Editor.**

- ▶ You can turn off delegate access to your Outlook by either deleting the delegate or changing the permission level to **None.**
- ▶ Depending on the level of permission granted, delegates can open, view, edit, and create Outlook items for other Outlook users.
- ▶ The **Trust Center** in Outlook allows users to customize the level of security employed in Outlook.
- ▶ With the use of a **Digital ID,** Outlook users can add a **digital signature** to messages and **encrypt** information included in an e-mail to secure the contents of the message.
- ▶ **Junk E-mail Options** helps control the amount of junk e-mail you receive. You can add senders and domain names to the **Blocked Senders** list to automatically move e-mails from these e-mail addresses and domains to your **Junk E-mail folder.**
- ▶ You can add senders and domain names to the **Safe Senders** and **Safe Recipients** lists to prevent e-mail from these e-mail addresses and domains from being treated as junk e-mail.
- ▶ **Instant Search** indexes e-mail items in Outlook for quick retrieval when searching for items that match specific criteria.
- ▶ **Advanced Find** can be used to search for all types of Outlook items that match specific criteria.
- ▶ **Outlook Today** is an introductory screen that is displayed in the Folder pane when Outlook is started. It displays upcoming calendar and task items and the number of unread e-mails in your mail folders.
- ▶ You can customize the layout and content of Outlook Today.
- ▶ You can customize the Navigation pane by choosing different large and small buttons and changing the order of buttons.
- ▶ Links to mail folders can be placed in the **Favorites** area to give you quick access to these folders.
- ▶ Outlook items displayed in the Folder pane can be **sorted** or **arranged** by a specific field. You can sort items in **ascending** or **descending** order.
- ▶ When viewing Outlook items in the Folder pane in list view, columns can be added by using **Add Columns** or **Field Chooser.**
- ▶ Outlook items displayed in the Folder pane can be **grouped** by different fields. Groups can be expanded or collapsed.
- ▶ Outlook provides many different preset views for each area of Outlook. Each of these views can be customized, and new custom views can be created.

What Do You Know About Outlook?

True/False Questions

T F   1. When an e-mail message that includes HTML content is received, Outlook by default blocks this content. [Objective 12.2]

T F   2. E-mail items identified by Outlook as junk e-mail are moved to the Deleted Items folder. [Objective 12.2]

T F   3. When items displayed in the Folder pane are grouped by a field or column, only that column of each item is displayed in the Folder pane. [Objective 12.4]

T   F   4. Outlook Today can display the most recently used contacts.
[Objective 12.4]

T   F   5. The delegate permission with the highest level of access is Editor.
[Objective 12.1]

Multiple Choice Questions

1. Which of the following is *not* a permission level that can be granted to
a delegate? [Objective 12.1]
   a. Creator
   b. Editor
   c. Reviewer
   d. Author

2. Instant Search searches for which type(s) of Outlook items? [Objective 12.3]
   a. Calendar items
   b. Tasks
   c. E-mail
   d. All the above

3. Which of the following lists are available in Junk E-mail options?
[Objective 12.2]
   a. Blocked Senders
   b. Blocked Recipients
   c. Safe Groups
   d. All the above

4. A delegate can be given access to which area of your Outlook?
[Objective 12.1]
   a. Tasks
   b. E-mail
   c. Contacts
   d. All the above

5. When using Instant Search, which of the following is true?
[Objective 12.3]
   a. A search folder can be created from the search criteria.
   b. The results are displayed in the Folder pane.
   c. Instant Search searches all Outlook folders for items matching the
   search criteria.
   d. All the above.

Short Answer Questions

1. Describe how using delegates differs from sharing in Outlook.
[Objective 12.1]

2. Explain how Instant Search differs from Advanced Find.
[Objective 12.3]

3. Explain how to add and remove fields displayed in the Folder pane in
list view. [Objective 12.4]

Putting Outlook to Work

In the following exercises, you will be giving access to areas of your Outlook to delegates, incorporating security features, using Outlook search features, and customizing Outlook user interfaces. In addition to using the new Outlook features covered in this chapter, you will be using some of the Outlook features learned in previous chapters. To use the delegates feature, you must be using an Exchange account.

Exercise 12.1 [Guided Practice]

Assign other Outlook users as delegates. *Note: This exercise requires that you are working on an Exchange server.* **[Objective 12.1]**

1. Click on the **File** tab, click on **Account Settings,** and choose **Delegate Access.** The *Delegates* dialog box will open.

2. Click on the **Add** button to add a delegate. The *Add Users* dialog box will open.

   a. Select your professor as a delegate.
   b. Click **Add.**
   c. Click **OK** to close the *Add Users* dialog box.
   d. The *Delegate Permissions* dialog box will open.

3. Set the following roles or permissions for your professor.

   a. Calendar: **Editor.** Deselect the check box for **Delegates receive copies of meeting-related messages sent to me.**
   b. Tasks: **Editor**
   c. Inbox: **None**
   d. Contacts: **Reviewer**
   e. Notes: **Author**
   f. Journal: **None**
   g. Check the box to **Automatically send a message to delegate summarizing these permissions.**
   h. Click **OK** to close the *Delegate Permissions* dialog box.
   i. Click **OK** to close the *Delegates* dialog box.

4. Assign the classmate sitting next to you as a delegate using the following roles or permissions.

   a. Calendar: **Author.** Deselect the check box for **Delegates receive copies of meeting-related messages sent to me.**
   b. Tasks: **Author**
   c. Inbox: **None**
   d. Contacts: **Reviewer**
   e. Notes: **Reviewer**
   f. Journal: **None**
   g. Check the box to **Automatically send a message to delegate summarizing these permissions.**
   h. Click **OK** to close the *Delegate Permissions* dialog box.
   i. Click **OK** to close the *Delegates* dialog box.

Exercise 12.2 [Guided Practice]

Create Outlook items for other users. *Note: This exercise requires that you are working on an Exchange server.* **[Objective 12.1]**

1. Click on the **Calendar** button in the *Navigation* pane.

2. Click on the **Open Calendar** button in the *Manage Calendars* group on the *Home* ribbon, and choose **Open a Shared Calendar.** The **Open a Shared Calendar** dialog box opens.

   a. Click on the **Name** button to open the *Select Names* dialog box.
   b. Select your professor, and click **OK.**
   c. Your professor's calendar will be displayed in the *Folder* pane and will also be listed in the *Shared Calendars* area in the *Navigation* pane.
   d. Drag two appointments or events from your calendar to your professor's calendar.
   e. Deselect your professor's calendar in the *Shared Calendar* list in the *Navigation* pane.

3. Click on the **Open Calendar** button, and choose **Open a Shared Calendar.** The *Open a Shared Calendar* dialog box will open.

   a. Click on the **Name** button to open the *Select Names* dialog box.
   b. Select your classmate who assigned you as a delegate, and click **OK.**
   c. Your classmate's calendar will be displayed in the *Folder* pane and will also be listed in the *Shared Calendars* area in the *Navigation* pane.

4. Create a new appointment on your classmate's calendar.

   a. Use **Outlook Review** as the subject.
   b. Set the date for **next Monday** from **8-10 a.m.**
   c. Use **Computer Lab** as the location for the appointment.
   d. Click on **Save & Close** to save the appointment.

5. Click on the **Tasks** button in the *Navigation* pane.

6. Click on the **Folder** tab and then on the **Open Shared Tasks** button in the *Share* group.

   a. Open both your professor's and your classmate's tasks. You will have to open these one at a time.

7. In the *Shared Tasks* area of the *Navigation* pane, click on your professor's tasks.

8. Create a new task in your professor's tasks.

   a. Use **Outlook Review Sheet** as the subject.
   b. Set the due date for this **Friday.**
   c. Set a reminder for **9 a.m.** this **Thursday.**
   d. Click on **Save & Close** to save this task.

9. In the *Shared Tasks* area of the *Navigation* pane, click on your classmate's tasks.

10. Create a new task in your classmate's tasks.

    a. Use **Outlook Review Sheet** as the subject.
    b. Set the due date for this **Friday.**
    c. Set a reminder for **9 a.m.** this **Thursday.**
    d. Click on **Save & Close** to save this task.

Exercise 12.3 [Guided Practice]

Send an e-mail through your Gmail account. Add senders and domain names to lists in the Junk e-mail options. [Objective 12.2]

1. Create a new e-mail message.

    a. Use `Outlook Review` as the subject.
    b. Send the e-mail to all your classmates' and professor's Gmail addresses.
    c. Include a brief message about the upcoming Outlook review.
    d. Include your signature.
    e. Mark as **high importance.**
    f. Set the message to expire at **8 a.m.** next **Monday.**
    g. Send the message through your **Gmail** account.

2. Click on the **Junk** button in the *Delete* group and then on **Junk E-mail Options.** The *Junk E-mail Options* dialog box will open.

3. Click on the **Safe Senders** tab.

4. Click **Add.** The *Add address or domain* dialog box opens.

    a. Type in the domain of your school e-mail address (e.g., @arc.losrios. edu).
    b. Click **OK** to add this domain to the *Safe Senders* list.

5. Click on the **Safe Recipients** tab.

6. Click **Add.** The *Add address or domain* dialog box opens.

    a. Type in the domain of your school e-mail address (e.g., @arc.losrios. edu).
    b. Click **OK** to add this domain to the *Safe Recipients* list.

7. Click on the **Blocked Senders** tab.

8. Click **Add.** The *Add address or domain* dialog box opens.

    a. Type in your professor's Gmail address.
    b. Click **OK** to add this domain to the *Blocked Senders* list.

9. Click **Apply** and then **OK** to close the *Junk E-mail Options* dialog box.

10. Open one of the **Outlook Review** e-mails from your classmates.

    a. Click on the **Junk** button in the *Delete* group and select **Never Block Sender.**
    b. A dialog box will open informing you that the sender has been added to the *Safe Senders* list.
    c. Check the box for **Please do not show me this dialog box again,** and click **OK.**
    d. Close the e-mail.

11. Right-click on one of the **Outlook Review** e-mails in the *Folder* pane.

    a. Choose **Junk** and then click on **Never Block Sender.**
    b. The sender will be added to the list.

12. Using one of the two preceding methods, add the rest of your classmates (Gmail addresses) to the *Safe Senders* list.

Exercise 12.4 [Guided Practice]

Customize Outlook Today, and customize views. [Objective 12.4]

1. Click on the **Mail** button in the *Navigation* pane.

2. Click on the **Mailbox** folder in the *Navigation* pane to display **Outlook Today** in the *Folder* pane.

3. Click on the **Customize Outlook Today** button in the *Folder* pane. The *Customize Outlook Today* screen will open in the *Folder* pane.

   a. Check the box **When starting, go directly to Outlook Today.**
   b. Click on the **Choose Folders** button in the *Messages* area.
   c. Check the **Gmail** folder and any **RSS feeds folders** you have.
   d. Click **OK** to close the *Select Folders* dialog box.
   e. In the *Calendars* area, choose **7** for the number of calendar days to display.
   f. In the *Tasks* area, choose **All Tasks** and sort **Descending** by **Due Date.**
   g. Choose a **Style** of your choice.
   h. Click on **Save Changes.**

4. Click on your **Inbox** folder in the *Navigation* pane.

5. Click on the **View** tab and then on the **Add Columns** button in the *Arrangement* group. The *Show Columns* dialog box will open.

   a. Click on the **Size** field in the *Show these columns in this order* area at the right.
   b. Click on the **Remove** button. The *Size* field is removed from this view.
   c. Click on the **Reminder** field at the right and then on the **Move Up** button until the *Reminder* column appears before the *Importance* column.
   d. Click **OK** to close the *Show Columns* dialog box.

6. Right-click on one of the column headings in the *Folder* pane and select **Field Chooser.** The *Field Chooser* dialog box opens.

   a. Click on the pull-down list at the top of this dialog box and choose **All Mail fields.**
   b. Scroll down to find the *Expires* field.
   c. Drag and drop the **Expires** field between the *Received* and *Categories* field.

7. On the *View* ribbon, click on the **More** button at the bottom right of *Arrangement,* and then deselect **Show in Groups.**

Exercise 12.5 [Guided Practice]

Use Instant Search and Advanced Find. [Objective 12.3]

1. Click on the **Mail** button in the *Navigation* pane, and select your **Inbox** folder.

2. Click in the **Search** box at the top of the *Folder* pane. The *Search* area will open and the *Search* ribbon will be displayed.

3. Click on the **Subject** button in the *Refine* group.

4. Type **Outlook** as the subject.

   a. The results of the search are displayed in the *Folder* pane.

5. Click on the **All Mail Items** button in the *Scope* group.

   a. The results of the search are displayed in the *Folder* pane.

6. Click on the **Close Search** button in the *Close* group on the *Search* ribbon, or click on the **Close Search** button (**X**) to the right of the *Subject* field. The *Search* area and *Search* ribbon will close.

7. Click in the **Search** box at the top of the *Folder* pane.

8. Click on the **Search Tools** button in the *Options* group on the *Search* ribbon, and choose **Advanced Find.** The *Advanced Find* dialog box will open. **Ctrl+Shift+F** will also open the *Advanced Find* dialog box.

9. Type **Outlook** in the *Search for the words* box.

   a. Notice Outlook will search for *Messages* in the *Inbox*.

10. In the *In* field, select **subject field and message body.**

    a. Click on the **Find Now** button.
    b. The results of the search are displayed at the bottom of the *Advanced Find* dialog box.

11. In the *Look for* area, choose **Any type of Outlook item.**

    a. A dialog box will open telling you your current search has cleared.
    b. Click **OK.**

12. Type **Outlook** in the *Search for the words* box.

    a. Notice Outlook will search for *Any type of Outlook item* in the *Mailbox*.
    b. Click on the **Find Now** button.
    c. The results of the search are displayed at the bottom of the *Advanced Find* dialog box.

13. Click on the **New Search** button.

    a. A dialog box will open telling you your current search has cleared.
    b. Click **OK.**

14. Click on the **From** box, choose your **professor's e-mail addresses,** and close the *Select Names* dialog box.

    a. Click on the **Find Now** button.

15. Close the *Advanced Find* dialog box.

16. Click on the **Close Search** button on the *Search* ribbon.

Exercise 12.6 [Independent Practice]

Customize the Quick Access toolbar, and create a custom view. [Objective 12.4]

1. Open an e-mail in your *Inbox* folder.

2. Add the **Quick Print** and **Spelling & Grammar** buttons to your Quick Access toolbar.

3. Close the open e-mail message.

4. In *Tasks,* open the **Manage Views** dialog box to create a new **Task** view.

   a. Hint: **View** ribbon, **Change View, Manage Views.**

5. Create a new view and name it *[your first name]*.

    a. The new view will be a **Table** view and can be used on **All Task folders.**

6. Include the following columns in the order listed: **Icon, Complete, Priority, Attachment, Subject, Assigned To, Due Date, Status, % Complete, Categories, Notes, Flag Status.**

7. **Group** by **Categories** in **ascending** order.

8. **Sort** by **Due Date** in **descending** order.

9. Apply the view and close any open dialog boxes.

10. Display your professor's tasks and apply the *[your first name]* view to the task list.

Exercise 12.7 [Independent Practice]

Edit Junk e-mail lists and delegates. Change Navigation pane buttons. [Objectives 12.1, 12.2]

1. Open the **Junk E-mail Options** dialog box.

2. Remove your professor's Gmail address from the *Blocked Senders* list. Note: Your professor's e-mail address was added to the *Blocked Senders* list in Exercise 12.3.

3. Open a message from your professor, and add it to the *Safe Sender* list.

4. Open the **Delegates** dialog box.

5. Remove your classmate as a delegate.

6. Edit the permission settings for your professor.

    a. Set the permissions level to **None** on all Outlook areas.

7. In the *Navigation* pane, add **Notes** as a large button below *Tasks*.

Exercise 12.8 [Independent Practice]

Use Advanced Find to search all Outlook items. Create a new view for e-mail items. [Objective 12.4]

1. Use **Advanced Find** to find any type of Outlook item with the word **"Outlook"** in the subject and from your professor.

2. Specify that *Advanced Find* look in all mailbox folders.

3. Create a new e-mail view, and name it *[your first name]*.

    a. The new view will be a **Table** view and can be used on **All Mail and Post folders.**

4. Include the following columns in the order listed: **Importance, Icon, Attachment, From, Subject, Received, In Folder, Categories, Flag Status.**

5. **Group** by **Received** in **descending** order.

6. **Sort** by **Received** in **descending** order.

7. Make any other desired changes to this new view.

8. Apply this view, and close any open dialog boxes.

9. Use this new view on your *Inbox* and your *Gmail* folders.

Appendix A

Setting Up Outlook for an On-site or Online Classroom Environment

Ideally, the course using this text will be taught as an on-site course. In an on-site course, students will be able to experience all the benefits of using Outlook in an Exchange environment and practice using the features of Outlook with classmates in a computer lab environment. But many Outlook courses are taught in an online environment. In this appendix, you'll be provided with some tips to help you set up your Outlook course whether it is an online or on-site course.

On-site Course

If you're teaching this course on-site, you should create a set of student accounts on an Exchange server. These accounts can be generic accounts that get recycled from semester to semester. It is probably best to have a separate domain for the classroom Exchange server so it does not conflict with your campus or district Exchange server. Using a separate server also helps prevent students from having access to the entire Global Address List of your school, district, or company.

 MORE INFO

The individual who manages the Exchange server at your school will be able to help you create a set of Exchange e-mail accounts.

Creating User Accounts

These accounts can easily be managed through *Active Directory* and *Exchange System Manager*. The student accounts are given a generic name (e.g., D01, D02, D03, and so forth), and a generic password is used (e.g., student). Once one account is created in Active Directory, it can be copied so that only the username and password need to be reentered. Here is the process that can be used to create the generic student accounts.

STEP-BY-STEP

1. Open **Active Directory,** and create a container to store the user accounts.

2. Create a **New User**. The name information and username can be generic rather than a specific student's name.

New Object/User dialog box in Active Directory

3. Click **Next**.

New user password and password options in Active Directory

4. Type in the **password** and **confirm password**.

5. You can set the password options to your preference. I've found it best to use the same password for all students and set the account to **User cannot change password** and **Password never expires**.

6. Check the box to **Create an Exchange mailbox**. This will automatically create an *Exchange* e-mail account with this user's information when the account is created in *Active Directory*.

7. Click **Next**.

New user alias, server, and mailbox storage options in Active Directory

8. Confirm the *Exchange* server and *mailbox storage* of the user, and click **Next**.

9. Confirm the new user information, and click **Finish**. The new user account will be created both in *Active Directory* and on the *Exchange* server.

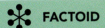

New user confirmation dialog box in Active Directory

10. You can create additional accounts by copying the new account and entering in the new username and password. All the other settings will remain the same.

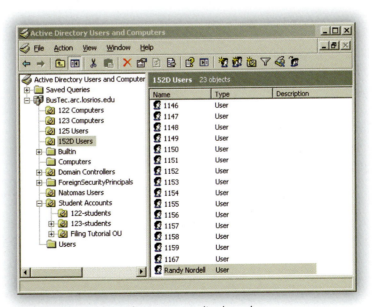

Active Directory with new user displayed

Recycling User Accounts

At the end of each semester, these Exchange e-mail accounts can be recycled so they can be used again for subsequent semesters. The recycling process consists of deleting the accounts from Active Directory, purging the deleted accounts from Exchange System Manager, and re-creating the accounts.

STEP-BY-STEP

1. Open **Active Directory,** and navigate to the folder containing the accounts to be deleted.

2. Select the accounts to be deleted, and **delete** them. This will not delete the *Exchange* accounts, but marks these accounts for deletion.

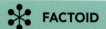
FACTOID

There are third-party software programs that will purge e-mail accounts without deleting and re-creating them.

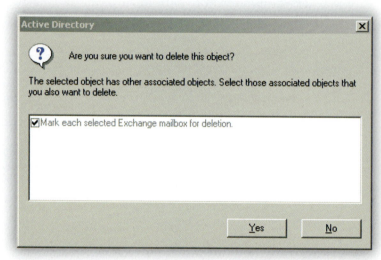

Deletion confirmation dialog box in Active Directory

3. Open **Exchange System Manager** and navigate to the **Mailboxes** folder in the proper server folder.

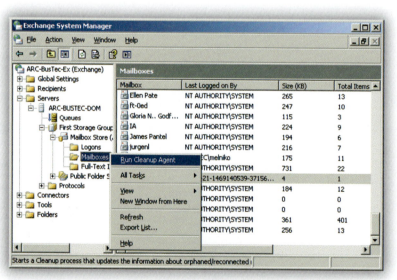

Run Cleanup Agent on Mailbox folder in Exchange System Manager

4. Right-click on the **Mailboxes** folder, and choose **Run Cleanup Agent**. This will mark with a red X all the accounts that were deleted in Active Directory. You can scroll through to see the disabled accounts.

5. Right-click on each account to be deleted, and choose **Purge**. This step has to be done individually on each account to be deleted.

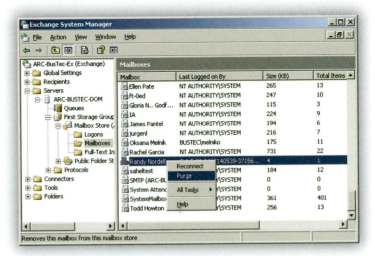

Purge each Exchange account to be deleted

6. Once the accounts have been purged, they are no longer on the *Exchange* server or in Active Directory.

7. Follow the steps previously outlined in the Create User Accounts section to re-create the new set of user accounts.

Although this might seem like a daunting process, it actually only takes about 15 minutes. Most likely this process will be done by the person who manages the Exchange server at your institution. This person can easily set up a separate domain in the forest for the class Exchange server.

Online Course

When teaching an Outlook course in an online environment, there will be some decisions that need to be made by the instructor, and it's important to think through some of these issues prior to setting up your class. The following are some issues to think about before setting up your course and some suggestions to help make your online course as effective as possible.

E-mail

One of the major issues of teaching a course such as this online is e-mail accounts. Do students use their personal e-mail account, school account, or a new e-mail account? Along the same line as e-mail are contacts. How do students get the contact information for other students in the course?

There are a couple of reasons why it is probably not a good idea to have students use their personal e-mail accounts for a course such as this. Students will be interacting via e-mail with others in the course. They do not necessarily want all students in the class to have their personal e-mail accounts. Also, there will be a large volume of e-mails being sent and received in this class. It will be much better if class e-mails are not intermingled with personal e-mails.

Below are a couple of suggestions:

- **Generic E-mail Accounts**. You can set up generic e-mail accounts for your class using one of the free e-mail services such as Gmail or Live Mail. You could use a generic format such as ARC-Student1@live. com, ARC-Student2@live.com, and so forth. At the end of the semester, you could recycle these accounts by deleting all e-mails and changing passwords.

At the beginning of the semester, each student would be given an e-mail account and a list of the e-mail addresses for other students and the professor in the class. Students would type in the e-mail addresses of other students and the professor until contacts are covered in Chapter 4.

- **Student-Created E-mail Accounts**. Students could create a new e-mail account to be used specifically for this course. These e-mail addresses could then be sent to the professor. A list of e-mail addresses could then be created and distributed to all students in the class.

- **School-Created E-mail Accounts**. Many schools provide e-mail accounts for students. Depending on the type of account, it is possible that these accounts can be set up and used in Outlook. If these school-created accounts are either POP3 or IMAP accounts, they can be set up in Outlook.

It would still be a good idea to have your e-mail administrator set up a unique set of student accounts that can be used specifically for this course. These accounts could then be recycled each semester.

In Chapter 8, students will be adding an additional account. At this point they will create a new account and share their e-mail addresses with other classmates. They will have enough knowledge of e-mail and contacts to easily get this new information to others in the class without the professor having to handle this administrative task.

Using SimNet

One of the difficulties of teaching an Outlook course in an online environment is that students are not on a common Exchange server. Also, students will not be able to experience all the benefits of using Outlook in conjunction with an Exchange server.

For an online course, I would highly suggest using this text in conjunction with **SimNet**, which will allow you to create lessons and tests that can be used with the students. The features that are unique to using Outlook in an Exchange environment can be covered in SimNet. Appendix D lists many of the features that are unique to Outlook in an Exchange environment.

Screen Shots

Many of the topics covered in this text, such as Calendar, Notes, Journal, and user interface, will not require students to send e-mails. The instructor might require students to take screen shots (Ctrl+PrintScreen). These screen shots could then be pasted into a Word document, saved, and submitted as an attachment to an e-mail.

Appendix B
Outlook Shortcuts

Global Outlook Commands

Activity	Shortcut
Go to Mail	Ctrl+1
Go to Calendar	Ctrl+2
Go to Contacts	Ctrl+3
Go to Tasks	Ctrl+4
Go to Notes	Ctrl+5
Go to Folder List	Ctrl+6
Go to Shortcuts	Ctrl+7
Go to Journal	Ctrl+8
New item	Ctrl+N
New e-mail message	Ctrl+Shift+M
New calendar appointment	Ctrl+Shift+A
New meeting request	Ctrl+Shift+Q
New contact	Ctrl+Shift+C
New contact group	Ctrl+Shift+L
New task	Ctrl+Shift+K
New task request	Ctrl+Alt+Shift+U
New note	Ctrl+Shift+N
New journal entry	Ctrl+Shift+J
New text message	Ctrl+Shift+T
New folder	Ctrl+Shift+E
Save	Ctrl+S
Save as	F12
Move item	Ctrl+Shift+V
Print	Ctrl+P
Open	Ctrl+O

(continued)

Activity	Shortcut
Close an open Outlook item or dialog box	Esc or Alt+F4
Copy	Ctrl+C
Cut	Ctrl+X
Paste	Ctrl+V
Undo	Ctrl+Z
Bold	Ctrl+B
Italicize	Ctrl+I
Underline	Ctrl+U
Select all	Ctrl+A
Select range of items	Shift+click on first and last item in range
Select nonadjacent items	Ctrl+click
Help	F1
Search	F3 or Ctrl+E
Advanced find	Ctrl+Shift+F
Find a contact	F11
Open Address Book	Ctrl+Shift+B
Switch between panes	F6
Context menu (same as right click)	Shift+F10
Activate ribbon/menu	F10
Send/receive all folders	F9
Move forward one field	Tab
Move back one field	Shift+Tab
Repeat command or typing	Ctrl+Y
Forward selected item	Ctrl+F
Delete selected item	Ctrl+D

Mail

Activity	Shortcut
Go to Mail	Ctrl+1
New e-mail message	Ctrl+N
New e-mail message (anywhere in Outlook)	Ctrl+Shift+M
Open selected e-mail	Ctrl+O

Activity	Shortcut
Close an open e-mail	Esc or Alt+F4
Reply	Ctrl+R
Reply all	Ctrl+Shift+R
Reply with meeting	Ctrl+Alt+R
Forward	Ctrl+F
Forward e-mail as an attachment	Ctrl+Alt+F
Send	Alt+S
Mark as read	Ctrl+Q
Mark as unread	Ctrl+U
New mail folder	Ctrl+Shift+E
Delete selected e-mail or folder	Ctrl+D
Ignore conversation	Ctrl+Del
Clean up conversation	Alt+Del
Display Address Book	Ctrl+Shift+B

Calendar

Activity	Shortcut
Go to Calendar	Ctrl+2
New appointment	Ctrl+N
New appointment (anywhere in Outlook)	Ctrl+Shift+A
New meeting request	Ctrl+Shift+Q
Open selected calendar item	Ctrl+O
Close an open calendar item	Esc or Alt+F4
Forward calendar item	Ctrl+F
Open Recurrence dialog box	Ctrl+G
Create new calendar	Ctrl+Shift+E
Delete selected calendar item or calendar	Ctrl+D
Display calendar in Day view	Ctrl+Alt+1
Display calendar in Work Week view	Ctrl+Alt+2
Display calendar in Week view	Ctrl+Alt+3
Display calendar in Month view	Ctrl+Alt+4
Display calendar in Schedule view	Ctrl+Alt+5

Contacts

Activity	Shortcut
Go to Contacts	Ctrl+3
New contact	Ctrl+N
New contact (anywhere in Outlook)	Ctrl+Shift+C
New contact group	Ctrl+Shift+L
Open selected contact	Ctrl+O
Close an open contact	Esc or Alt+F4
Open Address Book	Ctrl+Shift+B
New contact folder	Ctrl+Shift+E
Forward contact as a business card	Ctrl+F
Delete selected contact or folder	Ctrl+D

Tasks

Activity	Shortcut
Go to Tasks	Ctrl+4
New task	Ctrl+N
New task (anywhere in Outlook)	Ctrl+Shift+K
New task request	Ctrl+Alt+Shift+U
Open selected task	Ctrl+O
Close an open task	Esc or Alt+F4
Open Recurrence dialog box	Ctrl+G
New task folder	Ctrl+Shift+E
Delete selected contact or folder	Ctrl+D

Notes

Activity	Shortcut
Go to Notes	Ctrl+5
New note	Ctrl+N
New note (anywhere in Outlook)	Ctrl+Shift+N
Open selected note	Ctrl+O
Close an open note	Esc or Alt+F4
Forward note	Ctrl+F
New note folder	Ctrl+Shift+E
Delete selected note or folder	Ctrl+D

Journal

Activity	Shortcut
Go to Journal	Ctrl+6
New journal entry	Ctrl+N
New journal entry (anywhere in Outlook)	Ctrl+Shift+J
Open selected journal	Ctrl+O
Close an open journal	Esc or Alt+F4
Forward journal	Ctrl+F
Open Address Book	Ctrl+Shift+B
New journal folder	Ctrl+Shift+E
Delete selected journal or folder	Ctrl+D

Formatting

Activity	Shortcut
Copy	Ctrl+C
Cut	Ctrl+X
Paste	Ctrl+V
Undo	Ctrl+Z
Select all	Ctrl+A
Bold	Ctrl+B
Italicize	Ctrl+I
Underline	Ctrl+U
Align left	Ctrl+L
Align center	Ctrl+E
Align right	Ctrl+R
Align justified	Ctrl+J
Add bullet	Ctrl+Shift+L
Insert hyperlink	Ctrl+K
Increase indent	Ctrl+M
Decrease indent	Ctrl+Shift+M
Increase font size	Ctrl+> (Ctrl+Shift+.)
Decrease font size	Ctrl+< (Ctrl+Shift+,)
Clear all formatting	Ctrl+Spacebar

Appendix C
Outlook Quick Reference Guide

Global Outlook Features

Task	Action	Alternative Method	Keyboard Shortcut
Advanced Find	Click in the Search box above the Folder pane • Search ribbon • Options group • Search Tools button • Advanced Find		Ctrl+Shift+F
Archive—folder settings	Select folder • Folder ribbon • Properties group • AutoArchive Settings	Right-click on folder • Properties • AutoArchive tab	
Archive—global settings	File tab • Options • Advanced • Auto-Archive Settings		
Categories—assign	With Outlook item open • Tags group • Categorize button • select category	In list view, right-click on the Category column • select category	
Categories—create new	Home tab • Tags group • Categorize button • All Categories	Open Outlook item • Tags group • Categorize button • All Categories	
Categories—set Quick Click	Home tab • Tags group • Categorize button • Set Quick Click	File tab • Options • Advanced • Other section • Quick Click	
Delegate—assign	File tab • Account Settings • Delegate Access • Add		
Delegate—edit permissions	File tab • Account Settings • Delegate Access • select delegate • Permissions		

Task	Action	Alternative Method	Keyboard Shortcut
Delegate—remove	File tab • Account settings • Delegate access • Remove		
E-mail account—create new	File tab • Add Account	File tab • Account Settings • Account Settings • New	
E-mail account—edit	File tab • Account Settings • Account Settings • Change		
Empty Deleted Items upon exiting—default setting	File tab • Options • Advanced • Empty Deleted Items folder when exiting Outlook		
Empty Deleted Items—manually	Click on Deleted Items folder in the Navigation pane • Folder ribbon • Clean Up group • Empty Folder button	Right-click on Deleted Items folder • Empty Folder	
Export Outlook Data File	File tab • Options • Advanced • Export • Export to a file • Outlook Data File (.pst)		
Folder—create new	Folder ribbon • New group • New Folder button	In the Navigation pane, right-click on folder in which the new folder will be created • New Folder	Ctrl+Shift+E
Folder—delete	Folder ribbon • Actions group • Delete Folder button	In the Navigation pane, right-click on folder to be deleted • Delete Folder	Ctrl+D
Folder—move	Folder ribbon • Actions group • Move Folder button	In the Navigation pane, drag the folder to the desired location in the list of folders	
Folder—rename	Folder ribbon • Actions group • Rename Folder button	In the Navigation pane, right-click on folder to be renamed • Rename Folder	

(continued)

Global Outlook Features *(continued)*

Task	Action	Alternative Method	Keyboard Shortcut
Import Outlook Data File	File tab • Open • Import • Import from another program or file • Outlook Data File (.pst)		
Instant Search	Click in the Search box above the Folder pane		Ctrl+E
Modifying views	View Menu • Current View group • Change View button • Manage Views		
Navigation buttons	Configure Buttons • Navigation Pane Options	Right-click on a Navigation button • Navigation Pane Options	
Navigation pane options	Configure Buttons • Navigation Pane Options	File tab • Options • Advanced • Outlook Panes section • Navigation pane	
Outlook Today—customize	Click on Mailbox folder • Customize Outlook Today		
Outlook Today—default start window	File tab • Options • Advanced • Start Outlook in this folder	Click on Mailbox folder • Customize Outlook Today • check "When starting, go directly to Outlook Today"	
Quick Access toolbar—customize	Click on Customize Quick Access Toolbar button • More Commands	File tab • Options • Quick Access Toolbar	
Reading pane	View ribbon • Layout group • Reading Pane button		
Ribbon—customize	File tab • Options • Customize ribbon	Right-click on a ribbon or tab • Customize the Ribbon	
Security settings	File tab • Options • Trust Center • Trust Center Settings		

Task	Action	Alternative Method	Keyboard Shortcut
Shortcut group—create new	Right-click on Short-cuts • New Shortcut Group		
Shortcut group—delete	Right-click on Shortcuts • Delete Group		
Shortcut—create new	Click on Shortcuts button in Navigation pane • Folder ribbon • New group • New Shortcut	Click on Short-cuts button in Navigation pane • Right-click on Shortcuts • New Shortcut	
Shortcut—delete	Right-click on shortcut • Delete Shortcut		
Text message—create account	File tab • Add Account • Text Messaging		
View—add columns (in list views only)	View ribbon • Arrange-ment group • Add Columns button	Right-click on column heading in the Folder pane • Field Chooser	
View—custom view	View ribbon • Current View group • Change View button • Manage Views • New		
View—modify	View ribbon • Current View group • View Set-tings button	View ribbon • Current View group • Change View button • Manage Views • Modify	
View—show in groups	View ribbon • Arrangement group • More button • Show in Groups	View ribbon • View group • View Settings button • Group By	
View—sorting	Click on column header to sort by column • click to toggle between ascending and descending sort	View ribbon • Current View group • View Settings button • Sort	

Mail

The context of most of these commands is with a new e-mail open, or replying to or forwarding an e-mail.

Task	Action	Alternative Method	Keyboard Shortcut
Attach—file	Message ribbon • Include group • Attach File button	Insert ribbon • Include group • Attach File button	
Attachment—preview	Click on attachment • Attachment will be displayed in body of message		
Attachment—print	Click on attachment • Attachment ribbon • Actions group • Quick Print	Right-click on attachment • Quick Print	
Attachment—save	Click on attachment • Attachment ribbon • Actions group • Save As	Right-click on attachment • Save As	
Attach—Outlook item	Message ribbon • Include group • Attach Item button • Other Outlook item	Insert ribbon • Include group • Outlook Item button	
Bcc	Options tab • Show Fields group • Bcc	To button • Bcc	
Category	Select e-mail in Folder pane • Home ribbon • Tags group • Categorize	Right-click on e-mail in Folder pane • Categorize	
Change E-mail format—default setting	File tab • Options • Mail • Compose message in this format		
Change E-mail format—individual e-mail	Format ribbon • Format Textgroup • select format		
Delay Delivery	Options ribbon • More Options group • Delay Deliver button		
Delete E-mail	Home or Message ribbon • Delete group • Delete button	Right-click on e-mail in Folder pane • Delete	Ctrl+D

Task	Action	Alternative Method	Keyboard Shortcut
Delivery Receipt	Options ribbon • Tracking group • Request a delivery receipt	Message ribbon • Tags group • Expand button • Request a delivery receipt for this message	
Desktop Alert settings	File tab • Options • Mail • Message arrival area • Desktop Alert settings		
Direct Replies To	Options ribbon • More Options group • Direct Replies To	Message ribbon • Tags group • Expand button • Have replies sent to	
E-mail account— set default	File tab • Account Settings button • Account Settings • select account • Set as Default		
E-mail—change default delivery folder	File tab • Account Settings button • Account Settings • select account • Change Folder		
E-mail—options	File tab • Options • Mail		
E-mail—send through different account	Create new e-mail or choose Reply, Reply All, or Forward on existing e-mail • From button • Select account		
Expiration date/ time on e-mail	Message ribbon • Tags group • Expand button • Expires after	Options ribbon • More Options group • Expand button • Expires after	
Favorites—add folder	Select folder to add to Favorites • Folder ribbon • Favorites group • Show in Favorites	Right-click folder to add to Favorites • Show in Favorites	

(continued)

Mail *(continued)*

Task	Action	Alternative Method	Keyboard Shortcut
Favorites—remove folder	Select folder to remove from Favorites • Folder ribbon • Favorites group • Show in Favorites	Right-click folder to remove from Favorites • Show in Favorites	
Flag for Recipients	Message ribbon • Tags group • Follow Up button • Custom • Flag for Recipients		
Follow Up flag	Message ribbon • Tags group • Follow Up		
Font—default	File tab • Options • Mail • Stationery and Fonts • Personal Stationery tab		
Format text	Message ribbon • Basic Text group	Format Text ribbon	
Forward e-mail as attachment	Home or Message ribbon • Respond group • More button • Forward as Attachment		Ctrl+Alt+F
Importance	Message ribbon • Tags group • High Importance	Click on Expand button in Tags group • Importance	
Junk e-mail—block sender	Select e-mail to be blocked • Home ribbon • Delete group • Junk button • Block Sender	Open e-mail to be blocked • Message ribbon • Delete group • Junk button • Block Sender	
Junk e-mail—manage lists	Home ribbon • Delete group • Junk button • Junk E-mail Options • choose list to manage	Open e-mail • Message ribbon • Delete group • Junk button • Junk E-mail Options • choose list to manage	
Junk e-mail—never block sender or sender's domain	Select e-mail • Home ribbon • Delete group • Junk button • Never Block Sender or Never Block Sender's Domain	Open e-mail • Message ribbon • Delete group • Junk button • Never Block Sender or Never Block Sender's Domain	

Task	Action	Alternative Method	Keyboard Shortcut
Junk e-mail—options	Home ribbon • Delete group • Junk button • Junk E-mail Options		
Mark e-mail as read/unread	Click on e-mail in Folder pane • Home ribbon • Tags group • Read/Unread button	Right-click on e-mail in Folder pane • Mark as Read/Unread	Ctrl+Q (mark as read) Ctrl+U (mark as unread)
Out of Office Assistant	File tab • Automatic replies (Out of Office)		
Print e-mail	File tab • Print	Quick Print button on Quick Access toolbar	Ctrl+P
Quick Steps—create new	Home ribbon • Quick Steps group • Create New	Home ribbon • Quick Steps group • More button • New Quick Step	
Quick Steps—manage	Home ribbon • Quick Steps group • More button • Manage Quick Step		
Quick Steps—use existing	Home ribbon • Quick Steps group • select Quick Step to use		
Read receipt	Options ribbon • Tracking group • Request a Read Receipt	Message ribbon • Tags group • Expand button • Request a read receipt for this message	
Recall sent message	Sent Items folder • Open e-mail to be recalled • Message ribbon • Move group • Actions button • Recall This Message	Sent Items folder • Open e-mail to be recalled • File tab • Recall or Resend button • Recall This Message	
Reminder	Message ribbon • Tags group • Follow Up • Add Reminder	Right-click on e-mail in Folder pane • Follow Up • Add Reminder	

(continued)

Mail *(continued)*

Task	Action	Alternative Method	Keyboard Shortcut
Resend sent message	Sent Items folder • Open e-mail to be recalled • Message ribbon • Move group • Actions button • Resend This Message	Sent Items folder • Open e-mail to be recalled • File tab • Recall or Resend button • Resend This Message	
RSS feed—delete	File tab • Account Settings button • Account Settings • RSS Feed tab • select RSS feed • Remove	Right-click on RSS Feed folder to delete • Delete Folder	Select RSS feed folder to delete • Ctrl+D
RSS feed—share	Open an existing RSS feed e-mail • RSS Article ribbon • RSS group • Share This Feed	Right-click on an RSS feed e-mail • Share this feed	
RSS feed—subscribe	File tab • Account Settings button • Account Settings • RSS Feeds tab • New	In the Navigation pane, right-click on the RSS Feeds folder • Add a New RSS Feed	
Rules—create	Home ribbon • Move group • Rules button • Manage Rules & Alerts • New Rule	Right-click on e-mail message • Rules • Create Rule	
Rules—delete	Home ribbon • Move group • Rules button • Manage Rules & Alerts • select rule • Delete		
Rules—edit	Home ribbon • Move group • Rules button • Manage Rules & Alerts • select rule • Change Rule • Edit Rule Settings	Home ribbon • Move group • Rules button • Manage Rules & Alerts • double-click on rule	
Rules—order	Home ribbon • Move group • Rules button • Manage Rules & Alerts • select rule • Move Up or Move Down button		

Task	Action	Alternative Method	Keyboard Shortcut
Rules—run rules now	Folder ribbon • Clean Up group • Run Rules Now button • select rules to run • Run Now	Home ribbon • Actions group • Rules button • Manage Rules & Alerts • Run Rules Now button • select rules to run • Run Now	
Rules—turn on/off	Home ribbon • Move group • Rules button • Manage Rules & Alerts • select rule • select or deselect check box		
Save e-mail—draft	Save button on Quick Access Toolbar	File tab • Save	Ctrl+S
Save e-mail—outside of Outlook	File tab • Save As		F12
Save Sent Item To	Options ribbon • More Option group • Save Sent Items To button • Other Folder		
Search folder—create new	Folder ribbon • New group • New Search Folder	Right-click on Search Folders • New Search Folder	Ctrl+Shift+P
Search folder—customize	Select search folder • Folder ribbon • Actions group • Customize This Search Folder		
Search folder—delete	Select search folder • Folder ribbon • Actions group • Delete Folder	Right-click on search folder • Delete Folder	Ctrl+D
Security	Message ribbon • Tags group • Expand button • Security Settings		
Sensitivity	Message ribbon • Tags group • Expand button • Sensitivity	Options ribbon • More Options group • Expand button • Sensitivity	

(continued)

Mail *(continued)*

Task	Action	Alternative Method	Keyboard Shortcut
Signature—create	File tab • Options • Mail • Signatures • New	Message ribbon • Include group • Signature button • Signatures	
Signature—default	File tab • Options • Mail • Signatures • set default signature account and type	With e-mail open • Message ribbon • Include group • Signatures button • Signatures • set default signature account and type	
Signature—insert	Message ribbon • Include group • Signatures button • select signature	Insert ribbon • Include group • Signatures button • select signature	
Theme—individual e-mail	Options ribbon • Themes group • Themes button		
Theme—set default	File tab • Options • Mail • Stationery and Fonts • Theme		
Voting buttons—custom	Options ribbon • Tracking group • Use Voting Buttons button • Custom	Message ribbon • Tags group • Expand button • Use voting buttons • type voting buttons separated by a semicolon	
Voting buttons—preset	Options ribbon • Tracking group • Use Voting Buttons button • select preset voting buttons	Message ribbon • Tags group • Expand button • Use voting buttons	
Voting buttons—track responses	Open e-mail with voting response • click on InfoBar • View voting responses	Open original e-mail with voting buttons from Sent Items folder • Message ribbon • Show button • Tracking	
Voting buttons—vote	Open e-mail with voting button • Respond group • Vote button • select response		

Calendar

Task	Action	Alternative Method	Keyboard Shortcut
Add Holidays	File tab • Options • Calendar • Calendar options area • Add Holidays		
Appointment	Home ribbon • New group • New Appointment button	Type appointment on calendar in Day or Week view	Ctrl+N (when in Calendar) Ctrl+Shift+A (anywhere in Outlook)
Attach business card to calendar item	Open new or existing calendar item • Insert ribbon • Include group • Business Card • Other Business Cards		
Attach file to calendar item	Open new or existing calendar item • Insert ribbon • Include group • Attach File		
Attach Outlook item to calendar item	Open new or existing calendar item • Insert ribbon • Include group • Outlook Item		
AutoPick Meeting Times	Open new or existing meeting request • Meeting ribbon • Show group • Scheduling Assistant button • AutoPick Next		
Calendar—create new calendar folder	Folder ribbon • New group • New Calendar button	Right-click on the Calendar folder in the Navigation pane • New Calendar	Ctrl+Shift+E
Calendar item—copy	Select calendar item • hold down Ctrl key • drag to new location		Ctrl+C (copy) Ctrl+V (paste)

(continued)

Calendar *(continued)*

Task	Action	Alternative Method	Keyboard Shortcut
Calendar item—delete	Select calendar item • Actions group • Delete button	Open existing calendar item • Appointment, Event, or Meeting ribbon • Actions group • Delete button	Ctrl+D
Calendar item—move	Open calendar item • change date/time • Save & Close	Drag the calendar item to new location on the calendar	Ctrl+X (cut) Ctrl+V (paste)
Calendar View—Day	Home ribbon • Arrangement group • Day View button	View ribbon • Arrangement group • Day View button	Ctrl+Alt+1
Calendar view—Month	Home ribbon • Arrangement group • Month View button	View ribbon • Arrangement group • Month View button	Ctrl+Alt+4
Calendar view—other views	View ribbon • Current View group • Change View button • select view		
Calendar view—Schedule	Home ribbon • Arrange group • Schedule View button	View ribbon • Arrangement group • Schedule View button	
Calendar view—Week	Home ribbon • Arrange group • Week View button	View ribbon • Arrangement group • Week View button	Ctrl+Alt+3
Calendar view—Work Week	Home ribbon • Arrange group • Work Week View button	View ribbon • Arrangement group • Work Week View button	Ctrl+Alt+2
Convert e-mail to calendar item	Select e-mail • Home ribbon • Quick Steps • Create Appointment	Drag e-mail to Calendar button	
Event	Home ribbon • New group • New Appointment button • All day event	Type event on calendar in Event area of Day, Week, or Month view	

Task	Action	Alternative Method	Keyboard Shortcut
Forward calendar item	Select calendar item • Appointment ribbon • Actions group • Forward button	Open calendar item • Appointment, Event, or Meeting ribbon • Actions group • Forward button	Ctrl+F
Forward calendar item—as iCalendar	Select calendar item • Appointment ribbon • Actions group • Small arrow below the Forward button • Forward as iCalendar	Open calendar item • Appointment, Event, or Meeting ribbon • Actions group • Small arrow to the right of the Forward button • Forward as iCalendar	
Meeting—create	Home ribbon • New group • New Meeting button	Open existing appointment or create new appointment • Appointment ribbon • Attendees group • Invite Attendees button	Ctrl+Shift+Q
Meeting—respond	Open meeting request e-mail • Meeting ribbon • Respond group • select response		
Meeting—tracking	From your Calendar, open the meeting request you created • Meeting ribbon • Show group • Tracking button	From your Calendar, open the meeting request you created • tracking summary in the InfoBar	
Meeting—updating	From your Calendar, open the meeting request you created • Meeting ribbon • make desired changes • Send Update		
Print calendar	File tab • Print • select Settings • Print	Print button on Quick Access toolbar	Ctrl+P

(*continued*)

Calendar *(continued)*

Task	Action	Alternative Method	Keyboard Shortcut
Private calendar item	Open new or existing calendar item • Appointment, Event, or Meeting ribbon • Tags group • Private button	Right-click on calendar item • Private	
Publish calendar	Home ribbon • Share group • Publish Online button • Publish to Office.com	Right-click on calendar • Share • Publish to Office.com	
Recurring calendar item	Open new or existing calendar item • Appointment, Event, or Meeting ribbon • Options group • Recurrence button	Select calendar item • Appointment ribbon • Recurrence button	Ctrl+G
Reminder—default settings	File tab • Options • Calendar • Calendar options area • Default reminders		
Reminder—set reminder	Open calendar item • Appointment, Event, or Meeting ribbon • Options group • Reminder		
Scheduling Assistant—default settings	File tab • Options • Calendar • Scheduling assistant area		
Scheduling Assistant—use	Open existing or new calendar item • Appointment, Event, or Meeting ribbon • Show group • Scheduling Assistant button		
Send calendar via e-mail	Home ribbon • Share group • E-mail Calendar	Right-click on calendar • Share • E-mail Calendar	
Share calendar	Home ribbon • Share group • Share Calendar	Right-click on calendar • Share • Share Calendar	
Time zones	File tab • Options • Calendar • Time zones area		
Work time options	File tab • Options • Calendar • Work time area		

Contacts

Task	Action	Alternative Method	Keyboard Shortcut
Add multiple e-mail addresses	Open new or existing contact record • click on arrow next to E-mail button • select E-mail 2 or E-mail 3		
Change default Address Book	Home ribbon • Find group • Address Book • Tools menu • Options		
Change field name	Open new or existing contact record • click on arrow next to field name • select new field name		
Contact folder—new	Folder ribbon • New group • New Folder button	Right-click on Contacts • New folder	Ctrl+Shift+E
Contact group—add members	Open new or existing contact group • Contact Group ribbon • Members group • Add Members button		
Contact group—create new	Home ribbon • New group • New Contact Group		Ctrl+Shift+L
Contact group—delete	Select contact group • Home ribbon • Delete group • Delete button	Right-click on contact group • Delete	Ctrl+D
Contact group—remove members	Open new or existing contact group • select members to be removed • Contact Group ribbon • Members group • Remove Member button	Open new or existing contact group • select members to be removed • press Delete	
Contact options	File tab • Options • Contacts		

(continued)

Contacts *(continued)*

Task	Action	Alternative Method	Keyboard Shortcut
Contact—add from Global Address List	Open Global Address List • right-click on contact to be added • Add to Contacts	Open Global Address List • select contact to be added • File menu • Add to Contacts	
Contact—create new	Home ribbon • New group • New Contact button		Ctrl+N (when in Contacts) Ctrl+Shift+C (anywhere in Outlook)
Contact—from received e-mail	With e-mail open or in Reading pane, right-click on name or e-mail address • Add to Outlook Contacts	With e-mail open or in Reading pane, move pointer on name or e-mail address • click on + button • Add to Outlook Contacts	
Contact—new from same company	With existing contact open • Contact ribbon • Actions group • Small arrow next to the Save & New button • Contact from the Same Company		
Create mailing labels using Contacts	Home ribbon • Actions group • Mail Merge button		
Customize business card	Open existing contact • Contact ribbon • Options group • Business Card button		
Delete contact	Select contact • Home ribbon • Delete group • Delete button	Right-click on contact • Delete	Ctrl+D
Export contacts	File tab • Options • Advanced • Export • Export to a file		
Forward business card	Select contact • Home ribbon • Share group • Forward Contact • As a Business Card	Right-click on contact • Forward Contact • As a Business Card	Ctrl+F
Import contacts	File tab • Open • Import • Import from another program or file		

Task	Action	Alternative Method	Keyboard Shortcut
Include business card in signature	File tab • Options • Mail • Signatures • Business Card		
Map contact address	Open existing contact with address • Map It button	Open existing contact with address • Contact ribbon • Communicate group • More button • Map It	
Picture—add	Open new or existing contact • click on Add Contact Picture button	Open new or existing contact • Contacts ribbon • Options group • Picture button • Add Picture	
Picture—remove	Open new or existing contact • Contacts ribbon • Options group • Picture button • Remove Picture		
Send e-mail to contact	Select contact • Contact ribbon • Communicate group • E-mail	Right-click on contact • Create • E-mail	
Tracking contact activities	Contact ribbon • Show group • Activities button		

Tasks

Task	Action	Alternative Method	Keyboard Shortcut
Attach file to task	Open new or existing task • Insert ribbon • Include group • Attach File button		
Attach Outlook item to task	Open new or existing task • Insert ribbon • Include group • Outlook Item button		
Mark task as complete	Select task • Home ribbon • Manage Task group • Mark Complete	Right-click on task • Mark Complete	

(continued)

Tasks *(continued)*

Task	Action	Alternative Method	Keyboard Shortcut
Private	Select task • Home ribbon • Tags group • Private button	Open new or existing task • Task ribbon • Tags group • Private button	
Recurring task	Open new or existing task • Task ribbon • Recurrence group • Recurrence button		Ctrl+G
Reminder	Open new or existing task • check Reminder • set reminder date and time	Select task • Home ribbon • Follow Up group • Custom button • Reminder	
Task options	File tab • Options • Tasks		
Task Request—accept	Open task request e-mail • Task ribbon • Respond group • Accept		
Task Request—assign	Open new or existing task • Task ribbon • Manage Task group • Assign Task button	Right-click on task • Assign Task	
Task Request— create new	Home ribbon • New group • New Items button • Task Request	Open new task • Task ribbon • Manage Task group • Assign Task button	Ctrl+Alt+ Shift+U
Task Request— Mark complete	Select an accepted task • Home ribbon • Manage Task group • Mark Complete	Right-click on accepted task • Mark Complete	
Task request— send status report	Open an accepted task • Task ribbon • Manage Task group • Send Status Report		
Task—create new	Home ribbon • New group • New Task button		Ctrl+N (when in Tasks) Ctrl+Shift+K (anywhere in Outlook)
Task—delete	Select task • Home ribbon • Delete group • Delete button	Right-click on task • Delete	Ctrl+D

Task	Action	Alternative Method	Keyboard Shortcut
Task—new from e-mail	Drag e-mail to Tasks button	Select e-mail • Home ribbon • Move group • Move button • Copy to Folder • Tasks	
To-Do bar—options	View ribbon • Layout group • To-Do bar button • Options	Right-click on To-Do bar • Options	
To-Do bar—view	View ribbon • Layout group • To-Do bar button • select view	Click the small arrow at the top of the To-Do bar to toggle between Normal and Minimized view	

Notes & Journal

Task	Action	Alternative Method	Keyboard Shortcut
Journal options	File tab • Options • Notes and Journal		
Journal—automatically record	File tab • Options • Notes and Journal • Journal Options • select the items to automatically record		
Journal—manually record	Home ribbon • New group • Journal Entry		Ctrl+N (when in Journal) Ctrl+Shift+J (anywhere in Outlook)
Note options	File tab • Options • Notes and Journal		
Note—create new	Home ribbon • New group • New Note		Ctrl+N (when in Notes) Ctrl+Shift+N (anywhere in Outlook)

(continued)

Notes & Journal *(continued)*

Task	Action	Alternative Method	Keyboard Shortcut
Note—delete	Select note to be deleted • Home ribbon • Delete group • Delete button	Right-click on note to be deleted • Delete	Ctrl+D
Note—edit	Double-click on Note • make editing changes		Ctrl+O
Note—forward	Select note • Home ribbon • Actions group • Forward button	Right-click on note • Forward	Ctrl+F

Appendix D

Exchange Server versus Stand-Alone Usage

Outlook Features Available When on an Exchange Server

Some features of Outlook are available only when it is operating within an Exchange environment. Microsoft Exchange on a business network handles all the incoming and outgoing mail. Each individual user of Exchange is actually a client of this Exchange network, and the network administrator sets up an account for each individual user. In addition to handling e-mail, Exchange also stores all the data associated with calendars, contacts, tasks, notes, and journals. All this information is stored on the Exchange server.

Outlook in an Exchange environment has the same user interface as in a stand-alone environment, but Outlook with an Exchange server does allow you more functionality.

Global Address List

The Global Address List is the list of Outlook contact records of all the employees in an organization. If an organization is using an Exchange server,

MORE INFO

The Global Address List is covered in Chapters 4 and 9.

Address Book dialog box displaying the Global Address List

411

each individual in the organization has a unique e-mail address. This e-mail address, as well as other contact information such as title, department, and phone, is stored in the Global Address List. It usually includes contact groups as well. The Global Address List is maintained by the person who is responsible for maintaining the Exchange server.

Contact records that you use frequently can be added from the Global Address List to your Contacts folder.

MORE INFO

Tracking is discussed in Chapters 3, 5, and 8.

Tracking

Outlook can track the responses to meeting requests, task requests, and e-mails with voting buttons. When you recall an e-mail message, Outlook will also track whether or not the recall succeeded or failed. When you use one of these tasks in Outlook, you will be provided with a summary of responses to voting buttons, meeting requests, task requests, or success and failures of e-mail recalls. Tracking is a very powerful tool and is unique to using Outlook on an Exchange server.

Voting responses displayed in the body of an e-mail message

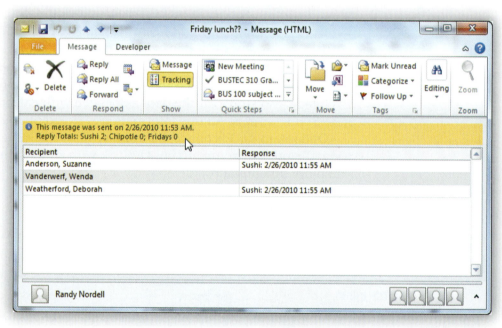

MORE INFO

Meeting Requests are covered in Chapter 5, and sharing calendars, the Scheduling Assistant, and AutoPick are discussed in Chapter 8.

Meeting Requests, Scheduling Assistant, and AutoPick

Meeting requests work only with those on your Exchange server. Because calendars are stored on the Exchange server, an accepted meeting request is automatically saved on your calendar, and the responses to the meeting request are available on this calendar item. When a meeting calendar item is opened from the calendar, you can view the attendees and their responses.

Also, the Scheduling Assistant and AutoPick meeting times are available when using Exchange. These features gather information from other calendars stored on the Exchange server. These features will only work if others have shared their calendar with you.

Meeting request with tracking displayed

Task Requests

MORE INFO

Task requests are covered in Chapter 6.

When a task request is sent to another user on your Exchange system and that task is accepted, it is recorded in your Tasks. You will see a different task icon displayed in the Task list to indicate that a task has been assigned and accepted. When an assigned task has been completed, the originator of the task will receive a message and the task will automatically be marked as complete.

Assigned task in the Task List

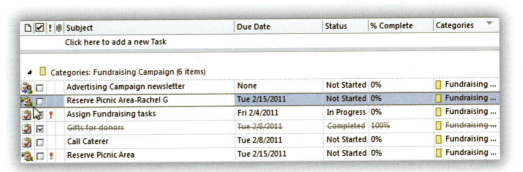

Voting Buttons

MORE INFO

Voting buttons are covered in Chapter 3.

Using voting buttons on an e-mail is a great way to get information from others. If you wanted to find out the restaurant preference for the members of your team, you could set up voting buttons with three choices of restaurants from which they could choose. The benefit of using voting buttons as opposed to having recipients just type their selection in the body of the message is that

Outlook will consolidate the voting results for you (see Figure D-2). For voting buttons to work properly, the recipients must be using Outlook on an Exchange server.

MORE INFO

Sharing calendars is covered in Chapter 10, and delegates are covered in Chapter 12.

Sharing and Delegates

One of the advantages of using Outlook in conjunction with an Exchange server is the ability to share different parts of your Outlook (Mail, Calendar, Contacts, Tasks, etc.) with others on your Exchange system. Since your Outlook information is stored on an Exchange server, you can allow others to access your Outlook information and control the amount of access they have by setting the permission level. This feature is particularly helpful for scheduling meetings and appointments. When you have access to view others' calendars, you can open a shared calendar in your Outlook to view available times and dates. Sharing and delegate permissions work in all areas of Outlook.

Shared calendar displayed in the Folder pane

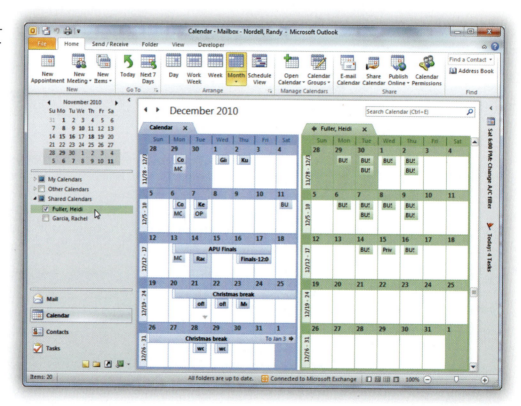

Outlook Web Access

If you have an e-mail account at work, most likely it is set up on an Exchange server. If so, then you most likely have access to your e-mail and other Outlook information through the Internet on Outlook Web Access (OWA).

If you are on a business trip, working from home, or away from your office computer, you can still access your Exchange mailbox by using OWA. You can connect to OWA through the Internet and a Web browser. You can log into your OWA account with your username and password. The information stored on the Exchange server is available to you in OWA.

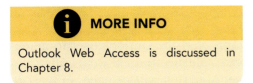

MORE INFO

Outlook Web Access is discussed in Chapter 8.

Outlook Web Access displayed in an Internet browser window

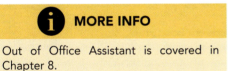

MORE INFO

Out of Office Assistant is covered in Chapter 8.

Out of Office Assistant

The Out of Office Assistant is available when using Outlook in a stand-alone environment. But, you are given additional Out of Office options when using Outlook in an Exchange environment. You can set up your Out of Office replies to those inside of your organization (on the same Exchange server) and those outside of your organization. You can set up a different message and different criteria for these two groups.

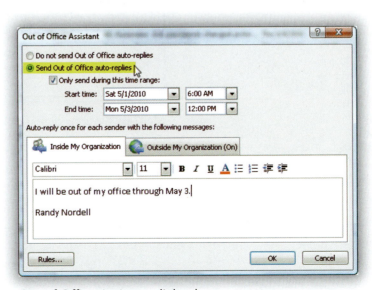

Out of Office Assistant dialog box

MailTips

MailTips are new to Outlook 2010. MailTips alert the Outlook user to potential issues with an e-mail to be sent. For example, if you press Reply All rather than Reply and the recipient list is large, MailTips will provide an alert to warn you that you are about to send an e-mail to a large number of recipients. MailTips will alert you if you are sending an e-mail to a recipient who is out of the office, to an invalid e-mail address, to a recipient whose mailbox is full, or to a recipient who is outside of your organization. MailTips will also alert you if you are sending an attachment that is too large or if the attachment is too large for the recipient. MailTips will only work in conjunction with Microsoft Exchange Server 2010.

MORE INFO

MailTips are covered in Chapter 8.

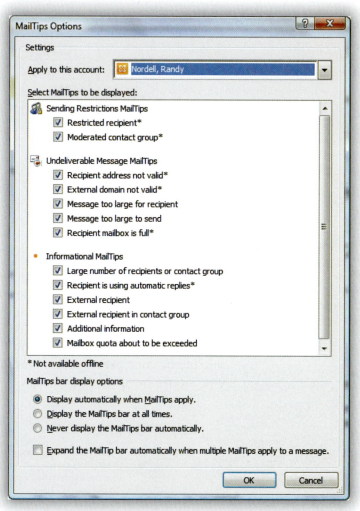

MailTips Options dialog box

A

action   What Outlook does when a condition to a rule is met.

add-ins   Third-party software programs that add functionality to Outlook.

address book   The collection of names and e-mail addresses from a Contacts folder or Global Address List. An address book can be used to populate an e-mail message, meeting request, or task request.

appointment   A calendar item that is less than 24 hours in duration.

arrangement   The way Outlook items are grouped or sorted for display in the Folder pane.

attachment   A file or other Outlook item attached to an e-mail message, contact, calendar item, task, or journal.

Auto Account Setup   An Outlook feature that can automatically detect e-mail account settings and use these settings to create an account in Outlook.

AutoArchive   The automatic process of removing older Outlook items and storing them in a separate set of folders in Outlook.

AutoPick   An Outlook calendar feature that will pick available meeting times.

B

BackStage   The window displayed when the Office button is clicked.

Bcc   Acronym for blind carbon copy; it can be used to hide a recipient's name and e-mail address from other recipients of an e-mail message.

business card (or electronic business card)   An Outlook item created from a contact record that can be sent to other Outlook users.

C

calendar snapshot   Displays calendar details in the body of an e-mail message.

category   A grouping tool that can be used on all Outlook items. Categories can be customized by name and color.

Cc   Acronym for carbon copy; it is used when someone is not the main recipient of an e-mail message.

Clean Up   A feature that will delete redundant items related to an e-mail conversation.

condition   The part of an Outlook rule for which Outlook is looking when an e-mail is received or sent.

contact   A group of related pieces of information (fields) about an individual or company.

contact group   A selected set of contacts that are saved together in a group. Contact groups were previously known as distribution lists.

contact linking   Links a contact to other Outlook items such as e-mails, calendar items, tasks, journals, or other contacts.

context sensitive   Groups and buttons will change based on the context of the selection. For example, the Home ribbon will display different groups and buttons depending on whether Mail or Calendar is selected.

conversation   An Outlook arrangement that groups together messages with the same subject.

D

Daily Task List   A list of current tasks that appears at the bottom of the calendar in the Folder pane when viewing the calendar in Day, Week, or Work Week view.

Data Execution Prevention   A security area of Outlook that protects your computer from malicious code being saved and run.

database   A file consisting of related groups of information (records); each record consists of individual pieces of information (fields).

Date Navigator   A calendar thumbnail that appears in the To-Do bar. Clicking on a date on the Date Navigator will display that day in the Folder pane.

default settings   Those settings that come preset in Outlook. Many default settings can be changed in the Options dialog box.

delay delivery   A feature used to delay the sending of an e-mail message.

delegate   An Outlook user who has access to the Outlook folders of another Outlook user.

delivery receipt   An Outlook feature that can be used to send a receipt to the sender of a message when the recipients receive the e-mail message.

desktop alert   A notification that appears when you receive an e-mail message.

dialog box   A separate window that opens and provides additional selection options.

digital signature   A method of authenticating an e-mail message.

draft   An e-mail message that has been created and saved but not yet sent. A draft message is stored in the Drafts folder.

E

e-mail   The commonly used term for an electronic message.

encrypt   An e-mail message option that scrambles the message and/or attachment to add security to a message.

event   A calendar item that is a full day or more in duration.

exception An optional part of the rule that would cause an action to not be performed when a condition is met.

expand button At the bottom right corner of some groups is an expand button that will open a dialog box with additional selections.

export The process of sending Outlook data to another file format.

F

Favorites The area of Outlook in the Navigation pane that contains links to commonly used mail folders.

field An individual piece of information.

Field Chooser The dialog box that allows users to choose fields to be displayed in the Folder pane.

File tab The tab that opens the Outlook BackStage. The File tab replaces the Office button from previous versions of Microsoft Office.

Flag for Recipients A flag and InfoBar message added to an e-mail that recipients receive.

Folder List The selection that displays all the Outlook folders in the Navigation pane.

Folder pane The section of Outlook to the right of the Navigation pane. The contents of the folder selected in the Navigation pane are displayed in the Folder pane.

Follow Up flag A flag that can be added to Outlook items that serves as a reminder for the user. When an Outlook item is marked with a Follow Up flag, that item will also be included in the To-Do List.

G

Global Address List The collection of contact records available when using Outlook in conjunction with an Exchange server.

groups Each ribbon has buttons and options categorized by groups. Some groups can be expanded to open a dialog box with additional options. Groups can also refer to how items are grouped and displayed in the Folder pane.

H

HTML (Hypertext Markup Language) A message format that is the standard format for e-mail messages. This format supports the use of different fonts, styles, colors, and HTML content.

HTTP (Hypertext Transfer Protocol) A web-based type of e-mail account. Hotmail is an example of an HTTP e-mail account

I

iCalendar A calendar format that can be sent via e-mail and is compatible with many other software programs.

ignore An Outlook feature that will move current and future e-mail messages related to a particular conversation to the Deleted Items folder.

IMAP (Internet Message Access Protocol) A standard Internet protocol for sending and receiving e-mail.

importance A tag that can be added to Outlook items. Importance can be set at high, normal, or low.

import The process of bringing data from another file into Outlook.

InfoBar An informational bar that appears above the From line in an e-mail message and provides additional information for the recipients.

Instant Search An Outlook feature to quickly search for Outlook items in a specific folder or all folders.

Internet service provider (ISP) A company that offers access to the Internet and provides e-mail accounts for users.

J

Journal An Outlook item to record the amount of time spent working on a document or other task.

junk e-mail An e-mail message that is identified by Outlook as potentially dangerous or from a unreputable source.

M

macro A set of programming instructions.

MailTips New to Outlook 2010, these alerts warn the user of potential e-mail issues.

meeting (or meeting request) A calendar item that can be used to invite other Outlook users to an appointment or event.

member A contact who is part of a contact group.

Microsoft Exchange Server A fileserver used to manage Outlook accounts and data within a company.

N

Navigation pane The section of Outlook at the left-hand side of the window used to navigate between the different Outlook features and provide access to the folders in each of these areas.

O

Out of Office Assistant An Outlook feature that will allow the user to create an automated response to reply to e-mail received.

Outlook Connector An add-in program that allows users to set up a Hotmail or Live e-mail account in Outlook.

Outlook data file Outlook stores user data in a .pst file.

Outlook Rich Text Format (RTF) A message format that is unique to Outlook and supports the use of different fonts, styles, colors, and HTML content.

Outlook Social Connector New to Outlook 2010, this feature allows Outlook users to keep track of friends and colleagues; related Outlook items are displayed in the People pane.

Outlook Today The opening window that is displayed in the Folder pane when Outlook is started.

Outlook Web Access (OWA)   The online environment to access your Outlook exchange account.

P

panes   Separate areas within the Outlook window, which include the Navigation pane, Folder pane, Reading pane, and People pane.

People pane   New to Outlook 2010, this pane displays Outlook items associated with the individual. The People pane appears below the Reading pane in the main Outlook interface and at the bottom of received e-mail messages, contacts, meetings, and task requests.

permission   The amount of access a delegate has to an area of Outlook.

plain text   A message format that supports only basic text.

POP3 (Post Office Protocol)   A standard Internet protocol for sending and receiving e-mail.

private   A tag that can be used on calendar items, contacts, tasks, and journal entries that hides details of these items from delegates or other users with whom areas of Outlook are shared.

private key   A tool used by the message sender to encrypt an e-mail message.

public key   An authentication tool used by the receiver of a message to unencrypt and view an encrypted message.

Q

Quick Access toolbar   The toolbar at the top left of the Outlook window that contains buttons for commonly used features. The Quick Access toolbar is available on all Microsoft Office products.

Quick Steps   New to Outlook 2010, these provide one-click access to e-mail actions.

R

read receipt   An Outlook feature that can be used to send a receipt to the sender of a message when recipients open the e-mail message.

Reading pane   The Reading pane can appear below or to the right of the Folder pane. The Reading pane displays the Outlook item selected in the Folder pane. The Reading pane can also be turned off.

recall   An Outlook feature used to recall a previously sent message.

record   A group of related fields about an individual or company.

recurrence   A calendar item or task can be set to recur at a specified interval.

reminder   A reminder can be set on Outlook items, and a reminder dialog box will open to alert the user.

resend   An Outlook feature used to resend a previously sent message.

ribbon   Each Outlook ribbon provides users with groups and buttons for easy access to Outlook features and commands. Each ribbon is accessed by clicking on its tab.

RSS feed   Headlines of new articles or information from a Web site that can be received in Outlook similar to an e-mail message.

rule   An Outlook feature that controls the handling of e-mail messages. Rules operate on a logical condition, action, and exception sequence.

S

Schedule view   A calendar view new to Outlook 2010 that displays calendars in timeline format.

Scheduling Assistant   An Outlook calendar feature that displays multiple calendars in timeline format to help facilitate meeting, appointment, and event scheduling.

ScreenTips   A small label that appears when the mouse pointer is placed on a button or area of a ribbon.

search folder   A virtual folder that will display e-mail items from other folders that match specified criteria.

sensitivity   A tag on an e-mail message that provides a handling message to the recipient.

signature   A stored group of text that can be automatically or manually inserted into an e-mail, meeting request, or task request.

stand-alone   Refers to Outlook being used without being connected to a Microsoft Exchange server.

T

tab   Each ribbon in Outlook has a tab that has the name of that ribbon.

Task List   A list of all the tasks in Outlook.

task request   A task that is assigned to another Outlook user.

theme   A set of fonts, colors, background, and fill effects in the body of an e-mail message.

To-Do bar   The area at the right of the Outlook window that displays a date navigator, upcoming calendar items, and the To-Do items.

To-Do items   All Outlook items marked with a Follow Up flag.

To-Do List   A list of Outlook items that have been marked with a Follow Up flag. This list is available in Tasks.

tracking   A Microsoft Exchange feature that provides the sender with a summary of responses to meeting requests, voting buttons, and read and delivery receipts.

Trust Center   The area of Outlook that allows users to customize the security settings.

trusted publisher   Reputable organizations that have a digital signature assigned to a macro or program to be run on a user's computer.

V

view   How items are displayed in the Folder pane.

voting buttons   These preset or custom buttons can be used on an e-mail message to gather responses from recipients.

PHOTO CREDITS

INDEX

A

Accept option, 131, 133
Accepted Task task list icon, 163
Accepting Task dialog box, 162
account, selecting to send e-mail through, 215
Account Settings button, 29
Account Settings dialog box, 209, 214, 230
  changing default delivery folder, 215, 216
  Internet Calendars tab, 296
action
  adding or deleting, 190
  delivering e-mails, 217
  of a rule, 177, 179, 180
action step, in the Rules Wizard dialog box, 182
Actions buttons, on the Message ribbon, 38
Active Directory, managing student accounts, 379
Activities, tracking for contacts, 246
Add a New RSS Feed, 230
Add Action button, 190
Add Columns button, 365–366
Add Contact Picture dialog box, 96, 97
Add digital signature options, 357
Add Holidays to Calendar dialog box, 284
Add Members, from the Member group, 106
Add Members button, in the Members group, 107, 109
Add New Account dialog box, 29, 208, 209, 210–211, 212
Add New Category dialog box, 193
Add New Member dialog box, 109
Add properties to attachments to enable Reply with Changes feature, 351
Add RSS feed confirmation dialog box, 230
Add this RSS Feed button, 232
Add to Contacts, in Global Address List, 94
Add to Contacts check box, 109
Add to Navigation Pane dialog box, 329
Add to Outlook Contacts option, 91
Add Users dialog box, 345
Add-ins, 348–349
address book, 88
Address Book dialog box, 93, 242, 411
Address Book pull-down menu, 103, 104
addresses, for contacts, 96
Addressing dialog box, 242–243
Advanced Find dialog box, 360

advanced rules, creating, 179–184
Advanced View Settings dialog box, 102, 368, 369, 370
All day event check box, 122, 127, 132
Allow button, sharing recipient's calendar, 291
Apply rule on messages I receive option, 181
Appointment button, in the Show group, 136
Appointment Recurrence dialog box, 130, 300
appointments, 121
  in the To-Do bar, 159
  forwarding, 288–289
  recurring, 129
Archive feature, 314
archiving, Outlook folders, 330
Arrange group, on the View ribbon, 102
arrangement, of e-mail messages in the Folder pane, 44–45
Arrangement group, on the View ribbon, 45, 364
arrangement options, for journal entries, 323
Assign Task button, in the Manage Task group, 160
Assigned Task task list icon, 162
Attach File button, 39, 40, 299
Attach File option, with a task, 153
Attach Item button, 43
attachment(s)
  handling, 39–43, 351–352
  icon indicating, 46
  inserting items as, 43
  opening and saving, 40–41
  previewing, 41–42
  sending large, 40
Attachment Preview feature, 352
Attachments ribbon, 40–41
Author permission, 344
Auto account setup, 29, 207–209
AutoArchive, 330–333
Auto-Complete List, 224
Automatic Download, in the Trust Center, 352
Automatic Replies (Out of Office) button, 226
automatic tracking, in the journal, 321–322
AutoPick, available from Exchange, 412–413
AutoPick meeting times, 302–303
AutoPick Next button, 302, 303

B

BackStage
  accessing, 49
  Export button on, 261

Import button on, 256
  Print options, 287–288
  window, 15, 29
Basic Text group, Message ribbon, 33
Bcc button, showing, 32–33
Bing Maps, 97, 98
blank rule, creating, 180
Blind copy (Bcc), 32
Block Sender option, 356
Blocked Senders list, 356
Blocked Senders option, 355
blue arrow, on the e-mail icon, 46
Body, in an e-mail, 33
bottom of Navigation pane, Shortcuts button, 328
Browse dialog box, 257, 262–263
Business Card button, on the Contact ribbon, 253
Business card format, 105
business cards, 249–255. See also electronic business cards
  attached to e-mail messages, 105
  attaching to tasks, 153
  customizing, 252–255
  including in signatures, 251–252
  sending, 104–105
By Category timeline view, for journal entries, 322, 323
By Category view, 244, 245

C

calendar(s). See also Outlook Calendar
  creating new, 280–281
  printing, 287–288
  publishing, 293–296
  quick reference guide, 401–404
  sending via e-mail, 291–293
  sharing, 290–291
  using multiple, 279–282
  viewing multiple, 281–282
  viewing shared, 297
Calendar button, in the Navigation pane, 131
calendar events, 122
calendar items, 121–123
  creating and editing, 126–131
  creating from an e-mail, 131
  deleting, 130–131
  moving and copying, 129
  private, 299–300
Calendar Options, 282–287
Calendar Permissions button, 291
Calendar Preview feature, 133
Calendar Properties dialog box, 332
calendar shortcuts, 387
Calendar Snapshot, 291

calendar views
   navigating, 123–126
   tasks in, 158–159
Cancel Meeting button, in the
   Actions group, 138
Card Design area, 253
categories
   assigning, 193
   customizing, 191–193
   grouping Inbox items, 47
   grouping tasks, 152
   for notes, 315–316
   removing, 193
   using, 191–195, 244–246,
     297–298
   viewing by, 194
Categories column heading,
   sorting by category, 194
Categorize button
   on the Home ribbon, 316
   in the Tags group, 192, 193, 244,
     245, 297
Categorize selected contacts, 245
Category feature, marking
   Outlook items, 191
cell phone, syncing with
   Outlook, 97
Change Picture option, 97
Change Rule button, 184
Change View button, 13, 158, 298
Check Address dialog box, 96
Choose default signature, 74–75
Clean Up, 16, 222
Clean Up Conversation
   button, 365
Clean Up menu, 48
Clear All Categories, 193
Clear Flag option, 197
Click to add prompt, in
   calendars, 285
closed envelope icon, 46
Color Categories dialog box,
   192, 193
colors, displayed for calendars,
   284–285
column heading, sorting
   using, 103
comma separated value (CSV),
   260, 265
communication capabilities,
   increased, 17
Complete check box, in the
   To-Do List, 197
Completed check box, 154, 156
completed tasks, 164–165
Compose messages area, default
   message format, 61
Compose messages section,
   in Mail options, 219–221
compressed (zipped) files,
   attaching, 39
compressed folders, 39
condition
   delivering e-mails, 217
   of a rule, 177, 180
   selecting for a rule, 179
condition, action, exception
   sequence, 184
Confidential sensitivity, 63

Configure buttons button, in
   Navigation pane, 319
Confirm deletion dialog box, 327
Confirm Sharing Request dialog
   box, 291
contact(s), 5–6, 88, 248
   adding, 91–94
   changing views in, 101–103
   creating, 89–95
   deleting, 101
   editing information, 95–101
   importing and exporting,
     255–265
   managing, 241–255
   merged into labels in Word, 269
   quick reference guide, 405–407
   sending as business cards,
     250–251
   shortcuts, 388
   sorting, 103
   updating, 247
   using, 103–110, 268–270
   viewed by category, 194, 245
   views, 101–102
contact activities, tracking,
   246–247
Contact Attendees button, 137
Contact folder, 243
Contact from Same Company
   option, 90
contact group, selecting
   members, 106
contact groups, 93
   creating, 103, 105–106
   modifying, 107–110
contact options, customizing,
   247–249
contact record, 88
Contacts address book, 88
Contacts button, in the Navigation
   pane, 89, 90, 102, 104, 105
Contacts folder, 88, 244, 255
Context sensitive tabs and
   ribbons, 11
conversation
   e-mails displayed in Folder
     pane by, 48
   grouping e-mail by, 16
Conversation arrangement,
   44–45, 365
Conversation Clean Up section,
   of Mail Options, 222
Copy (Cc), 32
copying, an appointment to
   another date, 129
Create a New View dialog box,
   369–370
Create New Folder dialog box,
   174, 175, 244, 280
Create New Quick Step
   option, 189
Create Rule dialog box, 178, 179
Ctrl key
   holding down, 31, 101
   selecting nonadjacent
     items, 250
Ctrl+1, 9
Ctrl+2, 9
Ctrl+3, 9

Ctrl+4, 9
Ctrl+5, 9, 314
Ctrl+6, 9, 13, 176
Ctrl+7, 9, 328
Ctrl+8, 9, 320
Ctrl+A, 269
Ctrl+Alt+1, 123
Ctrl+Alt+2, 124
Ctrl+Alt+3, 124
Ctrl+Alt+4, 125
Ctrl+Alt+5, 125
Ctrl+Alt+A, 358
Ctrl+Alt+F, 42
Ctrl+Alt+J, 356
Ctrl+Alt+Shift+U, 161
Ctrl+C, 129, 229, 230
Ctrl+D, 47, 101, 130, 176, 232,
   281, 327
Ctrl+E, 358
Ctrl+F, 36, 289, 318
Ctrl+F1, 11
Ctrl+G, 130, 301
Ctrl+N, 30, 89, 125, 126, 127, 150,
   315, 320
Ctrl+O, 35
Ctrl+P, 37
Ctrl+PrintScreen, 384
Ctrl+R, 36
Ctrl+S, 34, 41, 89
Ctrl+Shift+A, 127
Ctrl+Shift+B, 93, 242
Ctrl+Shift+C, 89
Ctrl+Shift+E, 244
Ctrl+Shift+F, 360
Ctrl+Shift+J, 320
Ctrl+Shift+K, 150
Ctrl+Shift+L, 106
Ctrl+Shift+N, 315
Ctrl+Shift+P, 325
Ctrl+Shift+Q, 132
Ctrl+Shift+R, 36
Ctrl+Shift+T, 218
Ctrl+Shift+V, 248
Ctrl+V, 129, 230
Ctrl+X, 129
Current View area, in the
   Navigation pane, 316
Current View group, 101, 194
custom AutoArchive settings, 332
Custom dialog box, 68, 196
Custom flag, 68
custom views, creating, 368–370
Custom Voting buttons option, 70
Customize dialog box, 325–326
Customize Outlook Today button,
   361–362
Customize Quick Access toolbar
   button, 363–364
Customize Quick Step dialog
   box, 188
Customize This Search Folder
   button, 325

D

Daily Task List, 124, 158–159
Data Execution Prevention (DEP),
   349–350
database terminology, 88

Date arrangement, 364
date navigator, 123, 125, 159–160
Day view, 123–124, 286
Decline and Propose New Time option, 134
Decline option, 131, 133
default address book, changing, 242–243
default e-mail account, setting, 214
default reminder, 283
default reminder time, 128
default search folders, 324
default setting, changing, 72
default theme and fonts, setting, 75–76
Delay Delivery button, 66
delegate permissions, e-mail summarizing, 346
Delegate Permissions dialog box, 345–346
delegates
    assigning, 344–346
    creating Outlook items as, 347–348
    defined, 344
    on a Exchange system, 414
    in Outlook, 153, 343
    removing, 348
Delegates dialog box, 344–345, 348
Delete button
    on the Appointment ribbon, 130
    in the Delete group, 47
    on the Folder ribbon, 176, 327
Delete Calendar button, on the Folder ribbon, 281, 296
Delete Folder button, 177
Delete Folder option, 176
Delete Group button, 109
Delete Group option, 329
Delete key, 47
Delete Occurrence option, 131
delete recurring calendar item, 130
Delete Series option, 131
Delete Shortcut option, 329
Deleted Items folder, 47, 48–49, 101, 131
Deletion confirmation dialog box, 382
Delivery and read receipts, 64
delivery options, 66–67
delivery receipts, 225
desktop, displaying a note on, 317
Desktop Alert(s), 76–77, 221–222
Details button, in the Show group, 163
Details section, of an open task, 163
Digital IDs (certificates), 351
digital signatures, 63, 351, 356–358
Direct Replies To button, 66
Dismiss All button, 152
Dismiss button, 152
dismissing, a reminder, 46
Display options, in Outlook options, 284–285

distribution lists. *See* contact groups
Do not AutoArchive this item check box, 64, 333
Do not deliver before box, 66
Do Not Forward permission, 69
Do Not Send a Response option, 133, 134
Draft folder, in the Navigation pane, 35
Drafts folder, 34, 223
Due date, selecting for a task, 150–151
Duplicate Contact Detected dialog box, 94, 95
duplicates, adding to contacts, 94–95

E
Edit Business Card dialog box, 253
Edit Quick Step dialog box, 189, 190
Edit Rule Settings, 184
Edit signature section, 73
Edit the response before sending option, 70, 71, 133, 134, 161
Editor Options dialog box, 220
Editor permission, 344, 345
electronic business cards. *See also* business cards
    adding contacts from, 92–93
    defined, 249
    sending, 249–251
electronic calendar. *See* calendar(s); Outlook Calendar
electronic mail. *See* e-mail
electronic receipt, 64
electronic sticky notes, 7
e-mail, 4–5
    calendar item attached to, 289
    creating a meeting directly from, 133
    creating calendar items from, 131
    customizing, 72–78
    deleting, 47
    displaying in Conversation arrangement, 365
    with Internet Calendar attached, 292, 293
    managing large volumes of, 16
    quick reference guide, 394–400
    sending a calendar via, 291–293
    sending through a different account, 215
    sending to contacts, 103–104
    summarizing permission levels, 346
    tasks created from, 156–157
    troubleshooting problems, 210–212
E-mail Account radio button, 208
e-mail accounts
    handling, 27–28
    multiple, 16, 207, 214–218
    for an online course, 383–384
    setting up, 28–30, 207–214

through Exchange, 209
    types of, 28
e-mail addresses
    storing multiple, 96
    supplying, 29
E-mail button
    in the Communicate group, 104, 107
    on a contact record, 96
E-mail Calendar button, on the Home ribbon, 292
e-mail delivery folder, changing, 215–216
e-mail draft, saving, 34–35
e-mail format, types of, 60–61
e-mail message(s)
    attaching a business card to, 249
    changing to Plain Text format, 61
    creating, 30–33
    displayed in groups, 367
    with embedded HTML content, 352
    forwarding as an attachment, 42–43
    marking as Read or Unread, 46
    with notes attached, 318
    opening, 35
    printing, 37
    recalling, 38–39
    resending, 39
    saving, 36–37
    sending, 34
e-mail options, customizing, 219–227
e-mail received, adding new contact from, 91–92
E-mail Security area, of the Trust Center, 350–351
e-mail sharing invitation, creating, 295
e-mail shortcuts, 386–387
Empty Auto-Complete List button, 224
Empty Deleted Items folder when exiting Outlook option, 49
Empty Folder button, in the Clean Up group, 48
encrypting, 63, 351
End time of an appointment, 127
events, 122, 129
Excel file, saving, 265
exceptions
    in a rule, 177
    to a rule, 180
exceptions step, in the Rules Wizard, 183
Exchange account, accessing through the Internet, 217
Exchange e-mail account, creating, 380
Exchange Server
    Outlook features available on, 411–416
    sharing a calendar on, 290
Exchange System Manager, 379
Expand button, 12, 62, 67
expand or collapse all groups, 367

Expires after feature, for
    e-mail, 67
Export Outlook Data File dialog
    box, 266
Export to File dialog box,
    261–262, 263, 264, 266
exporting, contacts, 260–265

F

F1 function key, 14
F12 function key, 37
Facebook, connecting to, 99
Favorites folders, 363
Field Chooser dialog box, adding
    a column, 366
field names, changing for
    contacts, 95
fields, 88, 255, 367
file(s), 39–40, 88
File Previewing dialog box,
    351–352
File tab, 15
Find Now button, 360
Finish rule setup step, in the
    Rules Wizard, 183
Flag for Recipients, creating,
    68–69
flag icon, 46
Flag to messages, preset, 68
flagged items, 148
flagging, items, 195–196
flags, removing, 197
Folder List, 13, 177
Folder List button, 13, 177
Folder pane, 8, 9, 44
    creating e-mail from
        contact, 104
    To-Do List displayed, 149
    imported records
        displayed, 260
    Outlook Today displayed in, 8
Folder Properties button, 326
folder type, confirming, 175
folders
    in Contacts, 88
    creating, 174–175, 217
    deleting, 176–177
    moving, 175–176
    types of, 174
    using, 174–177, 243–244
Follow Up button, in the Tags
    group, 68, 195, 197
Follow Up flags, 67–68, 152,
    195–197
Font dialog box, 33
For Follow Up search folder, 324
Format group, selecting message
    format, 61
Format Text ribbon, 33
formatting, shortcuts for, 389
Forward as Attachment
    option, 42
Forward button
    in the Actions group, 105
    on the Appointment ribbon, 288
    on the Home ribbon, 317

Forward Contact button, in the
    Share group, 105
Forward: FYI Quick Step, 187
Forward option, 35–36
forwarding, a message, 222, 223
Free/Busy Options, with Exchange
    server, 284
from people or public group
    box, 181
functions, 9

G

generic e-mail accounts, 383–384
Global Address List, 88, 93–94,
    242, 411–412
global features, quick reference
    guide, 390–393
global Outlook shortcut
    comments, 385–386
Gmail, 28, 207
gradient, changing page color to
    include, 75
groups
    creating in the Shortcuts area,
        328, 329
    deleting, 329
    editing, 329
    expanding or collapsing, 367
    of ribbons, 12

H

Have Replies Sent To dialog box,
    66
hierarchical rules, 186
High Importance, 46
High Importance e-mail
    message, 63
holidays, adding to an Outlook
    calendar, 284
Home ribbon
    Calendar Permissions
        button, 291
    Categorize button, 316
    Change View button, 158
    Current View group, 101
    E-mail Calendar button, 292
    Forward button, 317
    Junk button, 354
    New Appointment button,
        125, 127
    New Contact button, 89, 90
    New Meeting button, 131
    New Task button, 150
    Publish Online button, 293
    Respond group, 36
    Share Calendar button, 290
Home tab and ribbon, 11
Hotmail, 207, 212
HTML (Hypertext Markup
    Language) content, e-mail
    with, 352
HTML (Hypertext Markup
    Language) message format, 60
HTTP (Hypertext Transfer
    Protocol) accounts, 28

I

iCalendar format, 284, 289
icons
    displaying notes as, 317
    in the Folder pane, 44
if/then logical principle, 177
Ignore, in e-mail, 16
Ignore button, deleting selected
    e-mails, 365
Ignore dialog box, 48
IMAP accounts, 28
IMAP e-mail accounts, delivery
    e-mail received, 216
Import a File dialog box,
    256–258, 267
Import and Export Wizard, 261
Import and Export Wizard dialog
    box, 256
Import Outlook Data File dialog
    box, 267
importance, levels of, 46, 63
importing, contacts, 255–260
Inbox, cleaning up, 47–49
Inbox contents, in the Folder
    pane, 45
Inbox icon, for a meeting, 133
InfoBar
    clicking or right-clicking
        on, 245
    displaying flag details, 195
    meeting with response
        summary displayed, 136
    sensitivity notification in, 63
    voting responses displayed, 72
Information Rights Management
    (IRM), 69
Insert Business Card dialog box,
    250, 252, 299
Insert File dialog box, 40, 299
Insert Item dialog box, 43, 153,
    298–299
Insert tab, on a calendar item, 298
Instant Search, in Outlook,
    358–359
International option, 355
Internet calendar, 291
Internet Calendars, in the Account
    Settings dialog box, 296
Internet Message Access Protocol
    (IMAP) accounts, 28
Internet service provider (ISP),
    18, 28
Invite Attendees button, in
    the Attendees group, 123,
    131, 132
items
    attaching to a calendar item,
        298–299
    setting to not be archived, 333

J

Journal, 7, 314
    quick reference guide, 409–410
    using, 319–323
Journal button, 319, 320
Journal shortcuts, 389

Junk button, on the Home ribbon, 354
junk e-mail options, 353–356

L

Label Options dialog box, 269
Large Mail search folder, 324
Layout group, on the View ribbon, 159
LinkedIn icon, in People pane, 101
LinkedIn Web site, 99
linking, contacts, 248
Live, add-in for, 212
Location of an appointment, 127
Low Importance, 46
Low Importance e-mail message, 63

M

Macro Settings, in the Trust Center, 353
macros, 353
Mail button, 5, 10, 156, 161
Mail folders, 174, 209
Mail from specific people condition, 324
Mail Merge button, 268
Mail Merge Contacts dialog box, 268
Mail Merge Helper dialog box, 269
Mail Merge Wizard dialog box, 269
Mail options, in the Outlook Options dialog box, 220
Mail Options dialog box, 219
mailing labels, creating in Word, 268
MailTips, 17, 36, 416
MailTips Options dialog box, 224, 416
MailTips section, of Mail Options, 224
Manage All Views dialog box, 368–369
Manage Credentials permission, 69
Manage Quick Steps dialog box, 190
Manage Views option, on the View ribbon, 369
Manually configure server settings box, 210
map, opening for a contact address, 97–98
Map Custom Fields dialog box, 258–259, 263–264
Map It button, in the Communicate group, 98
MAPI (Messaging Application Programming Interface), 28
Mark All as Read option, 46
Mark as Not Junk dialog box, 356
Mark as Unread/Read button, 46

Mark Complete, using, 197
Mark Complete button, 154, 156, 165
Meeting button, in the Respond group, 133
meeting cancellation, sending, 138
meeting cancellation e-mail, 137
meeting organizer (creator), 137
meeting request respondents, tracking, 135–136
meeting requests, 122–123
    changing and updating, 137
    creating and using, 131–138
    proposing new times, 134–135
    responding to, 133–134
    working from Exchange Server, 412–413
meeting update, sending to attendees, 137
meetings
    picking new times for, 302
    recurring, 300–301
    scheduling, 17
Message arrival section, of Mail Options, 221–222
Message button, in the Show group, 65
Message format, of Mail Options, 225
message format, setting default and changing, 60–61
message options, for individual e-mail messages, 62–69
Message ribbon, 33, 62
Messaging Application Programming Interface (MAPI), 28
Microsoft Access documents, as attachments, 351
Microsoft Exchange accounts, 28
    on a business network, 411
Microsoft Exchange Server, 17, 18
Microsoft Office Communicator, 17
Microsoft Office Online Calendar Sharing Service, 293
Microsoft Outlook. *See* Outlook
Microsoft Word. *See* Word
modifying, rules, 184
Month view, 124–125
More button, in the Communicate group, 98
Move button, in the Move group, 131, 157
Move Down button, in Rules and Alerts dialog box, 187
Move Folder button, in the Actions group, 176
move it to the specified folder box, 182
Move Up button, in Rules and Alerts dialog box, 187
moving
    calendar items, 129
    folders, 175–176

MSN Connector for Outlook, 28
My Calendars, in the Navigation pane, 280, 281
My Calendars list, in the Navigation pane, 293
My Tasks area, of the Navigation pane, 148
MySpace, connecting to, 99

N

name of the individual, as condition of a rule, 182
Navigation pane, 8, 9–11, 44
    Calendar button, 131
    Calendar selected in, 123
    choosing buttons to displaying, 362–363
    Configure buttons button, 319
    Contact folder, 243
    Contacts button, 89, 90, 102, 104, 105
    Contacts folder, 88
    Current View area, 316
    Draft folder, 35
    Folder List button, 177
    Journal button, 319, 320
    Mail button, 10, 156, 161
    Mail folders, 209
    My Calendars list, 280, 281, 293
    My Tasks area, 148
    Notes button, 314
    Reset button, 362
    RSS Feeds folder, 228, 230
    Sent Items folder, 65
    Shared Calendars area, 291
    Shared Calendars list, 347
    Shortcuts view, 328
    Show Fewer Buttons option, 363
    Show More Buttons option, 362
    Tasks button, 149, 156
    Unread Mail search folder, 323
Navigation Pane Options dialog box, 319, 362
Never Block Sender option, 355
New Appointment button, 125, 127
New Calendar button, 280
New Contact button, 89, 90
New Contact Group button, 105
New contact record, 89
new contacts, creating, 89–91
New E-mail button, 30, 34
New E-mail Contact option, 109
New E-mail Delivery Location dialog box, 216
new e-mail message, opening, 30
new event, creating, 127–128
New Folder button, 216
    on the Folder ribbon, 174
    in the New group, 175, 244
New Journal Entry button, 320
New Meeting button, 131, 132
New Object/User dialog box, in Active Directory, 380
New Quick Step button, 189

New RSS Feed dialog box, 229, 230
New Rule button, 180
New Search Folder dialog box, 324, 325
New Shortcut button, on the Folder ribbon, 329
New Shortcut Group option, 329
New Signature dialog box, 73, 251
New Task button, on the Home ribbon, 150
New text message, 218
New Time Proposed e-mail, 135
New user confirmation dialog box, 381
New user password and password options, 380
No Date Follow Up flag, 195
Normal Importance, 46
Normal Importance e-mail message, 63
Normal sensitivity, 63
Not Junk option, 356
Notes, 7, 314
  categorizing, 315–316
  changing default settings on, 318–319
  creating, 314–315
  displaying as large icons, 317
  editing, 315
  forwarding as attachments via e-mail, 317–318
  quick reference guide, 409–410
  shortcuts, 388
  using, 314–319
  views for, 316–317

O

Office BackStage, 15
Office Theme, 75
online course, using this text with, 383–384
online templates, for business cards, 253–255
on-site course, using this text with, 379–383
Open a Shared Calendar dialog box, 346–347
Open button, in the Actions group, 41
Open Calendar button, 297
open envelope icon, 46
Open Recurring Item dialog box, 130
Open this Calendar button, 291
opening, an e-mail, 46
Optional attendees, 132
Options ribbon, on a new e-mail message, 62
ordering, rules, 186–187
Out of Office Assistant, 225–227, 415
Out of Office Rules dialog box, 227
Out of Office status indicator, 227
Outlook
  customizing, 361–370
  described, 3–4

with Exchange Server, 18
  navigating, 7–14
  Outlook Reference Guide, 390–410
  as a stand-alone program, 17–18
  what's new in, 15–17
  working with, 4–7
Outlook Calendar, 5, 120–121, 287–297. *See also* calendar(s)
Outlook Connector, 212–214
Outlook Contacts. *See* contact(s)
Outlook Data File, 265–267
Outlook Duplicate Items Remover (ODIR), 95
Outlook Help, 14
Outlook Item button, in the Include group, 298
Outlook items, searching for, 358–360
Outlook Journal. *See* Journal
Outlook Notes. *See* Notes
Outlook Options dialog box, 49, 60–61, 73, 219, 261
  AutoArchive Settings button, 331
  choosing Calendar in, 282, 283
  Contact options, 248
  Notes and Journal button, 318
  Task options, 165
Outlook panes section, in Mail options, 221
Outlook Reference Guide, 390–410
Outlook Social Connector (OSC), 10, 11, 16, 78, 99–101
Outlook Syndicated Content (RSS) Directory, 228
Outlook tasks, 6, 147–148. *See also* task(s)
Outlook Today, 8, 361
Outlook Trust Center, 348
Outlook Web Access (OWA), 217, 414–415
Outside My Organization tab, 227
overdue task, 154
overlay mode, viewing calendars in, 281–282

P

Page color, 75
panes, 7–8, 9, 44
paper clip icon, 46
paper sticky notes, 314
password, supplying, 29
pattern, changing page color to include, 75
people or public group link, 182
People pane, 8, 10–11, 16, 77–78, 98
% Complete, 163, 164
Permission option, 69
permissions, of a delegate, 344
Permissions button
  in Delegates dialog box, 348
  in the Properties group, 345
Permissions setting, for publishing calendars, 294

personal management software, Outlook as, 4
Personal sensitivity, 63
Personal stationery tab, 76, 220
Picture button, in the Options group, 97
pictures
  adding for contacts, 96–97
  changing page color to include, 75
plain text format, 60
POP (Post Office Protocol)
  accounts, 28
  enabling, 208
preset Quick Steps, 187
preset task views, in the Current View group, 158
preset views
  for calendars, 298
  for journal entries, 322–323
Print button, 37
Print dialog box, 288, 300
Print options, on BackStage, 287–288
Printing options, 37
Priority, of a task, 151
Privacy Options area, of the Trust Center, 350
private calendar items, 299–300
private key, 64, 351
Private marking, for a task, 153
Private sensitivity, 63
Problem Connecting to Server message, 210
Programmatic Access Security, 353
Properties dialog box, 12, 62, 333, 357
  custom voting buttons in, 70
  Receipt options, 65
  Security Settings button, 63
Propose New Time dialog box, 134, 135
Propose New Time option, 131, 133
.pst file, 265
public key, 64, 351
Publish Calendar to Office.com dialog box, 293–294
Publish Online button, on the Home ribbon, 293
Published Calendar Settings dialog box, 294
published Internet Calendar, subscribing to, 296
publishing, calendars, 293–296
pull-down arrow
  on the Save & New button, 90
  select from calendar thumbnail, 151
purging, Exchange accounts, 382–383
purple arrow, on the e-mail icon, 46

Q

Quick Access toolbar, 8, 363–364
Quick Click category, setting, 194–195

Quick Click flag, setting, 196
Quick Click Follow Up flag,
    setting, 166
Quick Reference Guide, 390–410
quick rules, creating, 178–179
Quick Steps, 15, 178, 187–191

R

Range of recurrence
    selecting, 130
    setting, 155, 301
read receipts, 65, 225
Reading pane, 8, 9–10, 35, 44
    interacting with Folder pane,
        221
    resizing, 10
    for Tasks, 158
read/unread e-mail, 45–46
really simple syndication. *See* RSS
    feeds
Recall feature, 38–39
Recall This Message dialog
    box, 38
Received meeting request, 134
received task request, 161
recipient notification, of a Read
    Receipt, 65
recipients, selecting, 31
records, 88, 255
Recover Deleted Items dialog
    box, 49
Recurrence button, 129
    in the Options group, 300
    in the Recurrence group, 155
Recurrence dialog box, 129–130
Recurrence pattern, setting,
    130, 301
Recurring appointments, 129
recurring meetings, 300–301
recurring tasks, 154, 155–156
Reminder pull-down menu, in the
    Options group, 128
Reminder window, 47, 128, 152
reminders, 128
    changing default, 283
    including with e-mails, 46–47
    setting for tasks, 151–152
Remove button, in Delegates
    dialog box, 348
Remove Member button, 109
Remove Picture option, 97
Rename button, 192
Rename Folder button, 326
renaming, a category, 191
Repair feature, in Outlook, 212
Replies and forwards section, of
    Mail Options, 222–223
Reply All button, pressing by
    mistake, 17
Reply All option, 35–36
reply e-mail, 36
Reply option, 35–36
Reply with Meeting button, 133
replying, to a message, 223
Required attendees, 132
Resend This Message option, 39
Reset button, in Navigation
    pane, 362

Reset Current View button, 103
Reset to Defaults button, 190
Reset View button
    in the Current View group, 368
    on the View ribbon, 103
Resource Scheduling dialog box,
    286–287
resources, including with a
    task, 153
Respond group, on the Home
    ribbon, 36
Reverse Sort button, in the
    Arrangement group, 364
Reviewer permission, 344
ribbons, 11, 15
Rich Text Format (RTF), 60
RSS feed e-mail, 232
RSS feed icon, 229
RSS feed links, 229
RSS feeds
    in the Account Settings Dialog
        box, 231
    managing, 207, 230–231
    sharing, 231–232
    subscribing to, 228
    unsubscribing, 232–233
    using, 227–233
Rule Address dialog box, 182
Rule Description, 185, 186
rule hierarchy, 186, 187
rule template, creating a blank
    rule, 180
rules, 177
    delaying delivery of e-mails, 66
    deleting and turning on/off, 185
    keeping simple, 184
    modifying, 184
    ordering, 186–187
    running, 185–186
    using, 217
Rules and Alerts dialog box, 178,
    179, 180, 182, 183, 185, 186,
    187
Rules button
    on the Message ribbon, 178
    in Out of Office Assistant dialog
        box, 227
Rules Wizard dialog box,
    180–183
Run Cleanup Agent, 382
Run Rules Now dialog box, 185,
    186
Run this rule now. . .box, 179, 183
running, rules, 185–186

S

Safe Recipients option, 355
Safe Senders list, 356
Safe Senders option, 355
Save & Close button, 90
Save All Attachments button, 42
Save As button, 36, 41
Save As dialog box, 36, 37, 41
Save button, 34, 36, 89
Save icon, 41
Save messages section, of Mail
    Options, 223
Save Sent Item To button, 66

Schedule view, 17, 125–126, 285
Scheduled meetings, deleting,
    137–138
Scheduling Assistant, 286,
    301–303, 412–413
school-created e-mail accounts,
    384
screen shots, 384
ScreenTips, 11
Search box, at top of Folder
    pane, 358
search features, 344
search folders, 314
    creating new, 324–325
    customizing, 325–327
    deleting, 327
    using, 323–327
Search Option button, 359
search options, for Instant
    Search, 359
Search Options dialog box,
    359, 360
Search ribbon, in the Scope
    group, 358
Search subfolders options, 326
security features, 343, 348–358
Security Properties dialog box,
    64, 357
security settings, in the Properties
    dialog box, 63
Select Attendees and Resources
    dialog box, 132
Select Folder(s) dialog box, 326
Select Members dialog box, 106
Select Names dialog box, 31, 32,
    89, 96, 103, 107–108, 325, 347
semicolon
    separating recipients' e-mail
        addresses, 224
    separating voting choices, 70
Send a Calendar via E-mail dialog
    box, 292
Send a Sharing Invitation dialog
    box, 295
Send button, 34
Send Cancellation button, 138
Send messages section, of Mail
    Options, 223–224
Send Out of Office auto replies
    option, 226
Send Status Report button, 164
Send the response now option, 70,
    71, 133, 134, 161
Send Update options, 137
sender, adding to contacts, 91
sensitivity, of e-mail, 63
Sent Items folder, 34, 36, 65
Set as Default button, 214
Set Quick Click category dialog
    box, 195
Set Quick Click dialog box, 196–
    197
Settings dialog box, for social
    networking sites, 100
Share Calendar button, on the
    Home ribbon, 290
Share This Feed button, in the
    RSS group, 231
shared calendars, viewing, 297

Shared Calendars area, in the Navigation pane, 291
Shared Calendars list, in the Navigation pane, 347
SharePoint, 11, 78
sharing
  on a Exchange system, 414
  Outlook with others, 344–348
sharing invitation e-mail, opening, 295
Shift key, holding down, 31, 101
Shift+Tab, moving back a field, 150
shortcut key combination, adding, 193
shortcuts, 314, 385–389
  adding to Quick Steps, 190
  creating new, 328–329
  deleting, 329
  editing, 329
  using, 328–329
Show Columns dialog box, 365–366
Show Fewer Buttons option, 363
Show in Favorites button, 363
Show in Groups options, 367
Show Message button, 42
Show More Buttons option, 362
Show work week option, 283
side-by-side mode, viewing calendars in, 281–282
signatures, 72–75
  in the body of tasks, 153
  including business cards in, 251–252
  inserting, 74
Signatures and Stationery dialog box, 73–74, 76, 220–221, 251–252
SimNet, using, 384
small bell icon, 46
S/MIME (Secure/Multipurpose Internet Mail Extensions), 351
SMS service providers, link to, 218
Snooze pull-down menu, 128
snoozing a reminder, 46
Social Network Accounts dialog box, 99
sorting, contacts, 103
specified folder link, 182
stand-alone program, 17
Start date, selecting for a task, 150–151
Start time of an appointment, 127
Start Timer button, 320
Stationery and Fronts button, 76
Status
  of a task, 151
  on a task, 163
  updating for a task, 164
Status pane, 8
student-created e-mail accounts, 384
Subject line, in an e-mail, 33
Subject of an appointment, 127
Subscribe to this Calendar option, 296

Success dialog box, 179
Suggested Contacts, list of, 248–249

T

tab delimited file, 265
Tab key, moving to the next field, 150
tabs, 11, 15
Tabs and ribbons, 8
Tags group, task options available in, 152
task(s), 148. *See also* Outlook tasks
  accepting, 161
  assigning, 160–161
  creating, 149–160
  editing, 151–153
  managing, 160–166
  marking as complete, 153–154, 164–165
  quick reference guide, 407–409
  recurring, 154–156
Task Accepted inbox icon, 162
Task Accepted message, 162
Task button, in the Show group, 164
task details, 163
task icons, 162–163
Task List, 148, 153–154, 159
Task options, in the Outlook Options dialog box, 165
Task Recurrence dialog box, 155
task reminder, 152
Task request e-mail, 160, 161
Task Request inbox icon, 162
Task request message, opening, 161
task requests, on an Exchange system, 413
Task status, 151
task status report, 163–164
task views, preset, 158
Tasks button, in the Navigation pane, 149, 156
Tasks folder, in the My Tasks area, 149
tasks shortcuts, 388
Team E-mail Quick Step, 187
Tell me if recall succeeds or fails for each recipient check box, 39
template, creating a blank rule, 180
Tentative and Propose New Time option, 134
Tentative option, 131, 133
Test Account Settings dialog box, 211
text, formatting, 33
Text message (SMS) account, setting up, 218
Text only, inserting items as, 43
texting, from Outlook, 217–218
texture, changing page color to include, 75
Themes, 75–76

Time zones, in Outlook Options, 285–286
timeline view, in the Folder pane, 125
To button, 31, 34
Today button, in the Go To group, 125
Today Follow Up flag, 195
To-Do bar, 8, 44, 148, 149, 159–160
To-Do items
  compared to Tasks, 148
  listing e-mails as, 67–68
  marked with a Follow Up flag, 197
To-Do List, 6, 148, 149, 197
Tooltip text area, for a Quick Step, 190
tracking
  in Exchange, 65
  voting responses, 412
Tracking button, 65, 136
Tracking group, on the Options ribbon, 65
Tracking Options dialog box, 225
tracking responses, for meeting requests, 131
Tracking section, of Mail Options, 225
troubleshooting, e-mail problems, 210
Trust Center, 348
Trusted publishers, 349
turning off, rules, 185
Type a new task area, 150

U

Undo button, 101
unencrypted connection, attempting, 210
Unread Mail search folder, 323, 324
Unread/Read button, 46
unsubscribing, from an RSS feed, 232–233
Update button, on the Contact ribbon, 247
Update duplicate contact, 94, 95
Update Now Button, in the Members group, 110
Use this color on all calendars box, 285
Use Voting Buttons button, 69, 70
user accounts
  creating, 379–381
  recycling, 381–383
user interface, 7–8, 15

V

View ribbon, 44, 126
View Settings buttons, 102, 368
View tab, 102
View voting responses, 72
views, 12–13
  for calendars, 298
  changing in contacts, 101–103

customizing, 368
for grouping and viewing tasks,
157–160
modifying, 102–103
Virus protection software, 35
Vote button, on a received e-mail
message, 71
voting buttons, 69
customizing, 70
on an e-mail, 413–414

preset, 69
reply using, 70–71
voting responses, tracking,
71–72, 412

W

week numbers, adding, 285
Week view, 124
Windows Live ID account, 293,
294–295

Windows Live Mail, 28, 207
Windows Security dialog
box, 294
Word, mailing labels, 268, 270
Work time options, 283
Work Week view, 124

Y

Yahoo Mail accounts, 207

QUICK TIPS AND TROUBLESHOOTING

E-mail Accounts: Outlook provides you with an e-mail account Setup Wizard to help you easily set up e-mail accounts. The following are some troubleshooting tips if your e-mail account is not working properly. (E-mail accounts are discussed in Chapters 2 and 8.)

- **Username and password.** Make sure your username and password are correct. Typically usernames are not case sensitive while passwords are case sensitive.

- **Repair feature.** If your account is not working properly, you might try using the **Repair** feature. In the *Accounts Settings* dialog box, there is a Repair button, and Outlook will automatically make account setting changes in an attempt to repair an existing e-mail account.

- **Default account.** If you have multiple e-mail accounts, the first account you create will be your default account. The default account is the account by which new e-mail will be sent. On each e-mail message, you can change the account through which the e-mail is sent. You can also change your default e-mail account in the *Account Settings* dialog box.

- **Address books.** A common error is confusing or not distinguishing between the Global Address List and Contacts. (Contacts, Global Address List, and address books are covered in Chapters 4 and 9.)

- **Global Address List.** The Global Address List is only available when you are using Outlook in an Exchange environment. You cannot add to or make changes to the Global Address List because this list is maintained by your Exchange server administrator.

- **Contacts folder.** Whether you are using Outlook as a stand-alone program or in an Exchange environment, you will have a Contacts folder. The Contacts folder is by default the folder in which new contacts are saved. You can add, edit, or delete contacts from this folder.

- **Default address book.** When using Outlook in an Exchange environment, the Global Address List is the default address book. You can change the settings to make your Contacts folder the default address book (see Chapter 9, page 242).

- **Address Book.** When the *Address Book* dialog box is open, you can select the address book to use from the *Address Book* pull-down list.

- **Save contact to a different folder.** By default new contacts will be saved to your Contacts folder. You can save to a different folder by clicking on the **File** tab to open the *BackStage*, clicking on the **Move to Folder** button, and selecting the desired folder.

- **Contacts folder not displayed in Address Book.** If you have multiple Contacts folders, these folders can be made available in your address book by changing the properties of the folders. Right-click on the contacts folder to add to the address book, choose **Properties**, click on the **Outlook Address Book** tab, check **Show the folder as an e-mail Address Book,** and press **OK** to close the dialog box.

Rules—Troubleshooting: See the following for some common errors pertaining to rules and some troubleshooting tips. (Rules are covered in Chapter 7.)

- **Incorrect folder.** Be sure to specify the folder on which the rule is to run. Normally this should be the Inbox, but a common error is having the rule running on a different folder. This will cause the rule to not function as intended.

- **Misspellings and extra spaces.** If the rule is looking for a word or group of words, a misspelled word or an extra space after the last word will cause the rule to not function properly.

- **Deleted folder.** If a Mail folder that is referenced in a rule is deleted, Outlook will recognize the error in the rule and the rule will not function properly. An error message will appear when you open the *Rules and Alerts* dialog box, and the rule will be marked as having an error.

- **Run rules after modifying.** After modifying a rule, you must select **Run Rules Now** in order for the rule to run on those items in your *Inbox* or the folder on which the rule is to run.

Rules—Effectiveness: It is important to create rules that are effective and efficient. See the following tips to increase the effectiveness of your rules. (Rules are covered in Chapter 7.)

- **Keep rules simple.** Rules are most effective when they are simple. The effectiveness of a rule can be diluted if there are too many conditions, actions, and exceptions.

- **Break up a complex rule.** If a rule has multiple conditions, actions, and/or exceptions, try breaking the rule into two or more rules.

- **Ordering rules.** Rules run in the order in which they are listed in the *Rules and Alerts* dialog box. When creating, editing, and managing rules, you must think about the order in which they appear and the conflicts that might occur.

Quick Steps: These are new to Outlook 2010 and can be used and customized to perform one-click actions on e-mail messages. (Quick Steps are covered in Chapter 7.)

- **Using default Quick Steps.** Outlook provides a number of preset Quick Steps. On some of these Quick Steps, you will need to set the criteria of the action. Once the criteria are defined, Outlook will remember and perform the action.

- **Modifying Quick Steps.** Quick Steps can be modified by clicking on the **More** button in the *Quick Steps* group and choosing **Manage Quick Steps.** You can customize an existing Quick Step or reset a Quick Step to its original default setting. A Quick Step can also be modified to perform multiple actions.

- **Creating Quick Steps.** A new Quick Step can be created, or an existing Quick Step can be duplicated and modified.